THE DOUGLASS CENTURY

THE DOUGLASS CENTURY

TRANSFORMATION OF THE WOMEN'S COLLEGE AT RUTGERS UNIVERSITY

Kayo Denda, Mary Hawkesworth, and Fernanda Perrone

Rutgers University Press

New Brunswick, Camden,
and Newark, New Jersey, and London

Names: Denda, Kayo, author. | Hawkesworth, M. E., 1952- author. | Perrone, Fernanda, author.
Title: The Douglass century : transformation of the women's college at Rutgers University / Kayo Denda, Mary Hawkesworth, Fernanda Perrone.
Description: New Brunswick, NJ : Rutgers University Press, 2018. | Includes bibliographical references and index.
Identifiers: LCCN 2017017005 (print) | LCCN 2017042974 (ebook) | ISBN 9780813585420 (E-pub) | ISBN 9780813585437 (Web PDF) | ISBN 9780813585413 (hardback)
Subjects: LCSH: Douglass College—History. | Douglass College—History—Pictorial works. | Women—Education, Higher—New Jersey—New Brunswick—History. | Women—Education, Higher—New Jersey—New Brunswick—History—Pictorial works. | BISAC: EDUCATION / Higher. | SOCIAL SCIENCE / Women's Studies. | HISTORY / United States / State & Local / Middle Atlantic (DC, DE, MD, NJ, NY, PA). | EDUCATION / History.
Classification: LCC LD7071.5 (ebook) | LCC LD7071.5 .D46 2018 (print) | DDC 378.749/42—dc23
LC record available at https://lccn.loc.gov/2017017005

A British Cataloging-in-Publication record for this book is available from the British Library.

∞ The paper used in this publication meets the requirements of the American National Standard for Information Sciences—Permanence of Paper for Printed Library Materials, ANSI Z39.48–1992.

www.rutgersuniversitypress.org

Manufactured in the United States of America

CONTENTS

FOREWORD

History is one of the most important assets of a college or university; the story of an institution's founding—its origin story—defines its mission; decisions over time reveal strategic intent. Critical events define community. Most institutions preserve at least pieces of their history in traditions and rituals that help build a communal identity. But fewer institutions think analytically about their history, seek to understand where they stand from whence they've traveled.

The Douglass Century: Transformation of the Women's College at Rutgers University seeks to provide such a history for Douglass College. Douglass has a remarkable story. It is the only college in America founded by an organization of women's clubs and by popular subscription. Mabel Douglass, the driving force of this movement, and the college's first dean, was a formidable and complex woman. When the college opened its doors in 1918 as the New Jersey College for Women, with fifty-four students and twelve books in its library, it was a brave but frugal venture. In reading *The Douglass Century*, I thought often of Virginia Woolf's *A Room of One's Own* with its contrast between the rich and sumptuous dinner of wine and partridge at an Oxbridge men's college and the beef and potatoes served at the newly founded women's college. Woolf calls this new college Fernham—a stand-in for Newnham and Girton, but it could well be Douglass.

Douglass College's feisty beginning gave it a distinctive legacy; it was founded not by a benefactor, like Matthew Vassar or Sophia Smith, but by a woman's movement—the campaign of the women's clubs—and it was founded as a public resource—together with the agriculture school, the most public part of Rutgers University. *The Douglass Century* traces the distinctive growth of the college and its complex relationship to its parent university, Rutgers, which was not always a kind father. The most tangled piece of this tale is the series of negotiations with Rutgers, over several decades, in which all the separate colleges at Rutgers, including Douglass, became one university, with separate residential campuses. The story of

Douglass offers an interesting variant on the history of women's colleges in the United States. No longer an independent women's college like Smith or Wellesley with its own admissions and faculty, it nonetheless continues to exist as a residential campus with distinctive programs, designed for women students, and its own dean.

One of the many pleasures of *The Douglass Century* involves understanding your years as a student through a different lens. I was surprised by all that I didn't know about what was happening at the college when I was a student there in the mid 60s. We all tend to assume that we understood our experience when we were living it. One of the gifts of history is perspective. It can show us how the communities in which we participated were distinctive, how they inhabited their own context, how they shaped their environment and were shaped by it. And histories help us preserve those communities not only through their origin stories but also through the narratives that unfold from them. *The Douglass Century* gives us such a gift.

CAROL T. CHRIST (DC '66)
Interim Executive Vice Chancellor and Provost
University of California, Berkeley

DEANS OF
THE COLLEGE,
1918–2018

....

MABEL SMITH DOUGLASS,
1918–1932

ALBERT E. MEDER,
acting dean, 1932–1933;
interim dean, 1933–1934

MARGARET TRUMBULL CORWIN,
1934–1955

MARY INGRAHAM BUNTING,
1955–1960

JOHN L. SWINK,
chief administrator,
May 1–June 30, 1960

RUTH ADAMS,
1960–1966

MARGARET ATWOOD JUDSON,
interim dean, 1966–1967

MARGERY SOMERS FOSTER,
1967–1975

PAULA P. BROWNLEE,
interim dean, 1975–1976

JEWEL PLUMMER COBB,
1976–1981

MARY S. HARTMAN,
1981–1994

CAROL SMITH,
acting dean,
September–December 1985

MARTHA COTTER,
interim dean, 1995–1996

BARBARA A. SHAILOR,
1996–2001

LINDA STAMATO DC '62,
interim dean, 2001–2002

CARMEN TWILLIE AMBAR,
2002–2008

HARRIET DAVIDSON,
interim dean, 2008–2010

JACQUELYN LITT,
2010–

THE DOUGLASS CENTURY

INVENTING DOUGLASS
The Challenge of Women's Higher Education

THE STORY OF THE FOUNDING AND
THE HEROIC STRUGGLES, AND THE
REMARKABLE PROGRESS OF OUR NEW
JERSEY COLLEGE FOR WOMEN, UNDER
THE ABLE LEADERSHIP OF DEAN MABEL S.
DOUGLASS, IS ONE OF THE ROMANCES
OF AMERICAN HIGHER EDUCATION.

—John M. Thomas, president,
Rutgers University, 1925–1930

In her 1932 message to the graduating class of the New Jersey College for Women (NJC), founding dean Mabel Smith Douglass noted:

In material things . . . the College started with nothing—that is the precise and literal truth. In things of the spirit—loyalty, friendship, encouragement, vision, faith, hope, yes, even love—we were rich. We were rich too in obstacles, in heartaches, in difficulties and troubles, and in overcoming these we built into our College a spirit of cooperation among the students, faculty, and staff, which if not unique is surely rare among colleges. NJC has been built by its students as has no other college. My earnest hope is that, as the years pass and the students of the future come and go, the old spirit of cooperation, helpfulness, and sacrifice for faith in an ideal may ever continue a living reality on this campus.[1]

Faith in the ideal of women's education continues to flourish at Douglass, renamed in 1955 to honor its founder. Douglass inaugurates its second century as a residential college for women, nested within Rutgers, the State University of New Jersey. As the only women's college in a major public research university, Douglass is home to 2,545 women students, who represent the rich demography of twenty-first-century New Jersey.[2] With 20.6 percent of the student population African American, 23 percent Asian

American/Pacific Islander, 19 percent Latina, 4.4 percent mixed race, and 31.2 percent white, Douglass Residential College embodies the diverse, intellectually engaged citizenry of the United States—providing an exhilarating education that is dedicated to mentoring women to lead the world with conviction, creativity, and critical insight.

Since its founding a century ago, Douglass has been in a state of perpetual transformation, incontestably living up to the "magnificent opportunity" that Mabel Smith Douglass envisioned, in which "all would have to be thought of, planned, built up, created."[3] As this sage innovator in women's higher education foresaw, the making of Douglass College would not be the work of one person or one generation. The transformation of the inaugural class (fifty-four pioneering women who "extemporized in college hall . . . studying with coats on and galoshes to keep out the cold")[4] into a vibrant college with thirty-nine thousand alumnae and a reputation for excellence in arts, humanities, science, technology, engineering, and math, as well as women's studies, has been the work of a century. Built through the ingenuity and persistence of ten permanent deans, eight acting/interim deans, hundreds of faculty and professional staff, and thousands of creative students with the support of the New Jersey State Federation of Women's Clubs, the Associate Alumnae of Douglass College (AADC), and manifold generous donors, Douglass is both a monumental achievement and an unfinished project.

To celebrate this achievement and chart the contours of this unfolding experiment in women's higher education is the task of *The Douglass Century*. As the number of women's colleges has plummeted from a high of 268 in 1960 to 38 in 2016, the very survival of a women's college is a historic accomplishment.[5] Within a nation still marked by gender, racial, economic, and religious inequality, the diversity of Douglass's student population is a singular achievement—one that signals an expansion of the boundaries of belonging that has eluded most formerly all-white institutions. Over a century during which women have become the majority of undergraduate students, while college and university administrations have remained predominantly in the hands of white men, Douglass has developed and maintained a tradition of women's leadership, while generating unparalleled knowledge production by and about women. For a century, Douglass has educated women, forging an ethos of empowerment, cultivating leadership, and nurturing individual talent, creativity, and growth, while also enabling community among women of different generations and heritages.

Whether measured in terms of longevity, scale, quality of critical engagement, depths of individual transformation, or of solidarity among students and alumnae, the significance of Douglass's achievements becomes apparent only within a specific historical context. The project of women's education makes sense only in relation to the historical practice of women's exclusion—from education, the professions, public life, and the rights of citizenship. To grasp Douglass's unique mission and the enormity of the challenges it has faced, then, it is important to consider women's changing roles over the past hundred years, recurrent debates about the nature and legitimacy of women's education, and the complex evolution of Rutgers from a private, religiously affiliated men's college to a major research university.

Women's Roles and Women's Education

The first comprehensive census of occupations in the United States, which was conducted in 1870, recorded 338 occupations. Although at least one woman was noted within each of those occupational categories, 93 percent of all women workers were employed in seven jobs: domestic workers, agricultural laborers, seamstresses, milliners, teachers, textile mill workers, and laundresses.[6] By 1920, the employment opportunities for women in New Jersey had changed only slightly. The vast majority of women continued to work as agricultural laborers, servants, clerks, saleswomen, stenographers and typists, textile workers, seamstresses, dressmakers, and teachers.[7] The narrow sphere of women's occupations reflected the "ideology of Republican motherhood," which had been carefully cultivated in the early American republic, fueling the belief that "the rearing of children, that is, the laying a foundation of sound health both of body and mind in the rising generation, has justly been insisted on as the peculiar destination of women."[8] Whether that "peculiar destination" required or benefited from education was a topic of considerable controversy during the nineteenth and early twentieth century.

Some women of the Early Republic such as Abigail Adams (1744–1818), Judith Sargent Murray (1751–1820), Lydia Sigourney (1791–1865), and Lydia Maria Child (1802–1880) harnessed the specific responsibilities of motherhood to an argument for women's education, insisting that women's access to education, the professions, and political rights would make them better mothers and more intelligent companions in marriage. Refusing cavalier denigrations of women's intellectual abilities, proponents of women's education suggested that any deficiency was the result of inadequate training rather than reduced aptitude.

To remedy flawed training, some women opened schools for girls. Variously called female seminaries, institutes, or academies, the schools offered languages, literature, mathematics, natural philosophy (i.e., science), and religious instruction. Although the exact number of these schools is unknown, two were operating in New Brunswick, New Jersey, in the early nineteenth century.[9] Yet these two schools took quite different approaches to women's education. Known for genteel arts, music, French, drawing, dancing, and rote memorization, a "seminary for girls run by Miss Sophia Hay, an Englishwoman, had pupils in the first two decades of the nineteenth century from as far north as New Hampshire and as far west as Tennessee," according to William H. Demarest's *History of Rutgers*. By contrast, the New Brunswick Female Academy offered a more rigorous curriculum than Miss Hay's seminary, one that included Latin, Greek, and mathematics, comparable to the curriculum at Queens College, the precursor of Rutgers, during the same period. Indeed, students from the New Brunswick Female Academy were examined by Rutgers faculty prior to graduation.[10]

Although the boundary between secondary and tertiary education was particularly blurry in the early nineteenth century, by the 1830s several colleges began to open their doors to women. In 1831, Mississippi College became the first coeducational college in the United States to grant degrees to women, conferring the "Bachelor of Arts" on Alice Robinson and Catherine Hall. Oberlin began admitting men and women students in 1833, declaring its mission "to educate gospel ministers and pious school teachers." Matriculating through the Female Department, forty-four women enrolled in the first class. According to its catalog, Oberlin aspired to "the elevation of female character by bringing within the reach of the misjudged and neglected sex all the instructive privileges which hitherto have unreasonably distinguished the leading sex from theirs."[11] Toward that end, the course of study for "young ladies" was similar to that for men: history, English literature, philosophy and the sciences, math, Latin, and Greek, although linear drawing was offered to women but not to men. Despite a shared curriculum, the education of women students was not identical to that of their male counterparts, either within or outside the classroom. Following the practice of the day to bar women from public speech, women were not allowed to speak in class or participate in public speeches or debates. At commencement, men read their essays before an admiring public, while a rhetoric professor read the women's essays. Beyond the classroom, women were required to serve men in the dining commons, clean their rooms, and launder their clothing. Noting the sex-specific constraints imposed on women's education, Oberlin historian Robert Fletcher suggested that the gender-specific pedagogy might have important life lessons:

> It is not improbable that one reason why the early Oberlin Fathers favored "joint education" was that it was hoped that thus the young ladies could be more readily kept in their proper relation of awed subjection to the "leading sex." Washing the men's clothing, caring for their rooms, serving them at table, listening to their orations, but, themselves remaining respectfully silent in public assemblages, the Oberlin "co-eds" were being prepared for intelligent motherhood and a properly subservient wifehood.[12]

In early coeducational settings, then, the education of women was thoroughly compatible with continuing gender and racial subordination.

In 1839, the Rutgers Female Institute opened as the first institution of higher education for women in New York City. Although it had no ties to Rutgers College, the all-male institution in New Brunswick, it shared a key benefactor. New York real estate magnate and Revolutionary War hero Henry Rutgers (1745–1830) provided the land for the facility as a bequest. Offering an intensive one-year course of study for its first three decades, the Rutgers Female Institute was authorized by the New York Board of Regents to change its name to Rutgers Female College and begin offering the four-year bachelor of arts degree in 1867. According to the 1867–1868 *Catalogue*, the college offered a "classical curriculum designed to match that of any male college in New York." The Rutgers Female College provides a fascinating model of single-sex education designed to emulate the standard of education established for men. Yet the college catalog included an additional course for fourth-year students unlikely to be found in any male college: "Legal Relations of Women," which provided "a general view of the legal condition and rights of both single and married women."[13] Beyond this innovative course in women's rights, the Rutgers Female College also embraced sex-specific pedagogical practices, supposedly honed through years of work with women students.

> Whatever may be the methods best adapted to young men, there is felt to be a wide and important difference in the case of young ladies. So delicate is the sensibility of the female mind and so serious is the evil of injuring or exciting it, that any system of individual prizes and of personal competition is felt to be deeply unhappy. It is moreover liable to unfairness, as many minor circumstances, wholly remote from the care and faithfulness of the student may exercise an important influence in determining individual rank. The whole system of medals and prizes has therefore been discarded in the institution, and the incentives to study held forth to the pupils are of a more general and more permanent character. The standing of the student is determined by a system of marks, ranging from ten for a perfect exercise to zero for a total failure. During the undergraduate years, a monthly report is furnished to the parent or guardian. . . . The grade of each alumna is not made public at commencement but is preserved in the records of the College, and may be ascertained by inspection, whenever for any important reason it is desired. In this system, all personal competitions are avoided, and no place is left for anyone to feel that, in the decisions of the College, honors have been unduly awarded or withheld.[14]

Like many early women's colleges, the Rutgers Female College did not publicly grade academic performance, thereby sparing its women students the ardors of competition, while providing another example of the complexities of providing an equal education for a "different" clientele.

In his 1867 presidential address to the first graduating class of Rutgers Female College, President Henry Miller Pierce offered biblical warrant for the equal education of women: "The question whether or not woman is the equal of man [was] authoritatively settled by Him [Christ], when he pronounces marriage a union as excludes the idea that there can be essential inferiority in one of the parties. His ideal of marriage, unknown alike in classical nations and to the Hebrews, is incompatible with the inequality of the sexes."[15] Pierce emphasized that "equality, though it excludes the idea of inferiority, is consistent with diversity."[16] According to the male educators who designed the curriculum for the Rutgers Female College, educational practices, which eliminate competition, orient the woman student toward the Bible, "the only source of true wisdom," and inculcate "true piety in woman that alone which really can draw out from the heart of man, the sentiment of lasting veneration," foster individual happiness, preserve families, and advance civilization.[17]

In 1856, the University of Iowa broke new ground, introducing publicly funded higher education for men and women. In 1862, the Morrill Act, passed by the U.S. Congress, established and financed "land grant colleges" to promote agriculture and mechanical arts. Thirty-one states moved quickly to build institutions with the land grant funds, vastly increasing the coeducational opportunities available.[18] By 1873, there were nearly 100 coeducational colleges; by 1890, 282; by 1902, 330—with nearly half in the Midwest.[19] At the turn of the twentieth century, 80 percent of colleges, universities, and professional schools admitted women.[20] In 1870, less than half the women in higher education attended coeducational institutions. By 1890, 70 percent of women college students were in coeducational institutions.[21]

As educational opportunities for women grew, however, new grounds were advanced *against* women's higher education. In the late nineteenth century, the "gender balance" in coeducational schools began to shift as more women graduated from secondary school than men. As Mabel Newcomer has documented, only 2 percent of seventeen-year-olds graduated from secondary school in the second half of the nineteenth century, but more women graduated than men, and in some years 60 percent of the graduates were women.[22] As the empirical evidence made it increasingly difficult to claim that women had lesser academic abilities than men, the grounds for excluding women from higher education shifted from assertions that women *could not* do the work to claims that they *ought not* undertake academic pursuits—for their own well-being, for the nation, or indeed for "the race."

As the number of women in higher education began to increase significantly, leading medical experts warned that a young woman could learn chemistry and botany as well as a young man, but she could not do so and "retain uninjured health and a future secure from neuralgia, uterine disease, hysteria, and other derangements of the nervous system, if she were to follow the same method that boys are trained in."[23] Harvard professor Edward H. Clarke warned that women seeking advanced education would develop "monstrous brains," "puny bodies," and "abnormally weak digestion."[24] According to Clarke, the human body has a finite reserve of energy. If women devote energy to academic pursuits, they divert to the brain energy necessary for development of reproductive organs. Indeed, women who indulged in extensive study were likely to suffer cessation of menstruation, failure to develop breasts, or even death from "brain degeneracy." Recalling one patient who had suffered this fate, Clarke noted, "She was unable to make a good brain that could stand the wear and tear of life, and a good reproductive system that should serve the race, at the same time she was continually spending her force in intellectual labor. Nature asked for a periodical remission and did not get it. And so Miss 'G' died [because] she steadily ignored her woman's make."[25]

Many men of Clarke's era imagined women to be fragile creatures, and used that fragility as a reason to exclude women from various fields of study and employment. In the words of one exclusionist, "It is obvious we cannot instruct women as we do men in the science of medicine; we cannot carry them into the dissecting room and hospital; many of *our* delicate feelings, much of *our* refined sentiment must be subdued before we can study medicine; in females they must be destroyed."[26] To spare women the corrupting effects of men's education, some doctors emphasized the importance of separate spheres. In *Sex in Mind and Education* (1884), Dr. William Maudsley insisted that "there is a sex in mind as distinctly as there is a sex in body." As a consequence of each sex having unique mental characteristics, Maudsley argued that separate forms of instruction were essential. As these quotations suggest, "Most of the opposition [to women's higher education] was less concerned with whether education was good for women, than whether educated women were acceptable to men."[27]

The number of women in higher education increased in coeducational institutions from 3,044 in 1875 to 19,959 in 1900 and from 9,572 to 15, 977 in women's colleges.[28] Although the women attending colleges and universities constituted only 2.8 percent of all U.S. women aged 18 to 21, their growing numbers raised increasing concern among academic administrators as women students began to outperform as well as outnumber male students. "By 1908, women outnumbered men in seven of the large Western universities."[29] In a 1908 address to the American Association of University Women, M. Carey Thomas, founder and president of Bryn Mawr College, provided an impressive overview of women's academic performance in coeducational institutions:

> The evidence proves women excel in the same courses as men; the only fields they avoid are those from which they are banned (e.g., pharmacy). Women do slightly better than men in daily recitations; in spite of their supposedly less good health, they are absent less often from college classes; and, on average, they get higher marks on their examinations. None of this is very pleasing to men students, especially in the East where young men have been taught to look down on women. Men are said in consequence—and with some truth I think—to show a tendency to prefer separate colleges.[30]

Male educators grew increasingly distraught that women were earning far more Phi Beta Kappa keys than expected. In 1901, Hugo Munsterberg, a professor of philosophy at Harvard, articulated the multiple dimensions of educated men's fear of "feminization":

> In colleges and universities men still dominate, but soon will not if things are not changed; the great numbers of young women who pass their doctoral examinations and become specialists in science will have more and more to seek university professorships, or else they will have studied in vain. And here, as in the school, the economic conditions strongly favour the woman; since

she has no family to support, she can accept . . . [wages] so much smaller that the man is more and more crowded from the field. And it may be clearly foreseen that, if other social factors do not change, women will enter as competitors in every field where the labour does not require specifically masculine strength. So as it has been in the factories, so in the schools, and so in a few decades, it may be in the universities."[31]

The "feminization of higher education" signified not only increasing numbers of women in colleges and universities—as faculty and students—but also the specter of falling wages and declining prestige as "any success man attained would be devalued because women had demonstrated equal achievement."[32]

Decrying the negative effects of the feminization of higher education, some university administrators began reconsidering coeducation. At Stanford, women had been 33 percent of the entering class in 1885, and they were 51 percent within a decade. Fearing that the university would be seen as the "Vassar of the Pacific," Mrs. Leland Stanford imposed a quota on women in 1899, shortly after her husband's death. Without consulting other administrators, she capped the number of women allowed to matriculate at Stanford at five hundred at any time. Women reached that limit by 1903, creating an unsavory unintended consequence for those concerned about feminization. Because of the quota, the competition for admission to Stanford grew increasingly intense among women applicants, reaching four women applicants for each admission. As a result, the entering classes of women after 1903 outperformed their male counterparts even more dramatically than they had before the quota was introduced.[33]

From the moment of its founding in 1892, the University of Chicago also admitted women and men without restriction. A decade later, President William Rainey Harper initiated a series of discussions with the trustees about the detrimental effects of coeducation, most notably the "effemination" of men, which he deemed "contrary to the best development of the intellectual forces of the country, the unhappy fact that women were consistently outperforming men in academics, despite their smaller number in the student population; and the loss of certain virtues, traits, matters of deportment, and the like, more or less distinct for either sex due to the commingling of men and women on campus."[34] To remedy these "problems," President Harper proposed the segregation of men and women in single-sex junior colleges for the first two years of instruction. Despite vociferous opposition from a significant portion of the faculty and Marion Talbot, the dean of women, the Board of Trustees voted to segregate the junior colleges in 1902 at the urging of President Harper.[35]

At this juncture, psychologists and education specialists once again offered "scientific" grounds to legitimate concerns about coeducation and vindicate segregation of the sexes. In 1903, noted psychologist G. Stanley Hall reported that coeducation has detrimental effects on both sexes, causing "sexual precocity in boys—one of the subtlest dangers that can befall civilization," and "over brainwork in girls."[36] To avoid such significant dangers, Hall recommended that education be reoriented to train women and men for their "separate roles in life." In *Adolescence* (1904), Hall insisted that girls should be educated for roles of wife and mother: "Now that woman has by general consent attained the right to the best that man has, she must seek a training that fits her own nature as well or better. The family and the home recognize the differences of the two sexes; they are differentiated by their occupations, their games, their tastes; why do our schools exert themselves to wipe out this distinction? Neither of the sexes should be a final model for the imitation of the other."[37]

Noted educator Julius Sachs, who had founded the Sachs Collegiate Institute for Boys and Girls, which was known for a curriculum that integrated classics, philology, archeology, and art, began advocating sex-specific curricula after joining the faculty of Teachers College, Columbia University. In a 1907 essay, "Coeducation in the United States," Sachs suggested that women must be trained as thoroughly as men, but in different areas: "hygiene of the home, of dress, the question of food values in the household, questions of public welfare, and above all, the entire field of esthetics that has hitherto been almost completely neglected."[38]

As debates about the dangers of coeducation circulated in the pages of scholarly journals, Stanford and Chicago were emulated by other private universities in the early twentieth century. The Northeast had been the slowest region in the United States to adopt coeducation. In 1872 Wesleyan admitted women students, the second institution in New England to do so, following the lead of Boston University in 1869. Tufts University, founded in 1854 as the first Universalist institution in the United States, opened its doors to women in 1890—after more than twenty years of consideration. In the early twentieth century, administrators at both Tufts and Wesleyan began to discuss the "cost" of coeducation, fearing that admission of women would deter men from attending.[39] By 1907, women composed 70 percent of the students at Tufts, fueling trustees' fears that the college was becoming unattractive to men. Drawing justification from the scientific discourses concerning the pitfalls of coeducation, Tufts created Jackson College as a sex-segregated unit in 1909.[40] At Wesleyan, male students and alumni spearheaded the movement against coeducation as the number of women students increased sixfold between 1872 and 1902. As alumni lobbied the trustees, male students organized a secret society to agitate against coeducation, posted antiwomen handbills across campus, and used their numbers as a voting majority to deny women recognition at Class Day. In response to this pressure, the trustees introduced a quota in 1900, limiting women to 20 percent of those admitted. Restricting the number of women on campus did not lessen male students' hostility to coeducation and the harassment of women students escalated. In 1909, the trustees voted to stop admitting women students, thereby ending the initial experiment with coeducation at Wesleyan with the graduation of the class of 1913.[41]

Rather than securing academic respect, women's outstanding performance in coeducational settings produced forms of backlash that ranged from campus harassment and the design of special curricular offerings for women to the end of coeducation and the creation of "coordinate women's colleges" within university settings. Harvard designated Radcliffe as its women's "Annex" in 1882. "Harvard's Annex provided women with lectures by Harvard's professors but refused to certify their hard-won learning by issuing a diploma. Columbia's Collegiate Course, in contrast, granted degrees to the women who passed a set of examinations on the prescribed syllabus Columbia men followed, but offered women no instruction or guidance on their studies."[42] In 1899, Columbia absorbed Barnard College (which had been created as a single-sex institution in 1889) as a coordinate women's unit, creating the possibility for women to complete university course work. Brown created Pembroke as the women's college in 1891. Although operating as sex-segregated units, the women's colleges within these male-dominated universities offered their students the full range of academic course offerings available to male students. But the antiwomen backlash of the early twentieth century also generated a new curriculum designed for women, variously labeled "domestic science" or "home economics."

In 1841 Catherine E. Beecher, a strong proponent of women's education, published *A Treatise on Domestic Economy, For the Use of Young Ladies at Home, and At School*, which celebrated the importance of women's labor in the home for the stability of American democratic institutions. In contrast to early proponents of women's education such as Fanny Wright and Harriet Martineau who made a case for equal educational opportunity, however, Beecher advanced a conception of "feminine domesticity" designed to preserve traditional gender roles among men and women, which she claimed would foster the stability and security of the new nation. By the late nineteenth century, proponents of women's rights provided a new rationale for domestic science, advocating training in home economics "to liberate women from the hardships of housework, teach them to guard their health and safety and that of their families and to simplify their lives."[43] In a series of lectures at the University of Wisconsin, Ellen Richards identified multiple ways that domestic science could promote women's freedom and family well-being. "Knowledge of what lurks in the dangers of food material" affords critical power to save lives. In addition, home economics can serve as a crucial component of social justice for it teaches students to "consume ethically and avoid products created under unsafe working conditions."[44] Pioneered by the University of Wisconsin's Professor Abby Marlatt, who championed every facet of "home management" as a science, home economics was considered one of the most rigorous courses at the UW campus in the early twentieth century. The curriculum included chemistry; physiology; bacteriology; linguistic training in English and a foreign language; technical topics on food, textiles, architecture; and household management. As early as 1911, Professor Marlatt introduced the "Practice Cottage" to subject every aspect of housework to constant study. She incorporated scientific management theories (Taylorism) in domestic science education, using the Practice Cottage as a technical tool to teach scientific management and time efficiency in the discipline of home economics. Imparting a "scientific approach" to the education of women as professionals, both as homemakers and as career women, the courses equipped graduates to become research chemists, nutritionists, bacteriologists, and government employees, as well as college and high school teachers of home economics.[45]

Although feminist proponents of home economics sought to develop an interdisciplinary field of study that could provide meaningful career education for women, university administrators concerned with the "dangers" of coeducation latched on to "domestic science" as a vehicle for the redomestication of university women. Following the University of Chicago, University of Wisconsin president Charles R. Van Hise decided to segregate the student body, establishing separate classes for women and men. President Van Hise insisted that segregating the women was imperative in ensuring that the rapid increase of women at universities would not "feminize" the men or drive the men from the fields in which women were heavily enrolled. He also suggested that sex segregation was important because men students were objecting to the attendance of women. In addition, claiming that male reason was more theoretical in nature, Van Hise argued that there was a need to devise "a peculiar education for a woman." Home economics fit his conception of this peculiar education perfectly.[46] Not content to allow women to elect their own course of study, male university administrators lobbied the federal government for legislation to encourage separate educational courses for women. In 1917, Congress passed the Smith-Hughes National Vocational Education Act as a supplement to the 1862 Morrill Act, which created the land grant colleges. Smith-Hughes not only appropriated federal money to state universities and state-aided colleges for teaching agricultural trades and home economics; it legally mandated land grant colleges to finance at least one full four-year collegiate course for women—a teacher training course in home economics.[47]

The attacks on and retrenchment from coeducation encountered spirited opposition from proponents of coeducation and from advocates of women's colleges. Noted American philosopher John Dewey denounced the attacks on coeducation as antidemocratic, suggesting that any retreat from merit-based education for women and men would give rise to "an undesirable spirit of aristocracy . . . attracting a class of students more interested in social diversion, and with the wealth necessary to indulge in it rather than those of a disposition to serious work."[48] President William Oxley Thompson of Ohio State University lampooned the specious fears fueling attacks on coeducation:

> The Chicago boys that desire to be vaccinated so they cannot take the girls, or to be educated in quarantine, will not be disturbed by the rest of the world. On the other hand, if there are boys who are not afraid of being "feminized" and who have the necessary courage, let us by all means retain institutions where they may face ruin at the hands of the weaker sex. . . . The girls have been taking too many prizes in the college classes and we are told that the boys conscious of their "ultimate superiority" feel discouraged over the condition in the first few years of the contest.[49]

Advocates of women's colleges also denounced the rampant misogyny circulating in the attacks on coeducation. In 1901, Smith College professor Elizabeth Deering Hanscom published a thoughtful critique of flawed notions of sex-specific virtues and calls for gender-differentiated curricula. "To avoid then," she wrote, "the debilitating sense of the moral inferiority and the deadening arrogance of moral superiority founded on assumptions of difference in sex, educational institutions require a more general view of virtue and the virtues."[50] Hanscom had no doubt that issues of domination and subordination lay at the heart of attacks on women's education and on the call for sex-specific courses of study. M. Carey Thomas also published widely about the dangers of "recent efforts to press women's colleges to develop special curriculum in domestic science, hygiene, sanitary drainage, child study—practical studies for married women." According to Thomas, "the argument that women's colleges should fit women for two great vocations, marriage and teaching/training of children is specious. Nothing more disastrous for the training of women, or for men, can be conceived of than this specialized education for women as a sex. . . . It will unfit women to teach boys, including their own sons and will lead to women being dismissed from the classroom."[51]

The Quest for Women's Higher Education in New Jersey: The Move toward NJC

New Jersey was "the last state in the union to open the way of higher education to women," and it trailed behind other states in provision of public education at all levels.[52] Although the largest growth in women's enrollments by far occurred in state universities, New Jersey took no action to facilitate women's access to college education. Under the auspices of funding from the 1862 Morrill Act, the New Jersey Assembly designated Rutgers the state agricultural school in 1864, and by 1890, federal funding for scientific and agricultural facilities covered 60 percent of Rutgers's budget.[53] In 1881, Professor George H. Cook, the first layperson to serve on the Rutgers faculty and the director of the "Scientific School" and the agricultural field station, and his colleague David Murray recommended that Rutgers admit women. Keenly aware of coeducational developments at other land grant institutions, they proposed that "young women of proper age and fitness" be admitted to the college to pursue a new course. The course was designed for students "who found the program of the Scientific School too specialized, but who did not wish to devote so much time to the classics and mathematics as was required in the classical course. By requiring only two years of Latin and two years of math, the 'Third Course' permitted more work in modern languages, social sciences, and philosophy."[54] Cook and Murray pointed out that in the numerous institutions that "had recently accepted coeducation, the experience indicated an elevation of standards of scholarship and deportment. . . . Nor ought it to be overlooked that there is everywhere among thoughtful people a growing conviction of the importance of providing for young women equally with young men, largely increased facilities for acquiring Higher Education."[55] Although the trustees approved the establishment of the "Third Course," they rejected the proposal for coeducation without any explanation.

As Rutgers president William H. Demarest noted in his *History of Rutgers College*, in 1891, "the admission of women to the college became again a subject of discussion ten years after its former discussion and rejection. An overture was even received from the Rutgers Female College in New York, which later went out of existence, proposing that it be brought into connection. Again all such proposal [*sic*] was rejected. The Trustees and the college body were positively opposed to coeducation."[56]

▲ 1913 PAMPHLET SOLICITING SUPPORT FOR A WOMEN'S COLLEGE IN NEW JERSEY

In 1911 when the New Jersey State Federation of Women's Clubs determined to take up the cause of women's higher education, they did not do so naively.[57] They were thoroughly familiar with the history of Rutgers and the anti-coeducation sentiment that pervaded the institution, just as they were keenly aware of the anti-coeducation backlash that was fueling the creation of "coordinate colleges for women" housed within larger universities. Yet they were also cognizant of the fact that New Jersey high schools were graduating 1.5 times the number of girls as boys and faced a severe shortage of women teachers.[58] New Jersey women lacked access to nonsectarian higher education where they could acquire credentials to teach in secondary schools. In the first decade of the century, the Roman Catholic College of St. Elizabeth, founded in 1899, was graduating four to five women a year. Mount Saint Mary College (later renamed Georgian Court), opened as a liberal arts school for women in 1908. Anti-Catholic sentiment, rife in the United States in the late nineteenth and early twentieth century, made these options unacceptable to many Protestant families. Rutgers College considered itself a private men's school, religiously affiliated with the Dutch Reformed Church, yet it also housed the "agricultural department," which as the land grant college for New Jersey, received both federal and state funds. Women could not matriculate in any degree-granting programs at Rutgers, but beginning in 1907, some women were allowed to participate in agricultural extension programs and summer institutes organized by the agriculture department. The College Club of Jersey City began raising funds for scholarships to send young women out of state for their education, but the number of scholarships they could fund did not compare with the seventy full-tuition scholarships that the state provided to deserving students to attend Rutgers.[59] Denied access to state-funded scholarships at Rutgers, and denied access to federally funded public education at Rutgers Agricultural Department, the land grant institution, the women of New Jersey faced a double dose of state-sponsored discrimination. Spurred on by such exclusionary practices, the New Jersey State Federation of Women's Clubs launched a campaign to create the New Jersey College for Women (NJC).

Under the talented leadership of Mabel Smith Douglass, proponents of NJC realized that an endowment for a totally independent women's college with private funds was not feasible financially. And they surmised that Rutgers trustees and President Demarest would never relent in their opposition to coeducation. To craft a viable strategy, they turned to the model of a "coordinate women's college," which had been successfully adopted by Barnard, Delaware, Virginia, Georgia, and South Carolina.[60] Mabel Smith Douglass was a shrewd tactician. In an arena in which men held final decision power over the fate of the proposed college, she knew she would gain nothing by appearing to threaten either state legislators or Rutgers trustees. For this reason, she urged Women's Club activists to assure the Trustees that they had no interest in coeducation, which "fostered 'unpleasant' social relations, a source of distraction to both professors and students, and led to unhealthy competition between the sexes."[61] Douglass wrote personally to President Demarest to insist that "as to co-education—I would

not worry about that—no one wants it, neither the parents of the girls nor the parents of the boys . . . I know that I would lose some of my best backers were I to propose coeducation."[62] To assuage fears further, the campaign for NJC avoided all militancy, adopting "a gentle feminine tone." Indeed, Douglass asked campaigners not to mention suffrage while rallying support for the college.

Framing the college in nonthreatening vocational language, pro-NJC forces blanketed the state, detailing the need for proper vocational training for New Jersey women, for "a technical college for women" that could offer young women the opportunity to prepare themselves for diverse careers—"librarian, secretarial, nursing, domestic science, art, physical training, and social and civic betterment."[63] Borrowing language from the debates about "domestic science," they suggested that graduates would be suited not only for "exciting new positions as court stenographers, and private secretaries" but also as managers of homes and institutions, inspectors of food supplies, expert buyers of fabrics, designers, assistants in research work, students of home economics and homemakers, caretakers of children and trained workers in charity."[64]

In advancing the campaign for NJC, Women's Club activists had to think carefully about how they addressed the issue of women's citizenship. In the final decades before the passage of the Woman's Suffrage Amendment, enacted by the U.S. Congress in June 1919 and ratified by three-quarters of the states by August 1920, women's citizenship remained a hotly contested issue. Neither the membership of the New Jersey State Federation of Women's Clubs nor the population of New Jersey was firmly pro-suffrage. Indeed, in October 1915, New Jersey voters defeated a referendum on women's suffrage by a 58 percent majority.[65] In this complex political environment, proponents of NJC adopted the rhetoric of republican motherhood, arguing that a "good general education . . . would suit women to be an efficient housekeeper . . . both a citizen and homemaker . . . for both of these major functions the times require the most extended education possible."[66] In this early twentieth-century context, a racial element was added to the conceptualization of republican motherhood. "Women of the state were urged to join the movement behind NJC in the interests of "their daughters and their race." Appeals for money and support were addressed to "every woman who realizes that in the little girl we have the potential mother of the race, and that the level to which the future of the race will attain depends upon the same little girl."[67]

As Patricia Palmieri has noted, the "Progressive era is typically associated with women's entrance to the professions of medicine, law, social work, and academe, but it was also a period of reaction—backlash against women's colleges. . . . Many male educators and doctors viewed women's colleges as 'institutions for the promotion of celibacy, producing a class of intellectual women who were not marrying and hence were committing 'race suicide.'"[68] Marriage rates for women college graduates were low (55 percent compared with 90 percent for the general population). Although proponents of women's rights linked these marriage rates to laws that prohibited married women from many occupations, thereby creating an unnecessary opposition between a career and family life, those opposed to women's higher education lamented "the decline of feminine charm and the rise of the mannish woman."[69] Alice Freeman Palmer (1855–1902), a graduate of the University of Michigan, president of Wellesley College, and later the first dean of women at the University of Chicago, pointed out that "it is not possible to annihilate the womanliness of our American girls by anything that you can do to them in education."[70] But her lucid arguments did not persuade opponents of women's education. In a 1905 speech to Congress, "President Theodore Roosevelt condemned low marriage rates and the equally scandalous practice of birth control. He popularized the term, 'race suicide,' insisting that the incapacity or unwillingness of the Anglo-Saxon race and particularly its highly educated members to marry and reproduce . . . would leave the nation in the hands of immigrants . . . whose fertility was quite high, but whose intellect was deemed inferior."[71]

Avoiding controversial issues like suffrage, proponents of NJC canvassed the state to build public sentiment and raise funds in support of the women's college. The campaign emphasized that NJC would train women

> "to be better citizens, better homemakers, and better club-women." . . . The early literature clearly set out the college's mission to meet the needs of just two groups of women: "those who have to earn their living by teaching or some kind of clerical work, and those who wish to have a good education together with a training that will fit them to be efficient housekeepers." Women's true vocation, motherhood, was celebrated in all the literature: the purpose of NJC was to prepare its students to be better mothers.[72]

Carrying this message to influential forces across the state, the campaign built a coalition of women's groups that extended well beyond the New Jersey State Federation of Women's Clubs, including "the D.R.s [National Society of the Daughters of the Revolution of 1776], the D.A.R.s [Daughters of the American Revolution], the Suffrage, the Anti-Suffrage, the Colonial Dames, the WCTUs [Women's Christian Temperance Union]."[73]

As George Schmidt recounts in his history of Douglass College, the Rutgers trustees were cajoled into supporting the coordinate women's college, "provided such an institution could raise its own funds and would not expect Rutgers to assume any financial obligations."[74] Savvy friends of Rutgers suggested that verbal endorsement without any commitment of financial support would seal the fate of the proposed college. Offering advice to President Demarest, U.S. senator and Rutgers trustee Joseph Frelinghuysen referred to Mabel Smith Douglass as "reasonable and intelligent. . . . She wants $100,000. . . . I think the thing should not be turned down or ignored, as her inability to raise her fund will be a sufficient deterrent without any opposition on our part, and if it could succeed, it would not be so bad as it would not be a coeducational college but an affiliated college."[75] In 1914, after three years of the federation's statewide campaigning, the Rutgers trustees went on record in favor of an affiliated women's college.

Senator Frelinghuysen clearly underestimated Mabel Smith Douglass. She proved to be a particularly gifted fund-raiser. Orchestrating a door-to-door fund-raising effort, she asked each household to donate one dollar for women's education. She persuaded James Neilson to donate large tracts of land as a site for NJC and Leonor Loree to provide $50,000 to grade the land to create an athletic field for the students. She negotiated a gift of property—the former home of Rutgers professor Jacob Cooper—from his son Drury W. Cooper on the condition that she could raise $23,500 in matching funds from the women of New Brunswick, a task she accomplished by 1918. She also succeeded in borrowing $50,000 from the Rutgers trustees to purchase the Carpender estate adjacent to the Cooper residence (a loan subsequently repaid by James Neilson through a gift of land to Rutgers College). Douglass also convinced the New Jersey State Legislature to appropriate $50,000 per year for the maintenance of NJC, a sum that increased significantly each year after the college opened. With these financial matters in place, the trustees passed a resolution in spring 1918 to "establish a Woman's College as a department of the State University of New Jersey maintained by the Trustees."[76] With the official approval of NJC on the books, Douglass also secured a commitment for a $1.6 million bequest from Elizabeth Rodman Voorhees to build a chapel for the new college, a sum that surpassed all the funds raised by President Demarest and the Rutgers trustees in their 150th-anniversary campaign.[77]

▲ PAGE FROM MABEL SMITH DOUGLASS'S LEDGER RECORDING DONATIONS TO THE FUND TO CREATE COLLEGE FOR WOMEN, 1913

Women's Education at NJC

As the product of a diverse coalition of interests, NJC harbored multiple and conflicting hopes for women's education. While some assumed that women would now have access to the same educational opportunities as men at Rutgers College, others aspired to shape an education attuned to particular conceptions of women's "sacred mission": marriage and motherhood. Although Mabel Smith Douglass and the faculty were committed to liberal arts education, "emphasizing the importance of being intellectually alive, saturating oneself with literature, philosophy, and the social sciences, before deciding irrevocably on a career," the curriculum included English composition and literature, Latin, Greek, French, Spanish, history, chemistry, biology, and mathematics, as well as "teacher education, and home economics—the bread and butter course in more ways than one."[78]

Supporters of the college disagreed not only about the content of the curriculum but also about the very nature of the college. The women in the New Jersey State Federation of Women's Clubs, who had fought for its creation, envisioned NJC as a "coordinate college" for women, equal in rank and importance to the "men's colleges" (Arts and Sciences, Agriculture, and Engineering) at Rutgers. Presaging the college's complicated relationship with Rutgers, President Demarest and the trustees "thought of it as a department of the Agricultural College, the recipient of Smith-Hughes Funds."[79] Supported by public taxation, the New Jersey Assembly conceived the college as nonsectarian, yet like their male counterparts at Rutgers College, the entering NJC students were required to attend chapel three times each week, including attending one weekly service that had a distinctly Protestant flair. As a recipient of federal funds under the Smith-Hughes Act, NJC was prohibited from any form of racial discrimination; however, it remained an almost exclusively white institution until the 1970s, although it experimented with national, religious, and ethnic diversity, opening its doors to a student from India in 1922, two Orthodox Jews in 1925, and a Puerto Rican student in 1926.[80]

From this welter of possibilities, life commenced at the New Jersey College for Women in the fall of 1918. *The Douglass Century* explores the vision of women's education devised by Mabel Smith Douglass and her colleagues in the New Jersey State Federation of Women's Clubs and how it has been transformed through one hundred years of ingenuity and growth. From the outset, the hybrid nature of the college was distinctive. It struggled for autonomy, yet it operated under complicated constraints. It was a "department" of Rutgers with a governance structure created by Rutgers trustees, who nonetheless frequently complained of the "peculiar independence" of NJC. Rutgers trustee Leonor F. Loree, a railroad magnate, adopted NJC as a favorite cause, serving on the Board of Managers until his death in 1940. Loree insisted that NJC be run like a business, giving priority to developing its infrastructure and cutting costs in order to run a surplus, a strategy that evoked the ire of Rutgers president John Thomas, who criticized the women's college for its "overemphasis on physical expansion at the cost of academic excellence and administrative efficiency, accusing it of hiring cheap labor."[81] In addition to the Rutgers administration and the NJC board, Mabel Smith Douglass had to deal with the politics of the New Jersey legislature, which since the 1860s had been embroiled in fraught exchanges with Rutgers over questions of accountability. With its own line item in the New Jersey budget appropriation, NJC developed intricate relations with state legislators—relations that were also a source of dismay to the Rutgers administration. Indeed, it was the report of the Duffield Commission, which was appointed in 1928 by the State Assembly to investigate all aspects of Rutgers's relation to the state that first officially designated NJC an autonomous college, one of the "coordinate and constituent colleges of the University."[82]

Juggling the often competing demands of an activist board, a suspicious administration, and a thoroughly political state legislature, Mabel Smith Douglass recruited faculty and students and launched the project of women's higher education. Between 1918 and 1929, student enrollment increased from 54 to 1,159. By 1929, there were 1,401 men at Rutgers and 1,159 women at NJC, and Dean Douglass boasted that in both 1928 and 1929, Douglass graduated more seniors than did Rutgers. The state appropriation for NJC increased from $50,000 to $430,000 in its first decade, and the faculty increased from sixteen to eighty.[83] With these resources in play, the arduous work of building and sustaining a women's college commenced.

Douglass historian George P. Schmidt noted that from its inception NJC was not "just another college." In contrast to coeducational institutions that sought to assimilate

▶ BOOK PLATE
DESIGNED FOR
THE NEW JERSEY
COLLEGE FOR
WOMEN LIBRARY

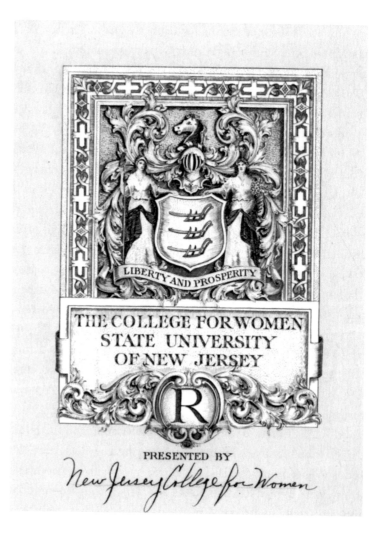

LIBERTY AND PROSPERITY

THE COLLEGE FOR WOMEN
STATE UNIVERSITY
OF NEW JERSEY

R

PRESENTED BY

New Jersey College for Women

women into norms derived from men's academic experiences, NJC took women's education as its fundamental mission, opening itself to the possibility that a women's college "should also involve changes in the content of the curriculum, what is taught, and the varieties of human experience examined. It might also affect the very creation of knowledge because a new group with new social perspectives would be recruited to research activities of the universities which are today the major creators of knowledge . . . [and it should promote] equal treatment for males and females [including] the same pattern of career development for men and women into the professional elites of society."[84]

The following chapters analyze the conception of women's education that evolved at NJC, a unique blend of curricular and co-curricular offerings devised to prepare women for life and for leadership. The challenges confronting a women's college have changed since 1918 as the roles of women, the nature of the world, and Rutgers University have been dramatically transformed. Enfranchisement, Prohibition, the Great Depression, World War II, the civil rights movement, Title VII of the Civil Rights Act of 1964, the Vietnam War, the women's movement, access to contraception, affirmative action, Title IX of the 1972 Education Amendments, *Roe v. Wade* (1973), the sexual revolution, the 1978 Pregnancy Discrimination Act, the Internet, the Beijing Platform for Action, gay marriage—all have left their mark just as have diminished state funding, the Rutgers Federated College Plan, coeducation, the 1981 University Reorganization, and the 2005 Transformation of Undergraduate Education. *The Douglass Century* traces the intricate means by which the college has preserved and enhanced its mission under these changing circumstances. Drawing upon its unswerving commitment to women's education, cherished values and traditions, loyal alumnae, astute administrators, and outstanding students as well as the support of a growing research university and of friends in the state legislature, Douglass has become a leader in women's higher education in the twenty-first century. The following chapters document that transformation.

NEW JERSEY COLLEGE FOR WOMEN
Establishing a Tradition, 1918–1929

THE LOVE I HAVE GIVEN MY GIRLS
HAS COME BACK TO ME MANY TIMES
OVER—PERHAPS I HAVE INSPIRED THEM
A LITTLE TO NOBLER THOUGHT AND
BETTER ACTION, BUT THEY HAVE GIVEN
ME COURAGE.

—Mabel Smith Douglass, March 1920

The New Jersey College for Women was founded at a tumultuous time in history. In fall 1918, the United States was still at war. By the end of the decade, the stock market had crashed and the world had plunged into the Great Depression. Although the Nineteenth Amendment was passed in 1918, in New Jersey women's struggle for the vote continued until the amendment was ratified in February 1920.[1] During the 1920s, the impact of World War I and women's suffrage, combined with economic prosperity, intellectual ferment, and the spread of new technology like the automobile, led to rapid social change. College students participated enthusiastically in the burgeoning youth culture of the Jazz Age. When the Eighteenth Amendment, prohibiting the sale of alcoholic beverages, proved unenforceable, the period became caricatured as the age of the flapper, whose bobbed hair, cigarettes, drinking, and sexual freedom shocked an earlier generation.[2] Female college students, particularly those in residential colleges, craved the new freedoms, while administrators who were considered in loco parentis and parents firmly believed that young women required protection. At NJC, Mabel Smith Douglass sought to maintain this delicate balance throughout the decade.

Mabel Smith Douglass and NJC

When Mabel Smith Douglass was appointed dean of NJC in May 1918, she had four months to set up the new institution. She designed a curriculum, hired faculty, recruited students, and found spaces for studying and living. She had just emerged from a long period of stress and grief that had led her to withdraw from the women's college movement in January 1915. After losing her husband to kidney disease in 1917, she ran his business in New York for one year and sold it, while raising two young children on her own.

On registration day, September 18, 1918, fifty-four students appeared and the college was under way. Almost immediately, Douglass faced a new challenge when the devastating 1918–1920 influenza epidemic reached New Brunswick. This new strain of influenza, which appeared in spring 1918, ultimately claimed fifty million deaths worldwide. Unlike in earlier epidemics, the death rate for adults between the ages of twenty and forty was shockingly high, almost half the total in the United States.[3] At Rutgers College, dozens of students were sent home and four died.[4] Surrounded by sick young women, Douglass was forced to close the college for three weeks, recalling that "it seemed to President Demarest and some of the faculty that it would mean the death of the college."[5] Happily, when she was able to reopen, fifty of the original fifty-four students returned.

Under Mabel Smith Douglass's leadership, NJC's curriculum, administrative structures, physical plant, extracurricular activities, and student traditions were developed during the 1920s. The college that Douglass created was heavily shaped by her own experience. Born Anna Mabel Smith on Wayne Street in downtown Jersey City on February 11, 1877, she was the elder of two daughters of James Weaver and Wilhelmine Joanne Midlige Smith, known as Minnie. James Weaver Smith was a successful merchant, the descendent of Dutch settlers who had come to Jersey City in the seventeenth century.[6] Mabel attended public elementary school number 3 and graduated from Jersey City High School (later Dickinson High School) in 1895. She moved on to Barnard College in New York, graduating in 1899.

Barnard College's origins came from the efforts of a group of prominent New Yorkers to open Columbia University to women in the late 1870s. Thwarted in this plan, the group, led by Annie Nathan Meyer, a young married Sephardic Jewish woman, proposed creating a Columbia annex, similar to the Harvard Annex (later Radcliffe), which had been founded in 1879. Barnard College opened in the fall of 1889 in a brownstone on Madison Avenue.[7] Six years later, Mabel Smith became one of several students who commuted to Barnard from New Jersey. Probably because of this commute, she did not participate in any student activities at college except at the Hap-Hazard social club.[8] In 1897, while Mabel was a student, Barnard followed Columbia to Morningside Heights, and began to build a new campus. Her Barnard experience would be an important influence on Mabel Smith, inspiring her to create an all-women's coordinate college at Rutgers.[9] In addition, her Barnard classmate Virginia Gildersleeve became dean of Barnard herself in 1911 and the two women's college deans frequently corresponded.

After graduation from Barnard, Mabel Smith taught in the New York City public schools for three years. In 1903, she married William Shipman Douglass, a New York commission merchant. The wedding, which took place at the Bergen Reformed Church in Jersey City and was followed by a reception at her grandparents' home on Summit Avenue, was reportedly "one of the large social gatherings of the early spring season." Two of the bridesmaids were Barnard friends, and the church was decorated in the 1899 class colors, green and white.[10] The young couple settled down to live a comfortable middle-class life. Their daughter, Edith, was born in 1905 and son, William, in 1907. Douglass's social background, religion, education, and early life had an important influence on NJC. This chapter will explore the foundation laid by Douglass and her allies in 1918 and its development during the 1920s.

Creating Spaces for Women

The most immediate concern for Mabel Smith Douglass was creating an adequate space for the new college. In 1918, practically the entire college—administration, classrooms, and dormitory—were located in College Hall. Constructed in 1855 as a private residence by Levi D. Jarrard, a local merchant and political figure, the property was purchased by John N. Carpender, a trustee and graduate of Rutgers, in 1880. In 1918, the building was leased from the Carpender family for the newly established College for Women and became known as College Hall. Laboratory courses were held in borrowed space in the Agricultural Building, while additional student rooms and a dining hall

▲ COLLEGE HALL IN THE 1920S

were carved into Cooper, the rambling Victorian house across the street from College Hall. The remaining students boarded with Dr. Jacob G. Lipman, dean of Agriculture.[11] The return of students and faculty from World War I in 1919 meant that the loaned space at the College of Agriculture was no longer available. With the college's future shaky, in January 1919, Douglass convened a group of representatives of New Jersey women's organizations to lobby the state legislature directly for support of the women's college. After a visit to the college, the legislators voted for an appropriation of fifty thousand dollars effective July 1, 1919; this sum would be the first direct state appropriation to NJC.[12]

The following year, Rutgers trustees created Boards of Managers to oversee the College for Women and the College of Agriculture. The NJC Board of Managers was made up of five Rutgers College trustees and five prominent women of the state, while the dean of NJC and the president of Rutgers served ex-officio. One of the five women's spots was reserved for the president of the New Jersey State Federation of Women's Clubs. The board supervised the expenditure of funds, oversaw the college property, engaged members of the teaching and clerical staff, prescribed the curriculum, and generally directed polices and management.[13] Trustee Leonor F. Loree of New York, the president of the Delaware and Hudson Railroad, installed (and paid for) one of his staff, Alfred Henderson, to serve as business manager. Born in Illinois, Loree grew up in Rahway, New Jersey. He commuted to Rutgers, graduating in 1877 with a bachelor of science degree. Loree was a lifelong Roman Catholic whose only daughter became a nun.[14] An active Rutgers trustee and supporter, Loree became a trusted adviser to Mabel Smith Douglass, although she did not always follow his recommendations.

▲ CORWIN DORMS

Another prominent trustee and benefactor, James Neilson, was also president of the Board of Visitors, the body that supervised all the state-supported units of Rutgers. The women members included New Jersey women's suffrage leader Lillian Feickert (1877–1945), who later became president of the New Jersey Women's Republican Club. Suffragists and feminists Miriam Lee Early Lippincott (1877–1947) of Camden and Florence Peshine Eagleton (1870–1953) of Newark both served on the Board of Managers and its successor committee for twenty-five years.

The Board of Managers had remarkable autonomy in running the college. Since his appointment as a trustee in 1909, Leonor Loree had been pressuring President Demarest to run Rutgers College in a more businesslike way.[15] At NJC, Loree had free rein to put his ideas into action. Loree's business plan initially involved renting houses and investing in an apartment house to be used as a dormitory. In 1919, the board rented five houses near the college on a three-year lease, while waiting for the apartment building on Suydam Street, christened Lorneil Hall after Loree and Neilson, to be completed by a local realtor. Loree and Mabel Smith Douglass had more ambitious plans, however. With the help of donations, a gift of land on Nichol Avenue from trustee William Leupp, and a loan of fifty thousand dollars from Rutgers College, the Board of Managers initiated the construction of twelve houses in the form of a horseshoe surrounding a tennis court. A mortgage was then taken out on the houses, which would be paid by way of the room fees charged to students. The loan was to be paid back when the mortgages were paid off.[16] Each house had a living room with a fireplace and beds for a maximum of seventeen students and a woman faculty member or administrator. Douglass wrote, "This method of accommodation has been so satisfactory from every point of view—of health, comfort, sociability, supervision, that any other method for this institution

would seem out of place. The large dormitory associated with many American colleges probably will never be built here."[17] Douglass was following the model of the small family house–like dormitory that had originated at Smith College in the 1870s. This model remained influential into the 1920s, informing, for example, George Kaufmann's design for Scripps College in 1926.[18] The small-house model proved successful at NJC as well: another horseshoe was built next to the first on what became the Douglass (later Corwin) campus, named in honor of the woman who originated the idea. The Douglass campus would be the first of many locations at NJC named after women. The Lodge, a recreation building, was placed at the center of one horseshoe, while a dramatic arts building, the Little Theater, became the focus of the other. Beginning in 1926, additional cottages were built on a parcel of land above the Raritan River donated by James Neilson, which became known as the Gibbons campus.

Douglass's creative use of space was further demonstrated by the transformation of the barn of the Carpender estate into a science building, and a series of extensions to Cooper Hall, which housed committee rooms and offices, the infirmary, student and faculty lounges, and living quarters. Most infamous was the "packing box" gymnasium constructed of surplus crates that were to have been used by the Wright Aeronautical Company in New Brunswick to ship airplane engines to Europe. As well as being employed for physical education, the packing box gym was used for concerts, plays, and dances and for assemblies and Sunday vespers before the erection of the chapel. Designed to be a temporary building, the gym was in use until 1963.[19]

Less quirky but more substantial, a zoology and botany building on Jones Street was built through funds raised by the New Jersey State Federation of Women's Clubs. Known as Federation Hall, the building later became the admissions office. The next major construction project, a home economics building, would be funded by the state. After the Agricultural Building was reclaimed by the College of Agriculture, home economics was housed in the Short Course Building on the College Farm. In 1924, Mabel Smith Douglass and her women's club allies successfully lobbied the state to secure an appropriation of $250,000 for a new home economics building and the completion of the Douglass (Corwin) campus. Douglass was aided by the fact that she had known Governor Edward I. Edwards in Jersey City, while the clubwomen were able to lobby assembly members from their respective districts. The new science building housed the chemistry and home economics departments and an expanded experimental cafeteria and lounge for the commuting students, the Bees. Douglass was able to repeat this feat in subsequent years, securing a state appropriation for what became known as the Recitation Building in 1926, and the Botany Building in 1927. As well as the botany department, Botany housed history and social sciences and, for a time, modern languages. Two floors of Recitation held the college library, as well as the English and art departments. The library would remain in this location until the opening of the Mabel Smith Douglass Library in 1961. In 1965, the three buildings off Bishop Street were renamed Chemistry, Biological Sciences, and Arts.[20]

THE CAFETERIA—THE SERVICE COUNTER

▲ THE COMMUTER CAFETERIA, ALSO KNOWN AS THE BEEHIVE, CA. 1930

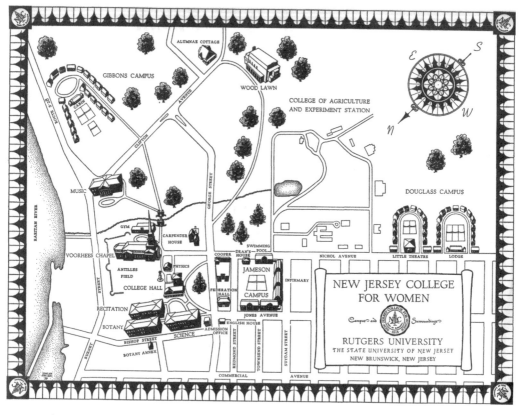

▲ MAP OF NEW JERSEY COLLEGE FOR WOMEN

Generous donors enabled several more buildings to rise on the NJC campus during the 1920s. After their success with Federation Hall, the clubwomen undertook an ambitious plan to raise money for a new music building. One hundred and three local clubs raised over one hundred thousand dollars for the imposing Georgian building located on Sonomon's Hill, later known as the Stephanie Morris Marryott Music Building. The largest single gift, however, was a bequest for a chapel by philanthropist Elizabeth Rodman Voorhees (1841–1924), whose family had already endowed the Rutgers College library in 1902. With its tall spire, the Georgian-style chapel became the signature of the NJC skyline. Voorhees's gift of $1.6 million also funded the purchase and maintenance of an organ manufactured by the Aeolian Company of New York. This organ was later replaced by a German Schuke model in 1976. The final construction project of the 1920s was a large residential red-brick complex similar to the buildings at Barnard, Vassar, and many other women's colleges. The land for the three-sided quadrangle that was ultimately built was donated by Rutgers trustee Edwin W. Jameson and named after his wife, Mary Gardner Jameson. As well as dormitory rooms, it contained a recreation lounge (Calumet), an assembly room (Agora), and a swimming pool. The complex built between 1928 and 1931 would be the last construction on the campus until the 1950s.[21]

Academic Life

FACULTY

The NJC faculty was initially primarily made up of professors from Rutgers College teaching part-time, a few full-time members, largely in home economics, and additional part-time lecturers and laboratory assistants. Distinguished Rutgers College faculty who taught part time at NJC included Louis Bevier, professor of Greek; William H. Kirk, professor of Latin; Irving Kull, in history; and Richard Morris, in mathematics. Most professors traveled across town to teach at the women's college, although a few classes were later taught at Rutgers College. Rutgers College faculty taught for free or received small stipends, which were probably welcome, since salaries at the men's college were notoriously low.[22]

The first full-time professor in the arts and sciences appointed directly to the NJC faculty was Ira D. Garard, who came to teach chemistry and oversee the development of the science program, and who would remain until 1957. Among the part-time faculty, a number of young women were employed as laboratory assistants in the botany and chemistry departments. Jessie Gladys Fiske, originally from Vermont, came to Rutgers

▲ CHEMISTRY LAB, 1920

as a graduate student in 1917 to work in seed analysis at the Agricultural Experiment Station. In 1918, Mabel Smith Douglass hired her as a laboratory assistant in botany. Douglass also asked her to live in one of the dormitories as a residence director. Fiske received her master of science degree in 1920 and was ultimately hired to teach full time at NJC in the department of botany. Fiske remained at NJC until 1960, was promoted to full professor, and was the chair of her department. She published on seeds, poisonous plans, and weeds, including marijuana, and was instrumental in establishing the teaching herbarium on campus, which emphasized local plants.[23]

There was quite a bit of turnover among the other part-time faculty, particularly in the department of home economics. Home economics courses were not even listed in the first few NJC catalogs. They were included in the announcement of the State University of New Jersey, which as of 1917 comprised the land grant college of agriculture and mechanic arts, along with several other departments such as ceramics that had been created by legislative action.[24] According to the terms of the Smith-Hughes Act, home economics students who were New Jersey residents paid no tuition (although they were charged certain fees), and the salaries of those teaching in the department were paid by the state. Because of the government appropriation, home economics had the highest budget of any NJC department (three thousand dollars in 1922–1923).[25] While beneficial for the students, this arrangement caused tension between NJC, Rutgers College, and the state over responsibility for the oversight of the department. The first department chair, Marie Casteen, complained to President Demarest about state inspectors constantly visiting her classrooms.[26] Further confusion arose among Rutgers professor of education Charles Elliott, the Board of Managers, the College of Agriculture, and Douglass herself over space, equipment, and finances. In a five-page letter to Demarest in 1922, the Dean wrote in frustration, "In the cooking and sewing departments . . . there is and has been constant friction."[27] Douglass was also pressured by Leonor Loree, who encouraged her to hire faculty as cheaply as possible. Hearing that twenty professors at the University of Chicago were retiring on pensions at age sixty-five, he urged Douglass to consider hiring them at NJC, for he expected that they could be had "at a very modest rate."[28] She ignored him.

Despite these pressures, Douglass was able to gradually build a stable and competent faculty, many of whom were women. By 1927, the total faculty had grown to eighty-three, thirty-five of whom were women.[29] In addition to Fiske and Garard, remarkably long-serving faculty appointed under Douglass included Oral Coad and Milton scholar Donald Dorian in English, distinguished scholar of the British constitution Margaret A. Judson in history, Dr. Leon Hausman in zoology, Evelyn J. Hawkes and Zora Klain in education, Helena M. Kees and Wilda Long in physical education, Helen W. Hazen in home economics, and Ethel Fair in library science. Douglass also hired an administrative team, including assistant dean Alice Aronoff, who arrived in 1918 and remained until 1953. The first registrar of the college, Mrs. Elisabeth N. Greene, assisted the dean from 1918 until her marriage in 1921 to Moncure C. Carpender, an engineer and nephew of John Neilson Carpender.[30] She was replaced by Esther B. Hawes, who would remain until 1952. Another long-serving administrator, dean of students Leah Boddie, from North Carolina, would serve with her assistant Elizabeth P. Thomas, from Nashville, Tennessee, until 1951. Dean Boddie was a formidable woman. According to one student of the 1930s, "She was the one with the social amenities and made sure everybody followed them."[31] Rounding out Douglass's team were director of admissions Sarah Tirrell and Fredericka Belknap, director of the Personnel Bureau, which arranged on-campus employment and provided career counseling for students.

The women administrators, faculty, and students created a vibrant women's community at the young college. Of women's colleges of the time, only Wellesley was committed to a total female professoriate.[32] At NJC, the number of women faculty members continued to grow, reaching 60 percent in 1928–1929.[33] Not all was peaceful, however, in the NJC community. According to college historian George P. Schmidt:

> Dean Douglass' regime took on a highly personal character. She chose her instructors and professors with considerable attention to personality factors, and while on the whole she assembled a capable and devoted faculty, not all her choices were wise. There were no regularities or gradations of salary or promotion, and tenure was unknown. Advancement came to those who, in the Dean's opinion, merited it. Without self-consciousness she habitually referred to "my students, my faculty, my college." Though consistently courteous, she did not like to be crossed and could be severe and sometimes arbitrary.[34]

Professor of history Margaret Judson, who held a bachelor of arts from Mount Holyoke and a PhD from Radcliffe, recalled that her job interview in 1928 consisted of a lunch alone with the dean. "Dean Douglass. . . . must have decided I met her requirements, whatever they were."[35] The brilliant Emily Gregory Hickman (1880–1947), who had a PhD in history from Cornell and had served as head of the history department at Wells College in Aurora, New York, was hired by Douglass as a full professor and assistant to the dean in 1927. By 1929, however, disagreements between Hickman and Douglass ended the former's administrative career, although Hickman continued teaching at the college until her death in an automobile accident in 1947. Hickman became an active member of the National Committee on the Cause and Cure of War, the pacifist educational organization founded in 1925. By the early 1930s, she became state chair and vice chair of the national organization. She was an outstanding and beloved teacher, and a new liberal arts building, Hickman Hall, was dedicated in her honor in 1964.[36]

Salaries at NJC were initially quite erratic. In 1924, they ranged from sixteen hundred dollars to six thousand dollars. As was typical of the time, men consistently earned more than women. In 1927, in response to criticism, Douglass hired a number of experienced faculty members at professorial rank with salaries up to five thousand dollars, many of whom were women whose salaries were comparable to men's.[37] In the early

1930s, the faculty continued to become more professionalized with the creation of committees, an executive council, and a faculty handbook.[38] In 1931, NJC was reaccredited, along with Rutgers, by the Middle States Association of Colleges and Secondary Schools. The acceptance letter noted that "the matter of faculty harmony had somewhat troubled the committee in making its recommendation." In her report, Douglass urged the faculty to be more harmonious.[39] Whether or not this actually happened is unknown.

CURRICULUM

The curriculum at NJC was similar to that of many other women's colleges of the time. In planning the curriculum, Douglass was influenced by those of her alma mater, Barnard, and the other Seven Sisters colleges, although she also sought comparisons to women's colleges at other state universities. In combining liberal arts with vocational subjects, Douglass was influenced by the reality of careers available to women at the time. In her notes, she listed the top careers for women based on the 1920 U.S. census—teaching, secretarial work, nursing, social work, art, and librarianship—and compared what was being offered and planned at NJC.[40] This hybrid approach was similar to that at Connecticut, Simmons, Skidmore, and William Smith Colleges—like NJC, these women's colleges were founded during the Progressive Era.[41] At NJC, students had a choice of three courses of study: liberal arts, education, and home economics. Liberal arts included required courses in English, mathematics, hygiene, and physical education, while electives were offered in French, Greek, Latin, Spanish, chemistry, history, and biology. Students preparing to be teachers majored in the subject that they planned to teach and took electives in education and psychology.[42] Those following the liberal arts course could prepare for the bachelor of arts, which required either Latin or Greek; the bachelor of letters, in which a modern language could be substituted for a classical language; or a bachelor of science.[43] This choice of degree course was also offered at Rutgers College.[44] While a few elite institutions like Bryn Mawr still required classical languages for graduation, this requirement was being quietly discontinued by the 1920s.[45]

Although Latin and Greek were losing their role as a required element of a liberal education, a thriving classics department developed at NJC under Shirley Smith. Smith was an Oberlin graduate with a PhD from Yale who was hired by Mabel Smith Douglass in 1927 and became chair after the withdrawal of the Rutgers College professors of Latin and Greek.[46] In her teaching, Smith and colleague Evalyn Clark used lantern slides of ancient sites from trips to Greece, Rome, and Turkey during the 1930s. Clark used her slides for teaching through the 1950s.[47] In contrast to the small classics department, English was NJC's largest. As department chair in the 1920s, Oral S. Coad assembled a group of younger colleagues, including Raymond Bennett, Donald and Edith Dorian, Eva Loudon, and Fred Rockwell. As well as English literature, the department's offerings featured courses in interpretive speaking and play production, which ultimately formed the nucleus of the Department of Speech and Dramatic Art. Another long-serving faculty member, Jane Inge, directed three plays a year at the Little Theater, which was open to the general public.[48]

NJC also became known for its offerings in modern languages. French, German, and Spanish were taught as early as 1919 and Italian was added by 1924. Modern language study at NJC emphasized language acquisition as a practical asset, as well as promoting understanding of new cultures. Douglass secured the services of native speakers like Alice De Visme in French, Emil Jordan in German, and Manuel Salas in Spanish, who introduced eclectic methods in which languages were taught as living languages.[49] Along with De Visme's colleague Marguerite Lentz Richards, these three were among NJC's longest-serving faculty. Trained in Middlebury College's innovative foreign language program, De Visme and her husband, H. W. Williamson, brought these concepts from the Vermont college to NJC. Language students embraced co-curricular features such as French-, German-, and Spanish-speaking tables in the dining room and language clubs in each department—Le Cercle Français, Der Deutsche Verein, and El Círculo Español. The establishment of language houses created yet another way to immerse students in language study. The first one, the French House, was founded in 1930 in one of the houses on the Douglass (Corwin) campus, and was soon followed by the German and Spanish Houses. Its founders hoped that the French House would provide "an opportunity for us to learn French so that we can improve in a small way international relations."[50]

Home economics differed from other departments in that it was a combination of academic and vocational training. The curriculum included hygiene, nutrition, money management, and principles of child development and family relationships. While household management was not a new concept, home economics was novel in that it provided *formal* instruction in dealing with the home and the family.[51] The funds provided by the Smith-Hughes Act were specifically designed to train teachers of home economics. Using the racialized language of the time, a brochure advertised the department: "Never has the American home had the great responsibility that it has today when thousands of immigrants from foreign countries are learning to make their new homes according to its ideals. The training of the foreign-born girl in Home Economics is one of the most effective agencies in Americanization. It is very necessary that we have specially prepared teachers for this work."[52] Although this legislation provided the key support that enabled NJC to be established, in reality home economics majors always remained in a minority at NJC, less than a quarter of the student body. Of the Class of 1922, twelve of fifty-four were studying home economics, six were pursuing a bachelor of science, ten were in the bachelor of letters program, and the remaining twenty-six were preparing for the bachelor of arts.[53] NJC resembled women's colleges like Mills, Goucher, and Vassar that offered home economics as one of many alternative courses.[54] Other vocationally oriented courses like journalism and library science were added later, in 1925 and 1927, respectively.

The home economics curriculum at NJC was similar to that at other women's colleges and coeducational land grant universities.[55] Home economics students at NJC followed a rigorous four-year program of study with limited time for electives. They were required to take basic science courses including general chemistry, organic chemistry, physics, and physiology. They also took science courses like Household Chemistry that were designed "to cover the most important applications of chemistry encountered in the home and its environment."[56] In the third year, home economics students were required to choose a major in Foods and Cookery or Textiles and Clothing. Upper-level courses in foods included Cafeteria and Large Quantity Cookery, Lunchroom Management, and Nutrition and Dietetics; courses in Textiles and Clothing included Dressmaking, Millinery, and Laundering. Students in the large-quantity cooking course got direct experience by running a cafeteria that was patronized by other students and staff. Textile and art students ran a costume shop where they sold garments bearing the label "product of the Junior Shop or Costume Shop of N.J.C."[57] In their senior year all students of home economics were required to live in the Practice House, a "charmingly-furnished" rented property where students lived as a family. When the Douglass (Corwin) campus was built, the Practice House moved to one of the houses. A final requirement was a Home Project, in which, during the summer vacation, students applied what they learned to their own homes. The catalog notes that "if for financial reasons the student cannot spend a part of the summer in her own home, her project work will be planned to fit her needs."[58] Home economics students also took courses in home nursing, civics, and sociology. The home economics specialist was expected to "carry her knowledge of real homeworking and good housekeeping into the outside world."[59] These courses reflected the Progressive Era ideal that through education and training in home economics and social science, white middle-class women could become "urban housekeepers," improving public health and welfare in their communities.[60]

Physical education was an important part of the NJC curriculum. Until 1937, when seniors were excused, all students were required to take four years of physical education. Physical education for women had its roots in the mid-nineteenth century when Elizabeth Cady Stanton and other feminists advocated physical activity to improve the health and well-being of girls and women. From their foundation, Vassar and Wellesley required students to engage in calisthenics. As more women entered higher education, promotion of physical activity and sports for women became a way to counter claims by Dr. Edward Clarke and others that higher education was detrimental to women's health. Both private and coeducational colleges rapidly developed departments of physical education and health, usually headed by women.[61] At NJC, one of the first people Douglass hired was Alice Aronoff to teach physical education.

Well aware of the arguments about the damaging effects of women's higher education, Mabel Smith Douglass and trustees Leonor Loree and James Neilson were all deeply concerned with students' health. Apparently Loree and Neilson were largely responsible for the four-year physical education requirement and a rule that students should attend all meals; those who cut gym classes were not allowed to go to dances.[62] The NJC infirmary began in one room in College Hall and moved to Cooper Hall in 1920. At the end of the decade, the Mary Kingsland Macy Willetts Infirmary, a three-story red-brick building on the Jameson campus, was proudly dedicated. Mary Maud Thompson, RN, who arrived at NJC in 1920 and originally lived in a room in Cooper next to the infirmary, would serve as director of the Willetts Infirmary until her retirement in 1951.

In the first years, physical education consisted of "marching tactics, calisthenics, Indian clubs,[63] the horizontal bar, gymnastic games, dancing, track, and team games played in the back porch or back yard of College Hall."[64] In early 1923, Loree gave fifty thousand dollars to grade, build a retaining wall on, and turn into athletic fields land near College Hall donated by James Neilson. NJC students played team sports on Antilles Field, named after the ship that brought Loree, his family, and his friends back from Europe in 1914. More sports were gradually added, including basketball, tennis, and swimming at the YWCA in New Brunswick before the Jameson pool was built. Another popular option was folk dancing and aesthetic dancing or "flit," described as "classical ballet, without toe dancing, with a little less drama and some added Isadora Duncan influence in the interpretation of classical music and the use of scarves to create a pattern of movement."[65] Herein lay the origins of Rutgers University's dance department.

Although Mabel Smith Douglass hoped to develop athletic instruction around the needs of individual students, Leonor Loree believed that "the time has come when both the institution and the individual student will be benefited by concerted movements. They act both as a stimulus and a strong disciplinary agency." He urged her to hire a Sokol instructor, whom he offered to help her obtain through the Czechoslovakian embassy.[66] Sokol was a form of gymnastics that originated in 1862 and was brought

▲ BASKETBALL GAME, 1920s

by Czechoslovakian immigrants to the United States. Loree did indeed bring Zdislava Prochazkova, AB (artium baccalaureus, the Latin for bachelor of arts), from the University of Prague, to NJC as a visiting faculty member. She arranged a demonstration of Sokol at the celebration of the tenth anniversary of NJC in 1928. The demonstration was covered by the *New York Herald Tribune*, drawing attention to the young college.[67]

Helena M. Kees took over the Department of Physical Education and Hygiene (later Health) in the mid-1920s and remained for over thirty years. Kees was trained at Wellesley, which after taking over the Boston Normal School of Gymnastics in 1909 became the most important institution of the day for training women college directors of physical education.[68] Under Kees's leadership, classes were developed in human anatomy, kinesiology, and therapeutic exercise, as well as principles and methods of teaching physical education to children. Classes in hygiene and health education focused on personal hygiene, school and community hygiene, the motivation of health habits, and how to measure success in health teaching.[69] Young women majoring in physical education looked forward to careers as public school teachers, recreation directors, or exercise supervisors at orthopedic clinics.[70]

The Department of Physical Education also played an important role in monitoring student's health. Infirmary director Maud Thompson worked closely with the deans and physical education faculty to make sure that students were following appropriate exercise programs. Upon admission, students were required to produce a medical certificate from a family physician and were examined by Dr. James Louis Fagan, the college physician, and nurses upon arrival. An October 1925 medical report revealed that several students were disabled, among them four suffering from the aftereffects of infantile paralysis or polio, one with an artificial leg, and two who were blind. In addition, thirty-four students had anemia, thirteen had heart problems, and numerous others suffered from various minor ailments. Students with medical issues were prescribed special diets and encouraged to rest between classes. They were also excused from more vigorous games and exercises. "Those suffering from disabilities such as permanent infantile paralysis, temporary bad posture cases, sprained ankles, etc.," were given "individual correctives."[71] NJC historian Rosamond Sawyer Moxon, who herself was part of the Class of 1929, noted that "when girls with grade C posture were required to take the work [corrective exercises], they often responded with marked reluctance."[72] NJC's physical education and medical staff were following theories about the importance of posture that gained currency at schools and universities during the early decades of the twentieth century. Posture testing for both men and women became especially prevalent at elite men's and women's institutions. Ultimately posture testing at women's colleges, which persisted long after medical opinion had moved on, would gain national attention when caches of photographs were discovered years later in college archives.[73]

NJC was also distinguished by its music and art programs. Douglass herself loved music and had studied violin as a girl. She was determined to include music as a required element in the curriculum. Soon after the college opened, she purchased a grand piano and secured an artist from New York to come down once a week to play it.[74] At Rutgers College, although the Glee Club became a permanent fixture in 1880, music courses were not offered until 1919 after the appointment of Howard Decker McKinney as music director.[75] Douglass boasted that the study of music at NJC predated that at Rutgers College; indeed she arranged for McKinney to teach at NJC in 1918. In 1919, History and Appreciation of Music was offered as an alternative to the History of Art to meet the fine arts requirement for graduation.[76] Other music courses developed at NJC included theory, composition, music education, and organ and piano performance. The first young women to graduate as music majors in 1925 included Stephanie Morris (Marryott), who later joined the faculty. This group established an honors music society, Delta Mu. The early music students wrote original college songs, including the NJC "Alma Mater," penned by Katherine Boynton ('22) with music by Howard McKinney, and the "Sacred Path Song," by Helen Kingman and Stephanie Morris. The first edition of the *N.J.C. Song Book* was compiled and published in the fall of 1922 by six members of the class of 1925 assisted by Howard McKinney.[77] Subsequent editions, the last of which was published in 1947, were compiled by McKinney, choir director and chapel organist J. Earle Newton, and Stephanie Morris Marryott. College songs continued to be printed in the student handbook.

NJC also developed a strong program in the visual arts. Unlike Rutgers College, which offered only art history, the NJC curriculum included preparation for teaching art at various levels, and a practical arts curriculum comprising classes in color, design, freehand drawing, and perspective.[78] One high school art teacher identified NJC along with Skidmore as one of the few colleges that provided good training in the practical arts.[79] As in music, co-curricular opportunities supplemented academic courses. Pen and Brush, the club for art students, was founded in the late 1920s. The *Quair* yearbook was another opportunity for NJC artists to show their talents: the 1929 *Quair* featured etchings of campus scenes by a student artist, while the 1930 yearbook had a striking art deco–inspired design. The real tour de force, however, was the 1931 *Quair* with its full-color Middle Eastern theme.

▲ ARTWORK FROM *QUAIR*, 1922

Student Life

WHO WENT TO NJC?

From fifty-four students in 1918, NJC grew rapidly. Each year the new freshman class was larger. Leonor Loree put pressure on Douglass to admit more students, complaining, for instance, that there were only seventy-five incoming freshmen in 1920, when "many are finding it impossible to enter such colleges as Vassar and Smith."[80] He was concerned with securing adequate student tuition, board, and lodging to support the dormitories that the college was building. The Class of 1925, boasting 114 members at the outset, titled their memoir *The Fourth Wall*: "Now for the first time, the college had a complete student body; the fourth wall had been set in place. Everyone felt obligated to reinforce any weakness and to help cement it firmly to the rest of the structure."[81] The college grew to 347 students in October 1922. Of these, 282 were in residence and 65 were commuters. While the vast majority of the students were from New Jersey, a few hailed from New York, Pennsylvania, Connecticut, Massachusetts, and Washington, DC.[82]

In the booming 1920s, NJC had no trouble attracting students. Its relatively low fees and free tuition for home economics students made it affordable for "students of modest means." Its convenient location appealed to young women from the thriving city of New Brunswick and cities and towns accessible by rail. The college continued to grow through the 1920s, reaching 540 students in 1924 and more than doubling to a peak of 1,157 in 1929, almost as many as the entire enrollment of the men's colleges of 1,401 students.[83] While striving to meet Loree's goals, however, the college staff became concerned that too many unprepared students were being admitted. The director of admissions wrote, "If twenty or thirty of the accepted students could be eliminated on the basis of scholarship, a tremendous growth in the intellectual morale of the freshman class would be noticed. I am not unconscious of nor have overlooked the administrative demands in meeting the expense of the new dormitories, but I am convinced that more students will want the thing harder to obtain."[84] To support academically struggling students, Emily Hickman chaired the unfortunately named "Deficient Students Committee." Under her leadership, struggling sophomores were divided into small groups and assigned to a senior mentor, who provided tutoring and closely monitored their progress.[85]

Part of these difficulties stemmed from the fact that Mabel Smith Douglass was reluctant to accept students, even if academically gifted, from working-class or immigrant backgrounds, including many Jews and Catholics. In fact, some of Emily Hickman's "deficient" students were Italian or German immigrants who struggled with the English language, came from poor families, or were forced by financial necessity to commute long distances.[86] As she wrote to trustee James Neilson, who had tried to intercede on behalf of some students who wanted to live with friends in New Brunswick, Douglass desired to have in college only students "who are willing to live at the same time a life of refinement and culture."[87] In the 1920s, with the exception of an international student from India, NJC was not racially, culturally or ethnically diverse.

This was a period, however, when an increasing number of daughters of the foreign born were entering college. Although women's colleges remained overwhelmingly white and Protestant, colleges in cities such as Barnard, in New York; Radcliffe, in Cambridge; and Goucher College, near Baltimore, enrolled increasing numbers of students from immigrant backgrounds because they could live at home.[88]

By the late 1920s, greater numbers of young Jewish and Catholic women were applying to NJC. Mabel Smith Douglass and her advisers attempted to restrict their numbers by trying to recruit students from small towns, rural areas, and outside the state.[89] Douglass feared that these newcomers would detract from the genteel middle-class atmosphere needed to attract desirable students and their families. Reports such as one from the dean of girls at Princeton High School alarmed her: "Apparently three girls she had sent to NJC recently were unhappy and wanted to transfer. They did not like the type of girl with whom they lived."[90] Douglass's attitude was typical of the nativism, anti-Semitism, and snobbery of her era. Michael Greenberg and Seymour Zenchelsky document similar efforts to restrict the admission of Jewish students at Rutgers College.[91] Historian Rosalind Rosenberg noted that Douglass's friend Virginia Gildersleeve, dean of Barnard from 1911 to 1946, "welcomed Jewish students and faculty as long as they were thoroughly assimilated, and she included African Americans only so long as they were well spoken and did not ask to live in the dormitories."[92]

Historically, elite institutions like Harvard, Yale, and Princeton admitted students almost entirely on the basis of academic merit. By the 1920s, however, academic requirements could no longer screen out scholastically accomplished students from working-class or lower-middle-class families, many of whom were from Eastern European Jewish backgrounds. This development occurred at a time when the national movement to restrict immigration was gaining momentum.[93] Indeed, at many U.S. colleges during the 1920s and 1930s, selective admissions policies based on amorphous notions of "character" were used as "tool(s) of discrimination against socially undesirable" students, many of whom were Jewish or from working-class immigrant backgrounds.[94] Mabel Smith Douglass's efforts were successful: the percentage of Jewish students at NJC declined to 11 percent in the Class of 1932 from an average of 17 percent in the Classes of 1928 through 1931.[95] Julia Feller Feist, Class of 1935, recalled, "When I was coming to school one of the rarities was a Jewish student. Black students were totally unknown."[96] It does not appear that similar attempts were made to limit the number of Catholic applicants. In fact, Helena Kees of the department of physical education, who was a Roman Catholic, was encouraged "to reach out to parochial schools and to talk to influential people in Catholic educational circles to try to gauge their opinion of NJC."[97]

TRADITIONS

The Class of 1922, the inaugural class at NJC, created a pattern of student life that would endure for many years. The pioneer class was aware that they were setting precedents. According to the compiler of a volume printed for the thirtieth reunion: "It was our job to tell the world what this college was, and where, and why, and to be sure that we didn't leave behind us a trail of bad starts that might wreck the hopes and plans of the anxious group of men and women who had worked for years to make the institution possible."[98] The first students arrived at an institution, known just as the College for Women, which did not even have a definite name, although they soon settled on New Jersey College for Women, shortened to NJC. The first class chose the college color, scarlet (the same as Rutgers College); the emblem, the pine tree, named after a majestic conifer in front of College Hall; and the Greek motto, roughly translated as "Wisdom and Self Control." The motto was chosen after consultation with Dean Douglass and the professor of Latin and Greek, who made suggestions, and was then voted on by the student body. Hazel Coddington and Florence Leonard from the Class of 1922 designed the first seal, of two concentric circles with "State University of New Jersey" and "College for Women" around the bottom and with "NJC" at the center, the pine tree draped around the "J." In 1931, the seal was modified, substituting "New Jersey College for Women" and "1918."[99]

The Class of '22 was keenly conscious that they were establishing college traditions. The most important of these were Campus Night in the fall, the Yule Log in December, and the Mother's Day celebration in the spring. Campus Night originated in a possibly apocryphal incident: a number of students had bought bright red tam-o'-shanters, or tams, hats that were a popular fashion item that year. Mabel Smith Douglass did not like these hats and convinced the students to burn them in a bonfire. Douglass decided to turn the ritual burning into an all-college hot dog roast and sing-a-long. The event grew over the years into an alumnae homecoming festival.[100] The college's "most beloved custom," the Yule Log ceremony, originated the first Christmas when students asked Douglass if they could have a tree and burn a Yule log in a fireplace at College Hall. They decorated College Hall and got permission to string electric lights on the famous pine tree, washing the windows of College Hall to earn money to pay the extra electric bill. The night was marked by carol singing and candle lighting.[101] This event inaugurated the yearly Yule Log ceremony, when, after lighting a Christmas tree in front of College Hall and the traditional log in the fireplace, the students marched across campus, singing carols, to enjoy a turkey and plum pudding dinner.[102] Yule Log was later moved to the Voorhees Chapel.

Spring brought the first Mother's Day celebration, at which students, dressed in white, danced around a maypole. Bouquets tied to their wrists were presented to their mothers at the end of the festivities.[103] This tradition developed from the English May Day festivities, which were celebrated at U.S. colleges—especially women's colleges—in the late nineteenth century. Bryn Mawr's famous May Day ceremony, first held in 1900, featured students in elaborate Elizabethan costumes and theatricals.[104] At NJC, the celebration was held the second week in May close to Mother's Day, first celebrated in the United States in 1908. Mother's Day at NJC was later known as Parents' Day.

The Class of 1922 saw the birth of commencement traditions. As the chapel had not been built yet, a baccalaureate religious service was held in St. John's Episcopal

▲ MOTHER'S DAY PAGEANT, 1920, SCHUMANN PHOTO

Church on George Street, near the college, presided over by the Reverend Edward W. Hall, the rector of the church.[105] Commencement itself was held in the packing box gym on June 10, 1922. The chief speaker was the Catholic essayist and biographer Agnes Repplier. Mabel Smith Douglass presided and President Demarest gave out the diplomas. The Gloria Trumpeters, an all-female trumpet quartet from New York hired by Leonor Loree, performed. Notably, a Phi Beta Kappa section of the Rutgers chapter was established at NJC and five young women were inducted.[106]

As student numbers rose, traditions became more elaborate and were increasingly geared to promote unity and identity among individual classes. Seniors enjoyed numerous activities during Senior Week—the final seven days before commencement—including Class Day, which featured music, readings, a public speaking contest, and presentation of the class gift. Juniors were required to write, produce, direct, and act in a musical production, the Junior Show. Florence Marshall (NJC '29) was elected chairman of the Junior Show in May 1927 for the coming year. She wrote in her diary that she was "thrilled to bits," but noted that "I have to watch my step & see that the administration would approve everything we do."[107] Throughout the year, members of the freshmen, sophomore, junior, and senior classes competed against each other in field hockey and soccer matches, canoe races, and debating and singing contests.[108] Each class sponsored a formal dance—the Senior Ball, Junior Prom, and Sophomore Hop. Freshmen and students who did not attend prepared early morning breakfasts for the dancers. NJC students also attended dances at Rutgers College, which provided a steady supply of dates.

Most striking was the tradition of freshmen hazing, which had its roots in practices at British boys' public schools and men's colleges. At Rutgers College in the late nineteenth century, elaborate freshmen customs—for instance, freshmen were not allowed to carry the canes popular at the time—resulted in pitched battles between freshmen and sophomores on the college lawn. At NJC, to show their "greenness" or inexperience, freshmen were required to wear a green feather and later a hat known as a dink. They were not allowed to walk on the grass, wear the college color, scarlet, and had to wait until the sophomores were seated in the dining hall before sitting down. Each freshman was assigned a "sister," from the junior class, with whom she was advised to make friends.[109] Although technically forbidden, freshman hazing existed at other women's colleges such as Bryn Mawr.[110] At NJC, Campus Night in October grew to mark the end of the two-month hazing period when the feathers or dinks were ceremoniously burned in the bonfire. The end of all freshmen restrictions was marked by the Sacred Path ceremony in early May. Freshmen were forbidden to walk on the Sacred Path, a shortcut across the lawn from College Hall to George Street. They were given access to the path after a ritual moving-up ceremony, when they gave school rings to the sophomores and in return the sophomores gave the freshmen the college blazer and the red hat. Juniors and seniors lined the path while the ceremony took place.[111] Freshmen hazing and costumes were ultimately banned in 1957, although the Sacred Path ceremony continues to mark the moving-up of classes.

STUDENT ORGANIZATIONS

Many enduring student clubs and societies were established by the first class. These included student publications: the biweekly newspaper *Campus News* (originally *Campus Chatter*) was founded in 1920, and the *Quair* yearbook was created to mark the graduation of the first class in 1922. The word *quair* or *quire* came from the Anglo-Saxon for a collection of leaves of a book. Amateur dramatics were extremely popular among members of the first class, led by Grace Webb, apparently the first student at NJC to have bobbed hair. The first production, directed by English professor Edna Barbour in conjunction with the Queen's Players, from the men's college, was J. M Barrie's *Quality Street*, performed in a rented auditorium at New Brunswick High School in April 1919. The production was followed by the official formation of the Mimes dramatic group. Another early organization was Philolathean, an honorary literary society introduced at NJC upon the initiative of members of Philoclean, the literary society at Rutgers College, first established in 1825 and revived in the early twentieth century.[112]

Musical clubs were among the many student societies established by the first few classes. These included the short-lived NJC drum and bugle corps, which had been created at the insistence of trustee Leonor Loree and was despised by Mabel Smith Douglass, and the Mandolin Club, where along with mandolins students played banjos, violins, saxophones, percussive instruments known as traps, and ukuleles. The Weeping Willows, soon shortened to the "Weepies" was a small group who sang to ukulele accompaniment at musicales and other entertainments. The various musical groups often performed together as the combined music clubs at the college and worked closely with the music department. The first class also created the Bees, the club for commuter students. The Bees' name was derived from their nonsensical theme song about a bee that sat on a wall and from the fact that many came from "Brunswick" or nearby. The Bees were initially assigned a room in the basement of College Hall, where they could eat lunch or change into gym uniforms or into party clothes before dances.[113] The only religious club was a college chapter of the YWCA. With the mission of promoting Christian fellowship on campus, the YWCA sponsored guest speakers and cooperated with the Red Cross, the Girl Scouts, and the New Brunswick YWCA on service projects. In the summer, the YWCA joined young college women from all over the country at the student conference at Silver Bay near Lake George in upstate New York.

Many co-curricular clubs were also formed in NJC's early years. Besides the language clubs and Pen and Brush, these included the Curie Science Club, founded in 1923; the Mathematics Club; the Pro and Con Debating Society; the History Club; and the Scissor Bowl, for home economics students. Later in the 1920s, the Varsity Debating Team competed with Syracuse, Swarthmore, Temple, and other colleges. Finally at graduation in 1922 the independent Associate Alumnae of New Jersey College for Women was established for graduates and former students of NJC, "to maintain the spirit of service and fellowship in every graduate and every former student[,] to foster active cooperation between the administration of the college and the alumnae, [and] to aid undergraduates and prospective students of the college."[114]

Athletics were very popular in the sports-mad 1920s, a decade that has been described as containing "the first wave of athletic feminism" for women.[115] NJC's Athletic Association organized all sporting activities, gave out varsity letters each year, and represented NJC at the National Amateur Athletic Federation of America. NJC fielded teams in basketball, hockey, soccer, volleyball, and archery. Uniforms were long black skirts, black tights, and white blouses with black ties. As at many women's colleges, participation in intercollegiate sports was a matter of debate at NJC. Leaders in women's athletics in the late 1920s were concerned about the unhealthy effects of competition, instead encouraging colleges to sponsor field days where athletes could demonstrate their skills.[116] An editorial in the *Campus News* explained that intercollegiate sports were expensive and opined that "the toll paid by the players themselves is far greater and more serious than any monetary loss" in nervous strain and excitement and time lost for studies.[117] At NJC, matches were between class years with the occasional exhibition game. In 1928, the college held its first track meet and "Canoe Carnival." Students also played golf at the Laurencebrook Country Club in East Brunswick and rode horses in a riding ring where Hickman Hall now stands. The riding club, Crop and Spur, was

SCIENCE · CLUB

Purpose: To stimulate interest in the various branches of Natural Science through discussion of scientific achievements and through the creation of a scientific museum.

MILDRED GREENE	*President*
ELIZABETH HUMMEL	*Vice-President*
EVA KAYHART	*Secretary and Treasurer*
RUTH POWELL	*Parliamentarian*

MEMBERS

The Class of 1925

M. CLERIHEW	R. POWELL	D. MINSCHWANER
M. SCHALAU	M. ROGERS	A. SEBESTYAK
M. GREENE	S. KAPLAN	H. TAYLOR

The Class of 1926

E. HUMMEL	J. KUDLICK	E. KAYHART
	E. TUNISON	

The Class of 1927

M. BEATY	C. DEVINE	H. STAHL

One Hundred Sixty-nine

founded in 1930. Professor Jessie Fiske, who was an accomplished equestrian, served as an adviser to the club.

In 1918, the first class formed a student governing association. In 1919, however, Mabel Smith Douglass decided that the students were not ready and the organization was disbanded.[118] In 1920, the first class adopted an honor system, which was modeled on those used at many elite colleges and universities.[119] Under this system, any student breaking one of the myriad rules and regulations codified in the college handbook, known as the *Red Book*, was obliged to report herself to the student-nominated Judicial Board, which would decide on an appropriate punishment. If she failed to do so, anyone observing her infraction had to report her. The honor system was a key component of the NJC Cooperative Government Association (Co-op), which was founded in the spring of 1923. Under its constitution, administrators, faculty, and students all shared in the governance of the college. Representatives and an executive board were elected from each residence and for the commuters. This shared governance model, in which students held limited power, was typical of women's colleges, where the administration, afraid that adverse publicity would hurt the cause of women's education, tried to keep tight control of student behavior.[120]

RULES AND REGULATIONS

In the early years of the college, Mabel Smith Douglass knew all the students by name, attended social functions, and provided personal guidance and discipline. Faculty members and administrators served as residence directors at College and Cooper Halls and Douglass herself presided at meetings of the Cooperative Association. With the rapid increase in student numbers during the 1920s, however, Douglass's personal style of governance was no longer tenable. In 1926, Leah Boddie was appointed dean of women and was able to dedicate her entire time to the extracurricular needs of the student body.[121] Administrators replaced the faculty as directors of residence "campuses," while seniors served as elected "chairmen" of individual houses. Boddie worked closely with the faculty and registrar, paying special attention to students who were on academic probation. At a time when colleges were in loco parentis for students, she was also in regular touch with the infirmary and department of physical education about women with special health and fitness needs.[122]

As well as orienting new students to college life, the *Red Book* listed rules governing academic integrity and student behavior. For instance, the 1922 *Red Book* enumerated approved restaurants in New Brunswick that could be visited without chaperones and decreed that no student could be seen off campus without a hat. Smoking was strictly prohibited, not for health reasons, but because it was deemed unladylike. Beginning in 1930, smoking was permitted in a designated room in Jameson Hall and by 1937 had been extended to additional locations.[123] All students were required to punctually attend all college exercises, including daily chapel or assembly and church services on Sunday. Like many colleges, NJC, although nonsectarian, had a distinctly Christian atmosphere.[124] Dean Douglass or Dean Boddie presided at daily chapel, which involved a talk, announcements, and a brief liturgy with music provided by a vested choir. Florence Marshall, who was Jewish, described attending a service at the Rutgers Kirkpatrick Chapel one icy February Sunday: "In church someone spoke about something but we didn't pay any attention—which proves the idiocy of compulsory church."[125] By 1924, however, the *Red Book* listed synagogues and Roman Catholic churches along with Protestant ones; Marshall herself occasionally attended services at a local synagogue.

Rules were particularly strict for women living in residence. In the early 1920s, students were required to be in their dormitories by 10:00 p.m. and lights were turned off at 10:30. Students were required to make their own beds, although the college employed servants to clean their rooms. Residence directors regularly inspected students' rooms, made sure students signed in and out, and kept a record of their church attendance. Male callers were not allowed past the reception room and had to leave by 10:00 p.m. Dancing was sanctioned "so long as it remains a clean, wholesome recreation. No exaggerated type will be tolerated. Vulgarity on the floor will not be permitted. Dancing is clean when the mind is clean."[126] Minor infractions of the rules were considered by the House Committees, while major infractions came before the Judicial Board of the college. Major offenses included "lying, false registration, cheating, plagiarism, stealing, drinking, and unchaperoned automobiling" and could be punished by expulsion.[127]

The 1920s, however, was a time of social change and student rebellion. "This was the still-talked-of era of the 'Flapper'—that gorgeous creature and daring young woman of the twenties!"[128] Women bobbed their hair, wore short skirts, and smoked cigarettes. Heterosexual dating without chaperones became more acceptable, while the advent of the automobile gave young people privacy and freedom.[129] Like their contemporaries, NJC students chafed against college regulations. As the Class of 1922 historian recalled, "We obeyed the rules that were laid down for propriety until they interfered too much with our freedom, then, like the college girl of today we either broke them or instated new ones."[130] To Mabel Smith Douglass's distress, an "epidemic" of bobbed hair broke out in fall 1918; "she wondered whether it was really worth the struggle to try to educate the young womanhood of New Jersey if this was the type of material she had to work with."[131] In 1923, the Pro and Con Club debated the ethics of bobbed hair. The "pros" defended the style as a "time-saver, becoming to most people, and hygienic," while the "cons" claimed that "bobbed hair was no time-saver if it had to be curled and that employers objected to it."[132] NJC students particularly objected to the cut system, where they were allowed only a very limited number of absences from classes and official college activities. According to Florence Marshall, "We had a history-making co-op meeting today about the awful cut system. . . . The hard thing about the system is that sickness is not excused and a whole lot of people lose credit who have no way of making it up."[133]

By the end of the 1920s, as standards changed, the NJC rules and regulations became more liberal. Students were allowed to stay out until 11:00 p.m. on weekends, and more "cuts" and weekends away were permitted.[134] The list of approved restaurants

was expanded, and restaurants outside New Brunswick were added. Even unchaperoned automobiling was allowed in certain instances, such as "when an automobile is
used within town limits solely as a means of conveyance."[135] In fact, college administrators encouraged heterosexual socializing within certain parameters. Florence Marshall's
diary describes dances, trips to see plays in New York, and weekend visits to other colleges. NJC women often dated Rutgers men, whom they met at club meetings, football
games, fraternity parties, and downtown venues. Stephanie Morris, who herself married a Rutgers man, Franklin Marryott, recalled that eight members of the class of 1925
married Rutgers undergraduates whom they met while at NJC.[136]

At the end of the 1920s, the New Jersey College for Women was a thriving institution that had just celebrated its tenth anniversary. With the young college still under the
leadership of its founding dean, Mabel Smith Douglass, its future looked bright. The
next decade, however, would bring unanticipated challenges.

CHALLENGES OF THE 1930s

THERE IS ABOUT THE COLLEGE, BOTH
AMONG THE FACULTY AND IN THE
STUDENT BODY, A SIMPLICITY OF LIFE,
A RESPECT FOR LEARNING AND A WILL
TO SERVE WHICH ARE TREASURES
BEYOND PRICE.

—Margaret T. Corwin, 1934

After the stock market crash of 1929, the United States soon found itself in the most devastating economic depression in the country's history. The Great Depression had a profound effect on colleges and universities. "This country lost a generation of college graduates in the classes of the early thirties. Almost everyone knew someone who couldn't go to college because of the Depression."[1] Those who were able to pursue higher education became more aware of the evils of American capitalism and many were radicalized, contributing to the launch of the United States' first student movement in the early 1930s. With the failures of capitalism more and more apparent, many students, intellectuals, and working-class labor activists were attracted to communism and socialism, which some conservatives characterized as the second "Red Scare."[2] By the middle of the decade, the rise of Hitler in Germany and Mussolini in Italy and the outbreak of the Spanish Civil War began to overshadow economic concerns. The threat of war and fascism gave a new urgency to the student movement. Although important women leaders like First Lady Eleanor Roosevelt, consumer advocate Frances Perkins, and civil rights activist Mary McLeod Bethune emerged in this period, women suffered badly during the depression. In times of hardship, young women were less likely to attend college than were their brothers. Viewed by society as breadwinners, men were often preferred for jobs over women. Women who did find employment earned less than men and had to stop working when they married or had children.[3]

During the depression, New Jersey College for Women students, many of whom were from families of modest means, struggled to stay in college. While enrollment fell, the college administration wrestled with the need to accommodate students from more diverse backgrounds. Far from an ivory tower, NJC became a locus of student activism, and it found itself in the national press as it was rocked by an unforeseen political scandal. Changing times challenged both faculty and students to become more aware of the college's place on the global stage. Meanwhile the usual round of classes, examinations, club meetings, dances, and social events continued. This chapter explores the particular challenges of this decade.

Last Days of Dean Douglass

RELATIONS WITH THE UNIVERSITY

Despite NJC's success during the 1920s, Dean Mabel Smith Douglass faced increasing personal and professional challenges. In the early 1920s, Douglass's two teenage children, Edith and William, seemed to be doing well. The family was living at 135 George Street, a dignified Victorian house near the entrance to NJC (more recently occupied by the Douglass Writing Center). Edith, the elder, attended the prestigious girls' school, Kent Place, in Summit, New Jersey, while William attended the Rutgers Preparatory School in New Brunswick. On September 3, 1923, tragedy struck when sixteen-year old William was found dead of a self-inflicted gunshot wound in the family home. His funeral was held on September 7 with Rutgers president William Demarest officiating, and the boy was buried in the family plot in Green-Wood Cemetery in Brooklyn.[4] Despite reeling from shock and grief, Douglass carried on with her college duties. Although the tragedy was kept quiet, Douglass's close friends and associates were aware of her suffering. In a letter discussing his support for the college's music program, trustee William H. Leupp wrote, "Please be assured that you have my deep sympathy in your late trouble. I am sure I can speak feelingly and trusting brighter days will soon come to you."[5]

Throughout her life, Douglass herself was afflicted by chronic ill-health, both mental and physical. She had largely withdrawn from the women's college movement from 1915 to 1918. According to college historian George Schmidt, "worn down by overwork and domestic worries, she had been ordered by her physician to give up all her club activities and left the state for an extended rest."[6] This period was punctuated by personal loss—Douglass endured the deaths of both her husband and her mother, Minnie Smith, during this time.

Apparently Douglass also suffered from chronic back pain. In December 1925, after a fall, an X-ray revealed a congenital deformity in her coccyx that may have contributed to the pain.[7] In August 1927, Douglass and her daughter, Edith, who had just graduated from NJC, took a trip to Europe, where they visited Prague, and Douglass took a cure at the Marienbad spa. Apparently Douglass was ill again in December 1929 and March 1930, and she did not preside at the 1930 commencement. A New York doctor diagnosed chronic arthritis or gout in her feet.[8] As professor of drama Jane Inge

wrote, "The College is not the same without you, now that you are ill everyone realized how very largely the College means you."[9] That Douglass's illnesses had mental as well as physical components would be borne out by later events.

Another cause of stress for Mabel Smith Douglass was the deteriorating relationship between NJC and Rutgers University. With the retirement of President Demarest in 1924, Douglass lost a valued ally and supporter. The new president, John Martin Thomas, was committed to making Rutgers a full-fledged state university. He created several cross-university bodies such as the University Council, made up of the five deans, who met weekly to plan and coordinate university policy; and a University Faculty, in which there was little participation from NJC.[10] More important, Thomas sought to present a unified budget request to the state, ending the practice in which Douglass and the other deans had petitioned Trenton directly for funds. Douglass wrote that as a woman and dean of NJC, she was the best person to represent the needs of the college noting, "The problem of the women students is quite distinct and apart. Their virtues, their desires, their needs: these are of a different sort."[11]

For the next five years, Douglass and the NJC Board of Managers, led by Leonor Loree, fought with Thomas over the autonomy of the women's college. In 1926, working with the U.S. Bureau of Education, Thomas commissioned a comprehensive study of higher education in New Jersey. Douglass found the resulting survey disturbing and intrusive, learning from Board of Managers member Marie Katzenbach, who served on the state Board of Education and whose husband, Edward, was the New Jersey attorney general, that the commission was critical of the education courses at NJC. Douglass noted correctly that teacher training was not the core mission of NJC: "We can never supply all the teachers needed and it would not be a good thing for the State if we could."[12] Notably, the survey was also critical of the excessive authority wielded by the Board of Managers.[13]

The final report of the commission, released in March 1927, found higher education in New Jersey as a whole woefully inadequate and noted that 80 percent of New Jersey students attended college outside the state. Because of complex factors, including inadequate tax revenues and doubt over the legal status of Rutgers's private Board of Trustees, an impasse was reached over the university's funding.[14] Mabel Smith Douglass was concerned about the implications for NJC's autonomy and status. Writing to Loree before a Board of Trustees meeting, Douglass warned him to beware of suggestions regarding "placing the college for women on a par with other colleges in the University or making the Dean of the College for Women coordinate in rank with the other deans of the University, as per recommendations of Survey Committee—recommendations being but a veiled attempt to cripple the growth of the College for Women."[15]

To try to break the impasse, in 1927, new governor A. Harry Moore and the legislature appointed a commission to examine the existing relation of the state with Rutgers University. Chaired by Edward D. Duffield, president of Prudential Life Insurance Company, it became known as the Duffield Commission. During the commission's deliberations, Douglass, Loree, and the New Jersey State Federation of Women's Clubs conducted a campaign to secure autonomous status for NJC. Testifying before a public hearing of the commission, Douglass declared, "We were created as a department of a State University. . . . We never were created as a part of old colonial Rutgers."[16] The commission's report, published in 1929, proposed establishing a state Board of Regents to oversee the university and, even more alarmingly, recommended studying the anomalous position of the college for women.

In May 1930, the newly created Board of Regents sought to bring NJC under more direct supervision by the Rutgers trustees. The resulting controversy led to the appointment of a special committee chaired by Edward Katzenbach to study the college for women. Meanwhile, President Thomas was increasingly concerned with NJC's mounting debts. In June 1930, the Board of Managers sought to borrow $340,000 from the Rutgers trustees to enable the Jameson dormitory complex to be completed. In his annual report for 1930, Thomas expressed his serious concern about this debt, attacked Loree's management of the college's finances, and criticized the college's low salaries and resulting high turnover in staff.[17] This annual report would prove to be Thomas's last. In September 1930, John Martin Thomas abruptly resigned to take a position with the National Life Insurance Company and trustee Philip M. Brett was named acting president.

The report of Katzenbach's committee, published in June 1931, advocated the continued separate status of the women's college with its own faculty, departments, and administration. The commission also recommended adding five women to the Rutgers Board of Trustees and replacing the Board of Managers by a trustees' committee that would include the five women, five additional trustees, and the president of the university. After several more months of wrangling, the recommendations were adopted and the Rutgers charter was amended in April 1932. In reality, many of the same trustees, including Chairman Leonor Loree, served on this new committee. Women members of the Board of Managers like Marie Katzenbach, Florence Eagleton, and Miriam Lippincott were elevated to trustee status. The president of the New Jersey State Federation of Women's Clubs continued to serve ex officio along with the president of the Associate Alumnae of New Jersey College for Women. A second alumnae representative was added in 1943. The main difference was that the committee was required to submit its annual budget to the Rutgers trustees.[18]

ECONOMIC DEPRESSION

The impact of growing state control coincided with the onset of the economic depression in the autumn of 1929. Between 1929 and 1933, enrollment at NJC dropped from 1,157 to 961, while at Rutgers College, student numbers fell from 1,400 to 1,200 during this time. The state appropriation was reduced from $430,000 to $272,000.[19] In the spring of 1931, the college had to borrow $175,000 to carry operations through the summer. Douglass noted an exceptional number of withdrawals from application for admission to the college because of lack of resources, four times as many as at the same time the previous year.[20] Support for the men's colleges was also drastically curtailed, as state revenues were redirected to care for the growing number of unemployed.[21] In spring 1932, Douglass joined the new Rutgers president, Robert C. Clothier, in bypassing the Board of Regents to lobby the legislature directly. "Proposed reduction of appropriation for Rutgers University including New Jersey College for Women would involve disastrous consequences disrupting faculty and seriously impairing our service to the state."[22]

The effect of the Great Depression on NJC was devastating. All plans for new construction came to a standstill and even routine maintenance was delayed. A $350,000 request for a new physical education and hygiene building was rejected, and plans for a much-needed library and student center were put on hold. In fact, after the completion of the Jameson dormitory complex in 1931, no new buildings rose on the NJC campus until a student center was finally built in 1953.

Still more damaging was the effect on faculty, programs, and students. The number of faculty was reduced from 131 in 1930–1931 to 107 in 1933–1934, where it remained for several years, primarily by not renewing the contracts of lower-ranked instructors and lecturers.[23] Similarly, at Rutgers College, salaries were reduced, and fifty staff members lost their appointments. Most academic programs were preserved, although several "special bureaus," including the Engineering Experiment Station, the Short Course in Engineering, and the Psychological and Mental Hygiene Clinic, were closed temporarily.[24] At NJC, a decision was made to close the new School for Child Study after only two years. The School for Child Study had opened in House DD on the Douglass (Corwin) campus in October 1930 with an enrollment of twelve children and a waiting list of thirty. Modeled on similar nursery schools at Smith, Vassar, and Yale, it provided a laboratory for the departments of psychology, home economics, physical education, and art.[25] Students taking classes in child development and child nutrition through the home economics department were scheduled for two hours a week at the school, "giving them an opportunity for observation and experience which they have lacked in the past."[26] The whole operation was overseen by Dr. Sidney Cook of the Department of Psychology. The staff included the director, Catherine Landreth (1899–1995), from New Zealand, who went on to become a distinguished professor at University of California–Berkeley and a pioneer in early childhood education; an assistant, NJC alumna Dorothy Hall; and a housekeeper. The school was supported by income from the children's tuition fees.

NJC students suffered worst of all from the economic depression. When a drop in enrollment of thirty students was recorded in 1930–1931, the college raised tuition to compensate. The following year, as enrollment fell even further, raising fees again was clearly out of the question, so total income dropped.[27] An editorial in *Campus News* urged students to stay in college. "Students who find themselves with scant financial resources for the continuance of their studies at N.J.C. are urged to remain in college even at the cost of personal hardship. . . . We are encouraging students to stay at college if they possibly can . . . because if they leave it will be very difficult for them to find employment sufficiently remunerative to meet present living expenses and to save enough to return to college."[28]

Many students who lived within commuting distance opted to live at home. The percentage of commuters rose to over one-third of the total enrollment in 1934. In that year, twenty cottages on the Douglass and Gibbons campuses were closed, as was one of the large dining rooms at Cooper Hall. Two units of Jameson followed later, leaving 42 percent of dormitory space unoccupied.[29] Private colleges with higher fees were losing even more students: some thirty-one women transferred to NJC because it was more affordable.[30] Lucille Bourath, Class of 1933, from Bayonne, New Jersey, lived on campus for her first two years and commuted for her last two. Like many of her contemporaries, she struggled to find a job after graduation. Fewer jobs in teaching were available and women faced discrimination as male "breadwinners" were preferred for existing positions.[31] A mathematics major, Bourath went on to Columbia University for a graduate degree but still could not find work. She was one of many graduates of the thirties who did not find steady employment until World War II.[32]

The college and its supporters mobilized to find financial support for students. The young institution had few scholarships, however, to offer them. In spring 1930, with 10 percent of the student body requesting aid, the college had only $950 available in scholarships and no loan funds. Fredericka Belknap, the director of the new Personnel Bureau, which had been created to advise students on vocational opportunities, found herself deluged by requests for immediate aid. Traditionally, the only "self-help," or work study, jobs that the college offered were waitresses in the dining halls, assistants in departments, and babysitting.[33] As Mabel Smith Douglass wrote to Loree:

> I really am greatly distressed over the possible decrease in our enrollment for the coming year. As I said at the Board meeting, many of the withdrawals which had already occurred [sic] were due to extreme financial embarrassment. We have had almost one hundred urgent requests from incoming freshmen for part-time positions through which they might obtain financial aid, and seventeen requests for scholarships. . . . The waitress position is almost the only remunerative field open to freshmen—at least in their first semesters—and the number of freshmen waitresses must necessarily be limited.[34]

The college created additional work opportunities for students whenever possible, including establishing campus agencies for newspaper delivery, caps and gowns, cosmetics, photographs, cleaning, flowers, candy, and cigarettes, although student purchasing power decreased during the depression.[35] The self-help crisis was solved only by the advent of federally funded programs in the mid-1930s.

Fortunately, the college was able to create a student loan fund of sixty thousand dollars from the income from the Elizabeth Rodman Voorhees endowment. The staff of the Personnel Bureau labored to find scholarships and loans for students from sources outside the college.[36] The barely ten-year-old Associate Alumnae mobilized, hosting dances, bridge, and theater benefits to raise money for student aid and beginning systematic fund-raising for the college. In 1926, the Associate Alumnae had established a magazine, the *Alumnae Bulletin*, and in 1931 created the office of paid secretary. The editor of the *Bulletin* and secretary of the association were admitted to faculty meetings ex officio. Alumnae clubs, which had been organized in a number of counties throughout the state, worked with local high schools to recruit more students for NJC.[37] The New Jersey State Federation of Women's Clubs cooperated with alumnae clubs to recruit and aid students. Over time, the college accumulated more scholarship funds, so was better able to support undergraduates.

TRAGEDY AND TRANSITION

The pressure of the early depression years took a physical and mental toll on Mabel Smith Douglass. In September 1932, Douglass, who had been ill since the previous spring, took a leave of absence. Albert E. Meder Jr., a professor of mathematics, was appointed acting dean until Douglass was able to return. Since June 1, 1932, Douglass had been a patient at Four Winds, a private mental hospital at Cross River in Westchester County.[38] On May 22, 1933, it was announced that for "reasons of health," Douglass had decided not to return to work and that Meder would continue as interim dean.[39] In fact, Douglass was still at Four Winds, where she would remain until July. Meder, who had been serving as Douglass's assistant since 1929, was a competent administrator who later became secretary of the university and dean of administration. He shepherded NJC through the difficult years of the early 1930s, the loss of the college's founding dean, and the appointment of a new dean in 1934. At that point, he returned to the faculty, teaching mathematics and serving on the Admissions Committee and as an adviser to the campus newspaper. In the early 1940s, he married NJC alumna Janet Davis (NJC '41). Meder had a long and distinguished career, ultimately serving as a trustee of Union County College in the 1960s. He lived until the late 1980s.[40]

▶ ALBERT E. MEDER JR., 1930

On June 3, the trustees accepted Douglass's resignation, granted her a generous pension, and formed a committee to search for a new dean.[41] Tributes poured in upon the news of Douglass's retirement. As one alumna wrote, "'N.J.C.' just never will mean as much without you there to those of us who were fortunate enough to be students when the college was small and we could learn to know you so intimately and to love you so much. My greatest hope for the future of 'N.J.C.' is that its beautiful spirit of friendship, loyalty, cooperation, courage and faith that you created and with which the students were imbued with live on forever."[42] In the years leading up to her retirement, Douglass received many honors. In 1931, she became the first woman ever to receive the Columbia University Medal, and in 1932, she was made an Officier d'Académie by the French government in appreciation of her influence in the teaching of French. She had received an honorary doctor of laws from Rutgers in 1924 and received a second honorary doctorate from Russell Sage College in 1932.[43] She had been appointed twice to the New Jersey State Board of Education.

After her release from Four Winds, Douglass spent the remainder of the summer 1933 with her daughter, Edith, at Onondaga, the Adirondack camp that she owned on the west shore of Lake Placid. On the afternoon of September 21, the day before she and Edith were scheduled to return to New Jersey, Mabel Smith Douglass rowed across the lake in a small boat. Later that afternoon, when she did not return and the boat was spotted drifting empty, Edith reported her as missing. The local police and divers searched the area, dragged the lake, and even set off dynamite to try to raise the body, but ultimately had to give up; Douglass was presumed drowned.[44] The college held a memorial service for Mabel Smith Douglass in the Voorhees Chapel on October 29, 1933. The Associate Alumnae organized a campaign to establish a scholarship in her memory (the Mabel Smith Douglass Graduate Fellowship), and Douglass's old Jersey City friend Mrs. Alvoni Allen commissioned local sculptor Archimedes A. Giacomantonio to create a bronze bust of the late dean. In February 1936, the Associate Alumnae dedicated a set of chimes and a bronze tablet in Mabel Smith Douglass's honor.[45]

Mabel Smith Douglass's death remained something of a mystery for thirty years, until September 15, 1963, when two recreational divers exploring the lake bottom discovered the well-preserved body of a woman dressed in old-fashioned clothes. The body was soon identified as Mabel Smith Douglass. The resulting inquest again attributed her death to an accident, despite the fact that the remains of a rope were found around her neck. According to the police report, "The investigation does reflect ill health and an extreme nervous condition of Mrs. Douglass; but since positive factual evidence is lacking, and the rope the skin divers saw around the neck disintegrated when touched, examination of a knot or accidental entanglement in an anchor rope cannot be determined."[46] By this time, Douglass no longer had any living relatives. Her daughter, Edith Douglass, had moved to New York City and worked in the insurance industry before marrying Swiss diplomatic courier Max Albert Roth in March 1943. Tragically, Max Roth was killed in a plane crash in Europe only four months after the wedding. Edith Douglass Roth herself committed suicide, jumping from an eighth-story window in Manhattan on April 30, 1948.[47] In the absence of other family, the college took responsibility for Mabel Smith Douglass's burial in Green-Wood Cemetery beside her husband, son, and daughter.

Taking into consideration Mabel Smith Douglass's family history and illness and the circumstances of her death, it is likely that she committed suicide. In 1933, suicide was considered shameful, so it was kept quiet. As George Ortloff writes in his rather sensationalized account of Douglass's disappearance and death, "In the final analysis, whether Mrs. Douglass's death was an accident—as the coroner ruled—or a suicide, doesn't matter. What really matters is that she was born and lived for 56 years before that last day of summer on which she died, and that in the interim, she left the world a better place for having passed through it."[48]

Margaret Trumbull Corwin

The credit for bringing the New Jersey College for Women through the Great Depression and World War II must be given to Margaret Trumbull Corwin, who became dean in January 1934. A descendant of an English family that had arrived in Massachusetts in 1633, Corwin was born in Philadelphia in 1889. Her family moved to New Haven, Connecticut, where her father, Robert Nelson Corwin, became professor of German at Yale University and served as chairman of the Board of Admissions from 1920 to 1933. Margaret graduated from New Haven High School and, like Mabel Smith Douglass, attended a Seven Sisters College, Bryn Mawr, where she majored in German and minored in French. Like her father, Margaret Corwin loved German literature and culture and visited the country many times. After graduating Phi Beta Kappa in 1912, Corwin worked at Yale University Press. During World War I, she was granted a leave of absence to serve as the executive secretary of the Connecticut Women's Committee of the Council for National Defense, and in 1918, she was sent to Beaune, France, by the YMCA. From 1919 until accepting the position at NJC, she served as executive secretary of Yale University Graduate School. Like Douglass, she was an active clubwoman, primarily through the American Association of University Women (AAUW). She became director of the North Atlantic Section of the association from 1924 to 1928, and in 1930 was AAUW delegate to the council meeting of the International Federation of University Women (IFUW) in Prague. Douglass also participated in the IFUW through her Barnard friend Virginia Gildersleeve. As was Douglass, Corwin was a world traveler; she visited China under the auspices of Yale Graduate School and later traveled extensively through her appointment as convener of the IFUW Exchange Committee from 1937 to 1947 and assistant treasurer from 1947 to 1950.[49]

Upon her arrival at NJC in 1934, Corwin found a college deeply in debt. The financial crisis came to a head in 1936. At the November Trustees Committee meeting, which Robert Clothier chaired in Leonor Loree's absence, the president stated, "The

▶ MARGARET TRUMBULL CORWIN, DEAN OF NEW JERSEY COLLEGE FOR WOMEN, 1934–1955

University is confronted with a financial problem of increasing seriousness arising out of the indebtedness of the College for Women."[50] NJC owed almost a million dollars. Clothier decided that the university comptroller would take over the college's finances and immediately introduce various economy measures. Clothier himself became chair of the Trustees Committee, whose authority over property, funds, and nonacademic employees was rescinded.[51] Loree's longtime lieutenant, Alfred Henderson, took a leave of absence and then resigned. In 1937, the bulk of NJC's debt was refinanced on favorable terms with a loan of six hundred thousand dollars from an insurance company. Loree himself resigned in early 1938.

From then on, Corwin served as a liaison between the college and the university. In spite of a certain amount of friction with the university comptroller, she was able to work fairly harmoniously with Clothier, whose term in office (1932–1951) would roughly parallel her own. In her internal management of the college, Corwin tended to operate more through faculty and administrative committees than had Dean Douglass. She worked closely with faculty, administration, and alumnae to curb costs while maintaining standards. Among other measures, Corwin launched a recruitment drive to keep up student numbers. In 1934, she appointed Lillian Gardner as assistant in public information to help lure prospective students to the college. The first Pre-College Guidance Conference at NJC in that year brought 317 high school juniors and seniors to the campus.[52] Under Corwin, enrollment stabilized and admissions standards rose; in the late 1930s, 95 percent of the freshmen were in the upper half of their high school graduating class, and 80 percent were in the top quarter.[53] Several students recalled Corwin as a "very gray-looking lady." "She always wore gray or blue. Gray stockings and gray shoes." Apparently she was a poor public speaker who "would trip over her words. . . . It was painful to listen to her."[54]

Under Corwin, the NJC curriculum was reorganized in a more rational and practical way. In 1928, the general requirements for each major had been abolished and replaced by thirteen separate academic tracks that caused considerable confusion. In 1934, Corwin reinstated the general requirements, which specified a certain number of courses in humanities, foreign languages, sciences, and social sciences for each student. Several specialized programs were abolished, leaving agriculture, home economics, physical education, and pre-medical training. Agriculture was later replaced by a combination of NJC and College of Agriculture courses.[55] An honors program—two years of independent study with a faculty member followed by comprehensive exams—had been introduced in a few departments in 1928 but was not functioning when Corwin arrived. In its place, she introduced graduation with distinction, later known as graduation with honors.[56]

Despite the financial challenges, Margaret Corwin and her administration undertook several new curricular initiatives during the 1930s. Seeing the economy crumbling around them, students were increasingly interested in economics and sociology. Several new faculty members were appointed in this area, among them Francis W. Hopkins, who took over the chairmanship of the Department of Economics and Sociology from Eugene E. Agger of Rutgers in 1932 and remained for thirty years, and Miriam E. West, a specialist in labor problems.[57] In 1935, Corwin appointed Professor Eleanor Flynn, whose "courses in Sociology, contacts with the social agencies of the state and wise counsel to students interested in social work have done much to meet an evident need."[58] In 1936, with a grant from the Carnegie Corporation, Corwin introduced a Social Information Center, which assembled data on social welfare programs, and encouraged students to volunteer at agencies in New Brunswick.[59] Under Flynn's leadership, one of the cottages was transformed into a small settlement, known as the Jane Addams House, which sponsored programs for local children and served as a laboratory for sociology students.[60] In establishing the Jane Addams House, NJC followed the example of many other women's colleges that founded settlement houses during the early twentieth century.[61]

Social work was one of several vocationally oriented programs that became popular at NJC in the 1930s. During the decade, interest shifted from modern languages and English towards the social sciences, with one-quarter of the students in the professional departments by the late 1930s, as opposed to just under one-fifth (in home economics) in 1924.[62] As early as 1930, the college had introduced noncredit classes in typing, stenography, and shorthand "so students could be prepared for positions requiring these skills."[63] With the decline in teaching opportunities during the 1930s, college women increasingly looked for positions in business, librarianship, home economics, and other fields.[64] In 1936, the NJC trustees approved a bachelor of science in nursing education in cooperation with Christ's Hospital in Jersey City. Although this plan did not prove practicable, the college established a two-year pre-nursing course where students could transfer to Columbia University to complete the five-year program.[65]

In a modest way, Margaret Corwin began to encourage the faculty to conduct scholarly research and publish. Like Mabel Smith Douglass, Corwin fundamentally believed that the primary mission of NJC was to educate undergraduates, but her outlook was more flexible and practical. When the Rutgers Graduate Faculty was established in 1932, the NJC Trustees Committee decreed that "the College for Women will not engage in graduate work now or in the future. Professors will be eligible for seats on the Graduate Faculty. With permission of the dean, professors can teach graduate courses up to 25 percent of their time through extension, summer session, etc. Permission can be withdrawn if work suffers."[66] By 1938, Corwin presented an urgent plea that means be found "to aid the faculty of this College to continue scholarly research in order that they may make contributions in their respective fields, and in order that they may come back to the classroom refreshed and inspired."[67] The Trustees Committee was discussing a request from history professor Margaret Judson, who had received a research fellowship from Mount Holyoke College, for a sabbatical with partial pay. Judson was ultimately granted the sabbatical, which enabled her to spend a year doing primary research for *Crisis of the Constitution* (1949), her masterful work on the English Civil War. She later wrote, however, that Corwin was reluctant to reduce her hours of undergraduate teaching or to allow her to teach graduate students. Only in the early 1950s did Judson begin to teach graduate courses through the support of young faculty members at Rutgers College.[68]

In the mid-1930s, Rutgers's financial situation improved. The state appropriation began to increase again, reaching the pre-1932 level in 1936, enabling salary cuts to be restored. From March 1934, funding became available through the Federal Emergency Relief Administration (FERA) to employ two hundred men and women students at various tasks for as much as fifteen dollars a month. The establishment of the National Youth Administration in 1935 expanded the program and placed it on a continuing basis. Federal funds were distributed through NJC's Personnel Bureau, which in 1937 also introduced a yearly vocational conference designed to encourage students to remain in college.[69] Part of the state aid took the form of full-tuition scholarships, which, beginning in 1937, were awarded to NJC students on the basis of financial need, personal qualifications, and academic merit.[70] In that year, NJC received a major windfall from the estate of former trustee James Neilson. A bequest of fifty thousand dollars was put aside for student loans. Neilson's mansion, Woodlawn, became a base for the Associate Alumnae. Rooms were also rented to groups and overnight visitors.[71]

Even with increased scholarship aid, life for many students of the 1930s was still hard. Alma Geist from Califon, New Jersey, had wanted to attend Antioch College in Ohio but won the NJC Hickman History Scholarship in 1934. In spite of her scholarship, she had to work as a waitress in the dining hall and type papers for other students at ten cents a page. At the end of her junior year, a physical examination revealed a slight curvature in her spine reputedly from carrying heavy trays, so she was given a job as a professor's assistant.[72]

Changing Demographics

The 1930s was marked by continuing tensions over the increasing numbers of Jewish applicants to Rutgers and NJC. In the early 1930s, in response to complaints from Jewish community leaders in New Brunswick, the percentage of Jewish students at both colleges increased. Like Mabel Smith Douglass, however, Margaret Corwin and the Trustees Committee put into place policies like the limitation of commuters to 25 percent of the student body, which effectively restricted the number of Jewish women.[73] Corwin and her advisers claimed that library and classroom space was inadequate to accommodate more commuters.[74] At the same time, they tried to recruit students from outside New Jersey, establishing new competitive scholarships based on College Board examinations, psychological tests, general character, personality, and financial need (in that order). Four regional scholarships with similar criteria were introduced "to encourage students from areas not in the immediate vicinity of the college."[75] Many Jewish families lived in New Brunswick and other urban areas within commuting distance. Ida Perlmutter from the Class of 1938 commuted to NJC from South River. She recalled that all the girls she knew at NJC were Jewish and a group rode the bus together every day.[76]

Margaret Corwin was likely influenced by her father's experience as head of admissions at Yale at a time when she herself was also working in the Yale administration. Apparently Robert Corwin was one of the first administrators to suggest limiting Jewish numbers at Yale. He referred to the growing number of young Jewish men who commuted to Yale from New Haven as an "alien and unwashed element." In 1924, Yale limited Jewish admissions at 10 percent, a quota that would stay in place for four decades.[77] In a similar vein, Frieda Finklestein (NJC '41) came to NJC when she was told that the Jewish quota at Smith College was filled and she was put on a waiting list.[78] Annette Greenblatt (NJC '45), an outstanding student from Vineland, was rejected by NJC initially. "When I applied to NJC, I was rejected, and my English teacher, whose name was Jane (Beakley?), at the time, was so infuriated that she went up to the school to speak to the admissions officer and told him that she knew why I hadn't been accepted, and that it was a state school, and that he had no right to do that, and that's how I went to NJC."[79] Other Jewish students of the 1930s complained about being expected to eat non-kosher food in the dining hall (the only alternative was cornflakes), and an orientation being scheduled on the Rosh Hashanah holiday.[80]

Discrimination against African American students was even more overt. In 1934, the first known African American student, Julia Baxter Bates, arrived at NJC. Julia Baxter was a light-skinned black woman who grew up in the predominantly white community of Bernardsville, New Jersey. Her grandfather was Newark's first African American school principal and her father and aunt founded the National Association for the Advancement of Colored People (NAACP) chapters in Morristown and Newark. Baxter, who wanted to be a teacher, applied to NJC in 1934 with the required photograph and was provisionally accepted. When she came to NJC for an interview, however, it became clear that she had been mistaken for white, because she was told that "she would be more comfortable" in a black college. Of the small percentage of African American students who attended college at that time, the vast majority attended black colleges (later known as historically black colleges and universities).[81]

Baxter, however, insisted that she had been accepted at NJC and had the right to attend. Through her activist family, she was probably aware that the NAACP was pursuing several cases of discrimination in higher education as part of mounting legal challenges to the *Plessy* doctrine of "separate but equal."[82] The admissions officer who interviewed her appealed to Corwin, who brought the matter to President Clothier:

> I can't see how we at a college with state subsidy could refuse to take a negro girl. Rutgers has taken negro students, and Smith [and] Radcliffe have had many. Bryn Mawr has had one or two pretty lonely souls I fear. I'm afraid this Bernardsville girl would be lonely too, but if she cannot be dissuaded, I think we must consider her application on its merits. I feel . . . that she would probably be happier commuting. I'd ever so much like your reaction in the matter. It isn't going to appeal to the Southerners in our Dean of Women staff.[83]

Baxter was admitted to NJC, but she was denied the right to live on campus, instead staying with family in Newark and commuting to NJC by train. She graduated with a degree in English but was unable to find work as a teacher because of her race. Ultimately, Julia Baxter Bates found a position at the NAACP headquarters in New York, serving twenty years as national director of research and information. During the 1950s, Bates researched and coauthored the winning brief in the historic *Brown v. Board of Education of Topeka, Kansas* decision, which the NAACP used to prove the scientific case against segregation in the nation's public schools in the U.S. Supreme Court.[84] The next known African American women to attend NJC were Lydia Benning Moss (NJC '42) and Constance Virginia Andrews (NJC '45).[85] The experience of black women at NJC during this period was similar to that documented by Linda Perkins in her study of African American women at the Seven Sisters colleges that Margaret Corwin, like Mabel Smith Douglass, attended and emulated. Perkins finds about five hundred black women at the seven colleges between 1890 and 1960. Like Julia Baxter Bates, many were light-skinned African Americans who were admitted unwittingly. At the Seven Sisters, as at NJC, black women were often denied campus housing and forced to commute.[86]

Student Life in the Depression Decade

Like their peers throughout the country, NJC students became increasingly engaged in politics during the 1930s. Observing the economic upheavals going on around them, students sought to understand and effect social and political change. The NJC branch of the League of Women Voters, founded in 1927, became more active. In 1935, for the first time the NJC branch was invited to send representatives to the Model Senate conference at Vassar College. Theresa Kunst (NJC '35), the branch president, wrote excitedly in her diary, "The conference was run very smoothly. The delegates were an extremely intelligent group. Oh did they know government upside down and inside out!!!!"[87] The following year the conference was held at NJC, bringing delegates from thirty colleges to campus for three days.[88]

Lecture evenings were exciting campus events at both NJC and Rutgers College. Prominent women like radical English professor Vida Scudder of Wellesley were invited to NJC to give lectures, while Eleanor Roosevelt spoke at the college on three different occasions. NJC students also attended events at the men's college, where the Rutgers Forum, organized in 1930, conducted meetings throughout the year on subjects such

▲ SMOKERS, 1936

as conscription, censorship, and socialism. The Rutgers Liberal Club, often in cooperation with such groups as the Rutgers Christian Association, the League for Independent
Political Action, the League for Industrial Democracy, and the local branch of the
Socialist Party, arranged a popular series of lectures that featured such speakers as Com-
munist Party of the USA secretary Earl Browder; American Socialist Party leader
Norman Thomas; antiwar activist, socialist, and communist Scott Nearing; and social-
ist and writer Harry W. Laidler.[89] In a political poll of the NJC senior class in 1934, the
Socialist Party drew the highest numbers of votes.[90]

As economic concerns were replaced by the threat of fascism in Europe and the fear
of war, many students at both Rutgers and NJC became involved in the peace movement. The compulsory Army Reserve Officer Training Corps (ROTC) at Rutgers
College was attacked and various types of peace pledges were circulated.[91] At NJC,
Emily Hickman of the history department, herself a leader in the moderate Committee
on the Cause and Cure of War, organized a Peace Club, which sponsored speakers, held
discussion groups, and organized international nights.[92] NJC women also participated
actively in the national student peace movement, a key component of the larger student
protest movement of the 1930s. The student rebels of the depression era have been
called "the most effective radical organizers in the history of American student politics."[93] On April 13, 1934, the anniversary of the day that the United States entered
World War I, the National Student League and the student arm of the League for Industrial Democracy held the first National Strike against War. Nationwide twenty-five
thousand college students walked out of class for one hour to hold peace assemblies.
The strike in 1935 was far larger, drawing 175,000 students.[94] At Rutgers, several hundred students assembled peacefully at the New Brunswick Theological Seminary on the
Rutgers College campus. Theresa Kunst wrote in her diary, "This morning at 11 we had
our strike for peace. A couple hundred of us went down to Rutgers—10 of us went in
Aimée's little five seater ford! The main meeting was indoors because of the rain. The big
lesson learned was 'wage peace'! as those interested in war are waging war!!"[95] The following year, 1936, when around 500,000 participated in the strike nationally, the NJC
Peace Club organized an alternative event in the Voorhees Chapel.[96]

Coinciding with the Peace Strike, NJC and Rutgers were rocked by a serious controversy that became known as the Bergel-Hauptmann affair.[97] In the spring of 1933,
Friedrich Hauptmann, chair of the NJC German department, informed Acting Dean
Albert Meder that he did not recommend promoting Lienhard Bergel, a young instructor who had been at NJC since early 1932. As was customary, Meder supported the
chairman's recommendation, which was communicated to Bergel in September,
although he was allowed until spring 1935 to find another position. In the economic
conditions of the early 1930s, junior faculty members were frequently let go, and Bergel's dismissal would have been unremarkable had not it occurred against the
background of Adolf Hitler's accession to power in Germany in January 1933. German-
born Hauptmann was cautiously supportive of the new Nazi government, while Bergel,

also German born, was an outspoken opponent of Nazism. After his nonreappointment was confirmed by Margaret Corwin in 1934, Bergel began to assert publicly that he had been dismissed because of his political views. The controversy escalated through the 1934 and 1935 academic years, with Bergel garnering support from students, New Jersey legislators, the Jewish community, and the American Civil Liberties Union, while Hauptmann was supported by most of the students living in the German House and various Rutgers administrators. As the Red Scare escalated on college campuses in the mid-1930s, Bergel's supporters were tarred with accusations of communism.[98] Theresa Kunst, who knew both men, emerged as a leader of the pro-Bergel faction at NJC. She was concerned, however, about the impact of the leftist groups supporting Bergel, writing in her diary:

> Cut cooking lecture after lunch & went to the "red den"—fighting for Bergel's retention. They were going to have a mass meeting in town—the League against War & Fascism, the National Student League, the Young Communist League, the Liberal Club, some N.J.C.ers, etc.—which Bergel would have been blamed for. . . . I told them they were "dopes" for bringing them to the meeting . . . that Clothier would merely have to make a statement to the press that the agitation was merely a "red problem"—Finally, I convinced them to hold off.[99]

When the conflict reached the national press in May 1935, President Clothier took the extraordinary step of charging a special committee of the Board of Trustees, chaired by Edward Ashmead, to investigate the allegations. From May to late July 1935, the committee heard the testimony of witnesses from both sides, including dozens of NJC students and faculty. Theresa Kunst approached her turn at the witness stand with trepidation: "I felt as if I were going to my execution."[100] The Ashmead Committee's final report, issued on August 18, 1935, supported the NJC administration's decision not to reappoint Bergel and found no evidence of political bias on Hauptmann's part. After two years of unemployment, Lienhard Bergel was appointed at the newly founded Queens College in New York where he went on to have a distinguished career in comparative literature. Hauptmann disappeared in November 1940. He was later discovered to have returned to Germany, where he joined the Nazi Party and was given a position as chief of the German Academy in Slovakia.[101]

As well as protesting against fascism abroad, the student radicals of the 1930s advocated for free speech and greater democracy on their home campuses.[102] Theresa Kunst and the editors of NJC's *Campus News* were among the student leaders at the forefront of these campaigns at Rutgers. As in the 1920s, NJC students chafed against college rules and regulations. Students particularly objected to compulsory chapel, which was still held four days a week and on Sundays. There were numerous complaints about poor student attendance and talking during chapel. In 1935, weekday services were reduced to a semi-religious service with a guest speaker on Tuesdays and a secular assembly on Fridays, while Sunday services were discontinued except for an occasional vespers.[103] Tuesday program topics from the 1930s included "The History and Liturgy of the Moravian Church," "Catholic Thought Today," "New Types of Mission Work," and "Jewish Thought Today."[104] Commuters were apparently not required to attend.[105] Some students still complained. According to an editorial in *Campus News*, "A spiritual need exists only if the individual feels this need. There can be no group need for an institutionalized religion. . . . Then we have regimentation of thought." In contrast, Adelaide Marcus Zagoren (NJC '40), who was Jewish, enjoyed chapel: "One of the Chapel sessions was sort of ecumenical with a wonderful speaker and the other was sort of religious and spiritual."[106] Two campus polls came out in favor of retaining compulsory weekday religious services, which remained until 1945, when Rutgers and all its divisions became the official state university of New Jersey.[107]

With the background of growing fascist influence in Europe, NJC students were sensitive to any policy that seemed undemocratic. As Theresa Kunst frequently wrote in her diary, "Democratic gov't here at college. That's a laugh!"[108] One example was the so-called seniors on the stairs controversy. At the yearly Yule Log ceremony, twenty-eight seniors were traditionally chosen by the dean to stand on a specially constructed staircase in the Voorhees Chapel. The ceremony, including the names of students honored, was actually covered by the *New York Times*.[109] The selection criteria, however, were unclear. A flurry of editorials and letters in *Campus News* critiqued the practice. According to a 1938 editorial titled "Democracy?":

> The difficulty of making any concrete suggestions for a change in this method of selection, [chosen by several members of administration] with which there was considerable dissatisfaction within the student body, was evident when discussion showed that opposition to the present method was based on a number of reasons. Perhaps the two most important were whether individuals who were not qualified by close acquaintance with the seniors could be fairly called upon to judge their intangible qualities, also whether the practice of setting up certain qualities as superior and then honoring these girls to whom certain individuals attributed these qualities was not questionable.[110]

In 1939, Dean Corwin, while refusing to change the method of selection, invited the students to vote on whether to eliminate the staircase part of the ceremony. The close vote was in favor of removing it, although it was reinstated several years after World War II upon student request.[111] Corwin had cleverly used the students' own faith in democratic processes to resolve the issue.

The constant critique of the college administration in *Campus News* eventually wore out the patience of Margaret Corwin and her advisers. During the Bergel-Hauptmann controversy, Albert Meder, the newspaper's faculty adviser, had instructed editor Marion Short not to print letters by students and alumnae about Bergel's dismissal and

▲ YULE LOG, VOORHEES CHAPEL

their experience in both professors' classes. Short believed, however, that she had an obligation to display student opinion. The incident marked the beginning of the tension between *Campus News* and the administration, which led Corwin to appoint a committee in October 1936 to investigate the relationship of the student newspaper with the college. This committee discovered that in March 1936, without consulting the administration, the newspaper had changed its 1928 constitution to weaken the role of the faculty adviser. Strongly committed to freedom of the press, the editors believed that the newspaper should represent the views of the student body and its democratically elected board of editors without interference from the administration.[112]

The committee completed its study in November 1937, marking the beginning of a protracted negotiation between the *Campus News* editors, Corwin, and the NJC Trustees Committee over the status and structure of the newspaper. The student editors wanted to adopt a model in which the newspaper would relinquish its support from student fees in return for greater independence. The administration's position was that regardless of its means of support, the newspaper still represented NJC and thus the administration wanted to oversee the budget and to approve the nomination of editors.[113] On March 22, 1940, when the editors refused to accept an ultimatum from the administration, Corwin informed the student body that *Campus News* would no longer serve as the college's undergraduate newspaper and that the administration would view any attempt to publish the newspaper "as a desire to resign from membership in the college."[114]

The abolition of *Campus News* attracted attention on other campuses. The *Daily Princetonian* supported the NJC editors, as did the Rutgers College newspaper, the *Targum*. The New Jersey Civil Liberties Union sent Corwin a letter, as did the National Student Federation of America—the umbrella organization for student governments—and many alumnae. Censorship of college newspapers was widespread in the 1930s, with major incidents at City College of New York and Columbia, among others.[115] NJC was without a student newspaper for nearly a year until the launch of the *Caellian* in February 1941. The *Campus News* editors of the 1930s were actually ahead of their time in that later many college newspapers, including the *Targum*, became independent.

Despite the tensions of the depression years, students of the 1930s remained engaged in traditional activities. Rutgers historian Richard P. McCormick noted that there were more campus activities during the thirties because students had no money to go elsewhere.[116] President Clothier and Dean Corwin founded the popular Freshmen Reception, which brought Rutgers men and NJC women together. Audrey Brown (NJC '38), a commuter from Metuchen, met her future husband at the first freshmen reception in 1934 and they remained together from then on.[117] At formal balls, students danced to the big bands of Tommy Dorsey, Hal Kemp, and Duke Ellington. Informal dances were held at NJC and Rutgers almost every weekend. With the repeal of Prohibition in 1933, bars like the Corner Tavern on Easton Avenue became busy watering spots. By far the most popular pastime, however, was the movies.[118] In the 1930s, New Brunswick had at least four downtown cinemas: Walter Reade's State Theatre, the Rivoli, the Strand, and the Bijou. Helen Erickson (NJC '31) recalled that when films ran past the NJC curfew, those forced to leave relied on commuters like herself to tell them the endings the next day.[119] Some students like Isolde Musterman (NJC '34) still managed to get to New York, going to Carnegie Hall and to the Metropolitan Opera with the Art and Music Club. Guest artists like Isaac Stern and the West Point Choir gave concerts at Rutgers.[120] New student clubs and organizations appeared at NJC and Rutgers in the 1930s. Although team sports were declining at NJC during this period, students increasingly pursued individual sports like swimming, fencing, and archery. Modern dance remained popular with the establishment of a dance group, Orchesis.[121]

The 1930s at NJC was a decade of retrenchment and consolidation. Faced with economic hardship, many students struggled to continue their education and find employment after graduation. In response to the economic crisis, the college administration sought sources of financial support for students and engaged more actively in recruitment and fund-raising. More vocationally oriented subjects, career guidance, and placement were offered with an eye toward the difficult job market. The young college experienced additional challenges in the loss of its dynamic founding dean, and tensions between the college, Rutgers University, and the state of New Jersey were exacerbated by economic hardship. As the international situation deteriorated, NJC students and faculty became more politically aware and participated in the debates, demonstrations, and controversies of the time. The Bergel-Hauptmann affair and the *Campus News* controversy produced serious divisions in the NJC family. By the end of the decade, however, the onset of World War II brought forth a new atmosphere on the campus, as students, faculty, and administration bonded in the face of a common enemy.[122]

WORLD WAR II
AND ITS AFTERMATH
New Jersey College for Women, 1940–1950

THE ESPRIT DE CORPS HAS BEEN SPLENDID.

—Margaret T. Corwin,
New Jersey College for Women,
Annual Report, 1942

The decade of the 1940s was a watershed era for the United States. U.S. participation in World War II (1941–1945) transformed the country militarily, politically, economically, and emotionally. With Europe devastated, the United States emerged from the war as a great power, although at a price of more than four hundred thousand American military and civilian lives lost.[1] American women participated actively in the war effort, both on the home front and in the new women's services first established in 1942, the Women's Army Corps (WAC), the Women Accepted for Volunteer Emergency Service (WAVES), the SPARS (Coast Guard), and the Women Marines.[2] On the home front, millions of women labored in war-related industrial and clerical jobs, taking the places of men who were serving in the armed forces, leading to an overall expansion of the female labor force from twelve million in 1940 to eighteen million in 1945.[3] Countless other women volunteered, planting gardens, rolling bandages, working in canteens, serving as air raid wardens, spotting airplanes, raising funds, collecting scrap metal, and carrying out dozens of other war-related tasks. At the same time, women kept families together in the absence of fathers, husbands, sons, and brothers, while dealing with rationing, shortages, and inflation. Black women did not participate equally in the new occupations that the war opened for women; they faced continuing employment discrimination and segregation. Overall, however, the war presented many new opportunities for women in roles previously restricted to men, although these gains did not necessarily extend beyond the term of the conflict.[4]

World War II had a profound effect on higher education. The American Council of Education (ACE), founded in 1918, served as a spokesperson for higher education during the war. Beginning in 1939, under the leadership of President George F. Zook, the ACE organized a series of higher education conferences, aggressively advocating the role that colleges and universities could play in the war effort.[5] Most dramatically, colleges and universities were rapidly depleted as male students joined the armed services, although new opportunities were created for women at some previously all-male institutions like the Rensselaer Polytechnic Institute in New York and Stonehill College in Massachusetts, which were forced to accept women students. The financial impact was mitigated at hundreds of institutions (including Rutgers) by participation in college training programs conducted by the army, navy, and army air force. The ACE issued a statement in January 1942 upholding academic freedom during wartime; colleges and universities did not experience the attacks on Germans, Italians, and German-language teaching that were seen during World War I. In the long term, the effect of World War II on universities was positive, contributing to the expansion of higher education opportunities and enhanced federal support for research.[6]

Women's colleges, of course, were not as severely affected by the war as were men's colleges and coeducational institutions. Nevertheless, the New Jersey College for Women, like other women's colleges, faced new challenges during World War II. Students, faculty, and staff participated actively in the war effort. The war presented new opportunities for students and graduates to work in industry or serve in the military. At the same time, all suffered from fear and anxiety as they witnessed the myriad tragedies of the war years. After 1945, the campus gradually returned to normal. Women students in the immediate postwar years received mixed messages about the relative importance of marriage, family life, and careers. While many NJC graduates took the traditional path of marrying and staying at home to care for children, the impact of the war years was not soon forgotten.

Early War Years

As the yearbook editors wrote, 1939 to 1940 was not only "a social year. It was a political year."[7] With the outbreak of war in Europe in 1939, the student leaders of the peace movement that had flourished during the 1930s were divided. Two new organizations emerged on campus, the Committee for the Support of the Allies and the Anti-War Committee. The Committee for the Support of the Allies favored sending aid to Britain while the Anti-War Committee feared that assisting Britain would lead to the United States' greater involvement in the war. Both groups held lectures, fund-raisers, and rallies in support of their respective positions.[8] According to NJC history professor and college historian George P. Schmidt, "Though the two groups engaged in some lively discussions, their clashes did not produce any deep divisions of opinion in the College for Women."[9] Together with Rutgers College students, NJC students continued to participate in the nationwide April rally for peace until the United States entered the war. In February 1941, a new student newspaper, the *Caellian*, replaced the banished *Campus News* after a one-year hiatus when NJC had no student newspaper. Caelian or Caellian is the name of the southernmost hill of the seven hills of Rome, continuing the classical theme of naming student spaces at NJC.

During the first year of the war, small adjustments and changes in curriculum were made. The faculty undertook a course of lectures on the background of the war. Many students were looking ahead to wartime needs in science and industry. In her 1940 annual report, Corwin noted that enrollment in chemistry, mathematics, and physics had all gone up significantly in the past five years, a trend that was also reported at Harvard and Yale. Remarking that these were "subjects for which women students have no especial aptitude," Corwin reaffirmed her commitment to the liberal arts: "The liberal arts college, symbol of the democratic freedom for which the U.S.A. has stood consistently since the days of the pilgrim fathers, must show whether it is still sound."[10] Corwin's thinking would evolve as NJC students were called on to study science and mathematics to meet the demands of the war industry.

By the fall of 1940, after a horrifying spring and summer in which Hitler overran one European country after another, NJC faculty and students were actively engaged in defense work. In early autumn, Corwin appointed a Red Cross Committee of faculty and students under the chairmanship of Helen Hazen, professor of home economics. She introduced a program of knitting garments for British soldiers and sewing items for refugees and classes in home hygiene and first aid taught by members of the staff, which led to a Red Cross Certificate.[11] The Red Cross program proved to be very popular and increased students' awareness of the international situation.[12]

In December, Corwin expanded the program, creating the Committee on Defense and Relief Work under the chairmanship of Professor Margaret Judson. In founding this committee, Corwin was following the lead of her peers at other women's colleges, who had established the Committee on Women in College and Defense in the fall of 1940. The chair, Meta Glass, was the president of Sweet Briar College and, like Corwin, a leader in the American Association of University Women.[13] The NJC committee developed a three-pronged approach: as well as continuing and expanding the existing relief program, it inaugurated defense work on campus and a series of noncredit courses. Money was raised for relief organizations, among them the British War Relief Society, American Friends Service, United China Relief Fund, the Greek War Relief Association, and the Finnish Relief Fund. Student-faculty bridge games, an alumnae food sale, and a faculty review that became a tradition for several years were a few of the fundraisers held. Among the classes, a course in auto mechanics proved to be the most popular, with over 400 students attempting to enroll for 162 places.[14] The purpose of the course was to "help people to be equipped to care for their own car should they need to drive at times when a service station and garage mechanics are not available."[15] Pearl Paterson Thompson (NJC '41) recalled, "I took one look at all that dirty gunk under the hood and decided I would join the Navy. It was a lot cleaner."[16]

In April 1941, Emily Hickman, chair of the Education Subcommittee, organized a series of lectures on the world situation, culminating in a speech by theologian and ethicist Reinhold Niebuhr of the Union Theological Seminary. Margaret Judson took particular pride in the lecture series, the purpose of which was "to present the college

▲ AUTO MECHANICS CLASS, *QUAIR*, 1943

community the nature of the world crisis and the various ways in which that crisis has created and will create a defense problem for the United States. It is evident that probably a majority of the students, and perhaps some of the faculty, are not really informed on the nature of the present crisis."[17]

Across town at Rutgers College, preparation for war was under way. In September 1939, a unit of the Civic Pilot Training Program was established at Rutgers, which provided basic flight instruction for two hundred students.[18] This program was open to women, but because of the required background in mathematics and physics, few applied.[19] With the passing of the Selective Service Act in October 1940, several hundred Rutgers students aged twenty-one and over registered for the draft. In January 1941, the College of Engineering, in association with the Extension division, launched the federally funded program, Engineering, Science, and Management War Training, which offered short courses in engineering. Established by Congress in 1940, this program offered free college-level courses in engineering, physics, chemistry, mathematics, and other defense-related subjects to both men and women. By the end of the war, more than 282,000 women had been enrolled at sites throughout the country.[20]

Because the Army Reserve Officer Training Corps (ROTC) was compulsory at Rutgers College, it was noticeable when the army began to expand and increasing numbers of advanced ROTC cadets went on active duty. Male enrollment dropped about 8 percent when the academic year began in September 1941.[21] Bernice Adler (NJC '41) met her future husband, who was a year ahead of her, in the second semester of her freshman year. She and her friends were aware that the young ROTC men would be among the first to be called up.[22]

The United States Enters the War

The Japanese attack on Pearl Harbor on December 7, 1941, followed by Franklin D. Roosevelt's declaration of war on December 11, brought sweeping changes to Rutgers and NJC. Ruth Sheeler (NJC '43) was pinned to a fraternity man and fellow Bridgeton resident, Bill Moncrief, who would become her husband. Bill was in advanced ROTC and would graduate in 1942 as a first lieutenant. She was at NJC when someone heard the news on the radio. "That news spread like wildfire." She recalled that "all the boys came over and commiserated with all the girls and talked about it and it was very upsetting and very exciting."[23] Barbara Waters (NJC '42) recalled that on Pearl Harbor Day, she was visiting her fiancé, Vince Kramer, who had graduated the previous spring and joined the marines. "He . . . was home, in Paterson, when it happened. Who could forget? . . . Yes, we were in the car, somewhere in Paterson, I remember. Had the radio on. So he had to dash right back to Quantico."[24] Since the attack occurred on a weekend, many NJC students were at home with their families when they heard the news. It was close to the end of the semester, so all waited with trepidation for what the new year would bring.

In January 1942, Dean Corwin and President Clothier attended an emergency meeting of college and university presidents sponsored by the ACE. There were few recommendations, however, for women's colleges apart from reiterating the importance of the liberal arts. Corwin was frustrated, noting that almost all the suggestions were applicable to only male students: "To the representatives of the colleges for women it was especially baffling to discover how little woman-power had been considered as an element in the man-power which was clearly so urgently needed."[25] In fact, at the end of the conference's first day, several members of the Committee on Women in College and Defense and others interested in women's education convened separately to discuss the role of women's students in the war effort.[26] Corwin continued to attend meetings of the committee throughout the duration.

At the men's colleges, President Clothier urged the students to remain calm and wait for further direction. The second term was shortened by five weeks and an expanded summer session was introduced to enable students to graduate in three years. When the 1942 academic year opened, Rutgers College welcomed the largest freshman class in the college's history, while the junior and senior classes had lost more than a quarter of their members. With the reduction of the draft age to eighteen, however, the situation changed drastically. Students rapidly withdrew and by May 1943, there were fewer than eight hundred undergraduates remaining in the men's colleges. Rutgers would have been in serious financial trouble had it not already been chosen as an Army Specialized Training Program (ASTP) site. The first group arrived in March 1943 and soon the college was once again overflowing with students, albeit uniformed ones. These students were selected from enlisted personnel on the basis of test scores and educational background. One group received training in engineering, another studied languages, while a later group took pre-medical and pre-dental courses. By April 1944, enrollment once again plummeted by one-third when the soldiers were withdrawn in preparation for the invasion of France. They were soon replaced, however, by participants in the Army Specialized Training Reserve Program (ASTRP), high school graduates who had not yet reached the age of eighteen who were enrolled and continued studying before being drafted. By early 1945, there were over four hundred young men attending classes in English, history, geography, mathematics, and science. Overall Rutgers educated nearly four thousand ASTP and ASTRP enlistees during World War II.[27]

Impact of the War on Academics at NJC

These war upheavals completely disrupted the curriculum at the men's colleges. Faculty members struggled to teach unfamiliar courses. The small number of civilian upperclassmen who remained had trouble finding courses, so were permitted to attend classes at NJC, an early instance of coeducation. The impact of war on the academic program at NJC and other women's colleges was, of course, much less pronounced. Overall, the demands of war temporarily promoted greater opportunities for women to study in traditionally male fields. The wartime emphasis on mathematics and science led to a 29 percent increase in bachelor's degrees awarded to women in these subjects during the war.[28] At NJC, the trend toward math and science that had begun in the late 1930s continued. In 1944–1945, NJC had the highest enrollment in advanced physics, chemistry, and mathematics in its history. At the same time, there were fewer women preparing to be teachers and librarians.[29] During the war, for the first time, NJC students were permitted to take classes in certain departments at the College of Engineering.[30] Students who were not majoring in science were encouraged to take science courses as electives.[31]

Only a few changes were made in the formal NJC curriculum as a direct result of the war. Unlike the men's colleges, NJC did not adopt a twelve-month academic year. A poll of students indicated that they relied on their summer jobs too much for income. A few students did arrange an accelerated program, and a special graduation exercise was held at the end of the fall semester, 1942.[32] A few new courses were introduced, including a public administration course to meet civil service requirements and a short course in calculus for nonmathematics majors.[33] The war stimulated student interest in international relations and cultures, contributing to the development of new history courses like Organization of the Post-War World and courses in Portuguese and Latin American studies. The latter built on an exchange program with Latin America, funded by the New Jersey State Federation of Women's Clubs, that had been introduced after 1939 when study abroad in Europe was no longer possible. Nancy Petersen Godfrey (NJC '44) recalled that "through history courses on the changing world and post-war problems, we [acquired] an awareness of such problems."[34] Other courses were adapted to wartime needs, such as Emily Hickman's Pacific World course, which incorporated material on Japanese history and civilization, and a new German course for translators, censors, and shortwave radio operators.[35]

Because of the wartime emphasis on physically toughening the younger generation, the physical education requirement was extended yet again to four years. New activities like gymnastics and cross-country running were added, while the more lady-like badminton and tap dancing were dropped. "Free election of activities has been limited in such a way as to ensure enrollment in *vigorous* class work for at least two of the three seasons of the year."[36] The new requirements were not universally popular. Jean Comeforo (NJC '45) recalled, "A lot of us got injured on that obstacle course, but we were supposed to jump over fences, and swing on the bars and all that kind of stuff to keep us healthy and strong, the homefront should be strong." A home economics major, she recalled that "all our recipes were for vitamins."[37]

The war was also hard on the NJC faculty, although they experienced far less disruption and uncertainty than did their colleagues at the men's colleges. Like the Rutgers College faculty, they were required to teach without compensation at the new extended summer session. Twenty-seven NJC professors and instructors, both men and women, left for various types of war service.[38] For example, economist Miriam West worked on defense housing under the Federal Works Agency before moving on to the War Labor Board. Those remaining were required to fill in where needed: Emil Jordan of the German department taught Portuguese, Jessie Fiske of the botany department took over some zoology courses, and Shirley Smith of classics taught elementary mathematics.[39] In subjects where enrollment had dropped, like library science, education, and Italian, Corwin was forced to ask instructors to work part time, although some were able to pick up teaching for the ASTP or ASTRP.[40]

New Career Opportunities

Like women throughout the country, NJC students took advantage of the new career opportunities provided by the war. Many graduates of these years found war industry-related jobs, while others took the places of men called up for service. In March 1942, the nearby Raritan Arsenal contacted NJC with an urgent request for fifty women with scientific or mathematical backgrounds to replace male section leaders who had been drafted.[41]

In 1943, Placement Bureau director Fredericka Belknap reported that 24 percent of the Class of 1942 was employed in war industries, the armed forces, or government. "Since last September, I have been besieged by prospective employers asking for permission to interview in particular our majors in mathematics, physics and chemistry, and the seniors who have taken drafting."[42] Home economics majors were also in demand for positions as dieticians in the military and in government, as experts tried to determine the dietary needs of troops and of civilians in case of rationing.[43] Six NJC home economics majors from the Class of 1942 found jobs as food inspectors at the U.S. Department of Agriculture, an area where few women had found employment in the past.[44] Liberal arts majors also easily found jobs during the war. Frieda Finklestein Feller, a Spanish and French major, worked in the Office of Censorship following graduation in 1941, ultimately specializing in "Secret Inks."[45] Nancy Squire Christensen (NJC '44), an English major, recalled that IBM came to the college to recruit, looking for people with a broad background. She was trained as a punch card operator and ultimately worked as a systems service representative.[46] At the same time, fewer NJC graduates took jobs in the more traditional roles of teachers or librarians, areas where there was still a great need during the war years.[47]

The need to replace men who were drafted led to new opportunities for women. Places in graduate schools opened up for women, particularly in the sciences. Phyllis Pollock Magat (NJC '44) was accepted into the doctoral program in chemistry at the Massachusetts Institute of Technology. She recalled, "Our entering class in the chemistry grad school in 1944 was small (about eight) and were mostly women. The professors were amazed but soon got over any prejudice."[48] Adelaide Marcus Zagoren (NJC '40), a journalism major, could not find a full-time job upon her graduation in 1940 and recalled that the only jobs available to women were writing for the society pages. The following year, however, she easily found a job for the *Home News*. "I could find a job in a newspaper in '41 because all the men had left."[49] Historian Margaret Rossiter notes that many of the new opportunities for women in science did not extend beyond the entry level and had an uncertain future once the war was over.[50]

Some NJC women joined the new women's armed services. According to Richard P. McCormick, 173 NJC alumnae and students entered military service during the World War II era.[51] Most NJC women joined the WAVES, although some joined the WAC, the Red Cross, or the Cadet Nurse Corps. The WAVES recruited heavily at NJC, and the 1943 commencement speaker was Mildred McAfee, the president of Wellesley College, who served as director of the WAVES from 1942 to 1946. Jean O'Grady Sheehan (NJC '43) overcame opposition from her father and her pastor to join in December 1942. O'Grady, from a strict Roman Catholic family, grew up a few blocks from NJC and had hardly been away from home. She recalled that her motives for joining the military were mixed: "You did feel very patriotic, but there were other issues besides the patriotism. There was a selfish issue there, the traveling, the being away from home, getting away from home, wearing the nice uniform. At age twenty, that was a big appeal. Yes, it was exciting for a young woman."[52] O'Grady became a recruiter for the WAVES based in Atlanta. She met her future husband, a military pilot, while in the service and they spent ten years living in Venezuela.

▲ WAVES RECRUITING POSTER AT NEW JERSEY COLLEGE FOR WOMEN, *QUAIR*, 1944

Like many of the college-educated women in the military, Jean O'Grady became an officer. Nancy Petersen Godfrey (NJC '44) also joined the WAVES after graduation, but remained in the ranks. She was offered the opportunity to apply for a commission, but her mother discouraged her because Nancy's fiancé, who was also in the navy, was an enlisted man. "My mother said, 'Well, you wouldn't want to do that, 'cause it would make Bill feel, whatever, lesser or something.'" After her education at NJC, which she described as "one place where you could sort of be yourself and you didn't have to compete with boys," this was "the first time I felt that it was different to be a woman."[53] Most NJC women found their experience in the military to be empowering. Margaret Harriet Waugh (NJC '44) recalled, "It gives you a lot of self-confidence, for some reason or other. . . . It was reassuring, in some way, to say, 'Oh, I was in the Navy for a year.'"[54] A science major, Waugh later worked in bacteriology at E. R. Squibb and Sons in New Brunswick.

Although military service offered new opportunities for women, some lost their lives during the conflict. At least four NJC alumnae died while serving. Anna Jane

Evans (NJC '35), president of her class, entered the Army Nurse Corps in 1944. She was posted to a regional hospital at Camp Lee, Virginia, where she was killed in an automobile accident in October 1945. Marian Carol Gillis (NJC '37) joined the WAC in 1943. Stationed in Guam, she died in a plane crash over Shangri-La in May 1945. Ruth Ballard Murdock (NJC '41), a music major from Montclair, and Cecil Florence Ritchie Nichols (NJC '39) both worked as staff assistants for the Red Cross. Murdock, who was attached to the Eighth Army Group in Munich organizing clubs for soldiers, was killed in an accident returning from leave on the Riviera, while Nichols died in a plane crash in Australia.[55]

Student Life during Wartime

Unlike the situation at the men's colleges, where virtually all extracurricular activities were suspended during the war, student life at NJC continued as it had before the conflict. As at other women's colleges, organizations were established to aid the war effort and existing clubs and societies redirected their activities to war-related work. Now enlarged and aptly renamed the War Services Committee but still chaired by Margaret Judson, the Defense and Relief Committee served as a clearinghouse for war-related campus activities, including recruiting volunteers for community projects and raising money for relief—a total of sixteen thousand dollars was raised by the end of the war.[56] Selling war bonds was popular; because students had little money, they tended to buy stamps until they collected enough to purchase the cheapest bond for $18.75.[57] In 1942, the *Caellian* editors undertook a two-year campaign to sell corsages made of war stamps, managing to raise five hundred dollars by 1944, despite an initial lack of enthusiasm.[58] Many students did war work off campus, including working in day care centers for the children of factory workers, serving as hostesses at the United Service Organizations (USO) club on Albany Street, and folding surgical dressings at Johnson & Johnson for a minimal sum, replacing regular employees who had been called up.[59]

In deference to the wartime mood, the gala celebration planned for the twenty-fifth anniversary of the college was replaced by a simple convocation in the chapel on October 9, 1943. At the ceremony, Margaret Corwin was awarded an honorary doctorate from Rutgers in commemoration of the anniversary and her ten years as dean. NJC's twenty-fifth anniversary was further marked by the publication of *Twenty-Five Years: Two Anniversary Sketches of New Jersey College for Women* by Rosamond Sawyer Moxon (NJC '29) and Mabel Clarke Peabody (NJC '31). Corwin sent copies of the book to fellow women's colleges.[60]

The Education Subcommittee, under Emily Hickman, offered an expanding number of noncredit war-related courses, including engineering drawing, secretarial work, first aid, nutrition, stagecraft, radio communication, and auto mechanics. In 1941–1942, 444 students enrolled in these courses. Hickman also organized a series of fortnightly talks by members of the faculty and distinguished visiting lecturers. These included anthropologist Margaret Mead; engineer and scientific management pioneer

Lillian Moller Gilbreth; and Eleanor Roosevelt, who first visited NJC in December 1940 under the auspices of the International Student Services. On January 17, 1944, she again addressed the students on the topic "why young women should remain in college in wartime." Prior to her lecture, she enjoyed a dinner at Woodlawn, the mansion that trustee and benefactor James Neilson had bequeathed to NJC, hosted by the Student Lecture Committee.[61]

In tune with the more serious atmosphere on campus, more frivolous or costly activities such as the freshman breakfast, parents' day, and junior show were dropped, some never to be revived. Club activities were more limited, and some clubs merged, like a new organization created from the history, economics, political science, and sociology clubs, called HEPS. The conviction that the war was being fought to safeguard democracy led some students to think more critically about the state of democracy at home. Race relations were in the news during the war as pressure mounted to desegregate the military and pass civil rights legislation to acknowledge the contribution of African Americans to the war effort.[62] In December 1943, HEPS established the Racial and Minorities Relations Committee, stating boldly, "Our primary purpose is to better relations between racial and minority groups on campus, our secondary aim is to carry this program further into the community and the nation."[63] To this end the committee

▲ ELEANOR ROOSEVELT AND NEW JERSEY COLLEGE FOR WOMEN STUDENT LECTURE COMMITTEE

created exhibits at Botany and Recitation halls on segregation and discrimination in education, labor, and housing; wrote articles for the *Caellian* dealing with racial prejudice; invited speakers; and collected and distributed pamphlets like anthropologist Ruth Benedict's *The Races of Mankind*, which attempted to set out the scientific case against racist beliefs.[64]

Most notably, the committee campaigned to permit African American students to live on campus at NJC. Since Julia Baxter Bates's time, a few black women had attended NJC but, like Baxter, were commuters.[65] As Chair Eleanor Oliven (NJC '48) cautiously noted, the committee members had been discussing the question for several years and they did not want to force the issue, but they believed active steps should be taken: "We need to have a few Negro girls living on campus, so those considering coming to NJC will not hesitate to live on campus. Actual contacts in houses will do a good deal towards breaking down prejudice."[66] Many of Oliven's fellow students supported the campaign. Nancy Petersen Godfrey recalled pointing out at an assembly that the administration did not allow black students to live on campus: "Anyway, I got called to the dean's [Boddie's] office and [was] asked to, I guess, repent, or something. What did she say? Maybe she said [that] I shouldn't feel that way, I should understand that they had to sort of bow to the will of the parents."[67] Irene Prager (NJC '44), in a letter to the *Caellian*, inquired why NJC did not admit more black women.[68] The first African American women to live on campus were Emma A. Warren, the younger sister of Constance Andrews (NJC '45), and Evelyn S. Field, both from the Class of 1949. They commuted their first year, but because of continuing support from HEPS, which found a scholarship to cover their room and board, they moved to campus the following year. At first they roomed together but later lived in separate dormitories. Field recalled that living on campus was "a very enriching experience." She found most people supportive, although one student reputedly moved out of a cottage when she heard that Field was coming. The Urban League of New Brunswick sponsored Friday night socials where NJC's African American women were able to meet black men from Rutgers College.[69]

Social Life on a Wartime Campus

During the war, heterosexual social life at NJC was much more limited. With the male students away, there were far fewer dances or other coeducational activities. Mary Lou Norton Busch remembered "no boys around to date during the war."[70] Nancy Squire Christenson (NJC '44) recalled that "there weren't many blind dates during the war." She and her friends "played bridge and went to the movies a lot."[71] Despite the fact that there were fewer men on campus, the marriage rate actually rose.[72] NJC students sometimes hurried to wed before their boyfriends were sent overseas. Mary Lou Norton Busch, who left NJC during the war to marry her high school boyfriend, "would never have thought of getting married if war had not occurred." She returned to finish her degree many years later.[73] This period marked the beginning of a long-term drop in age at marriage and increase in the birthrate, the "baby boom."[74] In her study of alumnae in

the twenty-fifth-anniversary volume, Mabel Peabody discovered that early marriage was reported much more frequently by the youngest classes than by any preceding class: in 1943, 18 percent of the students in the classes 1940–1942 had married before their twenty-second birthdays.[75] This pattern was similar to that at women's colleges in general during this period.[76]

Married NJC students, like those at other women's colleges, were not allowed to live on campus. Jean Comeforo (NJC '45) remembered that Dean Boddie called classmates who got married into her office for a talk. Her friend reported that "they had to live off campus, but . . . Dean wanted to be sure that they didn't talk about what you did in marriage to all these young innocent little girls who were on campus."[77] Nancy Petersen Godfrey's sister got married in her senior year and "had to live in a separate house with the black students." Another friend got married secretly.[78] Because so many women students were marrying servicemen, this prohibition was abandoned at most women's colleges, including NJC, by 1943.[79]

In the absence of male college students, some NJC women dated ASTP men or soldiers from Camp Kilmer, the embarkation camp that opened in nearby Piscataway in 1942. With thousands of servicemen passing through the camp, the atmosphere in New Brunswick changed dramatically. Although NJC was officially off limits to soldiers from Camp Kilmer, Corwin was concerned about security in downtown New Brunswick, requiring women students to travel in groups of four. Corwin hoped to persuade the Camp Kilmer commander to require soldiers on leave to return to camp by midnight rather than 6:00 a.m. It is doubtful if she was successful, although a guard was posted at the campus.[80] Most of the soldiers at Camp Kilmer were enlisted men rather than officers, which probably contributed to Corwin's anxiety, but there seem to have

▶ NEW JERSEY
COLLEGE FOR
WOMEN STUDENTS
WITH SAILOR, 1943

been relatively few incidents, considering the number of soldiers passing though the base. Jean Comeforo (NJC '45), who commuted to NJC by train from Metuchen, recalled being followed home by a soldier. She later discovered that another woman had been attacked nearby that night.[81]

With fiancés, friends, and brothers serving overseas, NJC women developed strong bonds with each other. As Richard P. McCormick wrote, the war's "impact was intensely emotional, for it touches everyone with the agony of death and the fervor of sacrifice."[82] Miriam Null (NJC '46), who lived on campus, stated, "I think our big . . . invasion was 1944 and friends of mine, my classmates at college, they all had boyfriends over there. They . . . were biting their fingernails at the quick waiting for the telegrams to come. One of them . . . was a bomber . . . in the 8th Air Force and they would go off to Germany every night. She was having fits. We were all having fits with her. . . . We were all her support group."[83] Some NJC women did experience losses, particularly those going out with ASTP men, many of whom were killed in the Battle of the Bulge. In all, 234 Rutgers men gave their lives during World War II.[84]

Postwar NJC: Era of Continuity and Change

The end of the war in August 1945 brought important changes at Rutgers. Before the end of the conflict, President Clothier approached state officials about crafting a new relationship between the state and the university, replacing the ineffectual Board of Regents. In 1945, the legislature passed a bill designating the whole of Rutgers—rather than just NJC, the College of Agriculture, and certain other departments—the State University of New Jersey. Rutgers University was now an "instrumentality of the state," without losing any of its autonomy.[85] The bill, which was supported by the Associate Alumnae, the New Jersey State Federation of Women's Clubs, and other women's organizations, had important consequences for NJC. In some respects, the college became more closely integrated into the university. As part of the reorganization, Rutgers created a Special Committee on Personnel Procedures, chaired by former NJC acting dean Albert E. Meder. Under Meder's leadership, appointments, promotions, and tenure were regularized at NJC and brought in line with procedures at the men's colleges, and a more equitable salary scale was adopted. For the first time, a retirement plan was introduced. Another consequence was that a state university could no longer demand compulsory attendance at chapel. NJC continued to hold two assemblies a week, but now only attendance at the secular assembly was required.[86] During the war, the students had approached Corwin about creating an interfaith committee, which sponsored diverse religious services at the college and organized regular trips to various churches and synagogues.[87]

With the end of the war and the passage of the Servicemen's Readjustment Act, better known as the G.I. Bill, in 1944, male students flocked to Rutgers. Fraternities, clubs, and social life resumed with a vengeance. Several new coeducational activities were introduced, including the WRSU radio station, the University Choir, and the Queen's Players theater group. Women cheerleaders began to appear at football games.[88] Enrollment skyrocketed at the men's colleges as veterans took advantage of the new educational opportunity, increasing from 750 in September 1945 to 3,200 in September 1946 and to a peak of 4,200 a year later.[89] Enrollment increased rapidly at NJC as well. By 1947, the women's college had 1,210 students, two hundred more than the college's physical plan could reasonably accommodate. In her annual report, Corwin noted that the college was accepting only a third of applicants, turning away many qualified young women.[90]

Although NJC was not as overcrowded as Rutgers College, the leaders of both institutions were keenly aware of the need for more classroom, office, and dormitory space. As early as 1943, the college purchased 23 Nichol Avenue from the estate of Frances Hall. Corwin moved there from the former dean's residence at 135 George Street, which was turned into office space.[91] In 1947, Rutgers began to lobby for a state bond issue to finance construction projects, including a new library, gymnasium, and student center at NJC, for which architectural plans had been drawn up several years before. The fifty-million-dollar proposal was also designed to aid the state colleges and welfare agencies. The measure faced opposition, as had the 1945 bill, from taxpayers' associations and religious groups that challenged Rutgers's legitimacy as a public university. In the end, the bond issue lost by more than eighty thousand votes in the November 1948 election.[92] The defeat was a severe blow for Margaret Corwin and NJC. Fund-raising efforts were refocused on the Associate Alumnae's campaign for a

▲ COOPER HALL WITH BICYCLES, CA. 1950

new student center, which proved difficult in the era of rising costs and economic retrenchment that followed the war. The campaign had not yet met its goal when it was folded into the university capital campaign launched in 1950. The end result was the completion of the student center in 1953, the first building to rise on the NJC campus since Jameson in 1931.[93]

The postwar period was characterized by a return to traditional gender roles. After the war, women experienced pressure to return to "normal," to marry, and to start families. The marriage rate peaked in 1946, while the age of marriage was decreasing and fertility rates rose.[94] College-educated women, including those at single-sex institutions, also felt pressure to marry early. According to distinguished historian of women's higher education Barbara Solomon, "A diamond ring on the fourth finger was the sign of success most valued in one's senior year at Vassar in 1949."[95] Mary Lou Norton Busch (DC '82), who ultimately returned to Douglass and graduated in 1982, recalled, "After the war, everybody was expected to go home and have kids and keep house."[96] To some extent, NJC administrators encouraged this trend. The home economics department offered a class in foods, which was open to only juniors and seniors majoring in liberal arts. The course description specified what students were taught: "Selection, preparation and serving of foods. Planning of balanced menus. Table Service for special occasions. Evaluation of publications available to the housewife."[97] Students nicknamed the class the "Bride's Course," describing the curriculum as "Cooking!"[98] In 1949, the Faculty-Student Service Council sponsored a series of lectures on marriage. Duke sociologist Hornell Hart advised students that "the most important aim in life between the ages of 14 and 24 is to find the right life partner and then to marry that partner."[99]

After the war, there was an overall drop in the number of employers looking for scientifically trained women.[100] By 1948, the number of women engaged in scientific work had decreased 2.5 percent from wartime levels. Ominously, reports surfaced that one employer was reluctant to spend time training women because they got married so soon, especially when more men were available. As of May 1949, almost one-quarter of the class of 1948 were already married.[101] The following year, there was growing unemployment among recent graduates. "No matter how excellent a woman's work may have been, when a choice is necessary, industry seems to prefer a man."[102] Many of those who had found work during the war were leaving to marry. Nancy Squire Christiansen left IBM in 1946, noting that her husband did not want her to work. "That was an era when your wife didn't work. If she did, it looked like you couldn't support her, almost that."[103] In her study of over three hundred alumnae of the war era, Laura Micheletti concluded that war service had long-term effects on women's confidence, showing them that they

▲ DANCE CLASS, *QUAIR*, 1956. PHOTO BY BRADBURY, SAYLES, AND O'NEILL

▲ STUDENTS ON THE STEPS OF VOORHEES CHAPEL, 1948

could fulfill roles traditionally reserved for men.[104] Many of these women returned to work much later, after their children had grown up.

Several alumnae credit their NJC experience with contributing to this confidence. Frieda Finklestein Feller (NJC '41) commented, "They brought in women like Margaret Mead to show us that you could do something."[105] After her stint in censorship during the war, Feller worked in her family's real estate business before returning to Rutgers to do a master's degree in education. She ultimately taught at the Rutgers Graduate School of Education. Evelyn Field (NJC '49) believed that NJC gave her "the opportunity to realize that as a woman, and even as a minority woman, as they say[,] 'you can do anything that you want to do.'"[106] Field went on to earn master's degrees in education and library service from Rutgers University. As well as an accomplished librarian and educator, she became a founding trustee of Raritan Valley Community College and a member of the Rutgers Board of Trustees and received numerous accolades for her contribution to women's advancement and civil rights.[107]

The early 1950s marked the end of an era for NJC. Many long-serving administrators retired, among them larger-than-life personality Leah Boddie and her assistant Elizabeth P. Thomas. Alice Aronoff, first appointed by Mabel Smith Douglass in 1918, librarian Ada English, and placement officer Fredericka Belknap also retired in 1954. Also retiring were many longtime faculty members, including Anna Campbell of the history department, C. Everard Deems of religion, and Helen Richardson of psychology, while Alice Schlimbach resigned her position as head of the German House and Jane Inge of drama stepped down from her role as department chair. Margaret Corwin's friend and ally President Robert C. Clothier retired in July 1951 and was replaced by Lewis Webster Jones. Corwin herself remained until July 1, 1955. In her last years as dean, Margaret Corwin continued to advocate for lighter teaching loads and greater research opportunities for faculty and for an expanded physical plant "to prepare for the rising tide of students that we know to be rapidly approaching." She constantly reaffirmed NJC's identity as a liberal arts college grounded in the example of elite private women's colleges like her own alma mater, Bryn Mawr.[108]

After her retirement Margaret Corwin returned to Connecticut, where she lived for many years in Guilford, keeping in close touch with the college. She died in 1983 at the age of ninety-three. By holding NJC together through the difficult years of the Great Depression and World War II, she ensured her legacy. By the 1950s, however, Corwin was increasingly out of step with the demands of a growing public university and a new generation of young women. An educated and highly accomplished leader herself, she was nevertheless bound by the limits of class, race, and gender of her upbringing. In her later years, she was loved by her former students, who credited her with instilling in them her dedication to service. As Adelaide Zagoren (NJC '40) recalled, "She always encouraged you to go beyond yourself and do what you could."[109]

5

FROM NEW JERSEY
COLLEGE FOR WOMEN
TO DOUGLASS COLLEGE

DOUGLASS COLLEGE IS IN THE
PROCESS OF EVOLVING FROM A
RELATIVELY SMALL, RELATIVELY
ISOLATED COLLEGE FOR WOMEN TO
A LARGE, WELL-INTEGRATED ORGAN
OF THE STATE OF NEW JERSEY.

—Mary Bunting, Douglass College,
Annual Report, 1956–1957

Women's colleges faced unique challenges in the 1950s. It became increasingly difficult to educate women for self-sufficiency and self-determination, as government officials and popular culture insisted that women's roles were exclusively domestic. J. Edgar Hoover initiated a propaganda campaign as World War II was winding down: "There must be no absenteeism among mothers. . . . Her patriotic duty is not on the factory front. It is on the home front."[1] Popular media shored up that message. One study documented that 90 percent of the women shown on the pages of women's magazines were depicted in familial roles—performing housework or child care.[2] These images of women were at some remove from the realities of women's lives, however. Although the return of soldiers from war service profoundly affected women's employment, it did not drive women out of the labor force. In 1950, women composed 29 percent of the U.S. labor force, half of women workers were over thirty-five years of age, and 40 percent of married women with small children held a job. By the mid-1950s, women's workforce participation matched World War II levels— what changed, however, was the nature of the jobs women held. Job segregation by sex was reinforced. By 1957, 70 percent of working women held clerical positions, assembly-line, or service jobs; 12 percent held professional positions; and 6 percent worked in management.[3] As employment horizons constricted, fewer women entered college in the 1950s, leading some women's colleges to redefine their mission. In the words of Lynn White Jr., president of Mills College, "The curriculum for female students should prepare women to foster the intellectual and emotional life of her family and community."[4]

Some women's organizations contested efforts to contain women within the domestic sphere. They formed coalitions with progressive organizations that welcomed women's time and talent, while relegating them to behind-the-scenes roles. The American Association of University Women, the American Friends Service Committee, the League of Women Voters, the National Council of Negro Women, and the NAACP actively promoted opportunities for women, an expanded welfare state, a powerful labor movement, civil liberties, racial equality, and a new equitable international order. Their efforts to advance a more egalitarian vision of the United States, however, conflicted with Cold War rhetoric that drew marked contrasts between Soviet communism, where women were consigned to waged labor and their children forced into depersonalized day care centers, and the "American dream" of stay-at-home mothers and breadwinner fathers, whose children experienced the full benefits of capitalism, freedom, and democracy.[5]

In the midst of these dueling visions of womanhood, NJC experienced its first leadership change in more than two decades, a crucial change in identity, and continued

▲ FIRST-YEAR STUDENTS IN THE EARLY 1950S WERE STILL REQUIRED TO WEAR "DINKS" DURING THE FIRST WEEKS OF CLASSES

challenges within Rutgers, as the university prepared for major growth. In 1955, thirty-seven years after its establishment, NJC changed its name to Douglass College to honor its founding dean and created a new "Alma Mater" and college seal to mark the occasion. The change in name coincided with the appointment of Mary Ingraham Bunting as the third dean of the college. Resisting domestic models of womanhood, Dean Bunting transformed the college by elevating academic standards, implementing structural changes, and reaffirming the responsibility of Douglass to meet the growing professional needs of young women in New Jersey. Dean Bunting urged students to raise their educational aspirations to include graduate and professional education. She pursued opportunities to collaborate with Rutgers College, the Graduate School, and central administration, under the presidencies of Lewis Webster Jones and Mason Gross.

In 1960, Ruth Marie Adams became the fourth dean of Douglass, ushering the college into a period of major growth, overseeing the completion of campus expansion, and providing critical leadership as the debates over the proposed Federated College Plan mobilized the university community. Dean Adams too set ambitious goals for the women's college at Rutgers. She reinvigorated the honors program and launched a Pilot Educational Opportunity Program for minority students. While preserving sacred NJC traditions, both Dean Bunting and Dean Adams sought to define women's education in terms of academic excellence and preparation for professional careers. This chapter chronicles their efforts to open the range of possibilities for young women in New Jersey, while safeguarding Douglass as a fully integrated unit of the university.

Mary Bunting and the Changing Vision of Douglass College

Mary Ingraham Bunting's path to the deanship at Douglass was precedent setting. For the first time, three members of the faculty worked closely with members of the university's Board of Trustees to select the third dean of Douglass College. This important step toward faculty governance led to the unanimous selection of Dean Bunting, a microbiologist with a PhD from the University of Wisconsin, Madison, who was also a widow with four children. Bunting came to Douglass from Yale University, having held previous positions at Bennington, Goucher, and Wellesley Colleges. Bunting's appointment at Douglass included faculty rank and an active laboratory. As a professor of bacteriology, she continued her research on grants she brought with her from the Atomic Energy Commission and the American Tuberculosis Association. During her deanship, Bunting received an additional major grant from the U.S. Public Health Service for research on *Serratia* bacteria. To assist her in running the lab, Bunting hired Ann Heuer, a Rutgers graduate student, who had worked in the bacteriology department at Douglass and helped with teaching and supervision of many Douglass students.[6]

Bunting inaugurated a new era of growth in the college. She envisioned Douglass as a "well-integrated organ of the State of New Jersey" and anticipated the need to expand to meet the needs of young women across the state: "If Douglass were to enroll its existing proportion of girls in senior high school classes of the state, it would have at least three thousand students by 1968."[7] The quality and purpose of Douglass students impressed the dean, "as nearly all of them graduated in the top quarter of their high school class," and the majority of students held summer jobs to earn wages towards their college education.[8] The dean appreciated both the students' intellects and their determination to work to support their college education. The students' capacity to juggle multiple responsibilities resonated with the dean's own demanding life. In the words of Rutgers University president Lewis Webster Jones, Dean Bunting "has successfully combined a distinct career in research and scholarship with the responsibilities of her family and, at the same time, made unusually valuable contributions to her community and its people."[9] Reiko Fukuyama Ohye and Lola Fuchs Kamp (both DC '56) recollected that Dean Bunting and her children introduced an "air of change" to the college and to campus. Compared with her predecessor, Bunting was informal and approachable, hosting meetings with students and events in her house, providing an opportunity for the students to relate to her own children, and as Sandra Harding (DC '56) noted, babysitting them on occasion.[10]

▶ MARY INGRAHAM
BUNTING, DEAN OF
DOUGLASS, 1955–1960.
PHOTO JUNE 1959.

Once settled in the dean's residence at the heart of Douglass Campus, Dean Bunting started a systematic attempt to build an efficient organization and to elevate the college's academic standards. She created the College Council, approved by the faculty in 1956, as a mechanism to advance her goals. The council combined the activities of four previously separate committees and greatly streamlined faculty committee obligations. The council consisted of the dean of the college as chair, the dean of student life, the assistant dean of administration, and four (later eight) faculty representatives appointed by the dean to represent the four academic divisions. Faculty representatives who served on the council received reduced teaching loads. This restructuring of the college's administrative bodies concentrated important decision-making processes in one place and streamlined the bureaucracy. After a slow start, the new organization received a vote of confidence from the faculty.

To counter cultural pressures to limit women's options to marriage and child-rearing and to repudiate popular tendencies to devalue women's intellects, Dean Bunting worked arduously to raise academic standards at the college. By 1950, two-thirds of NJC women were in the top tenth of their graduating classes, a far higher proportion than Rutgers men.[11] In 1951, NJC students had mobilized unsuccessfully to persuade the faculty to eliminate Saturday classes and implement a more research-oriented curriculum akin to the European model of higher education. The Government Association requested elimination of attendance policies and allowance of unlimited cuts, placing far greater emphasis on performance on exams and written work for grading purposes. The faculty refused.[12] Despite social changes precipitated by World War II and the postwar years, the values and academic curricula established in the early years of NJC remained unchanged. Dean Bunting introduced multiple changes. She strengthened the curricula by increasing student course options and encouraged the faculty to design and teach experimental and new courses. She saw the personal strengths and interests of Douglass women and emboldened them to explore career possibilities that involved research and professional training. She served as a role model and a mentor to prepare students for success. She wanted her students "to reach for lives that satisfied beyond a split-level in the Oranges."[13] She urged students to take advantage of the growing number of graduate scholarships and fellowships available to seniors with distinguished academic records. With her encouragement, the number of seniors pursuing graduate studies rose from 4 percent to 17 percent in just three years.[14]

In the mid-1950s, Rutgers was involved for the third time with negotiations in Trenton over its status as "the State University of New Jersey." As the final traces of the colonial college were being expunged by the emergence of a major public university, increasing attention and resources were devoted to research and graduate education. Within the men's colleges, the institutional focus shifted as faculty research changed from a supplementary to an essential task and graduate teaching was encouraged.[15] Yet faculty at Douglass were insulated from these developments by persistent devaluing of the women's college. As distinguished British constitutional historian Margaret Judson noted, Douglass had six PhDs teaching in its joint Political Science and History Department; Rutgers College had three PhDs. Yet when George Schmidt suggested that Douglass faculty teach in the Rutgers University Summer School, he was told they were not qualified, since Douglass professors were "only inflated high school teachers."[16] Dean Bunting sought to overcome such unwarranted bias against her faculty, exploring possibilities for collaboration with Rutgers College and other academic units in New Brunswick on graduate education. Her overtures met with considerable resistance. The Douglass faculty remained dedicated educators for whom teaching and the welfare of undergraduate students were the central concern—whether by choice or by exclusion from other possibilities. Douglass faculty also endured inadequate office spaces, poorly equipped classrooms, and heavy teaching loads, along with lower salaries.[17] Yet their service to the college and the university was exemplary; they devoted considerable effort to student academic advising and some made their homes among the students, serving as resident faculty in the dormitories.

In the interregnum between the Corwin and Bunting administrations, the Rutgers Board of Trustees initiated a comprehensive review of the college. In the words of Douglass historian George P. Schmidt, "efficiency experts swarmed the campus in 1954," searching for ways to economize.[18] Their final report combined the identification of pressing needs (e.g., a central heating system and better janitors) with some criticisms of the college, deemed misguided by friends of Douglass. Most notably, the high academic standards at NJC were considered to be untenable, creating an education for "highbrows only," which the report projected, would generate high dropout rates as student enrollment expanded.[19] The report recommended that fewer students be hired to serve in dining commons, jeopardizing a work-study opportunity that many students had relied upon to fund their college expenses. Another long-standing NJC tradition was also imperiled: the report endorsed the closure of the cafeteria run by the home economics department, which had served as a professional practice site for students specializing in food and nutrition, while also providing the best cuisine in New Brunswick for Douglass faculty and commuter students.[20] Concerned that the college was at risk because of the criticism, alumnae, the New Jersey State Federation of Women's Clubs, and the mother of the governor of New Jersey testified in Trenton about the importance of the women's college and the need to preserve its separate budget, autonomous student life, and integrity of the honor system, rather than succumb to centralization for the sake of purported efficiency.[21]

Dean Bunting took over the leadership of Douglass in the midst of this political turmoil. Although she was able to stave off some of the Trustee's recommendations, she could not withstand them all. As a result of the demands for heightened efficiency, NJC's library school was moved to the new Graduate School of Library Science, the education department was moved to the university's School of Education (but later reversed), and the physical education department merged with its counterpart at Rutgers College.[22] It was with mixed emotions, then, that Douglass joined the resuscitated

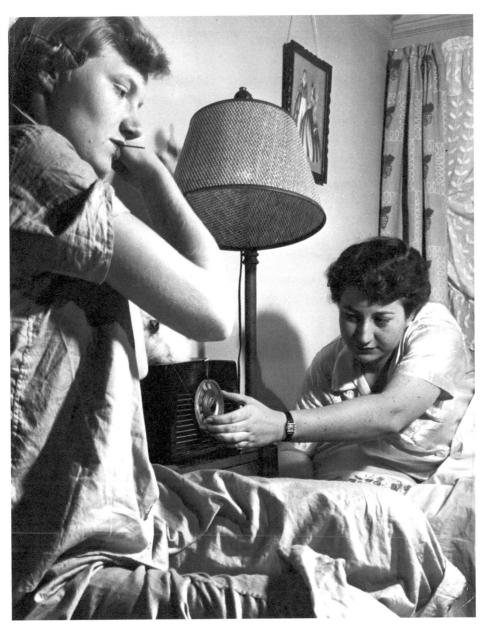

▲ STUDENTS IN RESIDENCE HALL, 1954

state university in 1956, as a full public corporation, directed by a Board of Governors accountable to the state. As articulated later in one of her final reports to the president, "Probably the most acute source of poor morale at Douglass has been a sense that University decisions of vital importance to the College . . . have been made without consulting those best informed at the College."[23]

There were additional sources of malaise at Douglass and across the university in 1956, as the Board of Trustees amended the colonial charter to create the state-mandated controlling body, the Board of Governors. The board comprised eleven members, six of whom were appointed by the governor, crystallizing the fact that the state of New Jersey would play an increasingly prominent role in key decisions pertaining to the university. Political control was particularly fraught at this moment when the nation was in the thralls of McCarthyism. Rutgers was in the unenviable position of being the first university in the country, whose faculty members were grappling with the limits of the Fifth Amendment guarantee against self-incrimination. Three Rutgers faculty—one in the College of Pharmacy, one at the Newark College of Arts and Sciences, and one in the Law School—claimed their Fifth Amendment rights when called to testify before the House Committee on Un-American Activities. From 1952 through 1957, the Rutgers board declared it "grounds for immediate dismissal . . . to refuse, on the ground of the Fifth Amendment to the Constitution of the United States, to answer questions propounded by any duly constituted investigatory body."[24] Although the board subsequently allowed faculty the option of resignation rather than dismissal, this policy cast a pall over free speech on campus. "Teachers and students alike resentfully but prudently recognized the temper of the times and grew cautious about expressing opinions that might provoke the charge of 'Un-American.'"[25]

Dean Bunting faced significant challenges as she sought to prepare young women to transcend the demands of the time and to develop plans for the proposed growth of the college. Despite insufficient university support, Douglass enjoyed a unique status within Rutgers in that it had "quasi-independent status," with its own state appropriation, its own distinct campus, and its own student services and business offices. The men's colleges, by contrast, shared academic and residential facilities, had a single dean of students, and relied on central administration for supporting services.[26] This unique autonomy afforded Douglass an agility that would be notably reduced in following decades. In the fall of 1958, however, as Bunting designed a plan for the future of the college, she made full use of her sphere of autonomy.

Dean Bunting could also draw upon the support of a dedicated and growing body of alumnae, who were fiercely loyal to the college. Their confidence in Dean Bunting's leadership was demonstrated through the creation of an unrestricted fund "for the good of Douglass," which enabled the dean to support innovative and creative initiatives on campus.[27] By 1958, more than 51 percent of the alumnae were contributing to fundraising drives. Two alumnae joined the college professional staff. When the Office of the Assistant Dean of the College was created in 1956, Dean Bunting appointed Edna M. Newby (NJC '31) to the position. With the exception of Rosamond Sawyer Moxon (NJC '29), a charter trustee of Rutgers and later a member of the Board of Governors, Newby was the first alumna to reach a high-ranking position in the college administration. She had served Douglass in one way or another since her graduation and was familiar with the administrative processes and challenges. She also understood the delicate relationship between the college and the university and could offer the dean sage counsel. Frances E. Riche (NJC '32) joined the staff of the Associate Alumnae of Douglass College (AADC), following her retirement from a career as a high school teacher of English. Serving in a dual role as executive secretary of the AADC and editor of the *Alumnae Bulletin*, she raised the effectiveness and the prestige of both endeavors. In 1951, Riche became the secretary of the college. Both Edna Newby and Frances Riche brought loyalty and invaluable perspective that grew with their longevity.[28]

In academic year 1958–1959, Douglass enrolled 1,480 students, the largest student population in the college's history. Dean Bunting anticipated that enrollments could grow to three thousand by 1965. The number of dormitories had not changed in twenty-five years, however. Thus Dean Bunting turned to increasing the number of commuter students as a solution, "since this was the only available means of admitting an increased number."[29]

Commuters, also known as "bees," had always been part of the student body from the early NJC years, a consequence both of the lack of campus housing and of racial and religious discriminatory practices that precluded students of different races or religions from rooming together. The "beehive," dedicated to the commuters (approximately 20 percent of the total student body), was located in the science building. It afforded a site where students studied between classes, connected with one another, and hosted social activities. In the late 1950s, as the college modified the admissions policy to increase the number of commuters, the beehive became increasingly crowded.

In the 1950s, the average age of marriage plummeted to nineteen for U.S. women and the number of families with three children doubled, while the number with four children quadrupled. Dean Bunting took bold action to expand the opportunities for higher education for women who married and started families early, establishing the first program in the nation designed to allow "older women" to attend college. In fall 1959, the college approved the enrollment of part-time students, which made it possible for women with family and work responsibilities to matriculate. Initially called "Sophias" to signify the wisdom achieved with age and later renamed "Bunting Scholars," these non-traditional-aged students enriched course discussions by sharing their rich life experiences, and their presence inspired many of the younger students.

Douglass College encouraged the development of new and interdisciplinary courses to increase student learning. Historian Margaret Judson, for example, coordinated the course Religious Heritage of Western Civilization, recruiting faculty from the Departments of Art, History, Music, Political Science, and Religion to give lectures and organize discussions, providing students an impressive overview of European history.[30] Other initiatives during the Bunting administration included the inauguration of the Department of Russian Language and Literature, with Ludmila Turkevitch as chair. The department successfully collaborated with the Rutgers College Russian Area Studies Program to expand the scope of teaching. The coordinated coeducational physical education program with Rutgers, under Helen Kees, the chair of the hygiene and physical education department, trained students to become physical education teachers. Financial considerations led Bunting to close departments when necessary. After the death of Wilford Jackson, the chair of the physics department, for example, Bunting

▲ THE COMMUTER CAFETERIA, ALSO KNOWN AS THE "BEEHIVE," 1950S

phased out the department because the college could not afford to provide state-of-the-art equipment for a handful of majors. All remaining Douglass physics students completed courses for their major at Rutgers College.

The Department of Religion was added in 1955 and remained popular as students searched for meaning in response to a changing society. Compared with the 1941 *Red Book*, which had listed no religion-based recognized student organizations, the 1953 *Red Book* listed twelve religious student organizations in New Brunswick, all Christian with the exception of B'nai B'rith Hillel Foundation. Religion captured the campus scene not only in classrooms but also in student life. When Mary Bunting took office, she elected to preside over the secular assembly in Voorhees Chapel on Thursdays and delegated the Tuesday religious service to the Department of Religion. This departed from the precedent Mabel Smith Douglass had set, which Margaret Trumbull Corwin had continued, using chapel time as a dean-taught, credit-bearing course and as a means of communication to build morale and a sense of community.

Dean Bunting's ability to inspire academic excellence quickly showed results. In spring 1959, 326 graduating seniors—17 percent of the class—planned to pursue graduate study; 41 of these students had secured prestigious fellowships and assistantships in national competitions to finance their graduate study. Refusing the domestic model of womanhood, Dean Bunting demonstrated to students that professional education followed by a career was desirable and possible for young women—even as they married and had children. Outstanding academic performance surfaced in other ways at the college through vibrant student-led intellectual initiatives. In 1958, students designed and peer-taught a new course on world poetry demonstrating their engagement with intellectual life on campus. Ten third- and fourth-year students designed the course, which had a comparative literature component, featuring international students, who taught poetry from their own countries. In addition to broadening students' learning, this initiative freed some faculty time for research and scholarship. The course won first prize in the Richard Welling Memorial Competition for Student Government Achievement, a national competition, valorizing Douglass students' creativity and pedagogical innovation. On the extracurricular front, the students added *Promethean*, a publication focused on current issues, to the *Horn Book*, which featured literature and poetry.

Although modest in number, international students were an important part of the Douglass community, following in the footsteps of Ruby Manikam, a student from India who received her bachelor of science degree in 1926.[31] Many international students, such as Nandita Kashyap (DC '57) from India, received an international scholarship offered by the college. Others received funding from the Ford Foundation and from the State Federation of Women's Clubs, which supported students from Latin America and the Caribbean with the Pan American Scholarship. Students from Argentina, Austria, Brazil, Canada, Chile, China, Cuba, Greece, Honduras, Hong Kong, Hungary, India, Iran, Ireland, Japan, New Zealand, Sierra Leone, Sweden, Yugoslavia, and Venezuela came to Douglass in the 1950s and enjoyed rich and valuable experiences during their time in New Brunswick. Assistant dean Edna Newby played a crucial role as adviser and mentor to Douglass's international students, whom she took "under her wing."[32]

Each year, the Douglass students, along with their Rutgers College counterparts, organized the International Weekend, a vibrant event that brought international students from other universities to campus for lectures, presentations and interaction with students and faculty. The annual themes reflected contemporary issues. In 1960, for example, at the height of the Cold War, the topic of discussion was "World without War." A panel presentation, titled "Minimum Requirements for Disarmament," drew a capacity crowd. Sharon Lindenfield (DC '61), chair of the Student Organizing Committee,

▲ INTERNATIONAL WEEKEND AT DOUGLASS, 1965

▲ "SOPHIAS," LATER RENAMED BUNTING SCHOLARS

characterized the event as stimulating and informative, designed "to promote friendly relations and to broaden the horizons of our students here and of our international guests."[33]

In February 1960, after five years guiding Douglass, Mary Ingraham Bunting announced her decision to resign at the end of the semester to serve as president of Radcliffe College. John L. Swink, then dean of administration and later vice president and treasurer of the university, served as chief academic administrator of the college from May 1 to June 30. Mary Bunting provided transformative leadership during a difficult decade at Douglass College. She introduced many innovative programs and departed from traditions that were no longer useful. She forged strong ties with faculty and students through an "open door" policy that capitalized upon casual interactions. Douglass students knew that if the porch light of the dean's residence was lit at night, they were welcome to visit her.[34] Many students visited the dean late at night for informal conversations that invariably took place in front of a warm fire. Her children, featured in many pages of yearbooks, were popular with the students and considered integral members of the college community. In addition, Dean Bunting introduced structural change, using the College Council as a source of advice and criticism. The faculty esteemed her and, with few exceptions, approved her overall objectives.

Ruth Adams and the Physical Expansion of Campus

Ruth Marie Adams, a scholar of Victorian literature, who had earned her bachelor's at Adelphi University, her master's from Columbia, and her PhD from Radcliffe, succeeded Mary Bunting as the fifth dean of Douglass in July 1960. Originally from New York City, Adams had risen through the academic ranks at the University of Rochester, where she also served as the director of the honors program. Appointed as professor of English and dean of the college, Ruth Adams was known to the students as a warm, interesting, and demanding teacher of Victorian literature as well as an avid traveler. She held her seminars on Dickens, Eliot, Hardy, and Conrad in the living room of the dean's house. In addition to inspiring the students with her insights into these authors' lengthy tomes, Adams offered the students advice about how to establish independent lives. In the words of Anne Spiegel Lipner (DC '62), Dean Adams insisted that "an education should prepare our minds so that if we were alone in a room without any external stimulation our minds should be able to provide sufficient stimulation."[35]

Dean Adams's era was marked by rapid growth in numbers of students and faculty, in the size of the physical plant, and in the complexity of Douglass's relationship with the university. Student enrollment grew from 1,079 in 1955 to 1,731 in 1960 to 2,844 in 1967, as faculty increased from 125 to 168 to 231 in the same period, increasing the student-teacher ratio from 10:1 to 12:1.[36] The academic excellence of Douglass

▲ RUTH MARIE ADAMS, DEAN OF DOUGLASS, 1960–1966. F. J. HIGGINS, PHOTOGRAPHER, 1964

students also grew impressively. By 1966, 80 percent of students admitted to Douglass were in top tenth of their graduating class. To accommodate this growth, the campus expansion initiated under Mary Bunting continued. Dean Adams also added new programs for gifted students and for minority students, which became hallmarks of her administration.

In its reaffirmed role as the State University of New Jersey, Rutgers was under considerable pressure to increase enrollments. At Douglass, this resulted in challenging situations. With creativity and patience, Dean Adams found "emergency housing... for 55 students in September" and rearranged "dining facilities at Cooper Hall to accommodate 1,400 students."[37] The growth of the student body also influenced college administration staffing. The Department of Student Life had to add a new counselor in residence to its permanent staff to meet the needs of the large number of incoming students. Faculty plans for the academic counseling of first- and second-year students were also negatively affected. The norm of close faculty involvement in student advising was becoming difficult to preserve as teaching responsibilities increased with the growing number of students.[38]

The building program begun during the Bunting administration was completed and several new projects were undertaken in response to unprecedented enrollments. President Mason Gross lobbied the legislature to pass a series of bond issues to expand all Rutgers's campuses. The university received twenty-nine million dollars for capital expenditure, and Douglass was targeted as a priority. Between 1959 and 1963, four residence halls were completed beyond Wood Lawn, bordering the College of Agriculture. Woodbury, Nicholas, Lippincott, and Katzenbach dormitories were each designed for 250 students. A new Neilson dining hall opened to serve the "Neilson Campus," which significantly increased the housing available in Corwin, Gibbons, and Jameson. The first students housed in Woodbury were overwhelmed by the "modern luxuries" compared with Corwin or Gibbons.[39]

The Student Center, later renamed the College Center, which had been constructed in 1953, was given a massive addition that nearly doubled the size of the facility. The addition, which opened in 1966, provided space for the roughly six-hundred "bees," who had been crowded into the forty-year old beehive, which itself had been shrinking as the chemistry and bacteriology departments expanded in the science building. The college center addition provided vital food services, including separate dining rooms for commuting students and for faculty. Corwin campus was modernized, and Gibbons was rebuilt to preserve the small student living communities, which had been a hallmark of the college.

On the academic side, a new library had long been a priority for Douglass. A one-million-dollar appropriation passed by the legislature in 1958 included funds for the "library study center" and the biology building. With an additional seventy-five thousand dollars contributed by the Associate Alumnae's Committee for Higher Education, the New Jersey State Federation of Women's Clubs, and student groups, the Mabel Smith Douglass Library finally became a reality in 1961.[40] Nicknamed "the Teahouse of the August Moon" by students for its Asian-looking sloped roof, the building was designed by Eleanor Larrabee, a specialist in library design with the firm Warner, Burns, Toan & Lunde, Architects, and received favorable recognition in architecture circles. Adjacent to the Voorhees Chapel, the new library became a focal point of the campus.[41]

▲ STUDENTS OUTSIDE JAMESON

The home economics and psychology departments benefited from new classroom buildings constructed under the bond issue of 1959, which also supported the first stage of construction on a new gymnasium named in honor of Leonor F. Loree, one of the early benefactors of the college. The home economics department had long outgrown its limited space in the science building. Its equipment was outdated and inferior compared to those in high schools in the state.[42] The psychology department had offices with other social science faculty in Carpender Hall, a multifunctional building that served as a residence and provided faculty offices and laboratories for animal experiments in the basement. The psychologists were pleased to relocate to a new building with modern facilities in 1963, even though they had to share it with the home economics department. In 1966, the new science building was renamed in memory of Margaret Brouwer Davison, a former resident of Englewood, New Jersey, and a benefactor of the college.

The new Loree Gymnasium expanded the teaching and performance capabilities of the dance and physical education department. The last of the academic buildings completed at this period was the classroom and office building for the liberal arts, Emily Gregory Hickman Hall, which opened in the fall of 1964. Occupying the site of the former riding ring used by the "Crop and Spur" student equestrian club, the six-story building became the new focus of the campus. It was the first building named after a faculty member.[43] Its thirty-two classrooms and two lecture halls, seating three hundred and five hundred students, respectively, accommodated courses with large numbers of students, and the upper floors provided modern offices for seventy faculty members. The faculty of English, History, Political Science, and Philosophy moved from Carpender Hall to Hickman, which sported modern amenities, such as elevators, and a sweeping vista of its surrounding areas. The new structure was superior in convenience and equipment, but the new Hickman Hall, with departments on different floors of the building, did not allow for casual encounters and exchanges among faculty to take place as easily as they had in Carpender Hall. As a consequence, contacts among colleagues from different departments diminished. Campus growth also affected the city's skyline, as high rise buildings, such as Hickman Hall, blocked the view of the river and the Watchung Hills beyond, previously enjoyed from Wood Lawn and other buildings at the edge of the campus.

Curricular and Co-curricular Innovations

In the 1960s, Douglass College revised its general curriculum. Although it preserved the principle of a general education core to provide a broad grounding in the arts and sciences followed by a major concentration, it introduced a wider range of course options and delayed decisions concerning the choice of the major.[44] The graduation requirements were left intact, but the individual departments changed the content of many required courses. The faculty also turned down a motion to substitute comprehensive departmental final examinations for the existing practices of examinations within specific courses.

The growth of the student body had implications for class sizes and teaching methods. Some classes became larger, and in some cases, multiple sections of the same course were necessary to meet demand. In 1964, the college enrolled a total of 2,604 students. Among the 925 first-year students, twenty-seven were part-time students and eighteen were nonmatriculated students. The academic interests of this cohort of Douglass women differed from the concerns of their predecessors. In 1926, for example, 26 of 93 graduates received the bachelor of science degree; by contrast, only 33 of 506 graduates earned a bachelor of science in 1965. The overwhelming majority of Douglass women pursued bachelor of arts degrees. Among the thirty-one majors offered by the college, the most popular were English (185 students), sociology (102 students), and history (93 students). In 1965, 145 full-time and 95 part-time faculty taught courses at Douglass.[45] Through the sustained negotiations of Dean Adams, an increasing number of Douglass faculty enjoyed the challenges of graduate teaching at Rutgers. In one semester, for example, the faculty taught sixty-four undergraduate courses and thirty-two graduate courses and supervised twenty-six master's theses and PhD dissertations. With heavy teaching loads, many faculty found it difficult to find time and energy for college service and for undergraduate academic advising. The once unquestionable dedication to undergraduate teaching and college service was slowly disappearing.[46]

Dean Adams was particularly interested in increasing academic opportunities and intellectual challenges for gifted students. She reinvigorated the honors program and remodeled the former physics building, across from Douglass Library, into an Honors House, a retreat for honors candidates from all departments for undisturbed study and exchange of ideas. The proximity to the library was particularly helpful for honors students, as were the special borrowing privileges that Dean Adams arranged, which extended the checkout period to the entire semester.[47] Building on the initiatives of her predecessor, Dean Adams strongly encouraged students to aim for graduate school and helped them to secure fellowships and scholarships to finance their advanced studies. During Adams's years Douglass women won major national fellowships, including the Woodrow Wilson Fellowship, the Atomic Energy Commission Fellowship, and two National Science Foundation Cooperative Fellowships. Another Douglass graduate was accepted into the Royal Academy for the Dramatic Arts in the United Kingdom.

From the early years, the Douglass curriculum included professional and practical training courses to address the needs of women who expected to provide "their own livelihood" and perform roles in the world of work. In addition to liberal arts courses, majors in home economics, physical education, and library science prepared students for careers that met the needs of the growing ranks of new schools, public libraries, and community health centers. The Departments of Biological Sciences, Chemistry, and Home Economics developed courses for students to enter business and industrial positions, areas of great potential in the late 1950s and 1960s. The music department offered music education in addition to performance. In art, traditional art history and appreciation was supplemented by credit-bearing courses taught by practitioners. "Practical art" and "studio art" courses prepared students to teach or to enter the field of industrial art. The idea that women's colleges could teach practical skills beyond traditional academic subjects was controversial, however. Reginald Neal, chair of the art department in the sixties, described the Douglass model as one in which artists taught college-level courses at a time when this was not the generally accepted norm. Indeed, the Douglass curriculum was a hybrid with elements taken from traditional liberal arts colleges combined with practical training.[48] Ironically, this innovation was possible only at a women's college where academic expectations were lower and the stakes were not deemed high enough to enforce the strictures of orthodoxy.

In the late fifties and early sixties, the art department at Douglass flourished, with its innovative pedagogy, which employed stellar artists as teaching faculty, allowing Rutgers to become one of the most experimental art programs in the nation. Unlike its counterpart at Rutgers College, Douglass art history was more expansive, with course offerings in "modern, Asian, Pre-Columbian, and Oceanic art," in addition to traditional European art.[49] Studio art had a full complement of studio courses in drawing, painting, sculpture, graphics, and ceramics and its faculty included major artists, who left lasting legacies in the modern art scene. The new art pedagogical practices at Douglass were an extension of similar vanguard movements in New York City. From 1957 to 1963, John Goodyear, Geoffrey Hendricks, Roy Lichtenstein, and Robert Watts at Douglass worked closely with Allan Kaprow and George Segal, their colleagues at Rutgers College. Their group also included Lucas Samaras and Robert Whitman, who were Rutgers students at the time. Following the Black Mountain College pedagogy, the artists explored interdisciplinary approaches and connections between performance and art objects, giving prominence to radical approaches to materials, art-making processes, and their connections to everyday life.[50] Kaprow, Lichtenstein, and Segal were collaborators on the "happenings" and installation art performed on Douglass campus. Their contributions to major artistic developments such as pop art and Fluxus expanded the dimensions of art into new frontiers. Hendricks, Watts, and Kaprow initiated an innovative master of fine arts program at Rutgers in the early 1960s, and by 1966, forty graduate students were enrolled. Letty Lou Eisenhauer (DC '57) experienced firsthand avant-garde art in all mediums, learning from artists whose experimental approaches opened a full range of new possibilities. Eisenhauer studied with Robert Watts and Geoffrey Hendricks and frequently appeared in Kaprow's happenings, including *Spring Happening*.[51] This rich art scene set the foundation for the launch of the Mary H. Dana Women Artists Series in 1971, which included women artists from the visual arts faculty at Douglass College, who sought to protest the invisibility of women artists in the art world.[52]

In 1962, Dean Adams broke new ground, organizing an interdisciplinary course for a coeducational audience. She recruited Henry Winkler, chair of Rutgers's history department, to co-teach Society and Literature in Nineteenth Century England. The course brought together Adams's specialization in nineteenth-century English fiction and social history and Winkler's expertise in nineteenth- and twentieth-century Britain, British diplomatic history, and modern European diplomatic history. Twenty-four Rutgers men and nine Douglass students took the course, reading novels by Dickens, Disraeli, and Thackeray to expand traditional approaches to the study of nineteenth-century England.[53] Dean Adams also transformed the nature of mandatory chapel. By 1967, the Department of Religion, under Chair Cyrus R. Pangborn, devoted chapel sessions to a course that examined the history and philosophy of Western religion and its relation to science and culture. The course fulfilled liberal education requirements for the core curriculum. Under the leadership of Professor Pangborn, a Voorhees Assembly Board of students and faculty chose an annual theme for "chapel" and built a program around it. These programs dealt with contemporary trends in theology, comparative religion, personal ethics, and contemporary social issues. Over the years, the chapel programs changed from religious services to general assemblies that featured experts on various topics, ranging from civil rights, race relations, and sexuality to politics. Befitting a secular academic community, the chapel program became a forum for critical examination and debate.

With funding from the Economic Opportunity Act and the Higher Education Act of 1965, Dean Adams introduced a new student diversity initiative at Douglass College. Twenty young African American women participated in the Pilot Education Opportunity Program. Recommended by their high school guidance counselors and principals, the students attended a special orientation program during the summer prior to matriculation as first-year students. To facilitate their academic success, students took a reduced course load of four classes, instead of five each semester, planning to obtain their degrees in five years rather than four. The students met their financial needs through federal and state grants and part-time work—up to ten hours a week during the academic year—and full-time summer jobs. A faculty adviser was assigned to mentor the students and supervise their educational, social, and work activities. The students were free to pursue any academic major within the allotted five-year period.[54] Many of the participating students were commuters, who lived with their families because they could not afford campus housing.

With changing times, rising enrollments, and a focus on employment and careers, the home economics department also introduced sweeping changes in course offerings. Courses to "strengthen the family life," such as the Bride's Course, were eliminated and courses in food preparation, nutrition, management, housing, clothing, child development, and family relationships were expanded and opened to liberal art majors, as well as home economics students. The major included three areas of study: teaching, nutrition, and clothing, which expanded to include consumer services and child and family services in the 1960s. Graduates found a range of professional career paths, including teaching positions in high schools, professions as nutritionists and dieticians, and work in fashion and costume design or merchandising. Faculty members such as Edna Sostman (NJC '43) and Beverly Mithen Savidge (NJC '38) taught undergraduate and graduate courses in the master of science program in home economics in New Brunswick and Newark, expanding the Douglass home economics legacy.

Home economics majors were required to complete an eight-week residential internship in the Practice House (renamed Home Management House in the early 1960s), located on the Corwin campus. Designed to perfect the homemaking skills learned in classrooms, Practice House activities included child care, preparing and hosting student teas, organizing an end-of-year dinner party for the seniors, and entertaining friends who didn't live in the house on a regular basis. Students also prepared food for events such as the International Weekend.[55] In 1950s, Home Management House added an innovation: "use of a baby, the son of a senior student, which gave students experience in caring for a very young child."[56] To heighten their expertise, students also had to complete two summer projects, each lasting six weeks. One was a homemaking project and the other was a commercial project. During World War II many of the summer projects had involved jobs at Red Cross centers, canteens, hospitals, and others locations related to the war effort. Home economics students also worked in the cafeteria in the basement of the science building, next to the beehive. The students created the menu, ordered food supplies, and prepared the food served in their cafeteria for the college community. Food service was both a form of professional development for the students and a source of income for the department. Invested in their reputations, the student chefs at the cafeteria produced the best food on campus. Students specializing in fashion design also sold items to the local community as a fund-raiser for the department.[57]

As in other women's colleges, participation in sports was an integral part of the Douglass educational mission. Physical education courses were mandatory and through the Athletics Association established in 1920, the college encouraged students to participate in different sports on Antilles Field and in other facilities. The 1951 *Quair* includes "hockey, basketball, softball, tennis, swimming and archery" as available options, along with Nereids, a "ballet swimming group." Douglass was a member of the state's Athletic Federation of College Women, which brought students opportunities to meet and connect with other students in New Jersey colleges. In 1952, Douglass expanded the physical education department to include dance. Six years later, Marjorie Myers Howes was hired in the department and started to coach basketball, inaugurating an era of college athletics. The basketball team competed against other women's teams in the area.[58]

Renamed in 1974 the Department of Health, Physical Education and Dance, the department played an historic role in Title IX compliance. Faculty members Nancy Mitchell and Janet Koontz served as chair and interim chair, respectively, of the Committee for Rutgers New Brunswick Campus Women's Intercollegiate Program, charged with the implementation of Title IX at the university. Their work documenting systematic discrimination against women in sports at the university led to the hiring of Rita Kay Thomas in 1974 as the first Rutgers director of women's athletics and assistant athletics director. In an interview conducted by Marissa Rodriguez, (DRC '11) in 2008, Thomas expressed her appreciation to the Douglass faculty and their athletics network for the invaluable support she received in her early years at Rutgers. Thomas credited Mitchell and Koontz with helping her launch the women's athletics program at Rutgers.[59]

The Department of Speech and Dramatic Art also flourished in the 1960s, conducting public performances of various plays at the "Little Theater," sometimes in collaboration with the music and art departments. Yet the department also expanded its course offerings in innovative directions with the advent of new technologies. It pioneered courses in radio and television broadcasting, as well as in speech therapy under the direction of department chair Dorothy Taylor Durand (NJC '40). Through extensive grant writing, Durand also ran a successful Speech and Hearing Center, where student majors gained clinical experience working with children and adults both on campus and at various community locations. Speech and therapy students provided remedial treatment to over one hundred children and young people in the community.[60]

In the late 1960s, the language houses on Corwin Campus included the Russian, German, French, Italian, and Spanish Houses, which fell under the administration of the Department of Romance Languages. All language majors were required to live for at least one year in their corresponding language house. Forerunners of "living-learning communities," the language houses had an academic component, while also contributing to campus awareness of the rich cultures associated with speakers of these various languages. Each house had a live-in house counselor, a graduate student or a staff member, who was a native speaker and who coordinated language learning and cultural events. Each house also had a house chair, a junior or a senior selected by the dean of students for her leadership accomplishments, who assisted the house director in organizing different events and initiatives.

With the exception of the physics department, which closed in 1959, the science departments flourished at Douglass. The bacteriology department, under the leadership of Hazel B. Gillespie, produced well-trained technical bacteriologists, many of whom continued on to graduate programs. In 1959, the Department of Biological Sciences, which included the fields of botany and zoology, was established under the leadership of Professor Jessie Gladys Fiske.[61] The faculty in biological sciences were the most successful grant writers on campus. For example, Charlotte Jo Avers, a prominent expert in the field of molecular cell biology in the department, initiated a project with colleagues at Rutgers College, on a grant from the National Science Foundation to support a course in biology offered via closed circuit television, a major innovation in pedagogy during this era.[62]

In the 1950s, the demands from local industries encouraged college administrators to increase course offerings in the areas of science, technology, and mathematics. As expressed by Ira Garard, chair of the chemistry department, "industries in New Jersey require a large number of chemists and women are more welcome than they were several years ago."[63] In 1959, Douglass received a Ford Foundation grant for the Mathematics Study Project at Douglass College. Led by Helen Marston, chair of the mathematics department, the project investigated professional opportunities for college-educated women, who wished to retrain themselves for jobs requiring knowledge in modern mathematics. With a follow-up grant from the Ford Foundation in 1961, Marston developed special mathematics courses taught in New Brunswick and Newark, to prepare women for job reentry opportunities, anticipating by a decade the development of "displaced homemaker programs" funded by the federal government in the 1970s. The mathematics department remained one of the larger departments at Douglass in the early sixties, attracting a considerable number of majors who obtained good professional positions after graduation.[64]

The English department continued to have the most majors and offered courses in literature, criticism, and creative writing. In 1962, Margaret F. Boyd succeeded Donald C. Dorian as chair. In addition to leading her department, Boyd offered a twelve-week television lecture series on the modern novel. Other faculty included Doris Falk, who taught Shakespeare and wrote a book about Lillian Hellman. Nelle Kroger Smither, who authored *A History of the English Theatre at New Orleans, 1806–1842*, taught modern drama. Anna Mary Wells, author of mystery books, taught creative writing. Elaine Showalter taught The Educated Women in Literature, the first feminist studies course at Douglass, while she was an instructor. She received a tenure-track appointment in 1970 and played a key role in launching the Douglass women's studies program in 1971. In the 1970s, the department recruited outstanding feminist scholars and writers, including Cheryl Wall, Carol Smith, Adrienne Rich, and Catharine Stimpson, who made profound contributions to the creation of the interdisciplinary field of women's studies.[65] (See Chapter 8).

As the unrest of the 1960s escalated on Rutgers campuses, they prompted the Douglass administration to consider the communal responsibility of educational institutions. The "Community Service" section was introduced in annual reports with a series of outreach efforts and activities undertaken by faculty and students. Students majoring in Spanish, for example, tutored Puerto Rican and Cuban children and adults who lacked English language proficiency, helping them to navigate the challenges of life in the United States. The physical education department offered swimming lessons in campus facilities to 147 children living in New Brunswick. The home economics department taught nutrition to local schoolchildren and assisted the nutrition programs of the local schools. Some of these interventions were strictly academic, such as those of the philosophy department, whose faculty worked throughout the state to interest secondary schools in introducing philosophy to their curriculum. Programs such as Upward Bound, a pre-college program designed to help disadvantaged students, were welcomed on campus, as were local children, who played on campus grounds. Activities bridging the college with the surrounding community were encouraged and considered central to the mission of Douglass and the university.[66]

Intercollege Cross-Registration and Its Impact

Since the mid-forties, Douglass and Rutgers students had enjoyed opportunities to participate in all-university coeducational student organizations. These student groups included university choir, the NAACP, religious groups of different denominations, and the WRSU student radio station. These groups grew in number and variety in the following decades. Intercollege cross-registration for courses increased the opportunity for Douglass and Rutgers students to be in close contact with one another in a classroom setting.

For Douglass students, intercollege course registration was permitted on an individual basis for courses or majors not offered at the college. In the sixties, male enrollment in Douglass courses increased, altering the teaching experience for Douglass faculty and the campus environment. In the classics department, for example, the only one in New Brunswick, 112 Rutgers students registered for classes. By the fall of 1962, the number of non-Douglass students taking Douglass classes totaled 479, more students than the entire Douglass senior class. Men's enrollment at Douglass continued to increase for the next few years.[67] Despite its identity as a women's college, in practice the classrooms manifested increased gender integration. Intercollege registration became much easier with the introduction of a new coordinated class schedule and in the early sixties the inauguration of the campus bus system, which facilitated cross-campus commuting.[68]

In 1966, 825 students from other colleges enrolled in courses at Douglass, while 564 Douglass students took one or more courses "across town." Sixty-two women studied at the School of Journalism, 51 took Hebrew courses, and 116 took physics at the Rutgers College of Arts and Sciences. Conversely, 201 Rutgers students enrolled in Greek and Latin courses, 174 in courses in religion and dramatic arts—subjects offered only at Douglass. Modern languages, which were offered on both campuses, had scarcely any cross-registration, particularly because the Douglass practice of conducting every upper-level class entirely in the foreign language discouraged students in other units from registering.

Both Mary Bunting and Ruth Adams left extraordinary legacies at Douglass College. They elevated the academic standing of Douglass students and established the college as an institution known for successfully preparing women for the job market and for graduate education. Bunting shepherded Douglass through major transformations at Rutgers, as it changed from a small liberal arts college into an integrated unit of the State University of New Jersey. With the growth of the alumnae population and their deep allegiance to their alma mater, Bunting forged strong ties with the Associate Alumnae of Douglass College, which led to the creation of an unrestricted fund for the dean that supported new academic programs and scholarships for students. The alumnae involvement in these efforts enhanced cross-generational interaction between NJC and Douglass women and afforded new opportunities for the students. For example, the *Douglass Alumnae Bulletin* added a student editor to facilitate flows of information critical to the establishment of a powerful intergenerational community of Douglass women. These efforts continued during Adams's leadership, which witnessed continued growth of the student population as well as campus expansion with the construction of new buildings. Dean Adams's major accomplishments included the reinvigoration of the honors program for academically talented students and the introduction of the Pilot Education Opportunity Program for minority students, a first crucial step toward expanding diversity on campus. The program included summer capacity-building programs to heighten academic success. Both deans encouraged faculty to create new interdisciplinary courses and new programs expanding the boundaries of traditional disciplines and encouraged students to engage with communities beyond the university. Their passion and commitment shaped Douglass as an innovative women's college, known for academic excellence and social engagement and well prepared for a new era of growth.

PRESERVING DOUGLASS'S SPECIAL MISSION

LIKE THE UNIVERSITY, THE COLLEGE
IS SUFFERING FROM GROWING PAINS,
SOME OF WHICH WILL PASS IN A DAY,
WHILE OTHERS REMAIN CHRONIC.

—Ruth M. Adams, Douglass College,
Annual Report, 1964–1965

For the two decades that spanned the presidencies of Mason Gross (1959–1971) and Edward J. Bloustein (1971–1989), the recurring themes at Rutgers were "expansion" and "reorganization." The number of students nearly tripled, from 7,100 to 21,000 undergraduates and from 1,800 to 4,800 graduate students, and thanks to funds from four state bond issues, federal support, and borrowing, the physical campus expanded to accommodate them.[1] The New Brunswick campus expanded across the Raritan River, absorbing 540 acres of the Camp Kilmer army base in Piscataway, which had been declared "surplus" by the U.S. Department of Defense in 1962.[2] The university administration grappled with the evolving educational needs of the rising numbers of students, the increased demands for efficiency in use of university resources, and growing pressure for coeducation. As faculty, administrators, students, alumni and alumnae engaged in "the Great Debate" over proposed models for university reorganization, successive deans of Douglass sought creative ways to preserve Douglass's "special mission" as a women's college.[3]

The New Jersey County Act of 1962 authorized the creation of nineteen county colleges throughout the state, providing broader access to education for high school graduates but also increasing competition for state funds for higher education. At the same time, student activism encompassing civil rights, women's liberation, and antiwar protests engulfed college campuses across the nation. The tragic assassinations of President John F. Kennedy, Medgar Evers, Malcolm X, Martin Luther King Jr., and Robert Kennedy profoundly affected student activism, including that at Rutgers. Framed by these dramatic events, the administrations of Ruth Adams (1960–1966), Margery Somers Foster (1967–1975), and Jewell Plummer Cobb (1976–1981) were marked by

117

intensive debates about the future structure of the university, the role of Douglass within it, and the importance of women's education in a rapidly changing world.

Ruth Marie Adams: From the Cluster College Concept to the Federated College Plan

In her inaugural essay in the *Douglass Alumnae Bulletin*, Dean Adams defined the role of the college as cultivating three interrelated capacities: "first, the accumulation of knowledge; second, the exercise of judgment; and third, the display of integrity.[4] The kind of college best able to foster these abilities in women became a subject of increasing controversy in the 1960s. Adams was keenly aware of the complex challenges facing Douglass as a women's college and in relation to its status within the university. She also understood that the Douglass community held divergent sentiments toward proposed changes. In the 1964–1965 Douglass College *Annual Report*, she aptly noted:

> Like the university, the College is suffering from growing pains, some of which will pass in a day, while others remain chronic. The faculty, students and staff, with a healthy lack of unanimity, think a lot about the "autonomy" of the College, the effect upon it of the new New Brunswick college, the demands and seductions of research and graduate teaching, the numbers of students to be accommodated, the quality and intimacy of the education offered them—all elements in the concerns of a growing university.[5]

During this time of extraordinary transformation at the university, Dean Adams placed the preservation of the women's college at the center of her planning for the future with support from faculty and staff who distinguished themselves by their dedication and commitment. Yet she faced significant challenges as debates about reorganization continued.

Unprecedented growth in student enrollments, the development of dispersed campuses, and the addition of the Camp Kilmer campus motivated President Mason Gross and Provost Richard Schlatter to consider systematic reorganization to address the needs of the university. Their initial proposal for reorganization introduced a distinction between a "college[,] . . . as an organization of students" with a focus on residence halls and student life, and "instruction," a realm governed by faculty within scholarly disciplines, involving the curriculum and general academic structure.[6] They recommended the creation of ten new coeducational residential colleges on the Kilmer Campus, each to accommodate fifteen hundred students, which would include dormitories, dining facilities, and classroom space, along with a core of central facilities. The colleges would not, however, have independent faculties. Instead, "the cluster college concept" endorsed the consolidation of faculty into discipline-based departments, which "would be responsible for teaching in Douglass, Rutgers, and Raritan (Kilmer) Colleges."[7] Each college would develop its own mission in terms of curriculum and student body. The president and the provost considered this option the best means to combine the advantages of a large university structure with the supportive features of relatively small college units. The Rutgers dean of arts and sciences supported this proposal, assuming that his unit would control instructional staff, curriculum, and standards for the new colleges. Ruth Adams objected on multiple grounds. She argued that a new coeducational school should have its own identity, faculty, department chairs and academic dean and she challenged the "imperialism" of the men's college as a threat to Douglass's autonomy.[8] Adams and the Douglass faculty mobilized serious opposition by faculty in all academic units and the scheme was abandoned.[9]

In 1962, President Gross appointed an Advisory Committee to plan for the new Kilmer campus. The committee included three faculty from Rutgers College and three from Douglass, and the deans of both units, coordinated by special assistant to the president Maurice Ayers. Participants from Douglass and Rutgers disagreed, however, about the educational programs to be offered at Kilmer. Rutgers College proposed the creation of a two-year coeducational junior college experience, named Queens College, after which students would enter either Douglass or Rutgers. Dean Adams and the Douglass representatives objected to the proposal, which they believed would vastly increase the power of Rutgers arts and sciences, and argued forcefully to preserve the integrity of Douglass as a four-year women's liberal arts experience. Douglass representatives also took issue with the president's proposal to increase student enrollment to 21,000 students by 1980, concerned that the quality of education would deteriorate with such a huge increase in students without a comparable increase in the number of faculty. Instead, Douglass proposed to limit enrollment growth to 14,000 students—6,000 women at Douglass and 8,000 men at Rutgers College of Arts and Sciences. Unable to bridge the fundamental differences between Rutgers and Douglass, Provost Schlatter suspended the planning process.[10]

Ruth Adams and the Douglass faculty perceived multiple dangers in the proposed reorganization plans. They worried that increasing centralization would erode the autonomy of the college, that a two-year college at Kilmer would undermine their integrity as a four-year liberal arts college, and that proposals for an independent four-year coeducational college at Kilmer might divert talented women students from Douglass. Following sustained debate, the faculty decided that a four-year independent, coeducational Kilmer College was the best of the available options. In May 1964, the Douglass faculty sent a petition signed by ninety-one faculty members to Provost Schlatter:

> We ... wish to be recorded as feeling strongly that the proposed new college on the Kilmer site should be set up with its own faculty, department chairmen, and an academic dean responsible to the provost. In other words, inasmuch as a decision has been made to move toward the creation of a coed school on a Kilmer site, we feel that every effort should be made to make it an identifiable entity, one that has the personnel resources of a full-fledged educational institution.[11]

Despite these dissenting voices, planning for the new campus continued within the Office of the President with the assistance of Provost Schlatter. The men's colleges were actively consulted in this process, but Douglass was excluded. In fall 1964, the president convened a critical meeting with the provost, the Rutgers College of Arts and Sciences Planning Committee, Rutgers College Associate Dean G. R. Bishop, and Ernest Lynton of the Rutgers College physics department. No one from Douglass was invited to attend or informed of this meeting. On the basis of these discussions, President Gross issued a confidential memorandum of understanding on October 28, 1964, which proposed that the "best solution for the expanding University in New Brunswick would be the emergence of single departments with single budgets in each discipline. These departments would be responsible for instruction in Douglass, Rutgers, and Raritan (Kilmer) Colleges."[12] The memorandum of understanding reflected a recent proposal made by the Rutgers College dean of arts and sciences, a proposal that was markedly similar to the cluster college concept, which had been vehemently opposed by Ruth Adams and the Douglass faculty. According to Richard P. McCormick, "No Douglass representatives participated in the meeting and there is no indication that the 'Memorandum' was shared with Douglass personnel."[13]

In March 1965, President Gross appointed Ernest Lynton inaugural dean for the Kilmer campus and gave him considerable freedom in shaping the new system.[14] Although Lynton had been central to the secret planning process, he quickly moved to create one coeducational college with its own faculty, equal to other undergraduate colleges, rather than a cluster of residential colleges whose instruction was provided by faculty in Rutgers College of Arts and Sciences.[15] Indeed, Lynton envisioned an innovative college designed to investigate and resolve pressing social, economic, and political problems—"an MIT of the social sciences."[16] With considerable funding from the Carnegie Foundation, Lynton began designing the new college, named to honor James Henry Livingston, who served as president of Rutgers precursor Queens College from 1810 to 1825.

As the plan for Livingston College moved forward and the future of Douglass remained uncertain, Dean Ruth Adams resigned in 1966 to become the president of Wellesley College.[17] Her era at Douglass was marked by the addition of new programs for gifted students and the new student diversity initiative; but perhaps most important, Ruth Adams foiled the cluster college concept throughout her tenure. She rallied faculty across all New Brunswick units to oppose the president's plan. Her insistence on preserving the integrity of the undergraduate colleges shifted the terms of debate. Rather than centralizing, the university adopted the Federated College Plan in 1965, which called for five independent colleges, each with a separate budget, a separate dean and faculty, and a separate campus. In developing the plan, Douglass became "the model for all the undergraduate colleges. . . . Each college was to have not only its own faculty but its own student life, student services apparatus and its own turf as well. In the process of devising a plan to coordinate a group of liberal arts faculties and strengthen the basic disciplines, the University ended up in 1967 with a number of relatively autonomous residential, multipurpose colleges."[18]

Margaret A. Judson, who had just retired after thirty-eight years of service to the college, was appointed acting dean and served in this capacity for one year as the dean search progressed. Judson was a renowned British historian who specialized in constitutional history. She was the first member of the Douglass history department to be allowed to teach a graduate course. Judson had also served as a member of the Graduate School Executive Committee. Although she was charged with representing Douglass in the planning process for the Federated College Plan, she discovered that many of the decisions were determined by a coalition of the dean of Rutgers College of Arts and Sciences and the dean of the Graduate School. Judson recognized the benefits of the proposed reorganization both in strengthening the Graduate School and building on the strengths of the distinctive liberal arts undergraduate colleges. Indeed, Judson

▶ MARGARET
ATWOOD JUDSON,
ACTING DEAN OF
DOUGLASS, 1966–1967

favored the concept, but she found that the deliberative process gave Douglass short shrift and warned that other university units drowned out the Douglass faculty's views. She noted in her 1966–1967 *Annual Report*: "I regret very much that a vote was taken by both Arts and Sciences and the Graduate Faculty. If now or in the future substantial changes in the Plan are made, the Douglass faculty wish to be consulted and allowed also to vote upon it."[19] Judson inherited the fruits of Ruth Adams's success in stymieing the president's cluster college plan. Just as Douglass administrators and faculty had been excluded from the president's planning process beginning in 1964, subsequent Douglass deans experienced bouts of exclusion from major university decision making.

Margery Somers Foster: The Struggle to Preserve Autonomy

In 1967, Margery Somers Foster arrived on campus as the fifth dean of Douglass College. As legend has it, she arrived in New Brunswick in a Mustang convertible with a speeding ticket for going eighty-five miles an hour on the New Jersey Turnpike.[20] An economist with a PhD from Radcliffe, Foster's scholarly research focused on public finance and the economic history of colonial America.[21] She had taught economics at Harvard and Mount Holyoke and served as dean of Hollins College in Roanoke, Virginia, before her appointment at Douglass. During World War II, Foster served in the WAVES (Women Accepted for Volunteer Emergency Service) in the U.S. Naval Reserve, rising to the rank of lieutenant. She was "not a compromiser on principle," and she was deeply committed to the preservation of Douglass as a women's college.[22]

For Dean Foster, the Federated College Plan represented both "an opportunity and a problem." She was aware of the pressures to increase student enrollments at the state university, but she was hopeful that university support for the plan would enable her to protect Douglass as a leader in public higher education for women. Within the college, she began revamping the curriculum and restructuring some departments—a move necessitated by continuing debates over distribution of faculty efforts between graduate and undergraduate teaching. Foster sought to secure Douglass faculty's contributions to the Graduate School, yet she was concerned about the repercussions of heightened research expectations both on undergraduate teaching and on faculty promotion and personnel actions.[23]

In 1968, the university finalized the Federated College Plan. Douglass and Rutgers were to remain single-sex residential colleges. The new coeducational Livingston College would open on the Kilmer campus in 1969. Although the men's college was to be the largest of these undergraduate units, rough parity was envisioned between the undergraduate colleges. This situation changed dramatically when President Gross appointed a committee to investigate the viability of another undergraduate college of about "3,500 students . . . with a special concern with environmental and applied science." Initially this new unit was proposed to be a second coeducational institution located on the Kilmer campus. Ralph A. Dungan, chancellor of the New Jersey Department of Higher Education, strongly advocated "a new co-educational multi-purpose undergraduate college composed of a community of faculty and students whose main educational objective would be the study of man and the opportunities of man's natural environment."[24] Dungan also insisted that the new college should be named to honor George H. Cook, the first layperson appointed to the faculty of Rutgers College, who played key roles in founding the land grant college and agricultural field station. Faculty in the College of Agriculture and Environmental Sciences (CAES) saw potential links between their research and the work of the proposed college and demanded that the new school should be located in proximity to the Agricultural Experimental Station facilities adjacent to Douglass.[25] Chancellor Dungan intensified his lobbying to locate the proposed Cook College on what he considered "idle space on Douglass Campus."[26]

▲ MARGERY SOMERS FOSTER, DEAN OF DOUGLASS, 1967–1975;
PICTURED WITH STUDENTS CAROL WEAVER AND LOIS BRODSKY, 1968

Facing budgetary problems and campus opposition to the creation of another independent college, this plan was put on hold, only to be resurrected in early 1970.

To overcome opposition to the creation of Cook College, CAES proposed an "innovative partnership" to Dean Foster. In this scenario, Douglass would offer the liberal arts components required for the baccalaureate, as well as academic support, such as library services, to the students enrolled in the new college. Although CAES envisioned this a "no cost" opportunity for Douglass, Foster saw things very differently. She voiced her strong objection to reducing Douglass to a service unit mandated to offer general education courses to students in another college. Douglass would be expected to "provide space and service and personnel to establish another college without anywhere nearly a proportionate addition of resources."[27] Beyond the presumptuousness of expecting Douglass faculty to teach whatever courses the faculty of the new unit preferred not to offer, and the mismatch of increased teaching for Douglass faculty while all the new resources would be devoted to Cook, the CAES proposal made it clear that the unique mission of a women's college was thoroughly misunderstood by many at Rutgers. Refusing the division of labor that CAES faculty suggested, Dean Foster denounced the "obnoxious stance" that she was being "forced" to counter "so continuously."[28] The dean's adamant objections precluded the division of labor suggested by CAES, but it did not derail the decision to create the new college on the Douglass campus. Cook College, located adjacent to Douglass residence halls and classroom buildings, became fully operational in 1973. The home economics department, which had been the best-funded unit in the college during the early decades, was transferred to Cook College in recognition of the ties between agriculture schools and home economics in land grant colleges forged by the Morrill and Smith-Hughes Acts.[29]

In 1971, Edward J. Bloustein succeeded Mason Gross as president of Rutgers and quickly resuscitated the question of centralizing the university's administrative structure. In 1973, he appointed a Commission on Effective Resource Allocation, charged to improve efficiency and economy. Kenneth Wheeler, former dean of University College, was appointed the New Brunswick provost with responsibilities to oversee the academic and budgetary issues of the federated colleges. Provost Wheeler appointed a task force to develop a master plan for New Brunswick to support a planned increase in enrollment from sixteen thousand to twenty-three thousand students over the next decade. Both the commission and the task force criticized the federated colleges as a "patchwork quilt which was expensive to operate, encouraged destructive collegiate rivalry and served the students ill."[30] Both endorsed the creation of a Faculty of Arts and Sciences that would integrate the formerly autonomous faculties of the undergraduate colleges in New Brunswick into large discipline-based departments.[31] Acting on the recommendations of these committees, President Bloustein granted a four-year extension to the federated colleges, while moving toward centralization that would eliminate "wasteful duplication of course offerings," increase student access to courses and majors, strengthen graduate programs, and enhance the research reputation of the university.[32]

In an important move toward centralization in 1973, President Bloustein appointed a vice president for student services, who assumed responsibility for admissions, financial aid, registration, scheduling, and health services, taking away these functions from the undergraduate colleges. This aspect of reorganization had an especially severe impact on Douglass as the only college responsible for handling its own student services operations.[33] As the reins of reorganization were tightening, Foster continued to advocate for Douglass's autonomy. The dean argued that autonomy was essential if the school was to carry out its "special mission," the education of women. In an effort to persuade Rutgers's administrators of the virtues of the federated college plan, Foster compared the organization of the undergraduate colleges at Rutgers to the Cambridge/Oxford model.[34] Drawing insights from the British university system, she argued that there were critical differences between a university and a business, differences that mandated that academic relations be conducted in an "un-business like" way. Efficient corporate structures conflicted with academic freedom, a value essential to excellence in teaching and research. To foster academic freedom within an institution of higher education, dispersed decision making and faculty governance were key. Foster also drew upon her own research on centuries of successful administration at Harvard University to support her view, concluding that the federated college system at Rutgers did not require radical transformation, merely some refinement. According to the dean, the problems confronting the university were the product of poor internal communications; the solution did not require a new structure, but rather a modification of the Federated College Plan.

Dean Foster insisted that Douglass, as a one of the federated colleges, had unique "Goals and Operating Objectives": "The over-riding objective of Douglass College, is (a) fully to participate in the graduate, research, and service activities of Rutgers University while at the same time (b) providing rigorous academic training and career orientation for women who seek distinction in their choice fields of post-graduate and professional career endeavor, and (c) serving as an experimental center and role model for furthering the development of women's talents."[35]

Although she had the support of her faculty, it became increasingly clear to Dean Foster that her vision for Douglass and the president's plans for reorganization were on a collision course. The reorganization promised to improve the national research profile of faculty by tightening standards for scholarship across all disciplines and colleges. It also promised to heighten efficiency by centralizing various student services such as admissions, financial aid, registration, and scheduling under the office of the vice President for student services. Yet these promises had budgetary implications that troubled the dean and the Douglass faculty. As resources were devoted to research and central administration, fewer funds were available to cover teaching. As early as November 1968, Douglass faculty submitted a statement to the Board of Governors deploring the absence of funds for new hires at Douglass, raising concerns about ominous changes in the student/faculty ratio. The Douglass faculty had completed a two-year study of its educational structure, resulting in the first complete overhaul of the college's curriculum since 1918. The proposed new curriculum, which included a complete revision of every department's offerings, was to become effective in the fall of 1969.[36] But the ambitious new curriculum required additional teaching resources, which the university's proposed budget omitted. In the absence of additional resources, the college had to abandon its proposed curriculum reform.

In the midst of these difficulties related to reorganization, Dean Foster pushed forward new initiatives at the college. She saw an opportunity to broaden the student population by extending admission to "people of varied backgrounds." Foster believed that Douglass could "integrate and educate well a small proportion of disadvantaged students." She was interested in admitting students with the "greatest potential" and "turning out the ablest and best educated graduates." Dean Foster also stated her full support for the development of the women's studies program, to put a "great deal of effort and emphasis on the full development of our woman students."[37] After Lois W. Banner and Mary S. Hartman hosted the first Berkshire Conference of Women Historians at Douglass in 1973, attracting national attention and an unprecedented number of participants, Foster congratulated Banner and Hartman enthusiastically: "You are the ones that deserve thanks for bringing honor to your discipline, your sex and your college."[38]

Separating from Speech, the theater arts department was inaugurated in 1970 with Jack Bettenbender as chair. A well-known actor, director, and playwright, Bettenbender inspired many students while elevating the quality of campus performances. According to Susan Cower Schwirck (DC '71), the production of *Threepenny Opera* in spring 1971 attracted a large audience, including Dean Foster. Schwirck, a returning student, was cast as a "whore" in the play. Dean Foster could not hide her disbelief at learning that the four children in the audience were enjoying their mother playing a dubious character in the play.[39]

With its autonomy under threat, and its intellectual vision hampered by inadequate funding, Douglass also faced increasing pressure to abandon its commitment to women's education and become a coeducational college. In 1970, Rutgers College voted to admit women with the incoming class in 1972. This decision had devastating implications for Douglass in terms of admissions. At a time when interest in single-sex colleges was waning among high school seniors, the college would have to compete for women students not only against coeducational Livingston College, but also against Rutgers College. And worse still, Douglass was asked to consider admitting men (see chapter 7). Debates within the president's cabinet became increasingly heated as Dean Foster argued forcefully for the preservation of Douglass as a women's college. Acutely aware that the president did not share her vision, Margery Somers Foster resigned in 1975.[40] She was joined by Charles E. Hess, dean of the recently created Cook College. In their letters of resignation, both voiced their strong objections to the university's usurpation of the autonomy of the undergraduate colleges, distancing faculty from student life, and creating a gulf between "instruction" and the all-round intellectual development of undergraduates.[41] The tenured faculty of Douglass voted no confidence in President Bloustein and Provost Wheeler, charging they had "systematically eroded the role of the New Brunswick colleges of the University and their faculties."[42] Paula P. Brownlee, professor of chemistry and associate dean of the college, was appointed acting dean and served until the arrival of Dean Jewell Plummer Cobb in 1976.[43]

Jewel Plummer Cobb:
Advancing the Special Mission through Diplomacy

A noted cancer researcher, and dean and professor of zoology at Connecticut College, Jewel Plummer Cobb was appointed the sixth dean of Douglass in 1976. As the first African American to serve as dean of Douglass, Cobb had firsthand experience of the challenges that confront women and minorities who enter nontraditional fields. Cobb initially matriculated at the University of Michigan, where she encountered systemic racial and gender discrimination, and chose to transfer to Talladega College in Alabama, a historically black college, to complete her bachelor's in biology. She applied for a teaching fellowship at New York University but was rejected because of her race. Rather than accepting this decision, Cobb traveled to New York and petitioned that her dossier be judged on its merits, rather than on racial grounds. NYU relented and Cobb completed her master of science in cell physiology in 1947 and her PhD in 1950.[44] Prior to her appointment as dean of Douglass, Dr. Cobb had been a fellow of the National Cancer Institute; director of the Tissue Culture Laboratory at the University of Illinois; and a research scholar at NYU, Hunter College, and Sarah Lawrence College and, subsequently, dean of Connecticut College. Her research focused on skin cancer and in particular the ability of melanin to protect skin from damage. She also investigated how hormones, ultraviolet light, and chemotherapeutic drugs could cause changes in cell division.

Although Cobb was under no illusions about the challenges facing her as dean of Douglass, she believed that Douglass offered unique opportunities to advance women's education, in general, and minority women's education in particular. She devoted her considerable talents to envisioning means to promote Douglass College's "special mission" as a women's college within the Federated College Plan. She tried to convince "Old Queens," the Rutgers vernacular for the university administration building and the administrators who inhabited it, that a college was far more than an organization of students. She championed women's studies for its innovative pedagogy, which countered the marginalization that women experienced in many mainstream disciplines, and she emphasized the importance of having women faculty in all academic disciplines. "There is no doubt that a women's college, at least at this moment, is the only place where one can see in the classrooms a significant number of women role models as professors. And there is a freedom for students to develop themselves in the total lifestyle of a women's college that many young women at 17 and 18 might be reticent to maximize in a co-educational environment."[45]

▶ JEWEL PLUMMER COBB, DEAN OF DOUGLASS, 1976–1981

Drawing on her success as a woman scientist, Dean Cobb introduced several model programs to encourage women and minorities to enter the fields of science, mathematics, and engineering. She designed the Science Management Program, which placed Douglass students in research labs on campus supplemented with internships in corporations that specialized in engineering, science, and technology (see chapter 9). She offered courses on tissue culture and actively promoted a proposal for the merger of the Cell Research Center and the biological sciences and microbiology, urging her colleagues to employ women students in their research projects. She conducted a survey to estimate the prevalence of "math anxiety" among Douglass students, which revealed that the mature women students returning to college were particularly leery of math courses. To address this problem, she initiated a Mathematics Anxiety Seminar.[46]

As the percentage of eighteen- to twenty-one-year-olds attending colleges and universities began to climb in the 1970s, a growing national debate erupted about the caliber of students entering colleges and universities, a perceived lack of proficiency in basic skills, and the need to develop remedial education programs to enable students to succeed. Dean Cobb appointed a Task Force on Basic Skills to explore these issues and organized a national conference on the topic.[47] In addition to her deep commitment to affirmative action programs to increase the number of students of color at Douglass, Dean Cobb sought to devise initiatives that would ensure the students' academic success, thereby making Douglass a national leader in the promotion of educational equity. Keenly aware of the challenges that bilingual students experienced in university, for example, she worked with the Douglass teacher training program to develop innovative bilingual programs for education majors—the first of its kind in the United States.[48]

In her interactions with Old Queens, Dean Cobb saw herself first and foremost as an advocate for Douglass's special needs and as an ambassador for its special mission. Lacking the autonomy enjoyed by presidents of other women's colleges and by previous deans of Douglass, she sought to enlist the support of central administration for her priorities at Douglass.[49] She also tried to demonstrate to President Bloustein and Provost Wheeler that Douglass was a resource for the university. She organized forums for women faculty and graduate students, inviting participants from Camden and Newark, as well as all New Brunswick units. She sponsored sessions on potential careers for women and encouraged all women students at Rutgers to attend. She argued that through its own pioneering practices, "Rutgers could make a national contribution to academic women."[50] She emphasized the growing national prominence of women's studies scholars at Douglass and launched a fund-raising campaign to build the Modern Women Writers' Collection, a manuscript collection, at Douglass library. The proposal included a budget request for acquisition of the manuscripts and a line for "one librarian for women's studies." Dean Cobb asserted that "the collection would not only be appropriate but would enhance the College's and University's reputation and create a new research resource."[51] Dean Cobb also drew attention to the various ways that Douglass and women's studies served the university community, providing support services for students and the local community such as the Douglass Feminist Collective, the Sophia Returning Student Organization, Douglass Advisory Services for Women, the Women's Crisis Center, and the University Coalition of Lesbian Feminists. Indeed, she emphasized that the Women's Studies Institute and the Center for the American Woman and Politics served statewide and national audiences, making special outreach efforts to scholars and elected officials.

In addition to the commitment to women's studies, Dean Cobb's vision for Douglas included an "intensified commitment to affirmative action."[52] Harnessing the dedication of alumnae, specifically black alumnae who had grown in number over the years, she persuaded Associate Alumnae of Douglass College (AADC) executive director Adelaide Zagoren to establish the Black Alumnae Network (BAN) as an AADC initiative. Since its inauguration in 1981, the BAN has organized special reunions and events, including outreach to and mentoring for incoming students of color, fostering deep relationships among Douglass women.[53]

Early Impacts of University Reorganization on Douglass

As Dean Cobb launched her diplomatic initiatives, Douglass began to feel the early effects of reorganization. In 1976, the School of Creative and Performing Arts, later renamed the Mason Gross School of the Arts, was created as an academic unit. Douglass faculty in the Departments of Dance, Fine Arts, Music, and Theater Arts—departments that Douglass had carefully nurtured and that had gained national recognition for pedagogical and artistic innovation—were moved administratively to the new school. Feeling that their college had been raided, Douglass students and faculty became increasingly vociferous in their opposition to reorganization.

Some of the most vocal opposition came from students, who complained that the university was misdiagnosing "the problem," blaming the federated college system for flaws of the administration. In a 1980 *Caellian* editorial, the Douglass newspaper staff noted, "The powers that be . . . seem to think that the screw-ups that plague us are endogenous to the Federated System. Well, there is nothing inoculating the Wheeler plan from these old problems, which are endogenous to a large University."[54] Appealing to democratic principles, Michele M. Guarino (DC '80) suggested that "a majority of the students and a good portion of faculty members do not support the plan. The reason I'm bringing this up to you is because the administration seems to be ignoring this fact."[55] Although the Douglass undergrads acknowledged that the proposed reorganization might benefit graduate students, faculty, and administrators, they argued that undergraduates constituted the vast majority of the university community and their voices were not being heard.

Corroborating the views expressed in the *Caellian*, the Douglass College Government Association (DCGA) offered a defense of the federated college system, enumerating its many successes. They emphasized that the "majority of undergraduate students support the present system" and advocated revision of the federated system rather than a comprehensive reorganization of the university. Faulting the proposed reorganization for failing to "retain vital components of the federated system—the missions of the colleges and the differing interdisciplinary perspectives of the departments," the DCGA also added an efficiency argument to support their opposition, noting that the proposal to create a dean of the Faculty of Arts and Sciences "seems extravagant and unnecessary at this time."[56]

Both the DCGA and the *Caellian* writers perceived that "the unique character and academic excellence which has come to be known as a Douglass tradition . . . and a heightened consciousness of our own individual identity . . . are threatened with a radically changing future."[57] With impressive prescience, Douglass students anticipated that reorganization would impose a significant travel burden on students, diverting time from studying to intercampus transportation. They also forecast that traditional disciplines might not be welcoming to feminist faculty recently hired by the interdisciplinary women's studies program, thereby jeopardizing women's studies courses that were highly popular among Douglass students.[58] To record their dismay at the proposed reorganization, on February 7, 1980, the DCGA unanimously voted to express no confidence in the provost's plan.

President Bloustein did engage the issues raised by the students, although his perspective differed markedly from theirs. He insisted that the federated college system unduly limited students to classes offered at their college, while dissuading faculty members from teaching at other locations within the university.[59] He also suggested that the federated system could not prevent course duplication across the colleges, thereby squandering teaching resources. Academic consolidation remedied these problems. It would "make a greater variety of courses available to undergraduates in each college. Students will have greater access to a more diverse, high quality faculty than is now possible under the restrictions of the federated system in its present form." In response to the claim that reorganization would result in greater student travel between campuses, Bloustein responded that the classrooms and laboratory instruction would not change significantly from the present pattern of scheduling. Indeed, he suggested that the extra travel involved would, for the most part, be faculty travel.[60]

Supplementing the criticisms advanced by Douglass faculty and students, Douglass alumnae led by Adelaide Marcus Zagoren (NJC '40) also articulated forceful opposition to the proposed reorganization. Emphasizing their experiences at Douglass, they called attention to greater leadership opportunities available at the women's college, the presence of women role models, superior sensitivity to women's special needs, and the cultivation of skills necessary for women's success "in a traditionally male-dominated world." Reorganization threatened to erase these hallmarks of the Douglass education. "The implementation of the proposed plan will impair pursuit of the educational missions of the five colleges, weaken their liberal arts focus, and ultimately bring about their dissolution." Indeed, AADC suggested that under reorganization Douglass would cease to be a women's college and become an institution "without the broad spectrum of educational offerings, without the administrators, faculty and alumnae who care about the special needs of women, and without a special recruitment program that brings the advantages of a women's college to the attention of high school students." To avoid this outcome, AADC drafted a list of principles to safeguard Douglass in the process of university transformation: "The Association believes that the particular mission of Douglass College to meet the educational needs of women and to be a strong advocate and voice for women's issues should be preserved." Drawing attention to persistent gender inequality in the professions, the alumnae insisted that "in view of the continuing special needs of women, the alumnae support the maintenance of a strong women's college at Douglass for the foreseeable future." They called for the continuation of the federated college system until 1984.[61]

The "Great Debate" about reorganization consumed the New Brunswick campuses in the spring of 1980. From the perspective of Old Queens, the reorganization would maintain the colleges' distinct missions through the establishment of College Fellows. Under the direction of the dean of the college, fellows would be responsible for creating

programs and classes that would achieve the mission of individual colleges by overseeing academics and student life. According to President Bloustein, the reorganization
could strengthen the missions of the colleges, since the deans would have reduced
administrative duties, enabling them to focus completely on the college's mission.

In a speech delivered at Founders Day on April 9, 1980, one month before the
Board of Governors was scheduled to vote on the issue of reorganization, Dean Cobb
cited national research that demonstrated that women's colleges afforded students specific advantages: "Research has shown us that graduates of women's colleges are far
more apt than women graduates of coeducational institutions to become outstanding
achievers in society."[62] The preservation of Douglass within a federated college system
would enable Rutgers to ensure that women students had the opportunity to develop a
strong sense of their own abilities, cultivate their leadership potential, and face the
future with confidence.

Despite vociferous objections, the Rutgers Board of Governors voted to reorganize
the New Brunswick faculty in their meeting on May 9, 1980. The reorganization guidelines stipulated that the Faculty of Arts and Sciences should be operative in the fall of
1981. Designed to create impressive strength in traditional academic disciplines, this
reorganization positioned Rutgers to become a "Research I Institution" under the
Carnegie classification of colleges and universities, a precondition for membership in
the elite Association of American Universities (AAU), which Rutgers secured in 1989.
Although faculties were consolidated in discipline-based departments, the undergraduate colleges were allowed to maintain their own campuses, admissions and graduation
standards, core curricula, approved range of majors, and distinctive missions.[63] Indeed,
the guidelines articulated a renewed commitment to the distinct missions of each of the
five undergraduate colleges, suggesting that the missions would be maintained by each
college's Faculty Fellows—representatives from various disciplines who would advise
the deans on academic matters, establish curricula, and approve candidates for degrees.
Faculty and staff members who held voting rights in the legislative body of the undergraduate colleges were designated fellows of their respective colleges. The roles and
responsibilities of fellows were left unspecified—to be determined by the fellows themselves through the development of college-specific bylaws. Dean Cobb successfully
fought for a strong fellows system that would preserve meaningful participation by the
faculty in the college affairs.[64] In keeping with the mandate for a state university, the
reorganization guidelines also articulated a renewed responsibility for the education of
racial and ethnic minorities, adult learners, and women.

For the majority of Douglass faculty, the new era introduced by reorganization
meant broader opportunities, but also more rigorous demands in terms of scholarship.
For those engaged in research, some advantages were immediately visible. The Rutgers
University Research Council offered grants for all faculty members for professional
improvement and the expansion of research agendas. Within large discipline-based
departments, the faculty were in close contact with scholars in similar and related fields,

ending college-centered isolation. Yet it was perceived that promotion criteria had become more strenuous. Previously, criteria for advancement emphasized successful teaching and general service to the college and university. After reorganization, however, promotion criteria required faculty members to have an active research agenda and publications with academic impact, which would be evaluated by the consolidated disciplinary department. The "publish or perish" environment added a new pressure to the majority of Douglass faculty, who regarded teaching as their chief priority. The model of faculty whose primary responsibility was teaching undergraduate students was no longer viable within a research university.

After reorganization became official, the former opposition became more conciliatory. A desire to work within the system prevailed even among those who had most fervently opposed the reorganization. The women's studies program, a former hotbed of opposition, took a strategic view and began to examine how it could fit into the new system. In the fall of 1980, Virginia Yans, the director of the women's studies program at Douglass, submitted a report coauthored with Judy Gerson and Michele Naples to the Discipline Identification Committee. The report provided an overview of the rich history of women's studies at the university, involving faculty at Douglass, Livingston, Rutgers, and University College, offering highly popular courses that introduced students to the new research on women. The report proposed the consolidation of these programs into an interdisciplinary department.[65] Viewing reorganization as a strategy to create a stronger future for the field, the report noted that department status could overcome difficulties associated with uneven development. "Women's studies had developed unevenly from campus to campus, without any central administrative structure (i.e. New Brunswick chairperson)." An "autonomous, interdisciplinary . . . New Brunswick-wide department . . . represented accordingly at the university level" could remedy these problems, enabling the emerging field "to award professional recognition and to create new formal structures and procedures."[66] Despite their ardent appeal, the Discipline Identification Committee did not grant departmental status to women's studies; faculty who had been hired on women's studies lines were assigned to traditional disciplines.

Douglass students demonstrated a similar pragmatism. Returning in fall 1980, the Alliance for Rutgers Federation, the student group that had organized the opposition to the reorganization, evolved into a new interest group, the Coalition to Protect the Colleges (CPC). The CPC's mission was to ensure that the implementation of the reorganization conformed to the Board of Governors' resolution. Douglass College Government Association (DCGA) president Nikki Thomas articulated the strategic resignation to the forces of change experienced by many Douglass students and supporters. In a letter to President Bloustein dated May 20, 1980, Thomas wrote that despite her opposition to reorganization, "I know I can no longer adamantly oppose the plan. I know that the only way I could help maintain my college, I must compromise and work with you on the plans." Thomas requested to serve as a student representative on one of the implementation committees. Following her example, other Douglass students served as members of other implementation committees.[67] Foreseeing that the college would be greatly altered by reorganization, Dean Cobb and her administrative staff began exploring ways to preserve the college's special mission by capitalizing on the rich possibilities of a major research university (see chapter 9).

Student Life, the DCGA, and the Honor System

Following precedents set by NJC, Douglass College preserved a strong government association (the DCGA) and an uncompromising honor system that involved faculty, staff, and students in shared responsibilities to govern and regulate academics and student life. Based on "cooperative integrity," the honor system stressed individual and collective responsibility in enforcing college rules. Each individual was expected to report any violation of the regulations—whether it was her own violation of the rules or another's offense.[68]

Small residential living units, one of the hallmarks of Douglass College, were particularly well suited to the demands of the honor system. The small number of students living together nurtured a communal sentiment and aided in the dissemination of college traditions, norms, and rules. The 1961 *Admission to Douglass College* pamphlet describes a structured system that guided students' lives on campus. Each house chair led a house unit with no more than forty students. The house units were grouped in four "campuses," each campus under the direction of the counselor in residence. This

▲ STUDENT MOVES INTO DOUGLASS RESIDENCE

"house model" was adapted to operate in large dormitories built in the 1960s. The house chairs were seniors or juniors, appointed by the dean of students, who had displayed leadership in previous years. Each house had a mix of students, ranging from first-years to seniors, creating an intergenerational community designed to encourage the older students to mentor the younger ones. The bees, or commuters, were also organized with a chair and a counselor for community students and considered a unit within the student body with representation in the Government Association. Each campus and house unit had the ability to organize social activities and events. This well-organized structure, considered the "Blueprint for Living," guided student life and facilitated the enforcement of general regulations, including the honors system."[69]

The DCGA provided leadership opportunities for students and empowered students to change practices within certain limits. Initiatives that expanded participation in governance were encouraged and enacted expeditiously. For example, the Campus Councils were created in 1963 to address specific concerns of individual campus communities within Douglass. Representing commuters, Corwin, Gibbons, Jameson, Katzenbach, Lippincott, Nicholas, and Woodbury, the Campus Councils had jurisdiction over issues such as "parties and fund-raising," relieving the DCGA of "individual campus concerns in order to allow it more time to work on issues concerning the student body as a whole." The DCGA organized debates on issues, which were then brought to the attention of the college administration. In spring of 1963, for example, the "smoking referendum" mobilized the largest student voter turnout in Douglass history.[70]

The 1964 *Quair* defined the Honor Board as

> one of the largest steps towards independence that a student will take during her four years at college. . . . A student soon . . . learns to understand that she is responsible for guiding her life according to a respect for the rights of fellow students, and for the principles of ethical academic procedures. The immediate freedoms of taking a cigarette break during an exam or of random browsing through the stacks are only a small part of the all-important value of having the opportunity to be led by one's own integrity in all facets of college life.[71]

The independence offered by the code also inspired new demands as students who understood themselves as adults and as moral agents perceived certain rules and regulations to be outdated. During the 1960s, students challenged the dress code, curfew, and rules governing smoking and drinking in dormitories. At Douglass, as at other Seven Sisters colleges, each relaxation of the rules was celebrated as a moral victory.[72] As challenges to the honor code increased, however, the norms underlying the system also began to shift.

In 1963, the *Caellian* conducted a comprehensive survey that listed the academic and social offenses mentioned in the *Red Book* and asked each student how frequently she had committed any such offense and whether she planned to report other's offenses in the future. The survey findings suggested that in the area of social regulations, the reporting clause was not effective. In the sphere of academic regulations, the results were somewhat better. Two of three students said they would report anyone cheating on tests, but less than one in four students planned to report infractions such as smoking in unauthorized places, nonobservance of study hours, taking an apple out of the dining room, or failing to sign out when leaving the dormitories in the evening.[73]

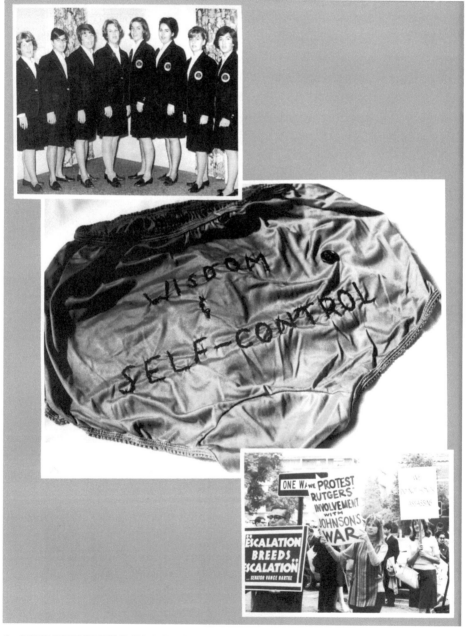

▲ *QUAIR* CAPTURES THE CHANGING TIMES AT DOUGLASS IN THE 1960S

As the sixties progressed, student mobilization against regulation of private conduct grew increasingly vociferous. On Thursday, December 5, 1967, Douglass students organized a teach-in to "evaluate the role of the individual in the university." Targeting increasingly unpopular rules concerning curfew, the meeting attracted three hundred students, who cast the issue as a matter of students' rights. The majority of participants asserted that administrative regulations of the college "violated their constitutional rights." Taking aim at the governance system that allowed administrative staff and faculty to veto proposals crafted by students, the students advanced a constitutional argument:

1. Responsibility over students' personal lives rightfully belongs to the students.
2. No one can surrender their civil rights to any authority.
3. Government Association is an inadequate avenue for responsible student participation in the determination of student affairs because of administrative veto.
4. Government Association is also inappropriate and undemocratic because it seeks to have three different groups govern only one of them.
5. Government Association is an illegal structure to work with because it gives a person or group of people the power to limit students' civil rights.[74]

Imitating the language of the Founding Fathers, the students called for a new "constitutional convention" that "will provide a unique and valuable experience enabling them to learn first-hand about American Democracy by being involved in the inception of a genuine and popular democratic government."[75] On February 22, 1968, forty-six students decided to resort to civil disobedience, violating curfew as a "declaration of students, human, and women's rights."[76] During this period of "revolt," the students also advocated that the Government Association change from a "community association," which included college faculty and staff, to "student government" to accord students greater self-determination.[77]

The college acceded to student demands, abolishing curfews and relaxing the rules governing smoking and drinking in dorms and cars, for seniors. In 1968, the faculty abolished mandatory attendance at Voorhees Chapel programs and the requirement that skirts be worn in the dining hall. But the termination of in loco parentis policies had unintended consequences. As part of an antiwar demonstration in November 1967, Nancy Sutula (DC '68) joined other Rutgers students in occupying the ROTC building to protest university complicity in the war effort. Old Queens referred the case to the Douglass Honor Board, demanding that Sutula be charged with a serious violation of university regulations. The Honors Board demurred, arguing that the purported offense was not included in the Douglass honors code; yet no alternative method existed for handling this new type of infraction in 1968.

In the midst of various student "revolts," Douglass celebrated its fiftieth anniversary. In the 1967–1968 *Annual Report*, Dean Foster noted that "overriding all the activity of Douglass College this year has been the realization that this is the fiftieth anniversary year of the College. . . . That Douglass's fiftieth year should be one of such unrest and significant change on the higher education scene in this country and abroad leads one to suspect that the second fifty years of Douglass will be very different from the first."[78] To mark the end of its first half century and to welcome its future, Dean Somers Foster was joined in special convocation by former deans Margaret Trumbull Corwin, Ruth Marie Adams, Mary Ingraham Bunting, and Margaret Atwood Judson, as well as other leaders of the Rutgers administration.

In the spring of 1968 as part of the fiftieth-anniversary celebration of the college, students organized an honor system conference that attracted participants from thirty-five colleges and universities in the Northeast. The consensus of the conference was that efforts to maintain a system of control that was losing force were futile.[79] Dean Foster commended the students for an "excellent honors system conference . . . numer-

▲ DOUGLASS DEANS CELEBRATE FIFTIETH ANNIVERSARY OF THE COLLEGE

ous discussion meetings and one very well run teach-in," and in fall 1968 appointed a "Commission on Douglass as a Resident College."[80] The fourteen-member commission concluded that "the community created by a resident college is invaluable because it provides the greatest number of opportunities for intellectual growth and personal development."[81] Contrary to the students' demands, however, the commission recommended that "the Honor System should be maintained as a central component in the learning process of this college." Addressing mounting pressure for Douglass to admit men, Dean Foster included an appendix to the report titled "Some Points for Coordinate Rather than Coeducation at Douglass & Rutgers," defending Douglass as a women's college and highlighting the advantages it offered to young women.[82]

The students did not accept the conclusions of the commission. In the spring of 1970, acknowledging that "many people do not want to understand or live under the honor system," the DCGA undertook a long and thoughtful deliberation. In 1971, DCGA issued a recommendation to abolish the honor system on the grounds that it no longer existed in practice. The students agreed that they should abide by all college regulations, but they insisted that they would no longer report on their own or others' infractions. The Douglass faculty were willing to accept a suspension of the honors code regulating private conduct but argued for the continuation of the code governing academic behavior such as plagiarism and cheating on exams. Ultimately the students prevailed: the honors system was abolished. To indicate what was to take its place, the revised *Red Book* included an ominous disclaimer: "The concept of in loco parentis has been abandoned as a definition of the student-institution relationship at Rutgers University. . . . [The] University is no longer a sanctuary: the student is no longer exempt from the normal regulations of the outside community."[83]

Service and Community Outreach

As the norms governing life inside the college were changing during the 1960s, student engagement with the outside world was also expanding. Noting that "the Douglass student today is faced with an increasingly complex environment, both on the campus and in the larger world," Sharon Lindenfield (DC '61), student editor of the *Douglass Alumnae Bulletin*, suggested that "Douglass women rejected the apathy and complacence of the 'beat generation,' and attempted to bridge their search for purpose in life with public service."[84] A decade later, Susan Jacobs (DC '70) envisioned a holistic approach to education that encompassed campus and community:

> The voice of the students in 1969 is a refusal to accept fragmentation of learning under the traditional university structure. It asks a correlation between the unity implicit in the process of living and the process of learning which must also be continuous and unified. It asks that dogmatic divisions between "education" and "non-education" be broken down so that all facets of university life combine in the same process of living and learning.[85]

Working with Douglass faculty and administrators and allies in state government, many students became more vocal on social issues and actively reached out to the communities outside the college campus.

The Douglass Migrant Project, for example, was a student-led initiative that focused on the hardships experienced by migrant farmworkers in New Jersey. The migrant worker population had grown significantly since the 1950s along with the growth of agribusiness, as seen in, for instance, the presence of Seabrook Farms and Food Processing Plant in Cumberland County. The large majority of farmworkers were Puerto Ricans, who numbered nearly twenty-three thousand in 1968.[86] With nine thousand dollars provided by the Dean's Unrestricted Fund, created by the Associate Alumnae of Douglass College, and with the cooperation of Senator Harrison Williams and of Commissioner Raymond Male of the New Jersey Department of Labor and Industry, sixteen students in this pilot work-study project offered assistance to farmers and their families. Faith LaGay (DC '64) and Susan Shill (DC '62) worked with William Dougherty, director of the Division of Preventable Diseases, New Jersey Department of Health, to organize community medical clinics for migrant workers. Following the drowning deaths of two children of migrant workers, Judy Kosakoll (DC '65), Arline Tyler (DC '63), and Ruth Stillwell (DC '64) collaborated with the Monmouth County Office of Social Services to introduce the "swim-mobile," which provided swimming lessons for migrant children. Two other students, Carole McDougall and Frances Profumo (both DC '65), surveyed eighty farms in the Cumberland area to assess the need for a day care center for migrant children, while also providing community first aid and safe-driving workshops for migrant workers. Phyllis Thompson (DC '64) and Margaret Klein (DC '65) assisted at the Fairton School for migrant children and gathered information about the economic problems facing the children's parents.[87]

One of the most successful community outreach projects was created in Burlington Country in cooperation with the Burlington County Public Health Nurses Association. Pat Carty, Elizabeth Ferrar, and Penny Friedman (all DC '64), and Judy Wurster, Marlene Mirabella, Beverly Tyree, and Ana Maria Colombo (all DC '63) organized two full-time day care centers for the children of migrant workers. With the help of local volunteers, including some alumnae who contributed work hours and supplies, the day care centers were offered on local farms for a period of seven weeks and served a total of thirty-one children. In these pioneering service-learning projects, Douglass students experienced firsthand the issues facing migrant families, including discrimination from local residents, inadequate access to medical care, and lack of social services, and they used their ingenuity to devise means to address these complex issues.[88]

The Dean's Unrestricted Fund also enabled students to engage global issues. Doris Wagner (DC '64) participated in a semester-long course on the work, structure, and influence of the United Nations, which included attendance at the United Nations General Assembly sessions in New York City twice weekly. Beryl Goldberg (DC '64) participated in Crossroads Africa, traveling to Bo, Sierra Leone, where she helped construct a dormitory for a secondary school. Goldberg established lasting bonds of friendship with several African students and gained a deeper understanding of the culture, history, and education system in Sierra Leone. Other students, such as Juanita Wade Wilson (DC '66), participated in the program, traveling to Africa in the summer to work on various projects.[89]

These outreach and cultural enrichment programs were made possible through the Dean's Unrestricted Fund. By 1967, there were 11,500 Douglass alumnae, many of whom took an active interest in the college. The Associate Alumnae of Douglass College (AADC) executive director and the editor of the *Alumnae Bulletin* attended all faculty meetings, keeping abreast of significant issues facing the college. Through the generosity of alumnae, AADC made regular financial contributions to the college, funding student scholarships as well as professional and cultural enrichment opportunities for the faculty.[90] The Dean's Unrestricted Fund also made possible educational programs and new co-curricular initiatives. In 1966, for example, Dr. Tsune Shirai, a Japanese psychologist and professor from the Tokyo Women's Christian College, became the first visiting associate alumnae lecturer, who spent a fulfilling year on campus.[91]

The AADC's development record provides one powerful indicator of how greatly graduates valued their NJC/Douglass experience. In the early 1960s, 50 percent of the alumnae were contributing annually to the college, almost twice the rate of contributions by alumni of state universities generally. In recognition of this achievement, the American Alumni Council awarded AADC the first prize for distinguished achievement in the development of alumnae support. AADC also won the top award for sustained donor performance among public institutions in 1966. AADC continued to play a significant role in supporting the college, providing new opportunities for learning and networking for Douglass students and alumnae through 2015 (see chapter 9). The ties forged across generations of Douglass alumnae remain one of the hallmarks of the college.

PENNY FRIEDMAN '64 splashes with a group of happy migrant children in a pond near a Burlington County center.

ANNA MARIA COLOMBO and Judith Wurster, both '63, pause during a busy session at one of two full-time nurseries.

▲ DOUGLASS STUDENTS CREATE DAY CARE CENTER FOR MIGRANT WORKERS

7

DOUGLASS IN TWO TURBULENT DECADES
Student Activism and Institutional Transformation

THE EARLIER INTEREST AT THE COLLEGE
IN DOING THE BEST EDUCATIONAL JOB
FOR WOMEN WAS GIVEN A NEW IMPETUS
THIS YEAR BY THE WOMEN'S LIBERATION
MOVEMENT.

THE UNIVERSITY IS OBVIOUSLY A SERVANT
OF THE STATE, BUT NOT THE SLAVE, AND A
PROFESSIONAL SERVANT IS EXPECTED TO
EXERCISE JUDGMENT IN DETERMINING
THE SERVICES NEEDED AND OFFERED.

—Margery Somers Foster, Douglass College,
Annual Report, 1969–1970

In his address to a joint session of the New Jersey legislature in November 1971, Rutgers president Edward J. Bloustein noted that the university must "learn to serve the cities and suburbs of this day as effectively as it served the farms of yesteryear."[1] Articulated at the end of a turbulent decade that included major mobilizations for civil rights ranging from mass marches to urban uprisings across the nation, President Bloustein's comment acknowledged that the demands for inclusive public higher education would require significant changes in long-standing academic and co-curricular practices in the federated liberal arts colleges in New Brunswick. The mission of Rutgers, as the state university of New Jersey, included far more than educating an affluent "elite." As a public university, Rutgers had a responsibility to devise innovative ways to educate students from all segments of the population, including African Americans, Asian Americans, Latinas and Latinos, Native Americans, low-income citizens, and nontraditional students. But the contours of inclusive education and the appropriate means to achieve that goal were the subject of enormous controversy among legislators, educators, and students themselves. Far more than in earlier decades, students across the

New Brunswick, Newark, and Camden campuses sought to engage the question of university transformation. Through articles in student newspapers, public debates, demonstrations, petitions, and protests, students engaged questions of inclusion spanning race, gender, ethnicity, and sexuality. Douglass women contributed mightily to these transformative debates, although their views were far from homogeneous. This chapter traces progressive student mobilization at Douglass around questions concerning the nature and extent of campus discrimination, strategies to eliminate the underrepresentation of students of color and create a supportive educational environment for all students, the comparative merits of coeducation versus single-sex education, the challenges of homophobia, and the complex changes required to ensure equal treatment on the basis of sexual orientation.

Student Activism

In the 1960s social protests concerning racial justice, the war in Vietnam, women's liberation, and gay and lesbian rights engulfed college and university campuses, including Rutgers, where students expressed their demands with great energy and conviction. Students participated actively in social justice mobilizations, often forming campus groups that worked with local community organizations. Yet how they mobilized was powerfully affected by gender norms and expectations. The 1960 Douglass *Red Book* clearly delineated the guidelines for student conduct on and off campus: "The Douglass objective of young women living graciously and courteously should enter into and be manifested in all facets of the student's life."[2] Constrained by norms of femininity and middle-class respectability, Douglass students were well mannered in their articulations of dissent, which were interpreted by many, including some Douglass faculty, as quiescence or lack of interest in activism generally. Yet Douglass women were increasingly concerned with social justice, expressing intolerance for what they perceived as injustice. They took leading roles in the university chapter of the NAACP; they manifested strong opposition to the Vietnam War; they fought intensively to preserve Douglass as a women's college; they created the Douglass Black Women's Congress, the Douglass Feminist Collective, Douglass Puerto Rican Students, and *Labrys* to advance the interests of diverse women; and they pressured the Rutgers Homophile League to represent lesbian as well as gay issues. They joined and led protests with students from other Rutgers units, contributing to seismic changes on campus and throughout the country.

Civil Rights Activism

Reliable data on the number of black students enrolled in predominantly white colleges and institutions prior to 1968 is remarkably difficult to find, and data for Douglass College is no exception.[3] Julia Baxter Bates (NJC '38) was the first known African American graduate from Douglass (see chapter 3). From 1922 to 1960, the yearbooks reveal fewer than twenty-five African American women among the graduating seniors. Even when international students and Asian American students, including two Japanese Americans who had relocated to New Jersey after their World War II internment experience, are tallied, the total number of women of color who graduated from Douglass prior to 1965 was negligible.[4] Beyond the numbers, the treatment of students of color reflected the segregationist practices of the nation. Emma Andrews Warren and Evelyn Sermons Field (both NJC '49) were roommates for two years, inaugurating the era of housing black students together in residence halls. In 1953, however, when African American Inez Phillips Durham (DC '57) entered Douglass, in the absence of other black students she was offered a single room, despite her expressed interest in having a roommate. Only in her junior year was she paired with a first-year black student.[5] It was not until 1962 when Douglass administrators confronted an uneven number (five) of African American students that they assigned a black student, Juanita Wade Wilson (DC '66), to room with a white student, Lydia Agnoli McMillan.[6] The gulf between claims of equal opportunity and actual practices loomed large. In the words of Wilson, "We were taught to be good citizens, to believe in the American way and American opportunity, and yet before our very eyes, we saw doors that were being shut in our faces."[7]

In fall 1963, the arrest of Donald Harris (RC '63), a former member of the Rutgers chapter of the NAACP and a member of the Student Nonviolent Coordinating Committee (SNCC), galvanized the New Brunswick campuses. Harris had been registering Blacks to vote in Americus, Georgia, when he was arrested along with two other SNCC members and charged with attempting to "incite insurrection," a capital offense in Georgia. Harris and his colleagues were incarcerated, pending bail, which was set at forty thousand dollars per person. Both the *Targum* and the *Caellian* dedicated pages to this issue, informing the college community of developments in the case and articulating outrage at such blatant injustice.[8]

The Douglass-Rutgers NAACP chapter, which had been established in 1959 as a racially mixed group, was among the first to respond to Harris's arrest. Three students from the Douglass class of 1964—Susan Kass, a white sociology major who was the chair of the NAACP Action Committee; Barbara Jaffe, a white sociology major; and Rita Murphy, an African American double-majoring in history and political science, along with Adrian Shreiber (RC '65), visited the SNCC office in New York to arrange legal representation for Harris. At Douglass, they created the Don Harris Co-ordinating Committee, chaired by Rita Murphy, which quickly expanded to include members from all Rutgers units. Sandi Cliadakis, a popular member of the Douglass history department, served as the faculty adviser for this recognized student organization. Cliadakis also helped organize a faculty committee in support of the coordinating committee. Together students and faculty circulated petitions and collected pledges and donations for Harris's legal defense.[9]

On September 26, 1963, the Douglass-Rutgers NAACP hosted a rally to build support for the Don Harris Legal Defense Fund, attracting an overflow crowd of fifteen hundred people to Voorhees Chapel and the old gym. Charles Sherrod, SNCC field secretary, joined Dean Ruth Adams and Harris's mother and father in addressing the

▲ DOUGLASS STUDENTS MOBILIZE IN SUPPORT OF DONALD HARRIS IN 1963

audience. Their presentations had a profound effect on the students. Editors of the 1964 *Quair* featured the Don Harris rally as a signal event in the "Douglass Life" section of the yearbook, along with other traditional college events such as convocation, campus night, homecoming, International Weekend, and Sacred Path.[10]

Douglass students distinguished themselves by their savvy strategy in the campaign to free Harris. Susan Kass and Rita Murphy brought Don Harris's arrest to the attention of U.S. senators Harrison Williams (D-NJ) and Clifford Case (R-NJ), who took great interest in the case. Indeed, Senator Case, a Rutgers graduate married to a Douglass graduate, sent a representative to the second collegewide Harris rally. Reverend Bradford S. Abernathy, university chaplain, and Nola Safro (DC '64), Douglass College Government Association president, had prominent roles in this event, which once again attracted a significant crowd. The Douglass Government Association gathered petitions protesting the arrest and delivered them to Burke Marshall, assistant attorney general in charge of civil rights. Prompted by a letter from a Douglass student, the *New York Times* covered the issue diligently, publishing articles almost daily to inform readers of developments in the case. In a letter dated October 19, 1963, addressed "To the Students of Rutgers and Douglass," Harris wrote, "I cannot adequately convey my deepest appreciation for the many, many things people have done to make our present situation more bearable and hasten our ultimate release."[11] Harris and his co-workers were ultimately freed in November 1963 after a federal court declared Georgia's insurrection laws unconstitutional.[12]

Under the leadership of Dean Adams, Douglass initiated a systematic effort to recruit and enroll minority students, creating the Pilot Education Opportunity Program in the fall of 1966. Twenty-six minority students—twenty-four of them black—enrolled at Douglass, constituting 1 percent of the total student population. With active involvement of these students in continuing recruitment efforts, the college doubled minority enrollment the following year. By the fall of 1968, minority students constituted 4 percent of the student population, 115 of 2,860 students. In contrast, only 95 of 6,416 students at Rutgers College were students of color, a fact acknowledged by the *Report of the Select Committee to Study the Issue of Rutgers College as a Multi-racial Community,* led by Rutgers College historian Warren Susman. The report found that Rutgers College and the university had failed to live up to its commitments to minority students. In her response to the report, Dean Margery Foster emphasized that Douglass had already implemented the committee's most important recommendations.[13] The recruitment of minority faculty and staff, however, did not keep pace with the recruitment of students. In the fall of 1968, Cecelia Hodges Drewry, of the Department of Speech and Dramatic Arts, was the only black faculty member at Douglass.

As civil rights marches and sit-ins encountered increasing violence orchestrated by white officials across the South, black activists began to question the merits of integrationist approaches to race relations. In 1964 when the Democratic National Convention refused to seat the Mississippi Freedom Democratic Party, which had been elected by black and white voters, in favor of the white supremacist Mississippi Democratic Party, student activists and SNCC members began to radicalize, advancing a vision of Black Power. With the election of Stokely Carmichael (aka Kwame Ture) as chair in May 1966, SNCC adopted a Black consciousness philosophy and expelled white activists from its membership. At Douglass, Karen Predow, who matriculated in fall 1966, introduced Black nationalism as an alternative to models of racial integration, which required Blacks to assimilate to white norms. Initially involved in the Student Afro-American Society, founded by Jerome Harris and Frank McClellan as a coeducational student organization, Predow and other black Douglass students founded the Douglass Black Student Congress in 1968, when the Afro-American Society decided to become an exclusively male organization.

In September 1967, *Caellian* published several articles in a series titled To Recognize Racism, which raised a host of questions about manifestations of individual, cultural, and institutional racism. To remedy these problems, the articles called for increases in the number of black students and faculty, as well as the introduction of Black studies courses. Later in 1967, *Caellian* produced a special issue, "Black Students in a White University," featuring stories about black student organizations and interviews with eight black Douglass women who spoke of their alienation in a white environment and the importance of forging a separate space within Douglass for the development of African American cultural identity. In March 1968, *Caellian* published a second special issue, "Focus: American Minorities Address Plight of Puerto Ricans, Native Americans, and African Americans."[14]

Following the assassination of Martin Luther King Jr. on April 4, 1968, racial tensions increased on campus as King's murder provoked an unprecedented sense of loss and a new determination for action and advocacy for social justice within a Black nationalist frame. Black Douglass women lowered the American flag and rehung it "upside down to register their distress, then marched to the College Ave. campus, where they met in Blacks-only session to discuss their grief."[15] The Douglass-Rutgers NAACP chapter subsequently ended its multiracial membership, reasserting the demands for black leadership and separate spaces within which to forge Black Power and cultural identity. As white students who had been active in NAACP migrated to Students for a Democratic Society (SDS), Black students joined an array of campus-specific black

▲ DOUGLASS STUDENTS HANG THE FLAG UPSIDE DOWN TO REGISTER THEIR DISTRESS AT THE ASSASSINATION OF MARTIN LUTHER KING JR., 1968

organizations, including the Black Organization of Students (BOS) at Newark, the Student African-American Society (SAS) at Rutgers College, and the Douglass Black Student Congress (DBSC).

After a series of unfruitful meetings, convocations, and debates with college administrators, members of BOS, SAS, and DBSC sought to meet with the Board of Governors. With the assistance of Bessie N. Hill, the sole black member of the Board of Governors, members of all three groups presented their grievances to the board. The students left the meeting without any confidence that their demands would be met anytime soon. DBSC presented a list of demands to both the college administration and the Government Association, calling for an increase of black faculty, students, and staff; the establishment of courses in black culture; increased financial support for black students; and increased black representation on Government Association committees. Many nonminority students joined in support for these demands.

On February 21, 1969, Rutgers, Douglass, and the Newark students developed a unified protest plan, which required careful timing and good communication between the different colleges. DBSC published a letter in *Caellian*, which charged Dean Foster with "callous indifference" and rearticulated "Black Demands":

> Dean Foster and Douglass College have refused to act upon the demands brought forth last year following the death of Martin Luther King. In the wake of possible disruption of the campus then, the administration was quick to agree to the demands of black students, but apparently because we have been relatively quiet on this campus, the administration has returned to its policy inaction. . . . We shall not tolerate the disregard of our demands and the treatment which we have received from members of the Douglass Community. We are forced to take action to insure the fulfillment of the needs of black students at Douglass.[16]

As tensions on campus escalated, culminating in the BOS takeover of Conklin Hall in Newark on February 24, 1969, DBSC coordinated protests to coincide with action by BOS in Newark and SAS across town. Sixty black Douglass students, acting in unison, filled their trays with double servings of food, then dumped them in the center of the dining hall and marched out in a gesture of protest. In multiple Douglass classes, "Black students hurled insults at instructors then walked out. They locked bathroom doors and clogged drains. They refused to speak to white students and declined to meet with the Dean for further discussions. They distributed leaflets airing their grievances and noting that the university had been unwilling to address their complaints."[17] Their message was unambiguous: "Blacks can no longer tolerate this."[18]

DBSC's demands generated intense interest on the Douglass campus. Twelve hundred students, staff, and faculty participated in a general meeting in Voorhees Chapel. At a special faculty meeting held on March 11, 1969, the faculty approved twenty-five

measures "related to the demands of black students and designed to improve the education of all students." These included recommendations to increase minority
representation among faculty, students, administrators, and staff; the creation of an
African American studies program; expansion of black content in campus programs
and events; and the creation of the African and Afro-American House, first envisioned
by Professor Cecelia Drewry, to coordinate cultural programs for students majoring in
or interested in the experiences of African Americans.[19]

Following the takeover of Conklin Hall and other disruptive protests, the Board of
Governors, President Mason Gross, and the chancellor of higher education, Ralph A.

▲ REPRESENTATIVE SHIRLEY CHISHOLM (D–NY) WITH DEAN MARGERY SOMERS FOSTER
AT DOUGLASS COMMENCEMENT, 1969

Dungan, met in mid-March 1969 to devise a "solution" for the underrepresentation of students of color—the establishment of the Urban University Program (UUP). Designed to support "educationally and economically disadvantaged graduates of the secondary schools in those communities where Rutgers has its primary location," the program pledged to provide remedial courses to help prepare students graduating from Camden, Newark, and New Brunswick high schools for college course work. Launched in September 1969 with seven hundred thousand dollars from the university emergency reserve funds, UUP registered six hundred students (more than 80 percent black), but the program never received adequate support from the state or from the Rutgers faculty and folded after only two years.[20] It was subsequently replaced by the Equal Opportunity Fund (EOF), which was created by state law in 1968 to ensure meaningful access to higher education for students from backgrounds of economic and educational disadvantage.

Racial tension persisted on campus, manifested particularly in interpersonal relations between black and white students, including verbal abuse, discourtesy, and pushing and shoving in the dining halls. Black students perceived white hostility and persisting negative stigmatization. Dean Foster appointed the Commission on Ethnic and Race Relations in April 1971 to explore ways to address issues of inequity and thereby reduce interracial tensions. After extensive public hearings, the commission's report, issued in January 1972, called on faculty, staff, and students to heighten their understanding of the effects of their own words and actions. The report charged the administration with taking steps "to facilitate the ready flow of accurate information about events of racial significance at Douglass so that we are less the victims of rumor than we have been in the past"[21] and to demonstrate "continuing commitment to a successful resolution of the tensions which divide the learning community.[22] Two black members of the commission, C. Maxene Summey (DC '70), who had been a leader of DBSC during her student days and who was then serving as assistant dean of Douglass, and Evelyn Daniels, the current chair of DBSC, noted that the report did not adequately address the original demands presented by black students and added an appendix to elaborate tactics to address institutional racism (see chapter 10).

Douglass moved quickly to implement recommendations of the commission, particularly in the areas of admissions and financial aid. The college introduced courses in Black studies and, to facilitate adjustment to college life, approved a proposal to eliminate first-semester grades from the cumulative grade point averages of all students, which was applied retroactively to all students who matriculated at Douglass beginning in fall 1968. The university administration also took the demands of black students seriously, introducing new initiatives across all campuses. By 1972, each college had an EOF program and staff. Black and Hispanic recruiters joined the admissions staff, working to increase applications from minority students. Five years later, twenty-five hundred black students were enrolled as full-time undergraduates, slightly more than 10 percent of the undergraduate population; nearly one thousand black graduate

▲ DOUGLASS AFRICAN AMERICAN HOUSE, 1973

students matriculated in various graduate programs, and eleven hundred African Americans were enrolled in the evening division. Blacks composed 5 percent of the full-time faculty and a slightly higher proportion of staff. Black student organizations proliferated, and the newspaper *Black Voice* joined other student publications.[23]

Campus militancy diminished during the 1970s as the number of minority students steadily increased. In 1979, a coalition of black student organizations again complained about recruitment and admission policies, financial aid, the small number of black faculty, "racist harassment," inequitable allocation of student activity fees, and high rates of attrition. Their central insight was stark: although black students were enrolled in record numbers, too few were receiving degrees. The first study of graduation rates completed in 1979 did not report on racial differences in degree completion, comparing only non-EOF and EOF students. Yet even these results were telling, as more than 60 percent of EOF students were black. The study reported that 62 percent of non-EOF students who entered the university in 1973 graduated in five years, while only 27 percent of EOF students received their degrees within the same period, an alarming disparity.

The seventies brought an unprecedented number of black and minority students to Rutgers, although the percentage of African Americans, Latinas, and Latinos in the student population declined in the 1980s and 1990s. In the 1980s, the New Jersey Department of Higher Education (DHE) began placing greater pressure on the university to recruit more minorities. In March 1986, Chancellor T. Edward Hollander (who had been appointed in 1977) sent a memo to the Board of Higher Education to set forth a program to boost minority enrollment. Rutgers was required to establish a "strategic plan to address minority enrollment," implement that plan, and report periodically to the DHE on its progress in meeting minority enrollment goals. The Board of Governors created an Ad Hoc Committee on Minority Recruitment and Retention to monitor the new initiatives. To encourage increases in minority enrollments, the DHE stipulated that college EOF programs must enroll at least 10 percent of each incoming first-year class or be placed on probation, which would entail a freeze in state funding until the situation was remediated. Five of Rutgers fifteen undergraduate units were affected by this policy. Within a year, Rutgers increased the number of EOF students, but black students constituted a declining proportion of EOF students. In 1986, the university also introduced special merit scholarships for outstanding African American and Puerto Rican high school graduates. Established in 1985 in honor of James Dickson Carr (RC 1892), the first black graduate from Rutgers College, these scholarships carried generous stipends. In combination with other scholarships designated for minority undergraduates who did not qualify for EOF assistance, the Carr scholarships helped attract and retain diverse students.

Antiwar Protests and Peace Activism

The University of Michigan in Ann Arbor organized the first teach-in against the Vietnam War, an educational innovation quickly adopted on college campuses across the United States and often accompanied by antiwar demonstrations. Rutgers and Douglass faculty organized a teach-in on Thursday April 22, 1965, in Scott Hall on College Avenue, which drew a large audience of students and faculty. A fierce debate between Douglass political scientist William Fitzpatrick and two Rutgers College historians, Lloyd Gardner and Warren Susman, ignited the crowd. But at a time when university faculty could be dismissed for membership in any communist organization, the comments of Rutgers history professor Eugene Genovese added an electrifying element as he stated support for the communist forces in Vietnam: "Those who know me, know I am a Marxist and a socialist. I do not fear or regret a pending Việt Cộng victory in Vietnam. I welcome it."[24] Student groups such as SDS and Young Americans for Freedom (YAF) organized subsequent teach-ins, which were characterized by vociferous disagreement.[25] A *Targum* poll in 1967 indicated that 52 percent of the students opposed the war, 41 percent supported it, and the rest remained "undecided"; but Douglass students voiced the strongest opposition to the war.[26] Douglass women demonstrated against the war and demanded the abolition of ROTC on campus and an end to research contracts funded by the Department of Defense. Six Douglass SDS members were arrested and faced suspension after storming a Board of Governors meeting to press for an end to all university complicity in the war effort, symbolized by the presence of ROTC on campus.[27]

As antiwar demonstrations galvanized the Rutgers community, peace activism became one of the largest preoccupations of Douglass women from 1968 to 1972. Although Douglass demonstrations were not as violent as those at Rutgers College and universities such as Kent State, both Douglass students and the faculty were deeply invested in efforts to end the war. The 1970 *Quair* indicates that antiwar protest at Douglass reached a pinnacle on April 30, 1970, when President Richard Nixon finally acknowledged the systematic bombing of Cambodia by the U.S. military. Students opted to participate in antiwar demonstrations rather than attend classes. On May 4, 1970, the Douglass faculty narrowly passed a motion to suspend classes and exams to enable the community to participate in a teach-in on peace in Southeast Asia. By a vote of 75–73, the faculty approved a resolution "to suspend classes (only six class days were left in the semester), cancel required papers and final exams, and distribute grades of pass or fail unless a student should ask for a numerical grade or a faculty member needed work in order to give a passing grade." The seventy-three opponents of the measure did not object to a collegewide demonstration against the war; they preferred to continue classes and exams, while granting moratoria on an individual basis, a position supported by the Rutgers College faculty.[28] Through the all-college assembly in Voorhees Chapel, Douglass joined colleges and universities across the nation in protesting atrocities committed in the war in Southeast Asia.[29]

In contrast to antiwar activism at Rutgers College, which often involved direct action and civil disobedience such as blocking bridges and disrupting traffic, Douglass College students protested for peace and sought to build unified public support to end the war.[30] In the three weeks preceding summer vacation in 1970, the students and faculty devoted themselves to intensive study of the history of the Vietnam War. The students made special efforts to reach out to alumnae and parents on Parents' Day on May 17. They organized educational meetings and presentations to share their knowledge of the issues with a broader community. The Douglass library was one of the busiest sites on campus during this time, arranging book displays and providing reading lists on this subject. In her *Annual Report*, Dean Foster applauded the students' initiatives and wrote proudly that "many students asked their teachers for special work or continued assignments in class. . . . Many worked on special projects to educate themselves and the community about the Vietnam situation. A group went to Trenton and was commended by the Senate for its rational approach." On May 11, the New Jersey Senate passed a resolution commending Rutgers and Douglass students for "working diligently and sincerely . . . through the accepted political process of our American democracy."[31]

Coeducation vs. Single-Sex Education

During the 1960s, both racial and gender segregation in schooling was called into question. Although the U.S. Supreme Court asserted without equivocation in *Brown v. Board of Education* that racial segregation imposed a "badge of inferiority" with lifelong consequences for African Americans, the effects of single-sex education were hotly contested. Public opinion tended to support coeducation as beneficial for both men and women.[32] When Princeton University commissioned a study of secondary school students about their college preferences in 1968, 78 percent indicated a preference for coeducation, while only 5 percent preferred single-sex schools.[33] Acknowledging this grim statistic, sixty-four women's colleges went coeducational or closed their doors between June and October 1968.[34]

Many women's rights proponents argued that in excluding women from admission, elite men's institutions of higher education denied women access to important pathways to power and prestige. In 1969, the American Civil Liberties Union (ACLU) and the National Student Association filed a lawsuit on behalf of women plaintiffs charging that the University of Virginia's practice of admitting only men to undergraduate programs violated the Fourteenth Amendment to the U.S. Constitution. In February 1970, a federal court approved a plan proposed by the university to admit women. In spring 1970, under the auspices of Executive Orders 11246 and 11375, which prohibited discrimination by federal contractors on the basis of race, color, religion, national origin, or sex, the Women's Equity Action League and the National Organization for Women filed a complaint with the Civil Rights Office of the Department of Health, Education, and Welfare over discrimination against women in forty-three colleges and universities, which had contracts with the federal government.[35] Rutgers was one of the institutions named in the complaint.[36] These lawsuits in combination with the social tumult of the late 1960s led some conservatives to characterize coeducation "as part of this massive assault on authority and traditional values."[37]

In 1969, when the Board of Governors again voted against the admission of women to Rutgers College, the college shared the dubious distinction of being one of only two state-supported all-male higher education institutions in the nation.[38] Facing growing pressure from the State of New Jersey to expand student enrollments, Rutgers students, faculty, and administrators debated the pros and cons of admitting women to the four undergraduate men's colleges and admitting men to Douglass. Plans were already in place to open Livingston College as a coeducational unit in fall 1969.

Although the Rutgers College faculty voted unanimously in fall 1968 to endorse coeducation, both the Student Council and the college athletic director opposed any quick movement to admit women. On February 2, 1969, the Rutgers College Student Council adopted a motion dissenting from the resolution of the Rutgers College faculty. The male students claimed to endorse "the idea of coeducation," but they argued that there had been insufficient "prior study of co-education," and the residence halls were totally unprepared to accommodate women. Instead of backing a hasty move to admit women, the Rutgers College Student Council supported the addition of "more coeducation classes through increased inter-college registration with Douglass College."[39] Albert Twitchell, Rutgers College athletic director, expressed his concern that coeducation would negatively affect the football team. In a letter addressed to Arnold Grobman, dean of Rutgers College, he wrote, "If we go co-ed . . . it will grossly affect our team strength. Most football squads come from Liberal Arts."[40] Twitchel assumed that women students with higher academic qualifications would take cherished spaces in the men's liberal arts college, reducing the number of places available for his athletes.[41]

Dean Margery Somers Foster was perhaps the most vociferous of all opponents to coeducation at Rutgers and at Douglass. To understand her opposition to the admission of women at Rutgers College, it is helpful to consider the campus climate at Rutgers College in the 1960s. Beauty contests dotted the Rutgers College calendar each academic year. Homecoming involved the election of a Queen and her Court. Nominees were put forward by Rutgers College students to be judged on their "beauty, personality, and charm." Nominations required full-length photos, and the specification of "vital statistics" (i.e., height; weight; measurements of breasts, waist, and hips). Candidates were judged by university officials, including the assistant directors of student aid, athletics, and the dean of men, along with one woman resident counselor at Douglass.[42] Rutgers College had an active ROTC program, which organized a weekend of military festivities each year that included parades, reviews, and a dance—the Military Ball. The "Queen" of the military ball was chosen "on the basis of grace, poise, verbal expression, grooming, good taste and beauty" by judges who included military men, administration officials, and on some occasions a religious leader.[43] The *Targum* organized an annual Miss Beautiful Secretary on Campus contest "to honor our industrious secretaries." The winner was chosen on the basis of "beauty and personality" and received "a pay raise, an air conditioner, and a rug in her office."[44] In addition, Rutgers men were renowned for their caricature of Douglass students. "Debbie Douglass" was depicted in white gloves and proper dress signifying "strong middle-class hang-ups." The stereotype included reserved sexuality ("mucho studios, mucho frigid!!!") and unattractive appearance ("glasses, overweight, and a bun"). According to the caricature, "99% are stuck up. . . . They never smile."[45] In this "chilly" campus climate, Dean Foster doubted that women could get an equal education.

In a letter addressed to President Mason Gross and the Board of Governors, Foster argued that women would get a far better education at a women's college, where

a. There is a climate of expectation that they should develop fully. Everything is there for them. . . .
b. There are role models—women with leading positions, women scholars, many of whom have husbands and children.
c. There is leadership experience—women will be officers of organizations, as they could be but aren't at coed places.[46]

Douglass faculty shared Dean Foster's fear that women would be treated as second-class citizens at Rutgers College just as they were in the United States more generally.

Women in this country are not first-class citizens. . . . There must be some division in the University where students are accepted as people; and not just men or women. . . . On a coeducational campus, women find themselves pandering to the notion that men are superior. . . . If a woman has no chance for leadership in college, we are undercutting her potential for contributing to society. . . . Rutgers does not want a woman student council president, a woman editor of the newspaper or yearbook.[47]

The commitment of the Douglass administration, faculty, and staff to preserve Douglass as a women's college within the coeducational university was clear. When the Rutgers College faculty voted again in 1970 to recommend that the college become coeducational, the Douglass Long Range Planning Committee undertook a study of the impact of such an action on the college. In response to the report of the committee, on April 14, 1970, the Douglass faculty voted two to one against a proposal that Douglass should follow suit, and three to one to affirm the college's mission "to educate women for full partnership and active participation in society."[48]

Douglass students were divided on the question of coeducation. In 1967, a Douglass Government Association Committee issued a report opposing coeducation. In a 1971 survey, however, Douglass women split evenly in their opinions: 1,093 respondents preferred to keep Douglass a relatively small women's college, allowing students to register for courses at Rutgers; 1,063 students indicated a preference to become coed and increase the size of the student body to seven thousand. Despite pronounced disagreement about the future of Douglass, students were clear that a merger with the College of Agriculture and Environmental Sciences—a possibility brought to the table by New Jersey chancellor of higher education Ralph A. Dungan—was not the way to achieve coeducation. The slight majority of Douglass women who sought to preserve the college as a single-sex institution drew attention to the intricate ways that a women's college facilitated intellectual growth and professional development. In a letter to the *Targum*, Douglass students Cheri Connell, Kathryn Conner, Janet Cottrell, and Barbara Oettle noted:

After approximately 18 years of male dominance including the effects of at least 12 years of coeducation, a girl needs the opportunity to develop as an individual, as a woman—not a man's idea of a woman. A woman's college is not a luxury; it is a necessity. Contrary to popular opinion, we are not here to preserve our virginity. We are here to develop our identity. . . . We feel that coeducation will make it even easier to preserve the myth of feminine inferiority. After all, most of us went to coed grammar and high schools. If men have failed in 12 years to realize that we are their equals, we doubt that another four years will convince them.[49]

Despite enormous pressure from the university, the state, and a substantial proportion of Douglass students, Dean Foster succeeded in securing the future of Douglass as a women's college. Her challenge then was to make good on her claims that a women's college offered the best environment for women's higher education, providing clear academic expectations, plentiful examples of accomplished women as role models, and leadership opportunities in student government and numerous student organizations. The coeducation debates challenged Dean Foster and the Douglass faculty not only to defend the validity of separate education for women but also to envision Douglass as a college specifically designed to compensate for the disadvantages facing women in society, to prepare them for positions of leadership, and to empower them for full and active participation in all spheres of public life. Doris Falk, chair of the English department, aptly captured this new focus: "The approach to women's education should be radically changed. I want to give my students the tools to liberate themselves—to create a job market in which men and women have equal pay for equal work, and have equal opportunity and mobility. I think Douglass must take the lead to find ways to make women think of themselves as free to fulfill themselves as people, not just as women."[50]

Toward a Feminist Model of Women's Education

The 1971 survey that tallied Douglass students' views on coeducation also revealed that the idea of women's liberation had not yet taken hold of the imaginations of all Douglass students. Although they believed that men and women were equally suited to most careers, with the exception of military service, the majority believed that if a working woman had a baby, she should stay home with the child until it started school. Many Douglass women believed that coeducation was a good way to promote equality of the sexes and disagreed with the notion that women should "break out of their exploitation through organized, unified activity, following the example of blacks."[51] Nevertheless, there is evidence that student leaders were anxious to take control of their own lives. In 1970, the Government Association changed its structure from a system of community governance involving students, faculty, staff, and administrators to a student government association. Although the students sought and accepted the invitation to attend faculty meetings, the Student Government Association withdrew voting rights from faculty representatives.

Although there had been no dramatic demonstrations for women's liberation on campus to this point, in 1970 the college committed itself to become a "leader in education for women, a college within a unique feminist identity."[52] To investigate how to educate women for leadership, Dean Foster appointed a ten-member Ad Hoc Committee on the Education of Women, led by two junior faculty, Elaine Showalter (English) and Mary Howard (Sociology). The committee included two students, Barbara Dildine and Lynn Tanenbaum (both DC '71). In what became known as the *Howard-Showalter Report*, the committee recommended that Douglass faculty take the lead in opposing discrimination against women at the university; expand courses on women's history, sponsor colloquia, conferences, and research on women's studies; and create a comprehensive education program for women beyond the ages of eighteen to twenty-two that gave priority to minority women and low-income women. The report envisioned a feminist approach to higher education that would "enable students to find the fullest satisfaction in rich and responsible personal lives and to serve usefully as citizens." The report urged Douglass to cultivate a feminist identity that would advance women's leadership by offering courses on women's history, status, and achievements, establishing a day care center to free women's time for intellectual labor, organizing programs for women in the community, supporting women artists and writers, improving career counseling for students and for women who sought to reenter the labor force after raising children, sponsoring research on women, creating sexual counseling services, and advocating for the abolition of all gender-based inequalities at Rutgers.[53] The Douglass faculty voted 90 to 32 to support the recommendations of the *Howard-Showalter Report*.[54]

The 1971–1973 *Red Book* enthusiastically embraced the new program for women's education at Douglass College: "With the coming of the 1970s, Douglass has dedicated itself anew to the special problems of women's education. A Women's Program has been initiated with emphasis placed on the role of women today—her personal satisfaction and her life within the larger community. Every student is given the fullest opportunity to make her decisions as an individual in the college environment with the hope that her years at Douglass will provide the basis for a rewarding future."[55]

In early 1972, President Bloustein also endorsed the *Howard-Showalter Report* and charged his deans to consider ways to meet the "need for women's studies, part-time and continuing education for women, graduate education for women, [and] part-time employment in relation to tenure and promotion."[56] At a time when the university was facing two sex discrimination complaints—a class action complaint filed by women faculty at Rutgers College of Arts and Sciences in Newark and an individual complaint filed by a woman faculty member at Rutgers College in New Brunswick, it was notable that President Bloustein made a verbal commitment to the concept of feminist higher education.[57]

Implementation of the feminist model of higher education took many forms at Douglass, from the creation of the Center for the American Woman and Politics at the Eagleton Institute, the development of the women's studies program, the Mary H. Dana Women's Artist Series, and the Women's Studies Institute (later renamed the Institute for Research on Women) to the establishment of the Training Institute for Sex Desegregation of the Public Schools at Douglass (see chapter 8).[58] One powerful example of the effect of this new feminist focus occurred with the opening of the Douglass Fine Arts Center, located next to the Voorhees Chapel and the ravine. Designed by the architect Pietro Belluschi, the Fine Arts Center provided "students in art, music and theater arts needed facilities to house expanding programs."[59] The building provided art and music studios, classrooms, a rehearsal hall, an art gallery, and an experimental theater. To celebrate the opening of the center, Dean Foster appointed a committee to organize a Year of the Arts, a year-long series of exhibitions, programs, and events involving the campus and the local community. Events included a film series; an exhibition of women artists' works; and an opera production of *The Faerie Queen*, a joint effort of the music and theater arts departments. During the dedication ceremony in April 1971, Susan Sontag spoke in Voorhees Chapel to a packed audience. The Douglass Year of the Arts increased Douglass's visibility as a major resource in the field of interdisciplinary aesthetics, providing high-level creative arts training for students and community members. It also added flair to the thirtieth-anniversary celebration of Rutgers as the state university.

The Women's Center, one of the key recommendations in the *Howard-Showalter Report*, was established at Douglass College in the early seventies under the leadership of Adrienne Anderson (NJC '45). Although it was intended primarily to serve Douglass community, the center also provided services to women in the local community, serving as a bridge between the campus and the community. The center included an office to assist women who sought retraining to reenter the job market or to pursue higher education. Staffed by professional counselors who organized workshops and provided individual consultations, the office offered abundant information about nontraditional careers for women. The center publicized its programs and activities broadly through its newsletter, *Women's Space*. The staff and the Douglass student volunteers worked closely with the University Counseling Centers and the Office of Career Development to provide updated information for its university and community clientele. Under Anderson's leadership, the Women's Center hosted numerous career conferences, earning statewide recognition, which helped it forge additional community partnerships. Anderson served as the Douglass representative to the New Jersey College and University Coalition for Women's Education. In 1976, the mission of the Women's Center at Douglass was expanded to meet the needs of a larger constituency—women on all the New Brunswick campuses. The center was renamed the Rutgers University Women's Center, whose staff worked to serve the needs of an expanded constituency with only slightly enhanced resources.[60]

In 1973, Douglass students formed the Douglass Feminist Collective "to raise consciousness at both Douglass and Rutgers." Members of the collective emphasized that women choose Douglass because of the women-centered focus, not in spite of it. They worked with the college to design a new orientation program that explored what it means to be a woman at a women's college, drawing attention to careers and opportunities in areas generally considered taboo for women. Through course work and co-curricular programming, the collective suggested, Douglass destroys the myths of women as second-class citizens. The 1973–1974 *Announcement* echoed these feminist themes: "Douglass recognizes its special responsibility with regard to women's roles in society and in higher education. The College is pursuing this challenge in a variety of ways."[61] The high percentage of women faculty, dedicated to raising the aspirations and career expectations of women students, while cultivating their intellectual potential and their desire to serve their communities, was characterized as central to Douglass's educational mission.

In academic year 1975–1976, the college introduced two seminars in women's studies, which were required for all students in the women's studies program. Although grounded in women's history and women's writing, the seminars were interdisciplinary. Titled Topics in Women's Studies, and Women and Contemporary Problems, they sought to cultivate students' capacities to critically engage inequitable social structures and relations. In 1976–1977, two further women's studies courses were added to the curriculum: Current Issues in the Women's Movement, and Women, Medicine, and Health, this latter taught by a physician; these supplemented the existing seminars Women and the Contemporary Arts, and Women and the Law. Participation in the seminars, usually in the senior year, gave "advanced students a chance to share experiences and concerns, to practice skills, to move from theory to action."[62] The language of critique also entered the 1976–77 *Red Book*: "The face of education is rapidly changing. Priorities must be reevaluated and reordered by the entire Douglass community. We as students must find new avenues to insure the maintenance of the high quality of educational experience our academic community so highly values. . . . The greatest responsibility we have facing us is to continue to question, to reevaluate, and to dissent in the creative process."[63]

Douglass students turned their feminist lens on various Rutgers traditions, including the *Targum*. In 1977, the Feminist Collective, which included Douglass and Rutgers students, launched *Labrys*, an alternative feminist newspaper. In the words of Sondra Korman (RU '77), one of founding editors of *Labrys*, the "traditional Rutgers newspaper, *Targum*, was not doing an adequate job of covering women's issues."[64] The students recruited feminist poet and critic Adrienne Rich, who taught in the Douglass English department, to serve as faculty adviser for the publication. The inaugural issue of *Labrys* featured a front page article by Cheryl Clarke titled "Assata Shakur: Strength Behind Bars." Clarke, a black feminist poet and theorist, later served as dean of Students at Livingston College and as director of the Office of Diverse Community Affairs and Lesbian/Gay Concerns at Rutgers (renamed the Office of Social Justice Education and LGBT Communities in 2004). She also taught in the Department of Women's and Gender Studies until her retirement in 2013. Through her poetry, pedagogy, and activism, Cheryl Clarke had a significant impact on black, lesbian, and women's communities at Rutgers and beyond.

▲ MASTHEAD OF *LABRYS*, AN ALTERNATIVE FEMINIST NEWSPAPER, LAUNCHED IN 1977

Puerto Rican Student Protests

The April 3, 1970, issue of *Caellian* drew attention to the forthcoming Puerto Rican Fete, the first Puerto Rican Cultural Festival in the state of New Jersey. The event included traditional folk dances by Estampas de Borinquen and a reading of *Las Calles de Oro*, a play by Piri Thomas, who grew up in New York's El Barrio. Considering that only five Puerto Rican students had been admitted to Douglass College from 1967 to 1969, this initiative demonstrates the extraordinary leadership and determination of the student organizers. Zaida (Josie) Torres (DC '73), one of festival organizers, became a leader of the Puerto Rican student movement and worked tirelessly to secure more support for Puerto Rican students from the Douglass administration. She pressed Douglass to recruit and retain more Puerto Rican students and to hire staff of Puerto Rican ancestry. And she supported the 1969 mobilization of sixteen Puerto Rican students in the inaugural class of Livingston College, who demanded the establishment of the Program in Puerto Rican Studies.[65]

▶ PUERTO RICAN STUDENT PROTEST

In the late sixties, Puerto Rican students experienced a degree of isolation and alienation on campus similar to that of African American students. They were labeled "special admits" and perceived by some white students, faculty, and staff as ill equipped for the demands of university courses. As Diane Miranda (DC '71) noted, although she graduated 18th in a class of 410 students at her high school, she was routinely discriminated against during her years as an undergraduate student, treated as deficient "because she was a recipient of an EOF grant."[66] Disillusioned by their treatment, some students transferred to other institutions, which appeared to be less fraught with racial tension. In 1969 those who remained at Rutgers created United Puerto Rican Students (UPRS), a university-wide organization that involved students from the New Brunswick, Newark, and Camden campuses. UPRS afforded students a sense of community, solidarity, and mutual support. They met with Puerto Rican high school students and encouraged them to apply to Rutgers. UPRS also sought to increase white students' awareness of Puerto Rican culture, identity, and traditions, drawing attention to the history of Spanish and U.S. colonialism. Toward that end, Puerto Rican students at Douglass lobbied for the creation of Casa Boriqua, a residence hall that bore the name of Puerto Rico prior to colonization. As part of its co-curricular programming, Casa Boriqua offered Douglass students opportunities to learn about the arts, culture, economics, history, and politics of Puerto Rico and the complex situation of Puerto Ricans as U.S. citizens living and working in the United States.

Josie Torres (DC '73) and Virginia Class (DC '74) were leaders of Douglass Puerto Rican Students (DPRS), a UPRS chapter. Using strategies adapted from the black student protest movement, DPRS presented a list of demands to Dean Foster and Provost Richard Schlatter.[67] Noting that the EOF program offered them very little assistance, the students' demands included hiring Puerto Rican staff to work on recruitment and retention, hiring bilingual staff to assist students with academic counseling, hiring Puerto Rican faculty, developing a bilingual college prep program, and creating bilingual education training for future teachers. When neither the Douglass nor the university administration responded to these demands, DPRS worked with UPRS chapters at Rutgers, Livingston, Newark, and Camden to organize a protest, which involved forty students—a very high proportion of the Puerto Rican students enrolled at Rutgers at the time.

Partially in response to the demands of the Puerto Rican students, Douglass College inaugurated Casa Boriqua in 1972. The new residential facility located in the Corwin BB building on Nichols Avenue accommodated twenty students. Following the model and structure of the language and culture houses at Douglass, Casa Boriqua featured three house leaders: Rosalina de la Carrera, the house counselor, who was recruited because of her Puerto Rican heritage; a house chair, selected by the dean of students; and a house historian, elected by house residents. Each year, the house historian created a scrapbook documenting the house residents, activities, and media coverage. As in the language houses, Casa Boriqua included an academic component drawn from the offerings in Puerto Rican studies, while also providing Puerto Rican students a culturally rich and empowering space within the college. Residents of Casa Boriqua organized an annual cultural festival at Douglass, which attracted Puerto Ricans from all regions of New Jersey. Over time, the festival expanded to celebrate Hispanic Caribbean cultures. The 1980 festival program, for example, displayed the flags of the five nations in the Hispanic Caribbean and featured performances and food from each of these nations, with particular attention to Afro-Caribbean traditions.

In 1974, Dean Foster reported to the Board of Trustees that African American and Hispanic students constituted 12.9 percent of the Douglass student body and that "our relationships with minority students have been quite good." Despite that optimistic assessment, issues of identity and subjectivity continued to preoccupy Douglass Puerto Rican students, who were racialized and marginalized by their white peers. In the 1973–1974 house scrapbook, Lourdes Santiago (DC '77) shared her poem, "Who I Am? What I Am? Where Do I Belong?" which captures a feeling of isolation shared by Puerto Rican students.[68] Race relations continued to trouble Douglass students and *Caellian* published an issue in 1973 titled "Racial Identity Dilemma," featuring articles by Casa Boriqua residents.[69] Ivette Mendez (DC '75) authored the essay "Is It True What They Say about Those People?" Other articles addressed "mistaken identity" experienced by Puerto Rican students.[70] To alleviate some of their sense of isolation, Puerto Rican students forged alliances with African American students on campus. The *Black Voice*, originally an African American student newsletter, changed its name to *Black Voice and Carta Boriqua*, signifying the evolving coalition of minority students on campus, as racial tensions continued to erupt periodically at Douglass and other units of the university.

In 1975, for example, Michael Meyers, a Rutgers law graduate and NAACP National staff member, petitioned the Board of Governors to "abandon special-interest housing university wide." Referring specifically to the Afro-American House and Casa Boriqua on the Douglass campus and to an unofficial clustering of black students within the Livingston College dormitories, Meyers filed a complaint with the U.S. Department of Health, Education, and Welfare (DHEW) alleging that such housing segregation was discriminatory and did not advance the education of minority students. Drawing upon language developed by the cultural houses at Douglass, university president Edward Bloustein countered Meyers's allegation, declaring that Douglass's special interest houses served an academic and cultural purpose. In the words of Douglass assistant dean of students Janet Yocum, "The houses were set up to enhance Black and Puerto Rican culture study and are still fulfilling that role."[71] Nancy Richards, Douglass dean of students, affirmed that "the cultural houses, like the language houses, were established by the faculty as part of an academic program," and "its residents receive a pass-fail grade for credit and are supervised by a directress, who is either a faculty member, teaching assistant, or a graduate student."[72] After completing an investigation, the U.S. Department of Health, Education, and Welfare determined that there was no violation of equal treatment guarantees in Douglass houses. The university, however, soon ended the unofficial housing arrangement at Livingston that allowed African American students to occupy rooms in a particular wing of the residence hall.

Gay and Lesbian Student Activism

Homophobia was rife in the United States throughout the twentieth century, incorporated in laws banning certain same-sex erotic practices and relationships. Accusations of homosexuality could cost one a job, a house or an apartment, or even one's freedom. In the early sixties, it was particularly difficult for gay and lesbian students to locate a community of support on or off campus. As Elizabeth Fraenkel (NJC '44) noted, when she "came out" in 1962 "after working as a scientist in industry for almost 20 years," she was not aware of any lesbian networks or organizations. Although the New York chapter of Daughters of Bilitis (DOB) had been in existence since 1958, it was unknown to Fraenkel. As a lesbian, keenly aware of her own "oppression," Fraenkel "joined the only group then in existence: the civil rights movement." She later became involved in DOB, serving in various capacities before becoming a lesbian counselor, a role that enabled her to help lesbians achieve a healthy and happy attitude toward their sexual orientation.[73]

As the civil rights, antiwar, and women's liberation movements swept the nation, the policing of sexuality and the criminalization of homosexuality came under increasing scrutiny by young, left-leaning activists. As a new counterculture began to flourish, "sexual minorities" created clandestine spaces to gather and forge supportive ties. When police raided the Stonewall Inn on Christopher Street in Greenwich Village in the early morning hours of June 28, 1969, they encountered a series of spontaneous, violent demonstrations by members of the gay community in protest of prolonged harassment. The Stonewall riots marked a turning point in the struggle for gay and lesbian rights, as proponents of "gay liberation" demanded the same constitutional protections afforded heterosexual citizens.[74]

In 1969, several months after Stonewall, Lionel Cuffie (RC '69) established the Rutgers Student Homophile League (RSHL), the first gay student organization in the nation. An African American who had been an active member of the Youth International Party, an offshoot of the free speech and antiwar movements, Cuffie turned his skills as a grassroots organizer to the issues of gay rights. Serving for two years as the chair of RSHL, Cuffie developed a vibrant organization that sought to challenge homophobia at Rutgers. Although Rutgers gay men composed the majority of members, lesbian students at Douglass, Livingston, and Rutgers Colleges became involved with the organization and its activities, helping to organize dances; staffing the advice hotline; running peer support groups and public engagements; and attending the numerous "coffeehouses," which attracted students and members of the larger New Brunswick community.[75]

Modeling its activism on the black student movement, RSHL organized marches, teach-ins, sit-ins, and other forms of public demonstrations to protest discrimination on the basis of sexual orientation and to topple common stereotypes. The RSHL's priorities also included the creation of a social space for its members and outreach to the community that marginalized gay and lesbians. In spring 1971, RSHL hosted the university's first Gay Liberation Conference, which featured the best-known lesbian and gay activists in the country, including Barbara Gittings of the Homophile Action League, Franklin Kameny of the Washington Mattachine Society, Barbara Love of DOB, and Isabel Miller, the author of *A Place of Us*. Attracting more than two hundred students, the conference presented twenty-two sessions on the gay liberation movement, gay lives, and strategies to promote equality for gays and lesbians at Rutgers and beyond.

Building on the success of the first conference, RSHL sponsored annual conferences to affirm the rights of gay and lesbian students and increase their visibility on campus. During the festivities of RSHL's fourth anniversary in 1973, there was a performance by lesbian a cappella group the Oral Tradition, featuring two Douglass students, Nancy Dean and Paula Schoor (both DC '74), and two Douglass alumnae, Joanna Labow (DC '70) and Kay Turner (DC '71). In 1974, the first Blue Jeans Day was launched in conjunction with the fourth annual conference to encourage gay and straight people to wear jeans to show solidarity with gays and lesbians. The conference included workshops designed to address lesbian and gay issues, such as "The Lesbian Mother and the Law," led by Anne Elwell; "Lesbian Separatism," led by Julia P. Stanley; and "Queens' Liberation," led by Bebe Scarpie, and lectures by Jeanne and Jules Manford, the founders of the organization Parents of Gays. The conference drew nearly three hundred attendees to the workshops and five hundred to the Saturday night dance.[76]

From its earliest days on campus, RSHL encountered significant hostility. In September 1970, pamphlets calling for the creation of the Rutgers Student Heterophile League belittled the issues that LGBT students confronted on campus. In April 1976, members of the Delta Kappa Epsilon fraternity hung the first of a series of gay effigies in front of their house on College Avenue, accompanied by homophobic signs ("Homos Back in Your Closet," "The Only Good Gay is a Dead Gay"). Although RSHL petitioned the university to take action against such menacing conduct, the university did nothing. In December 1977, following additional anti-gay eruptions on College Avenue, the Rutgers Student Government Association passed a resolution urging the "Administration to establish more visible means of reaching out to help gay students realize a more positive environment at Rutgers." Again, the university made no response. On April 23, 1979, during a demonstration for gay and lesbian rights on the College Avenue campus, a gay graduate student was struck in the head by a rock thrown from a fraternity house, but the university took no action.[77]

In the absence of interventions by the university administration, RSHL (later renamed Rutgers Gay Alliance [RGA]), forged relations with other progressive campus groups and individuals, including students from Douglass, who participated in events typically held on the College Avenue campus. RSHL cultivated political ties with the Livingston Feminist Coalition, and later with Douglass Feminist Collective, coordinating campus demonstrations and co-sponsoring dances and other events. Although the radical organization College Avenue Feminist Terrorists (CAFT), was not formally affiliated with RSHL, it had strong personal ties with some of the RGA members. Ingrid Wilhite (RU '82), for example, was a CAFT member living in Demarest Hall, known as a "hotbed of homosexuality" during this time.[78] In addition to creating the Pheminist Phunnies for the Douglass *Caellian*, Wilhite served on the board of RGA.[79] Inspired by radical feminism, CAFT staged protests against sexism. Their most famous action was a bomb threat called into a fraternity house that was showing pornographic films as a fund-raiser. CAFT also disrupted a pornographic film showing at Scott Hall by spraying ammonia throughout the facility.

As collaborations with lesbian groups became more frequent, RSHL renamed itself the Rutgers University Lesbian & Gay Alliance (RULGA).[80] RULGA co-sponsored an annual Gay/Lesbian Awareness Week, and an annual Black and White Dance, which attracted students from colleges and universities across New Jersey. They also co-sponsored film showings (e.g., Pink Triangles) and protests, such as Women Against

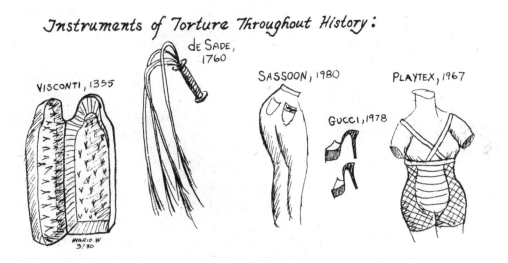

▲ INGRID WILHITE'S "PHEMINIST PHUNNIES." *CAELLIAN*, MARCH 26, 1981, P.3

Pornography, designed to disseminate the message "Pornography is not harmless entertainment. Pornography is propaganda against women." In addition to their collaborative programs with RULGA, Douglass lesbians published journals, such as *The Furies, The Common Woman: A Journal of Feminist Literature*, and *Beyond Polarities: A Student Handbook on Queer Issues for All*, and they contributed to Amazon Space, a weekly column published at Livingston by the Rutgers Coalition of Lesbian Feminists. RULGA became increasingly engaged with issues of gender violence against gays and lesbians, and in fall of 1983, it co-sponsored a controversial program with the Gay Men's Health Crisis in New York and the Rutgers Department of Health Education about the new threat of AIDS.[81]

Following intensive RULGA lobbying for more than a decade, in February 1988 President Bloustein appointed the President's Select Committee on Gay and Lesbian Concerns to investigate virulent homophobic episodes on campus.[82] Noting that "passive homophobia—turning one's back on the face of injustice—had been the norm at Rutgers," the Select Committee emphasized that the University had failed to enforce its

▶ DOUGLASS
FEMINIST
COLLECTIVE,
FLIER FOR
WOMEN AGAINST
PORNOGRAPHY
SLIDE SHOW,
UNDATED
(RULGA, BOX 4)

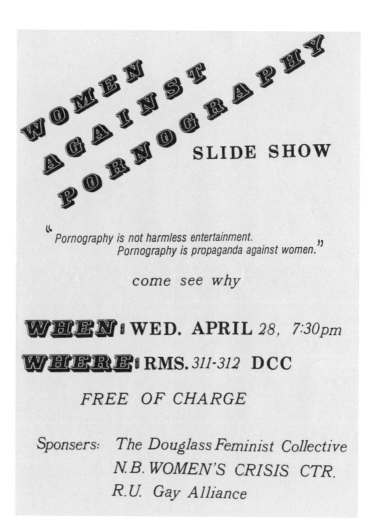

WOMEN AGAINST PORNOGRAPHY SLIDE SHOW

" *Pornography is not harmless entertainment.*
Pornography is propaganda against women. "

come see why

WHEN: WED. APRIL 28, 7:30pm

WHERE: RMS. 311-312 DCC

FREE OF CHARGE

Sponsors: The Douglass Feminist Collective
N.B. WOMEN'S CRISIS CTR.
R.U. Gay Alliance

THE

COMMON WOMAN

75c

JOURNAL OF FEMINIST LITERATURE

Volume 1   Number 1

[1977]

◀ INAUGURAL
ISSUE OF
*THE COMMON
WOMAN:
JOURNAL OF
FEMINIST
LITERATURE*

own provisions banning discrimination on the basis of sexual orientation. "To date, it is an empty promise of civil rights on paper. It is urgent that Rutgers University translate these paper-thin gay rights into institutional reality." Following its investigation of blatant homophobic discrimination on campus, the select committee published a manual, *In Every Classroom*, which identified constructive ways to ensure the equal treatment of gay and lesbian students in the educational process.[83] To implement the recommendations of the select committee, the university created the Office of Gay and Lesbian Concerns, which worked to transform the campus into an environment free of fear, violence, and harassment.[84]

Activist Transformations of Douglass College and the University

As founding dean Mabel Smith Douglass stated in her remarks at the college's tenth anniversary, "Higher education is powerfully influenced by the desires and ambitions of youth."[85] Courageous student activism from the sixties through the seventies had a powerful influence on all areas of Douglass College. Activists transformed the demographic profile of the student population; created new services; demanded new courses that would investigate the lives of women, African Americans, Puerto Ricans, gays, and lesbians; and made innovative outreach to the New Brunswick community and to women across the state. They created publications that expanded the boundaries of knowledge and introduced co-curricular programs and student organizations that have contributed to a more diverse and welcoming college environment for all students. From the standpoint of student experience, these activist initiatives have had as profound an effect on the transformation of Douglass and of the university as any "reorganization" or the state's expansion of the mission of a public institution of higher education.

CREATING KNOWLEDGE ABOUT, BY, AND FOR WOMEN

DOUGLASS COLLEGE IS THE ONLY EDUCA-
TIONAL INSTITUTION TO DATE THAT HAS
TAKEN A HOLISTIC APPROACH TO THE
ROLE OF WOMEN IN HIGHER EDUCATION
AND ITS IMPLICATION FOR SOCIETY.

—Mary Howard and Elaine Showalter, 1971

On April 24, 1970, Dean Margery Somers Foster appointed an Ad Hoc Committee on the Education of Women to survey the existing situation at Douglass College and formulate proposals for change.[1] Under the leadership of Mary Howard (sociology) and Elaine Showalter (English), the committee endorsed "a bold experiment in feminist education" that offered Douglass an "exciting opportunity to take the lead in a national re-definition of women's education."[2] The *Report of the Ad Hoc Committee on the Education of Women* is a visionary document grounded in the belief that "the first and most important step in achieving equal education for women is . . . overcoming the negative self-image of the female produced by years of conditioning by family, peers, and teachers."[3] To provide an educational milieu especially suited to the realization of women students' abilities, Douglass must not only transform the content of its curriculum but also "open up new areas of research and new interpretive approaches . . . to enlarge current knowledge."[4] Noting that academic subjects across the disciplines contain "many sex biases" that have debilitating effects on women students, the committee called for the creation of "at least five new courses . . . which deal with the experience of women," co-sponsorship of a regional conference called "Women in the Academic Community," and establishment of "centers for research on problems affecting American women."[5]

The feminist vision for women's education developed by the Ad Hoc Committee generated unprecedented programs to cultivate women's self-confidence and leadership potential, research the complexity of women's lives and livelihoods, document and celebrate the work of women artists, and develop a curriculum that would incorporate pathbreaking and paradigm-changing research on women. This chapter traces

the work of Douglass faculty and administrators to transform the known world by creating programs, centers, and institutes that produce knowledge about women: the
Center for American Women and Politics, the Mary H. Dana Women Artists Series,
the Institute for Research on Women, the Women's Studies Program, the Center
for Women's Global Leadership, the Institute for Women's Leadership, the Center
for Women and Work, and the Institute for Women and Art. Douglass dean Mary
Hartman fostered cross-fertilization between these units, generating innovative interdisciplinary projects like the New Jersey curriculum transformation project, which
worked to incorporate feminist and critical race scholarship in university curriculum
and in the public school curricula across the state by providing grants to high school
teachers to improve their teaching through adoption of these innovative materials.
Individually and collectively, these programs transformed teaching at Douglass, provided vibrant research opportunities and internships for Douglass students, and gave
new meaning to "women-centered education."

Researching Women's Lives

The *Report of the Ad Hoc Committee* challenged scholars to use their research skills to
investigate sex discrimination on campus and in all aspects of higher education. It
mapped out a transformative agenda that encompassed admissions, academic programs, student life, career counseling and job placement, maternity leave, and day care
facilities. And it engendered intensive conversations among women administrators and
faculty in New Brunswick about how to develop women's studies as a new interdisciplinary field and simultaneously improve women's status within the university and
within society. In the early 1970s, a group of Rutgers women administrators formed a
Women's Caucus, a loosely organized group that met monthly and that was convened
by Alice Evangelides, the university counsel. Other key players included Nancy Winter-
bauer, Jean Ambrose, Margaretta (Guida) West (University Extension Division), and
Adrienne Anderson (director of the Women's Center at Douglass and later chair of the
Rutgers Board of Governors). The caucus envisioned a three-pronged strategy for
women's advancement: the caucus itself would serve as the activist arm to address gender inequities on campus; a new Women's Studies Institute would be created as the
faculty base for feminist research and activism—drawing on and expanding the wom-
en's studies programs—and the Women's Center would do community outreach,
especially targeting Douglass alumnae.[6]

In 1970, three women's studies courses were taught at Douglass: two in the Department of English, The Educated Woman in Literature and The Woman Writer in the
20th Century, and one in sociology, The Role of Woman in Contemporary Society.[7]
Douglass faculty moved quickly to increase the women's studies course offerings. By
1973 Douglass had twelve courses in five disciplines.[8] It created a women's studies program and built a strong working group of faculty, who shared resources, and advised
students. By 1974, with more than fifty faculty and administrators affiliated with the

program and nineteen women students enrolled in the new certificate program, Douglass was gaining national recognition as a site for the development of feminist studies.

The *Report of the Ad Hoc Committee* stressed the significance of these courses for
women's positive self-understanding, but it went further, to suggest that interdisciplinary research on women had the potential to transform the academy itself, and urged
Douglass to be in the forefront of this new scholarly movement. Research on gender
inequity could give Douglass a distinctive role within the university. Because Douglass
led the university in women faculty (43 percent of all women faculty at the university in
1971 were employed at the college), the report insisted that Douglass had a stake in
feminist debates about discrimination, equity, and change.[9] It could give voice to wom-
en's concerns and fight to promote women's interests on campus.

To help establish the Women's Studies Institute proposed by the Women's Caucus,
feminist faculty volunteered to coordinate the initiative. Nancy Bazin, English professor and coordinator of women's studies at Rutgers College, received one course release

▲ THE *TARGUM* EMBRACES THE NEW MODEL OF WOMEN'S EDUCATION, 1971

for fall semester 1974 to organize the Women's Studies Institute. She convened the coordinators of women's studies at the undergraduate colleges (Elaine Showalter, Douglass College; Kate Ellis, Livingston College; Judith Walkowitz, University College) to establish the goals for the Women's Studies Institute. These included the creation of an interdisciplinary graduate program in women's studies, coordination of undergraduate women's studies courses, creation of a New Brunswick–wide undergraduate major in women's studies, development of a summer session in women's studies for high school teachers, and the creation of a semester exchange program that would enable students from other colleges in the United States to pursue a semester of course work in women's studies at Douglass. They also proposed that "the Institute will encourage scholarly research, organize faculty seminars, and perhaps sponsor and finance a scholarly journal."[10] Taking a leadership role in campus programming in women's studies, the Women's Studies Institute began coordinating the Rutgers University Women's Series, which had formerly been organized by the Women's Caucus.[11]

Judith R. Walkowitz, a British historian and pioneer in women's history, who served as acting director of the Women's Studies Institute in spring 1975, created a successful series of faculty-graduate student seminars, featuring papers and talks on feminist work in progress by professors in the Departments of English, Religion, Spanish, History, French, and Sociology. The seminars "helped to foster the kind of intellectual atmosphere that would encourage research and publication in Women's Studies."[12] In addition to the seminar series and coordinating women's studies course listings, Walkowitz attempted to create a women's studies certificate at Rutgers College and worked with the University Extension Division and Douglass College Women's Studies to present outreach workshops on sexism in education to parents and teachers in Central New Jersey.

Bylaws of the Women's Studies Institute of Rutgers University of New Brunswick, dated May 1975, describe the transformative objectives of the institute: "to increase opportunities for women in all areas of Women's Studies, by encouraging New Brunswick Units of the University to provide graduate and undergraduate offerings in all appropriate departments; and encourage curriculum innovation and diversity that will establish Rutgers University-New Brunswick as a nationally recognized center for Women's Studies." From its earliest days, the institute sought to be as widely inclusive as possible. It included "all members of the faculty, who hold the rank of instructor and above in the New Brunswick area, and who teach or are actively engaged in research in the area of women's studies. . . . other interested persons could apply for associate membership."[13]

In 1975, faculty from Rutgers College, Livingston College, Douglass College, and University College wrote to Provost Kenneth Wheeler as representatives of the "incipient Rutgers University Women's Studies Institute," suggesting Mary Hartman for the position of institute coordinator. Hartman had joined the Douglass history faculty in 1968. A specialist in modern European history, she introduced the first course in women's history to be taught at the university, The Comparative Roles of Women. In 1973, she organized the first Berkshire Conference on Women's History, which convened at Douglass. Her first book, *Victorian Murderesses: A True History of Thirteen Respectable French and English Women Accused of Unspeakable Crimes* (1977), demonstrated the potential of feminist scholarship to capture the public imagination when it was chosen as a selection of the Literary Guild book club. With the provost's approval, Hartman served as director of the Women's Studies Institute from 1975 to 1977. Helped by graduate student Jack Fisher, she produced the first directory of affiliated scholars of the Women's Studies Institute and organized a speaker series. The university provided the

◀ DOUGLASS WOMEN'S
STUDIES BROCHURE, 1976

institute a telephone line and an annual budget of three hundred dollars. Jean Ambrose, assistant to Douglass dean Jewel Plummer Cobb, was instrumental in getting space for the new institute on the corner of George and Jones Streets. From its earliest days, leadership of the institute rotated among feminist faculty, forging ties between scholars in departments of history, English, and sociology. Dee Garrison, a historian who specialized in peace and labor movements, directed the institute from 1977 to 1979. She was succeeded by E. Ann Kaplan, a specialist in English literature and film studies. During her tenure, Kaplan introduced a new project for the institute, which extended Douglass's reach into the community. With funding from Title IX of the Education Amendments of 1972 and an external grant from the Women's Educational Equity Program, she developed an initiative to promote nonsexist physical education in New Jersey middle schools.

As the number of women's studies courses continued to grow, the New Brunswick Women's Caucus lobbied the university to allocate a faculty line for a full-time faculty director of the Women's Studies Program. In 1978 following a national search, Virginia Yans, whose scholarship focused on Italian immigrants to the United States in the late nineteenth and early twentieth century, was hired as the first full-time director of the Douglass Women's Studies Program with a tenure home in the history department. A division of labor emerged as the Women's Studies Institute focused more on research, grant-writing, and community outreach, and the Women's Studies Program concentrated on course development, teaching, and student advising.

The *Report of the Ad Hoc Committee on the Education of Women* urged Douglass to partner with other university units to establish centers for research on problems affecting American women, specifically mentioning the Eagleton Institute's proposal to create the Center for the American Woman and Politics. The Eagleton Institute had strong roots at Douglass. It was housed in Wood Lawn, the mansion that James Neilson (1784–1862) had donated to NJC to provide a home for the alumnae association. And it was funded by a bequest from Florence Peshine Eagleton (1870–1953), a leader in the woman suffrage movement, founder of New Jersey's League of Women Voters, an advocate for women's higher education, one of the first women to serve as a trustee of Rutgers University, and a devoted member of the Douglass Board of Managers for more than twenty years. Upon her death, she bequeathed nearly two million dollars to establish the Wells Phillips Eagleton and Florence Peshine Eagleton Foundation at Rutgers, stipulating that the funds be used to endow an institute to provide education in practical politics for "young women and men" and to foster responsible, problem-solving leadership in civic and governmental affairs.[14] Founded in 1956, the Eagleton Institute of Politics quickly established a reputation for excellence in the study of American politics, with a strong specialization in state politics and the politics of state legislatures.

In 1970, fourteen years after the creation of the Eagleton Institute, Don Herzberg, the institute's first director, appointed a prestigious advisory committee to investigate the possibility of creating a center for women and American politics. The fifty-member advisory committee, co-chaired by Lucia Heffelfinger Ballantine and Shirley Smith Anderson, included U.S. representative Martha Griffiths (one of just ten women in the House of Representatives at the time) and three women who later entered Congress, Millicent Fenwick, Helen Meyner, and Eleanor Holmes Norton; attorney/activist Harriet Pilpel; scholars such as anthropologist Margaret Mead, sociologists Suzanne Keller (the first woman to receive tenure at Princeton) and Arlie Hochschild, and feminist literary critic Elaine Showalter; union leaders Myra Wolfgang and Edith Van Horn; social activist Rachel Cowan; and New York City consumer affairs commissioner Bess Myerson. The Advisory Committee endorsed Herzberg's plan to include funding for a Center for the American Woman and Politics in a grant proposal he was preparing for the Ford Foundation. The justification Herzberg offered for the new center emphasized the systemic inequality that structured women's lives in the United States.

> In these times of resurgent minorities, it does not seem out of place that women, too, are protesting their treatment. That is, it does not seem incongruous until one recalls that they are not a minority, are indeed a majority—even as eligible voters—and thus, curiously enough, those who protest must consider themselves part of an oppressed majority. Women in the United States make 60 cents for every $1.00 a man makes; they do not benefit from fair employment practices acts because these laws do not recognize discrimination on the basis of sex; when employed outside the home they still perform the housekeeping duties; they are nurses but not doctors, secretaries but not executives, researchers but not writers, workers but not managers. They are almost non-existent in government; they almost never hold policy- or decision-making positions. One does not have to be a Feminist to acknowledge these facts or to realize the importance of examining their significance. Some would hold that the position of women has not changed since the Code of Hammurabi.[15]

The Ford Foundation provided a two-year grant of fifty thousand dollars to launch the first center in the nation established to study women's political participation. Herzberg consulted Dean Margery Somers Foster for advice in staffing the new center. Foster recommended Ida F. S. Schmertz, who, following the assassinations of Martin Luther King and Robert Kennedy in 1968, had devoted two years to the successful creation of the National Organization for Gun Control.[16] To supplement Schmertz's acumen in political organizing, Herzberg recruited Ruth B. Mandel, a scholar specializing in women's writing in the Victorian era. As co-directors, Mandel and Schmertz officially launched the Center for the American Woman and Politics (CAWP) in July 1971, devoting their intellectual energies to creating the center's mission and programs at a time when only one book had been written on the topic, Martin Gruberg's *Women in American Politics* (1968). Their first task was to identify and study women elected officials to discover who they were, what offices they held, whether and how their paths to elective office differed from those of their male counterparts, what interests they hoped to serve, how they understood their relationship to women citizens, and what challenges they faced as women in positions of political power. Because governments at most levels did not (and in many cases still do not) maintain data about officeholders by sex, CAWP developed the National Information Bank on Women in Public Office, which includes information on current and past women officeholders and candidates; provides demographic and political data on individual officeholders; and analyzes trends in women's political participation, particularly at state and national levels. CAWP published the first national directories and statistical profiles of women in public office in the late 1970s.[17]

CAWP's early projects included a national conference for women state legislators in May 1972, which laid the groundwork for a study of women state legislators. CAWP recruited political scientist Jeane J. Kirkpatrick (who later became the first woman to serve as U.S. ambassador to the United Nations) to design a study that combined data gathered at the conference with additional research on politically active women, including the delegates to the 1972 Democratic and Republican National Conventions. Kirkpatrick's findings were published in her *Political Woman* (1974). In addition to

Presentation of WIPO II   White House   fall 1978

▲ SARAH WEDDINGTON (CENTER) HOLDING *WOMEN IN PUBLIC OFFICE: A BIOGRAPHICAL DIRECTORY AND STATISTICAL ANALYSIS* (1978), PRESENTED BY CAWP DIRECTOR RUTH B. MANDEL, ACCOMPANIED BY RUTGERS PRESIDENT EDWARD J. BLOUSTEIN

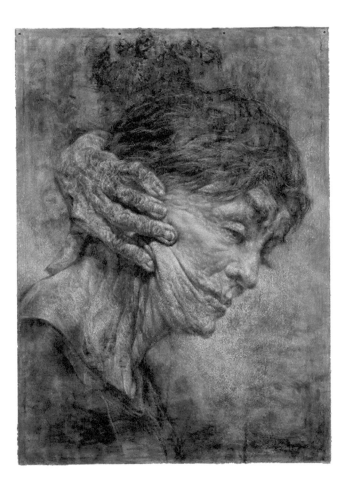

◄ MARGARET (BAILEY) DOOGAN, *FIVE-FINGERED SMILE*, 2010. CHARCOAL ON PRIMED PAPER, 72 X 52 INCHES. COLLECTION OF THE TUCSON MUSEUM OF ART. USED BY PERMISSION.

documenting the critical roles women were playing in American political life, Kirkpatrick's research indicated the range of inequities confronting women in the American polity, concluding that "for women to achieve de facto political equality . . . both a cultural and a social revolution are required."[18] Kirkpatrick's study was the first of a series of important research projects conducted by CAWP to investigate the political behavior of American women, the routes to power for aspiring women officeholders, women's issue agendas, and the impact of women in elective offices.

Echoing ongoing campus discussions about the underrepresentation of women artists in museum collections, the art market, and the Douglass art department, the *Report of the Ad Hoc Committee* also recommended that Douglass launch an annual Symposium on Women and the Arts to celebrate the achievements of women artists and investigate their relation to feminism.[19] The report envisioned a symposium that would include performances by feminist theater groups and women musicians; exhibitions of works by women painters and sculptors, panel discussions, poetry readings, and lectures. Feminist artist and Douglass alumna Joan Snyder (DC '62) had been lobbying for several years for just such a celebration of women artists. In spring 1971, she worked with Douglass Library director Daisy Brightenback Shenholm (NJC '44) to launch a Women Artists Series that would make visible the work of emerging and estab-lished contemporary women artists.[20] The series inaugurated an annual curated show at the Mabel Smith Douglass Library. Later renamed the Mary H. Dana Women Artists Series in memory of Dana (NJC '42), the series was initially coordinated by Lynn F. Miller.[21] During its first twenty-five years, close to two hundred artists, both acclaimed and emerging, exhibited their works in the Douglass Library gallery space, which has become the oldest continuously running exhibition space for women artists in the United States.[22] To recognize the momentousness of that accomplishment, in 1986, the Women's Caucus for Art of the College Art Association bestowed a Lifetime Achieve-ment Award on the series, the only time that the award was given to an organization rather than to a woman.

Changing Institutions

By the early 1980s, women's studies faculty at Douglass were gaining national and inter-national acclaim for their pathbreaking scholarship. The research and outreach programs of CAWP and the Women's Studies Institute were winning Rutgers a transnational reputation as a leader in feminist research. Under the direction of historian Phyllis Mack, the institute introduced the Annual Celebration of Our Work, a conference that attracted feminist scholars and activists from across the Northeast to discuss new direc-tions in feminist scholarship. During 1980–1981, the Women's Studies Institute was reorganized and renamed the Institute for Research on Women (IRW).[23] In addition, in early 1981, an ad hoc Nominating Committee (Judith Gerson, Ann Kaplan, Domna Stanton, and Ginny Yans) wrote to the provost to recommend the appointment of Catharine Stimpson, professor of English and founding editor of *Signs: Journal of Women in Culture and Society*, as the next director of the institute.[24] Pressing for a sig-nificant increase in funding, the Nominating Committee also endorsed the appointment of Domna Stanton, a scholar of seventeenth-century and early modern French studies, as associate director.[25] The strategy worked and both were appointed.

In 1984, the IRW expanded its mission. The new purpose was to "advance the development of Rutgers University as an internationally known center for women's studies; and to support and sponsor scholarship and research on topics pertaining to women, including attention to inequities and their implications for changes in policies, institutions, attitudes, and social structure."[26] Toward that end, the IRW expanded its membership, reaching out to faculty, graduate students, and staff on the Camden, New-ark and New Brunswick campuses of Rutgers, who "through their teaching or research demonstrate an active interest in women's studies."[27] The revised bylaws indicated the IRW would "forge links across disciplines among scholars, activists, and practitioners."[28] By 1985, the IRW had secured increased funding from the university, including a half line for Executive Officer Ferris Olin (DC '70), who served in that capacity until 1994.

During Catharine Stimpson's four-year term as director, the IRW entered a new stage of institutionalization. To heighten the profile of the IRW both on campus and on the national stage, Stimpson chose an intellectual theme each year as a focal point for visiting lectures and a national conference as well as research and grant-writing. For example, in 1986, women's labor, waged and unwaged, was the theme. With support from the Russell Sage Foundation, Stimpson partnered with economist Lourdes Beneria to organize a national conference on women and the economy, which generated their coedited volume, *Women, Households, and the Economy* (1987).[29] She inaugurated the annual Thinking about Women lecture series, which brought eminent scholars to Douglass to share their work. She won a three-year Rockefeller Humanists-in-Residence grant, which brought leading feminist researchers to Rutgers to nurture the burgeoning feminist intellectual community on campus.

The Rockefeller Humanists-in-Residence grant to the IRW created a new legitimacy for feminist scholarship. The grant from one of America's most important foundations sent a clear signal that women's studies was coming of age and that Douglass was helping to shape this new interdisciplinary field. The competitive faculty fellowships, which were advertised nationally, provided salary and benefits for two promising academics each year to come to Rutgers to pursue their research. While in residence, the Rockefeller scholars shared their research questions and findings with faculty and students, stimulating exciting intellectual debates, which fueled future research not only by the visiting scholars but also by Rutgers faculty and graduate students. The Rockefeller grant also enabled the IRW to support research involving historically disadvantaged groups. For example, Rockefeller fellows included Mae Henderson (now professor of English, University of North Carolina, Chapel Hill), whose project was titled "A Form for Their Fictions: A Study of Black Women's Narrative, 1859–1985"; Barbara Bair (currently associate editor of the Jane Addams Papers at Duke University and historian in the Manuscript Division of the Library of Congress), whose research resulted in "Our Women and What They Think: Amy Jacques Garvey and the Negro World"; and Veena Talwar Oldenburg (currently professor of history, Baruch College and CUNY Graduate Center), whose Rockefeller project, "Death by Dowry," challenged orientalist conceptions of dowry murder by tracing the complicity of British colonialism in the emergence of the practice.

In addition to generating innovative research on the lives, literatures, and social practices of diverse racial, ethnic, and national groups, the IRW used the Rockefeller grants to support the emerging field of feminist science studies, supporting the work of Londa Schiebinger (now John L. Hinds Professor of the History of Science at Stanford) in her project, "The Sexuality of Plants," and Carole S. Vance (now associate research scientist and clinical professor, sociomedical sciences, Mailman School of Public Health, Columbia University), in her project, "A Vagina Surrounded by a Woman: Sex, Gender, and Symbolic Conflict in the Attorney General's Commission on Pornography (1985–1986)." The Rockefeller grant also created space for scholars whose work challenged dominant paradigms in literary criticism, such as Felicity Nussbaum (currently Distinguished Professor of English, University of California, Los Angeles), who devoted

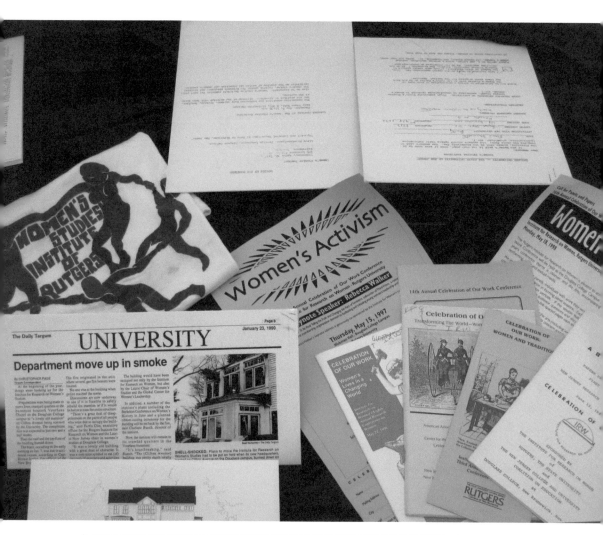

▲ PUBLICITY MATERIALS DEVELOPED BY THE WOMEN'S STUDIES INSTITUTE, RENAMED THE INSTITUTE FOR RESEARCH ON WOMEN (IRW) IN 1980

her year as a Rockefeller fellow to "Rethinking Eighteenth-Century Autobiography: Gendered Subjects." Through the Rockefeller fellowships, the IRW helped craft an expansive approach to feminist scholarship that encompassed critical race studies, postcolonial studies, and science studies—a breadth that has continued to inform the women's studies curriculum at Douglass.

During Carol H. Smith's tenure as IRW director, 1986–1992, the institute launched an ambitious effort to transform the curriculum in schools and colleges throughout the state by integrating new scholarship on race, gender, and ethnicity. The New Jersey Department of Higher Education provided funds to carry out faculty development and "gender integration projects" at colleges across the state. Through the "New Jersey Project," Carol Smith worked with Ferris Olin to develop materials and organize statewide conferences and workshops that presented pathbreaking scholarship to large audiences.

They also created an annual two-week summer residential institute for faculty teams from nine state colleges and nineteen county colleges in New Jersey. The summer institutes created an intensive forum for the sustained presentation of "state-of-the-art knowledge of gender research in a wide spectrum of disciplines provided by leaders in their fields."[30] New Jersey chancellor of higher education T. Edward Hollander (1977– 1990) described the New Jersey Project as a "quiet revolution" in the state's education. To share the content of the institute with wider audiences, Carol Smith and Ferris Olin published an overview of the proceedings of the first three years, *The New Jersey Project: Integrating the Scholarship on Gender 1986–1989*.[31] In 1987, English professor and Douglass Fellow Cheryl Wall organized a national conference on black women writers, featuring Paule Marshall as the keynote speaker, which culminated in the collection *Changing Our Own Words: Essays on Criticism, Theory, and Writing by Black Women* (1989), a major contribution to the emerging field of black feminist studies. In addition to bringing innovative scholarship to classrooms across the state, the New Jersey Project enabled the IRW to create a network of feminist scholars across the state, which proved vital in sustaining the New Jersey Project for more than two decades.

As more scholars were coming to Douglass to participate in and contribute to a growing world of feminist and critical race scholarship, Mary Hartman, then dean of Douglass, and Joan Burstyn, director of women's studies, secured a three-year grant from the Fund for the Improvement of Post-Secondary Education to develop a junior year program in women's studies at Douglass. Under the leadership of Ellen Mappen, students from Appalachian State University, Bard College, Butler University, Goucher College, Hamilton College, LeMoyne College, Southwestern University, St. Andrews College, University of Massachusetts–Amherst, University of Missouri–St. Louis, University of Wisconsin–La Cross, and Wesleyan University came to Douglass to take women's studies courses, complete internships at CAWP, and take advantage of the rich co-curricular programs like the Mary H. Dana Women Artists Series and the IRW lecture series.[32]

In the second half of the 1980s, feminist faculty formed Gender Groups in literary criticism, history, and the social sciences (political science, sociology and anthropology), which brought faculty and graduate students together to discuss work on women and gender in an interdisciplinary context. The New Jersey Department of Higher Education funded a grant to review and revise the introductory interdisciplinary women's studies course. Under the direction of Judith Gerson, faculty and graduate students developed an innovative syllabus for use in all sections of the introductory course, which in turn stimulated a broad revision of the women studies major.

In 1987, internationally renowned feminist theorist and activist Charlotte Bunch was recruited to the Laurie New Jersey Chair in Women Studies at Douglass College. Long before transnational feminist activism had become a field of scholarly investigation within women's studies, Charlotte Bunch was inventing the practice. While many feminist activists in the United States restricted their focus to national issues, Bunch

▲ MARY HARTMAN, CAROL SMITH, AND CHERYL WALL

began mapping the benefits of transnational activism in the late 1970s. Capitalizing upon the conferences organized by the United Nations in conjunction with the Decade for Women, Bunch began forging networks of feminist activists around the globe. Teaching women's studies courses in Peru, Chile, and the Dominican Republic and presenting workshops in Nairobi, India, and Sri Lanka, Bunch gained an international reputation for innovative approaches linking feminist theory with activism especially around questions concerning violence against women in general and trafficking in women in particular. Through these efforts, Bunch began framing women's issues, particularly violence against women, as human rights issues, a strategy that she continued exploring in her years as the Laurie Chair. Interest in and excitement about this project created the impetus for the creation of the Center for Women's Global Leadership (Global Center).

Recognizing the critical importance of Bunch's feminist theory and activism on the global scene, Douglass dean Mary Hartman and CAWP director Ruth Mandel began conversations with Bunch about the possibility of remaining at Rutgers on a permanent basis and launching a center that would work on women's leadership internationally. With the enthusiastic support of the faculty of the Women's Studies Program, Dean Hartman secured the agreement of President Bloustein to retain Bunch on the faculty for an additional year as planning for the Global Center continued.

To launch the Global Center, Dean Hartman suggested that the center be introduced as a project of Douglass College and she promised to assist Bunch in seeking additional university support. In 1988 Dean Hartman presented the idea of the Global Center to Rutgers University president Edward Bloustein, who agreed to the idea in principle and authorized the allocation of funds to provide some staff assistance. With these funds, Bunch hired several international graduate students to work on various Global Center initiatives. Associate Provost Barbara Callaway worked with the dean and faculty of the newly founded Bloustein School of Public Policy to secure a tenured faculty appointment and a reduced teaching load for Bunch to enable her to assume the responsibilities of founding director of the center. With these pieces in place, the Global Center was officially founded as a project of Douglass College in 1989 with the mission of developing and facilitating women's leadership for women's human rights and social justice worldwide.

As one of her first actions, Bunch formed a Rutgers-based policy committee to shape the mission of the center and to devise strategies to realize this mission. The committee included scholars with expertise on all major regions of the globe: Abena Busia (Africa), Lourdes Bueno and Roxanna Carrillo (Latin America), Niamh Reilly (Western Europe), Mary Hartman and Ruth Mandel (North America), Joanna Regulska (Eastern and Central Europe), and Heisoo Shin (Asia). The scope of the Global Center's early initiatives was broad; it included Global Gatherings at Douglass to raise awareness about women's human rights around the world, an International Planning Meeting, the Women's Global Leadership Institute (WGLI), a publications series, and the development of a global feminist resource center.

In May 1990, women's rights activists from all regions of the globe came to Douglass for an International Planning Meeting to discuss a range of possible initiatives for the Global Center in the years ahead, including mobilizing under the rubric of "women's rights as human rights." Coordinated by Roxanna Carrillo, the International Planning Meeting drew twenty-one women from various regions and backgrounds to identify activities that could provide the greatest benefit for women and for women's rights activism in their local areas. They were particularly concerned with strategic questions: how to make violations of women's rights a public policy priority both globally and within existing nation-states, how to develop international awareness of the devastating effects of violence against women, and how to design an international campaign that could be used by local activists to pressure their own governments to address violence against women.

Through discussions at the WGLI, the Global Center began to define its major projects. As one strategy to build awareness about gender-based violence and facilitate networking among women leaders working in this area, for example, the WGLI participants established the "16 Days of Activism Against Gender Violence Campaign," choosing to symbolically link November 25 (International Day Against Violence Against Women) and December 10 (International Human Rights Day). As a prime illustration of how local activism translates into global action, more than 5,167 organizations in 187 countries have organized activities around the 16 Days Campaign, generating significant international attention to the issue of gender-based violence.

A worldwide petition drive urging the United Nations to recognize women's rights as human rights was launched in 1991 as part of the 16 Days Campaign. Professor Bunch targeted the UN World Conference on Human Rights to be held in Vienna in June 1993 as the appropriate global forum through which to take the campaign for women's rights as human rights to a larger public arena. In preparation for the Vienna meeting, women's rights activists collected signatures through two cycles of the 16 Days Campaign and launched a series of other innovative strategies to bring visibility to this issue in both regional and global planning meetings for the conference. By the time of the Vienna World Conference, approximately half a million signatures from over eighty countries had been collected. When such overwhelming evidence of world concern with violence against women was presented to the Human Rights Office at the UN and to the World Conference, the massive number of signatures along with the other advocacy initiatives helped secure the international consensus that "women's rights are human rights," which was formally articulated in the Vienna Declaration in 1993.

During its first twenty-five years, the Center for Women's Global Leadership made significant contributions to global feminist activism and policy making in the area of human rights. It played a crucial role in initiating and shaping the global movement for women's rights as human rights. The center trained a generation of women leaders from all regions of the globe to use the human rights framework to achieve strategic objectives. It engaged in campaigns, tribunals, networking, and strategic planning around the United Nations World Conferences on Women; Human Rights; Population; and Against Racism, Xenophobia, and Related Intolerance, helping to set the agenda for global women's activism. The Global Center, now co-directed by Radhika Balakrishnan and Krishanti Dharmaraj, continues to be consulted by many UN agencies and interna-

▲ CHARLOTTE BUNCH AND NIAMH REILLY OF THE CENTER FOR WOMEN'S GLOBAL LEADERSHIP, ACCOMPANIED BY MEERA SINGH (INTERNATIONAL WOMEN'S TRIBUNE CENTER) AND DOREEN BOYD (WORLD YWCA), DELIVER PETITIONS FROM AROUND THE WORLD TO THE UNITED NATIONS DEMANDING THAT THE UN WORLD CONFERENCE ON HUMAN RIGHTS RECOGNIZE WOMEN'S RIGHTS AS HUMAN RIGHTS

tional leaders and activists on a wide array of women's rights issues, most notably, how to use economic and social rights as a frame for poverty elimination.

The growth and success of women's studies, CAWP, the IRW, and the Global Center brought national and international prominence to Douglass College and to Rutgers. The extraordinary work of the Douglass-based centers and institutes captured university attention as well. In 1996, the university's strategic plan, A New Vision for Excellence, identified gender studies as one of twelve university-wide "areas of excellence." Yet how to convert this recognition into palpable resources for the women's programs was an intensely debated topic at Douglass.

The heads of the various units, including Ruth Mandel, Carol Smith, Ferris Olin, Cora Kaplan, Alice Kessler-Harris, and Charlotte Bunch, began meeting regularly in the late 1980s to explore possibilities for the future and to work collaboratively to address challenges. Convened by Mary Hartman, the dean of Douglass College, this "Think Tank Committee" crafted a vision for women's education that would build on established success and address the next great challenge for women—advancing to leadership and decision-making positions in all arenas. This vision was the impetus for the creation of the Institute for Women's Leadership (IWL).

Conceived as a means to amplify the voices and trumpet the accomplishments of its constitutive units (Douglass College, Women's Studies, CAWP, the IRW, and the Global Center) and foster women's leadership at local, state, national, and global levels, the IWL adopted the advancement of women's leadership in education, politics, the workplace, and the world as a unifying theme. Officially launched in 1991, the IWL Board of Directors comprised the directors and associate directors of the constitutive units, including the dean and associate dean of Douglass College.

Through the synergies developed within the IWL board, Douglass took a "global" turn, a decade before other colleges and universities. Women's Studies director Alice Kessler Harris initiated a systematic review of the curriculum to increase the global content. With the support of a grant from the Ford Foundation, Women's Studies consulted with outside experts about the best means to "globalize" the curriculum and devise pedagogical strategies to assist U.S. women's studies students to learn about the complexities of globalization. The grant generated new requirements for Women's Studies majors and minors, including a course on comparative feminisms, and a revised text for the introductory course that had a global focus, as well as a proposal for an master's program that focused on transnational feminism. An external review of Women's Studies in 1994 ranked the program as one of the top three in the United States. With this affirmation, the faculty began planning for a PhD program and department status. In 2001, the university authorized the creation of a Department of Women's and Gender Studies, and the president and the Board of Governors approved the creation of the PhD program in women's and gender studies, one of eighteen in North America. From 2005 to 2014 under the editorship of Mary Hawkesworth, the department served as the editorial home of Signs: Journal of Women in Culture and Society, the leading journal in interdisciplinary feminist studies. With editorial offices in the basement of Voorhees Chapel, *Signs* involved four to five Douglass students in the work of the journal each semester through work-study jobs and internships.

The IRW also developed global themes and initiatives. During her term as director of the IRW, Cora Kaplan (1992–1995) worked with the IWL to strengthen the IRW's international visibility by featuring internationally acclaimed feminist speakers and inviting visiting scholars from abroad for year-long residencies at the Institute. Partnering with Joan Scott at the Institute for Advanced Studies in Princeton, Kaplan coedited *Transitions, Environments, Translations: Feminisms in International Politics* (1997), which includes innovative scholarship generated within the IRW seminar. Marianne De-Koven (1995–1998) secured a second four-year Rockefeller Humanists-in-Residence grant, which again brought outstanding scholars to Douglass and which provided enhanced support for the IRW seminar. Incorporating scholarship presented at the IRW during her years as director, DeKoven published *Feminist Locations: Local and Global, Theory and Practice* (2001) and produced a volume in the IRW Working Papers series, *Power, Practice, and Agency* (1999). Bonnie Smith (1998–2001) won support from the National Endowment for the Humanities to conduct a prestigious NEH Summer Institute for High School Teachers at Douglass to foster integration of global and transnational feminist research into high school curricula. Working with IRW associate director Beth Hutchinson, Smith also produced *Modes of Knowledge and Action: Working Papers from the Women in the Public Sphere Seminar* (1998–1999) and published *Gendering Disability* (2004). Dorothy Sue Cobble (2001–2004) initiated a series of conversations between scholars and activists, focusing on gendered inequities in the workplace, labor struggles within immigrant communities, and the role of class in contemporary American society, which culminated in the publication of a special issue of the *Journal of International Labor and Working-Class History* titled "Working Class Subjectivities and Sexualities" (spring 2006) and a book, *The Sex of Class: Women Transforming American Labor* (2007). Nancy Hewitt (2004–2007) offered the annual IRW seminars Diversity: Expanding Theory and Practice; Diasporas and Migrations; and Health and Bodies—covering issues of increasing concern in this era of globalization—and published *No Permanent Waves: Recasting Histories of U.S. Feminism* (2010). Dorothy Hodgson (2007–2010) explored women's rights as human rights and the prospects for gender justice, publishing *Gender and Culture at the Limit of Rights* (2011). Yolanda Martínez-San Miguel (2010–2013) broke new ground with the seminar's focus on critical sexualities, embodiment, and transgender scholarship, culminating in the publication of *Trans Studies: The Challenge to Hetero/Homo Normativities* (2016). Nicole Fleetwood (2013–2016) chose themes engaging the intersections of race, class, gender, and sexuality, offering Decolonizing Gender/Gendering Decolonization; Feminist Optics: Gender and Visual Culture; and Poverty.

In 1993, the IWL expanded its membership with the creation of the Center for Women and Work (CWW), which was the inspiration of Dorothy Sue Cobble, a professor of labor studies, women's studies, and history. An expert in women's labor history, Cobble was keenly attuned to changes in employment and work practices under globalization. Having been active in the national movement to make higher education more accessible to low-income and union workers, Cobble had helped to create residential institutes at Douglass to provide educational opportunities to low-income and union women. Envisioning CWW as a mechanism to build upon and enhance these forms of university outreach and assistance, Cobble worked with Sue Schurman, director of Extension Programs in the Labor Education Department, to develop a proposal for CWW and to enlist support from John Burton, director of the Institute of Management and Labor Relations (later renamed the School of Management and Labor Relations).

"Dedicated to advancing the needs of working women, both in the U.S. and internationally, through the development of relevant research, education and public policy," CWW during Cobble's term as director organized conferences, symposia, residential institutes, and noncredit educational programs open to the public. The inaugural public forum, "The Glass Ceiling and Beyond" (November 17, 1993), featured a lecture by Joyce Miller, executive director, U.S. Department of Labor's Glass Ceiling Commission, and former president of the Coalition of Labor Union Women. The forum also included the release of a new series of studies on working women in New Jersey, called NJ WomenCount, and panel presentations by Gloria Bonilla Santiago, director of the Hispanic Women's Leadership Institute; Marlene Kim, Labor Education Department at Rutgers; and Alice Kessler-Harris, director of Women's Studies and author of *A Woman's Wage* (1990).

Barbara Lee, professor in the School of Labor and Management Relations and an expert on sex discrimination law, became the CWW director in 1996. In addition to releasing *Boxed In and Breaking Out: New Jersey Women and Work in the 1990s*, the second report of the NJ WomenCount series, Lee developed a publicly accessible database on working women, which documented women's changing status in the labor force. Through a series of meetings with state legislators and Henry Plotkin, executive director of the New Jersey State Employment and Training Commission, Lee secured funds to construct the database on working women in New Jersey. Working collaboratively with state government, CWW was named the "research arm" of the newly established Council on Gender Parity in Labor and Education, which was created by the legislature to provide gender equity in labor, education, and training. As CWW's research became increasingly visible across the state, it also sponsored public programs on campus. To commemorate the landmark sex discrimination lawsuit on behalf of six hundred women at the *New York Times*, CWW sponsored a symposium, "20 Years Later: Women's Progress in Journalism Since *Boylan v. The New York Times*" and organized a lecture, "Affirmative Action and Meritocracy: Myths and Realities," by Harvard sociologist Barbara Reskin.

Eileen Appelbaum became the director of CWW in 2002. An internationally known expert on gendered workplace practices, work/family policy, and labor market experiences of women, Appelbaum had served as director of research for the Economic Policy Institute in Washington, DC. Under Appelbaum's leadership, CWW developed a wide range of interventions to enhance women's equality in the workforce and identify best practices to promote racial and gender diversity within organizations. Working with the New Jersey Department of Labor with the support of the Women's Bureau at the U.S. Department of Labor, Employment, and Training Administration, CWW explored the potential for online educational programs to enhance the skills and the quality of employment of single working mothers. In a project led by Mary Gatta, CWW developed an online curriculum to help 128 low-income women develop their capacity to work in information technology and thereby increase their incomes. The online pedagogy enabled the participants to complete the program, while working full time, raising children, and dealing with the many demands in their lives. The pilot project was so successful in helping women escape poverty that the Alfred P. Sloan Foundation provided CWW with a grant of nine hundred thousand dollars to replicate the program in other states. The results of this innovative research were published in Mary Gatta's *Not Just Getting By: The New Era of Flexible Workforce Development* (2005).

Sociologist Dana Britton became director of CWW in 2013. An expert on gender and work and gender and social control, she expanded CWW's research to examine work/life balance issues and to investigate inequities in academic employment. Under the auspices of a grant from NSF ADVANCE PAID (Partnerships for Adaptation, Implementation, and Dissemination), CWW conducted a national study of gendered transitions from associate professor to full professor for faculty in science fields.

The final research institute anticipated by Douglass's Ad Hoc Committee on the Education of Women took women and art as its focus. Longtime curator of the Mary H. Dana Women Artists Series and founding director of the Margery Somers Foster Center at the Douglass Library Ferris Olin and Mason Gross professor of art and founder of the Rutgers Center for Innovative Print and Paper Judith Brodsky strategized for two decades to create the Institute for Women and Art (IWA). In 2004 in preparation for the thirty-fifth anniversary of the Dana Women Artists Series, they began planning a Year of Women Artists celebration that would feature curated exhibits in Camden, Newark, and New Brunswick. Learning of these exciting developments, several major figures in the feminist art world, including Judy Chicago, Arlene Raven, and Susan Fisher Sterling, approached Olin and Brodsky about ways to capitalize on Douglass's role as a center for feminist art. Advancing a proposal for what would become IWA, Olin and Brodsky met with Isabel Nazario, then Rutgers associate vice president for academic and public partnerships in the arts and humanities, and vice president for academic affairs Philip Furmanski. They suggested that the IWA should continue long-established Douglass programs like the Dana Women Artists Series and the Women Artists Archives National Directory, which Olin had created with support from the Getty Foundation, while also coordinating new initiatives such as the administrative offices of the Women's Caucus for Art, the Feminist Art Project, and the Miriam Schapiro Archives on Women Artists. With the support of Isabel Nazario, Furmanski, and Marianne Gaunt, Rutgers vice president for information services and university librarian, Olin and Brodsky launched the IWA with a broad mission: "to transform values, policies, and institutions to ensure that the intellectual and aesthetic contributions of diverse communities of women in the visual arts are included in the cultural mainstream and acknowledged in the historical record."[33]

To heighten the visibility of women artists, Olin and Brodsky worked with prominent feminist artists, curators, and art historians to create the Feminist Art Project, an international collaborative initiative to promote diverse feminist art events, education, and publications through its website and online calendar. By using social media to disseminate information, the IWA facilitated global networking and regional program development among women artists. *The Fertile Crescent: Gender, Art, and Society* provides one powerful example of the use of IWA networks to create a series of exhibits, lectures, screenings, literary events, musical performances, and presentations exploring contemporary Middle Eastern women in society and culture. Organized at venues in New York City, New Brunswick, Princeton, and Trenton in fall 2012, *Fertile Crescent* showcased the work of Muslim and other Middle Eastern women artists, filmmakers, writers, musicians, and composers, tracing their contributions to art, literature, and film and demonstrating how artists, filmmakers, and writers contribute to critical dialogues on contentious issues.

Joining the IWL in 2007, the IWA has enriched Douglass and Rutgers with a host of feminist archival materials, art projects, exhibitions, lectures, and performances. Through their expansive network of women artists, Olin and Brodsky have brought thirty-seven manuscript collections of outstanding women artists and influential feminist art organizations to the Meriam Schapiro Archives on Women Artists. Curating shows through the Mary H. Dana Artists Series, IWA has featured the works of Louise Bourgeois, June Wayne, Betye Saar, Diane Burko, Joan Snyder, and Faith Ringgold, among others. Through the Estelle Lebowitz Endowed Visiting Artist Award, IWA brings renowned contemporary women artists to campus to give lectures and teach master classes, as well as exhibit their work. Lebowitz Award recipients have included Carolee Schneeman, Siri Berg, June Wayne, Hung Liu, Miriam Schapiro, Molly Snyder, Mary Stevens, Berni Searle, Renée Cox, Cecilia Vicuña, Joan Snyder, Audrey Flack, Ariane Littman, Martha Wilson, Grimanesa Amorós, Chitra Ganesh, and Laura Anderson Barbata. These rich programs in combination with special exhibits curated by Olin and Brodsky, such as *How American Women Artists Invented Postmodernism: 1970–1975*, retrospectives of Faith Ringgold and of the Guerilla Girls, and *Fertile Crescent* have made Douglass and Rutgers the leading center for study of the feminist art movement.

To share scholarship on feminist art with students, the IWA partnered with Women's and Gender Studies to introduce an unparalleled series of visual arts courses, including Gender, Art and Society; Homosexuality and Visual Culture; Gender, Race and Contemporary Art; and Gender and the Body: Representations and Pornography, which attract hundreds of students annually. The IWA also worked with Douglass assistant dean Rebecca Reynolds to create the Women and Creativity Living Learning Community at Douglass. In 2015, the IWA expanded its mandate to become the Center for Women in the Arts and Humanities.[34]

Advancing Women's Leadership

To move forward with women's leadership development, CAWP (the Center for the American Woman and Politics) created the National Education for Women's Leadership Program (NEW Leadership), supplementing the Public Leadership Education Network, which was restricted to students at a select group of women's colleges. With the support of a million-dollar, four-year grant from the W. K. Kellogg Foundation, CAWP designed NEW Leadership to encourage college women to participate in politics and equip them with the knowledge and skill to pursue political careers. Organized as a summer residential institute, NEW Leadership provides women undergraduate students with an immersion program in practical politics. The weeklong residential program at Douglass introduced the world of women's political leaders to college students. Through skill-building workshops and exercises, lectures, panel discussions, and a range of informal activities featuring distinguished women leaders and scholars, participants received an intensive education in the complex demands of political leadership. Student participants for the program were recruited from colleges and universities across the United States. Through their daily interactions with women elected officials, party activists, political operatives, and legislative staff, college women learned about the challenges of running for political office and the equally demanding challenges of serving in public office. Many of the participants reported on program evaluations that they found the NEW Leadership experience "life transforming."

When the initial grant for the national program ended, CAWP redesigned the program to address the unique political challenges faced by women in New Jersey. Each year since 1995, NEW Leadership–New Jersey has recruited thirty to forty young women to participate in a six-day residential institute held at Douglass. Recruiting students from public and private colleges and universities, as well as community colleges across the state, NEW Leadership participants come from families at all socioeconomic levels, and more than half the participants have been women of color. Keynote speakers have included congresswoman and Democratic Party vice presidential nominee Geraldine Ferraro (D-NY), U.S. senator Mary Landrieu (D-LA), Massachusetts governor Jane Swift, Congresswoman Robin Kelly (D-IL), Congresswoman Grace Meng (D-NY), New Jersey lieutenant governor and former secretary of state Kim Guadagno, and New Jersey senate majority leader Loretta Weinberg. Surveys of NEW Leadership–NJ alumnae indicate that the program has increased their understanding of politics (91 percent) and their desire to participate in politics (83 percent); 21 percent indicate that they plan to run for elective office.[35] Over the past two decades, CAWP has trained university faculty and administrators in nineteen states to run NEW Leadership programs at their home campuses.[36]

CAWP also designed programs to encourage New Jersey women of all ages to seek elective and appointive offices. Although New Jersey holds a unique place in U.S. history as the first state to enfranchise property-owning women (a right granted in 1790 and revoked in 1807), the state's record in electing women to the state legislature in the second half of the twentieth century was abysmal. From 1970 to 2002, New Jersey ranked among the ten worst states in the country for the percentage of women in the state legislature. Indeed, women held the same percentage of seats in the state legislature in 1927 as in 2002. The record was similarly poor at other levels of office. To counter the reluctance of both the Democratic and the Republican Party to recruit women candidates, CAWP devised the program Ready to Run. The program offers training for potential women candidates, featuring workshops conducted by prominent elected and appointed women leaders, campaign consultants, and party officials, who discuss the rigors of campaigning, fund-raising, and winning elections. Since its creation in 1998, Ready to Run has trained over twenty-five hundred women to run for office, seek appointed positions, and manage campaigns. Many women have benefited from the training, subsequently running for and winning elective office and thereby changing the gender makeup of public institutions in the state. In 2016, women held 39 percent of the seats in the New Jersey's Assembly and Senate, moving the state to eleventh highest in the nation for percentage of women in the legislature.[37] To maximize its impact, CAWP has trained partners in twenty states to replicate the program.

To supplement Ready to Run, which focuses on increasing the number of women in elective offices, CAWP helped form the Bipartisan Coalition for Women's Appointments, which seeks to increase the number of women in appointive offices. Convened in anticipation of each gubernatorial election, the coalition is made up of women leaders from both parties who advocate the appointment of women to prominent positions in government, as well as to less visible boards and commissions. Collecting biographical information from women interested in being considered for appointments, the coalition makes résumés available to the transition team of the governor-elect in order to diminish the reliance on old-boy networks and discredit the claim that "we don't know any qualified women."

To address the broader problem of women's underrepresentation, CAWP launched initiatives specifically aimed at increasing the number of women of color in elective offices in the United States. Beginning in 2002, CAWP director Debbie Walsh partnered with the National Order of Black Elected Legislative Women (NOBEL Women) to create a yearlong series of weekend recruitment and training programs to prepare African American women to run for office. Within New Jersey, CAWP has collaborated with the LUPE Fund and leaders in the Latino community to conduct "Elección Latina." Working with African American women leaders, it has launched "Run Sister Run: Women of the African Diaspora Changing the Political Landscape." And in collaboration with Asian American women leaders, CAWP sponsors "Rising Stars: Educating Asian American Women for Politics." Each of these programs helps to identify, recruit, and train women of color to run for political office.

To emphasize the importance of "women's leadership for a just world," the Global Center created the Women's Global Leadership Institute (WGLI), convening nine institutes at Douglass and three regionally—in Istanbul, Lagos, and Warsaw—between 1991 and 2002. Charlotte Bunch envisioned the WGLI as a means to strengthen and enhance women's international leadership, particularly in the area of women's human rights. The Global Center designed the WGLI to create opportunities "for individual leaders from different regions around the world to exchange experiences and to look for global responses that complement their local actions."[38] Through the WGLI, the Global Center sought to advance women's collective leadership, "so that their diverse voices can be channeled to forge a feminist transformation of perspectives on all global issues—not just 'women's issues.'"[39] Participants in the first WGLI, representing all regions of the world, engaged in strategic discussions about how to raise awareness of violence against women as a global human rights issue. One of their most lasting interventions is the international campaign, 16 Days of Activism against Gender Violence, which is organized annually in nations around the world, mobilizing thousands of women to speak out against gender-based violence.

Learning from the initiatives of CAWP and the Global Center, the IWL designed a leadership program for undergraduate women with a broad remit: to redress the persistent underrepresentation of women in positions of power across the domains of politics, business, education, arts, law, and science. In partnership with the Department of Women's and Gender Studies, IWL created a two-year, credit-bearing program to prepare women students to be informed, innovative, and socially responsible leaders. The IWL Leadership Scholars Program brings students to the Douglass Campus for nineteen credits of course work combined with research and policy internships and an independent "social action project," which affords students a distinctive leadership learning experience. Open to students in any academic program at Rutgers, the courses deepen understandings of women's leadership, draw attention to women's manifold contributions to social change, and encourage strategic thinking about transformative practice. The program connects participants with women community activists and leaders through internships and mentoring, enabling students to gain hands-on experience in various organizations, agencies, and corporations, as they develop their leadership capacities and undertake their chosen social action projects.

Partnering with CWW, the IWL has built a mentoring program for students interested in corporate careers, as well as an elite leadership program for corporate women. With sponsorship from Deloitte & Touche, the IWL and CWW launched WINGS (Women Investing in and Guiding Students) in 2002. This program links diverse undergraduate students from Rutgers with successful career women to provide a college-to-career bridge that increases students' awareness of work opportunities and challenges. The Executive Leadership Program for Women, inaugurated in the fall of 2000 at Douglass, is a leadership development program for senior corporate women, designed to assist them in moving up the corporate leadership ladder.

In addition to training programs, the IWL has published multiple books on women's leadership. *Talking Leadership: Conversations with Powerful Women* (1999) includes interviews with women who have made a mark in feminist theory (bell hooks), higher education (Ruth Simmons), journalism (Anna Quindlen), politics (Christine Todd Whitman), philanthropy (Susan Berresford), and transnational feminism (Peggy Antrobus and Jacqueline Pitanguy)—among other fields. The IWL's National Dialogue on Educating Women for Leadership series was launched in 2000 to encourage a national conversation about the development, meaning, and social impact of women's leadership. The series analyzes best practices for educating women for leadership, offers reasons why women's leadership should be a matter of public concern, examines leadership as a collective endeavor rather than an individual mission, and identifies strategies to promote young women's leadership. Contributors to the debate include Charlotte Bunch; physician and internationally acclaimed nuclear disarmament activist Helen Caldicott; third wave feminist activists Jennifer Baumgardner and Amy Richards; and distinguished scholars Deborah Gray White, M. Elizabeth Tidball, Patricia J. Williams, Ruth B. Mandel, and Nancy Hewitt.

IWL's most recent scholarship series, Junctures: Case Studies in Women's Leadership, uses the case study method to explore the diverse ways that women around the world exercise leadership, often overcoming rigid cultural and societal expectations about gender. The volume *Junctures in Women's Leadership: Social Movements* (2016) investigates critical decisions made by women such as Eleanor Roosevelt, Gloria Steinem, Dazon Dixon Diallo, Wangari Maathai, Mirna Cunningham, and Thuli Madonsela in their struggles for social justice. Engaging social movements from the 1940s to the present, the book analyzes women's leadership for indigenous peoples' rights, gender equality, reproductive rights, labor advocacy, environmental justice, and other causes.[40] The volume *Junctures in Women's Leadership: Business* examines how some women have managed to break through the glass ceiling of the business world, the management techniques they employ once they ascend to the upper echelons of power, the challenges they face, and the strategies they have used to resolve those challenges.[41] Researching women from diverse backgrounds who have achieved key leadership positions in the private sector, the volume illuminates how women work to improve the climate for women in male-dominated industries and exercise transformative leadership in business.

Since 1970, Douglass has been the catalyst for the creation of an unparalleled set of research centers and institutes designed to promote women's equality. Building upon and reshaping Douglass's rich tradition of women's education, these research centers provide supportive, stimulating, and cutting-edge intellectual environments for women; they ask new questions about the nature of power and systems of disadvantage grounded in race, gender, class, nationality, sexual orientation, and disability; they generate strategies to improve women's condition within and across nations; and they afford leadership training opportunities to diverse disadvantaged groups. Like Douglass College itself, these innovative programs were created by women leaders who envisioned mechanisms to educate and enhance the power of diverse populations of women and found creative ways to realize those visions. The faculty and administrators who have created the new academic programs, research centers, and institutes at Douglass have transformed knowledge—altering the curricula at colleges and universities across the world. By taking women's lives, interests, and intellects seriously, they have generated research that has transformed dominant paradigms in the humanities, social sciences, and natural sciences. Through their collaborative efforts they instantiate a new kind of university that is more inclusive and less stratified by race and gender hierarchies. In so doing, they have contributed to Douglass's distinctive role in U.S. higher education. What was first said in 1970 is still true today: "No other college in the country has taken steps as an institution to create a new environment for the advancement of women."[42]

REINVENTING DOUGLASS
From University Reorganization to the Transformation of Undergraduate Education

DOUGLASS MUST BE A NEW BREED OF
WOMEN'S COLLEGE, ONE THAT PROVIDES
ALL OF THE BENEFITS OF A TRADITIONAL
WOMEN'S COLLEGE, WITH NONE OF THE
TRADITIONAL WEAKNESSES.

—Dean Carmen Twillie Ambar, 2005

In *Rutgers: A Bicentennial History*, Richard P. McCormick notes that Rutgers, then comprising the Colleges of Arts and Sciences, Agriculture, and Engineering (the men's colleges) and NJC, began calling itself a university in 1924.[1] That language fit well with Mabel Smith Douglass's vision, as she testified before the Duffield Commission in 1928: "We were created as a department of a state university.... We never were created as a part of old colonial Rutgers."[2] Officially known as the Commission on Relations between Rutgers and the State of New Jersey, the Duffield Commission recommended "two reorganization plans, both calling for the establishment of a State University and providing for the government of the same."[3] In response to intensive lobbying by New Jersey women, orchestrated by Dean Douglass, the *Duffield Commission Report* designated NJC as an "autonomous college," one of the "coordinate and constituent colleges of the University."[4] The 1930s reorganization was the first of many as Rutgers grew exponentially over the course of the twentieth century.

The sustained transformations undertaken in the 1960s and 1970s left Douglass firmly entrenched within the State University of New Jersey, yet it was no longer autonomous and it lacked a faculty—two characteristics typically associated with a college. The challenge confronting Douglass Dean Jewel Plummer Cobb and her successors—Mary S. Hartman, Martha Cotter, Barbara Shailor, Linda Stamato, and Carmen Twillie Ambar—was the reinvention of women's higher education without many of the stock tools of the trade. This chapter traces the ingenuity of Douglass deans in devising means to offer outstanding educational opportunities to Douglass women within a markedly changed and constantly changing university. Individually and collectively, they worked to produce "a new breed of women's college, one that provides all of the benefits of a traditional women's college, with none of the traditional weaknesses."[5]

Reaffirming and Expanding
Douglass's Mission as a Women's College

In August 1980, Douglass dean Jewel Plummer Cobb wrote to Douglass students, alumnae, parents, and friends to assure them that despite reorganization, "Douglass will retain its identity as a women's college dedicated to the liberal arts and the preparation of women for challenging careers." Taking an upbeat tone, she emphasized that Douglass was and would remain a "winner," just like the nine Douglass women who led the Rutgers women's basketball team to place first in regional competition, gaining recognition as one of top ten women's teams in the country.[6] Indeed, Dean Cobb emphasized that Douglass would use reorganization as an opportunity to implement innovative curricular and co-curricular programs to increase opportunities and enrich instruction for Douglas students. Crafting a new brochure for the college in 1980, Dean Cobb noted that Douglass was beginning a new chapter, emerging stronger as a "place where students have the academic and career advantages of a women's school while still enjoying the opportunities for coeducation at other divisions of Rutgers U."[7]

Celebrating Douglass students as "new women for a new world," the College recruiting materials offered what would later be called "the benefits of dual citizenship in both the college and the university. The women have their own student government and nearly 100 Douglass clubs and organizations. There are also many more university wide clubs and organizations that bring men and women from all the New Brunswick campuses together."[8]

To fulfill its distinctive mission as the women's college, Dean Cobb moved quickly to appoint a committee to concretize the role of Douglass Fellows. At the end of the 1980–1981 academic year, 150 Douglass faculty who were being reassigned to discipline-based departments in the Faculty of Arts and Sciences pledged to dedicate themselves to the "Douglass cause"—innovative education for women—as Douglass Fellows.[9] Yet exactly what that might mean remained to be determined. Dean Cobb hoped that the fellows would assist her in devising academic initiatives and function as the "governing body of the College."[10] She particularly hoped that the fellows would help expand course offerings for the Douglass Scholars Program, launched in 1978 as the first honors program in New Brunswick. Douglass Scholars were outstanding students who were awarded full-tuition scholarships for four years and offered a special academic curriculum including two first-year seminars, intensive faculty-directed tutorials in the sophomore year, and junior and senior honors projects completed as independent studies under faculty supervision.

Dean Cobb introduced co-curricular programs designed to enhance students' professional development. For example, drawing on her expertise as a cell biologist and cancer researcher, she created a Science Management Program, which offered students majoring in biology, chemistry, computer science, and mathematics semester-long internships in local science-based industries. She secured funding to support Douglass students' participation in a Federal Summer Intern Program and a journalism and urban communications intern program and worked with Associate Alumnae of Douglass College to launch an Externship Program that allowed Douglass students to "shadow" a Douglass alumna in her place of work for a week during winter or spring break.[11]

Working with the associate and assistant deans in College Hall, Dean Cobb set clear objectives for the student affairs program in the 1980s:

> to support standards of academic integrity and provide avenues for grievance; facilitate informal faculty and student gatherings; provide auxiliary advising and career counseling; serve as a resource for addressing racial or sexual harassment in the classroom; provide safe quiet and pleasant places to study, assist students in coping with university bureaucracy; create an atmosphere where students can try out new behaviors, challenge old ideas and explore new ones in a supportive environment; break down prejudices and stereotypes which demean groups/individuals; provide leadership opportunities and training; help students examine values, build character, and develop a sense of community.[12]

In short, she sought to ensure that Douglass students would continue to experience the manifold benefits of an elite women's college, while also gaining access to the enormous intellectual resources of a major research university. In particular, she envisioned an institution that harnessed the intellectual power of the Faculty of Arts and Sciences, while crafting co-curricular and student life opportunities designed for women.

Jewel Plummer Cobb also made Douglass a resource for women faculty and staff at Rutgers. In spring 1980, she founded the Rutgers Women's Organizational Network (WON) as an "umbrella group to provide support for women in the university community and communicate their diverse scholarly interests to the greater society." Recruiting a twenty-member steering committee of well-known feminist scholars and administrators, including Jean Ambrose, Joan Burstyn, Barbara Calloway, Judith Gerson, Mary Hartman, Ruth Mandel, Ellen Mappen, Judith Walkowitz, Virginia Yans, Catharine Stimpson, and Linda Stamato, Dean Cobb began building bridges between Rutgers women in Camden and Newark, as well as New Brunswick. In the first *WON Newsletter*, published in December 1980, she identified the primary purpose of the network:

> to assist women at all levels—undergraduate, graduate, and non-matriculated students, faculty and professional staff—in their academic careers by providing such support as advising, counseling, mentoring, and facilitating; formulate and encourage broad programs to have significant impact on women at Rutgers; encourage scholarly research on or about women in many disciplines;

and to provide communication and visibility for research and action programs on women both within and beyond the university.[13]

This first *WON Newsletter* provided a systematic catalog of women's programs on campus, in the state of New Jersey, and at other universities in the United States. To bring Rutgers women together, WON scheduled open meetings each semester on the Douglass Campus, and organized lectures on feminist topics. The second *WON Newsletter*, published in April 1981, also began introducing "new women at Rutgers" and providing brief bios of women scientists and humanists who had joined the university community. By the time the second newsletter was circulated, there were hundreds of Rutgers women on the mailing list.

In a later issue of the newsletter, Julia Cameron, the newsletter's editor and a member of the Douglass dean's staff, coauthored an essay with Adrienne Scerbak, a PhD student in history, titled "Academic Feminism: A Contradiction in Terms?" The essay begins by clarifying the conception of feminism that WON hoped to foster at Douglass and at Rutgers:

> While all feminists agree that the bottom line is an equal sharing of societies' responsibilities and rewards between women and men . . . feminism should imply more than an equality between women and men in the world as it now stands. First, we doubt that our present society could survive without the oppression of a large number of women at home, in the workplace, and elsewhere. . . . Society is stratified by race and class and this stratification impinges on the lives of women. The feminism to which we subscribe transcends equal rights for we do not choose equality to men of our class and race, if it means the perpetuation of the oppression of our sisters from other backgrounds. . . . We do not wish only to participate in the public forum, but to bring to that forum those values and characteristics which have traditionally been described as "feminine." These include a preference for cooperation rather than competition, nurturance and compassion and a respect for the emotional and intuitive.[14]

With an impressive record of accomplishments, Dean Cobb left Douglass at the end of the 1980–1981 academic year to become president of California State University, Fullerton.[15] Her final note to the Class of 1981, published in *Quair: Yearbook of Douglass College*, is a testament to her vision of the "new" Douglass woman: "You are expected to become less provincial, more tolerant, less angry, more critical of all you read and hear in the media, more independent emotionally and academically. . . . You have always upheld a traditional expectation of top performance . . . as Douglass women. We expect that you will be not simply a writer or a surgeon or a judge or a teacher or a scientist, a corporate manager, or a civic leader, but we expect you to be the best of the lot."[16]

The Hartman Era

Mary S. Hartman, who had achieved a national reputation for research excellence and successful institution building in women's studies (see chapter 8), was tapped to serve as the acting dean of Douglas in July 1981 and appointed seventh dean of Douglass College in 1982. She was the first—and the only—Douglass faculty member to serve as permanent dean of Douglass.

With the consolidation of all New Brunswick faculty into the Faculty of Arts and Sciences in 1981, Dean Hartman's first order of business was to preserve a strong faculty presence at Douglass. Although in principle, all former Douglass faculty retained the status of Fellows of Douglass College, the demands of their new roles within Faculty of Arts and Sciences departments, the increased pressure to publish, and their dispersion across the Busch, College Avenue, Douglass, and Livingston campuses led most to treat the title as largely honorific. Using her ties with Douglass faculty and her powers of persuasion, augmented by enticing social events at the Dean's House, Mary Hartman recruited an inaugural class of twenty-five Douglass Fellows to perform the traditional role of college faculty, serving as academic advisers for first- and second-year students, planning programs, overseeing admissions and graduation requirements, and participating in student recruitment. Representing all major Faculty of Arts and Sciences

◀ MARY S. HARTMAN, DEAN OF DOUGLASS, 1981–1994

204 THE DOUGLASS CENTURY

disciplines, the fellows participated actively in the governance of the college, setting academic policies and curricular offerings, serving on college committees, recommending degree candidates to the Board of Governors, teaching honors seminars, supervising undergraduate research, developing special programs, organizing lecture series, and representing the college in university-wide bodies. Celebrating Douglass's resiliency in the aftermath of reorganization, Provost Kenneth Wheeler praised Douglass in 1983 for being "on the forefront of the collegiate units designing their organization, establishing standards and directions for the college, and initiating selected activities."[17]

To flesh out her commitment to women's leadership, Dean Hartman worked with Ruth Mandel, director of the Center for the American Woman and Politics, to secure Douglass's membership in the Public Leadership Education Network (PLEN).[18] Founded in 1978 by Frances Tarlton (Sissy) Farenthold, a Texas state legislator, gubernatorial candidate, and contender for the 1972 Democratic Party vice presidential nomination; the founding president of the bipartisan National Women's Political Caucus; and the president of Wells College, PLEN was an alliance of women's colleges committed to educating women for public leadership. With funding from the Carnegie Corporation of New York, Farenthold; Ruth Mandel; and Betsey Wright, director of the National Women's Education Fund, developed campus-based programs to prepare women students for leadership in the public arena. Douglass developed a three-credit PLEN course that combined an overview of American women and politics with guest lectures by three elected women officials each semester. The women politicians shared with the students their paths to power and discussed the challenges of public office. PLEN participants also traveled to Trenton to meet state legislators and policy makers. And beginning in 1983, PLEN students could attend seminars in Washington, DC, where they met with women in Congress and the executive agencies of the federal government. In 1985, Dean Hartman established the Emerging Leaders course, designed to promote new models of leadership by assisting students to develop a philosophy of leadership through experimentation with various leadership techniques, models, and theories, while gaining practical experience in building community partnerships.

Following precedents set by Deans Margery Somers Foster and Jewel Plummer Cobb, Dean Hartman continued to provide space—one of the university's most precious and limited resources—to feminist initiatives and serve as an invaluable resource for women faculty at Rutgers. In 1982, the college provided desperately needed office space in Voorhees Chapel for women's studies and the Institute for Research on Women, at a time when the university had withdrawn resources for the programs and assigned them to share two small basement offices in Carpender Hall. Throughout the 1980s, Hartman supported initiatives focusing on women's lives, initiatives that were moving forward in multiple sites at Rutgers. Within discipline-based departments such as English, history, anthropology, political science, and sociology, as well as within the Institute for Research on Women and the Center for the American Woman and Politics, feminist scholarship was advancing with energy and verve. Coming together at Douglass College, with its special mission to promote educational opportunities for women, feminist scholars worked collaboratively with Dean Hartman to strengthen and expand support from Rutgers and to address challenges posed by more subtle yet persistent gender stereotypes, exclusionary practices, and assumptions about power in society that thwart women's advancement to leadership.

Mary Hartman also brought celebrated women speakers with diverse specializations to campus, among them Sarah Weddington, Eleanor Holmes Norton, Eleanor Smeal, and Betty Friedan. In 1984 she inaugurated the annual Frances B. L'Hommedieu Lecture, which featured distinguished speakers such as British primatologist, ethologist, and anthropologist Jane Goodall; author Frank McCourt; Jody Williams, founding coordinator of the International Campaign to Ban Landmines (who later went on to win the Nobel Peace Prize in 1997); and *New York Times* health columnist Jane Brody. Dean Hartman created the Annual Women's Conference to explore important contemporary women's issues and she continued to host the Dana Women Artists series. To introduce Douglass students to the emerging field of feminist scholarship, new curricular requirements mandated two courses in women's studies for all Douglass students.

Dean Hartman recruited the directors of women's studies, CAWP, and the IRW to engage in strategic brainstorming sessions about how to heighten the visibility of women's research and educational programs, meet new challenges created by reorganization, and devise strategies to promote women's leadership. These discussions set a pattern of collaboration among women's units that became the hallmark of Douglass. Through collective initiatives to promote structural, curricular, and program changes at the university, Dean Hartman worked to ensure that women played a central role in and benefited from all aspects of university transformation. In these endeavors, Dean Hartman built a reputation for ingenuity and entrepreneurialism, working within as well as around the system.

In 1981, Dean Hartman began a series of discussions with university administrators and board members as well as state officials to create a chair in women's studies at Douglass College. Through contacts on the Rutgers Board of Governors and through CAWP's connections, she formed a legislative "study commission" consisting of female board members, state elected and appointed officials, and heads of New Jersey organizations focused on women. This study commission, chaired by state senator Anne Martindell and vice chaired by Hazel Gluck, then director of the State Lottery Commission, proceeded to recommend the creation of a state-supported chair in women's studies at Douglass. When Governor Thomas Kean approved the proposal, it was celebrated in a packed Assembly chambers in Trenton, with remarks delivered by Rutgers Board of Governors chair Linda Stamato (DC '62), Governor Kean, chancellor of higher education Ted Hollender, Dean Hartman, and others. The governor then challenged Douglass to supplement state support by finding a private donor. Before "leveraging" became a routine practice of university development offices, Dean Hartman worked with executive director of the Douglass Associate Alumnae Adelaide

Zagoren to approach potential donors with a proposal to "match" the state appropriation. New Brunswick philanthropist Irving Laurie agreed to give a quarter of a million dollars to establish an endowment for the joint venture, which was named the Blanche, Edith, and Irving J. Laurie New Jersey Chair in Women's Studies at Douglass College. At the dedication ceremony in 1983, President Bloustein and Governor Kean cele-

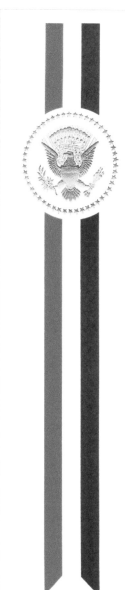

The Presidential Award for
Excellence in Science, Mathematics,
and Engineering Mentoring

is presented with the gratitude
of your fellow citizens by

The President of the
United States of America

to

Douglass Project for Women in Mathematics,
Science and Engineering
Rutgers, The State University of New Jersey

for embodying excellence in mentoring
underrepresented students and encouraging
their significant achievement in science,
mathematics, and engineering.

William J. Clinton

THE WHITE HOUSE
DECEMBER 1999

▲ CERTIFICATE OF PRESIDENTIAL AWARD FOR EXCELLENCE IN SCIENCE, MATHEMATICS, AND ENGINEERING MENTORING WON BY DOUGLASS PROJECT FOR WOMEN IN MATHEMATICS, SCIENCE AND ENGINEERING

brated this signal victory for Douglass and for women's studies as a model for future public-private partnerships.

With the support of Douglass alumnae, Dean Hartman launched the Douglass Project for Rutgers Women in Mathematics, Science and Engineering in 1986 to encourage young women to enter scientific and technical fields. Building upon the internship model of Dean Cobb's Science Management Program, the Douglass Project, led by Ellen Mappen, developed mentoring opportunities and various curricular (e.g., a three-credit course, Introduction to Scientific Research) and co-curricular programs to create a community of support for undergraduate women pursuing science and math majors. When the Douglass science departments were moved to the Busch campus, Dean Hartman transformed the science building into the Bunting-Cobb Math, Science, and Engineering Residence Hall, the first of its kind in the nation, which provided a living-learning community for one hundred Douglass women in STEM (science, technology, engineering, and math) fields. Over the next decade, with the support of major corporations and foundations, the Douglass Project created a range of pipeline programs, including the Douglass Science Institute for high school students, which brought students in grades 9 and 10 to campus for weeklong programs that featured workshops in math and computer science, field trips to AT&T Engineering Research, and meetings with women scientists from Colgate Palmolive. Science Career Exploration Day and the Douglass Science Academy were designed for high school juniors and seniors to reinforce commitments to science careers and strengthen research skills. The Douglass Project gained national recognition for its innovative initiatives, first in 1990, as the recipient of the American Association of University Women's Progress in Equity Award; then in 1991, as a National Research Council Model Program; and again in 1999, as the recipient of the Presidential Award for Excellence in Science, Mathematics, and Engineering Mentoring.

During the 1980s, Dean Hartman provided resources for community outreach programs, supporting Douglass Advisory Services for Women (DASW). Informally known as the Women's Center, DASW offered to women in Middlesex and surrounding counties an array of services, including career, educational, legal, and personal counseling to twelve hundred women a year (40 percent women of color). It operated a hot line for those in need of referrals to local and state agencies, and it organized workshops, seminars, and conferences.[19] Like women's centers at many colleges and universities across the United States, DASW afforded space to Douglass students concerned with social justice activism. From concerns about sexual harassment and acquaintance rape to strategies to address sexist jokes in some classes and insufficient material about women in others, students turned to DASW to organize Take Back the Night marches, campus escort services (the Green Lantern Guides), and pickets against pornography.

In the *Dean's Newsletter* (August 1987), Mary Hartman quoted the judgment of alumna Madeline Schetty (NJC '27) that Douglass provides "the best a good college can offer." Characterizing the college's ties with central administration of Rutgers as "tighter

▶ TAKE BACK THE
NIGHT MARCH
ORGANIZED BY
DOUGLASS
WOMEN'S CENTER

than they once were," Dean Hartman emphasized that closer ties "have enriched us academically. . . . There is no question that Douglass continues healthy and strong. Applications were up 8% despite a decline in high school graduates, reflecting the end of baby boom era. Efforts to recruit students of color have paid off, 22% of entering students are Black or Latina. . . . The physical plant has expanded enormously as have academic programs."[20] The dean also mentioned that the fifteen hundred responses to a Residence Hall survey were "gratifyingly positive: students were generally pleased with and supportive of efforts to maintain racial harmony; roommate relationships were notably strong; professional and student staff were perceived as generally fair and concerned."[21]

Douglass's successes won praise across town at Old Queens. In its report, the Provost's Committee on Undergraduate Education, chaired by Barry Qualls, noted:

> Most striking of all is praise of students for the work of Douglass College and its Deans. This college—"like having Vassar at Harvard"—clearly has found a way of personalizing its services, of knowing its students individually, while also fostering a learning environment that students define as genuinely intel-

lectual. Whether it be the Douglass Scholars Program, or the Dean's lecture series, or the Bunting Cobb Center, or the programs in women's studies, Douglass students see that their College provides "an education for undergraduates equal to that available at any private college in the country.[22]

In the 1990s, Douglass was the largest college for women in the United States, and the only one that was part of a state's flagship university. The *1994 Money Guide to Best College Buys Now* ranked Douglass twelfth in a field of one thousand schools and first among the top eight women's colleges. The Douglass Project won a half-million-dollar grant from the Sloan Foundation to establish Project SUPER (Science for Undergraduates: A Program for Excellence in Research), which created new forms of research collaboration between Rutgers faculty and undergraduate students. Building on its long history with the living-learning communities in the Language and Culture Houses, Douglass created the Global Village in 1992, consolidating the residences in a single area and revising their house courses to engage with issues of gender, migration, and globalization.[23]

New scholarship on women's life-writing inspired English professor and Douglass Fellow Carolyn Williams to suggest a new mission course for Douglass students. Dean Hartman charged the Curriculum Committee with exploring the possibilities. Following extensive planning by the Douglass Curriculum Committee, chaired by Associate Dean Louise Duus, and including Fellows Carolyn Williams (English), Robert Loveland (biology), Leslie Fishbein (American studies), Bonnie Smith (history), and Barbara Reid (journalism), the college created a first-year course, Shaping a Life, designed to help undergraduate women think about their future lives and livelihoods. Using a range of women's autobiographies as its primary texts, the course theme emphasized "shaping a life—in the living and in the telling"—as faculty encouraged students to analyze "how women live their lives—*and* how they talk about and write about them—living forward in time, then shaping the life retrospectively."[24] In fall 1994, Professor Williams taught a pilot version of the course to one hundred randomly selected students, combining weekly lectures and presentations by faculty members with eminent guest speakers. Women of achievement, such as Jill Ker Conway, the first woman to serve as president of Smith College, and Hazel Gluck, chair of the New Jersey Lottery Commission, spoke with the students about how their lives took shape; students analyzed both the content and the style of their narratives, while also learning to conduct oral history interviews. After the successful pilot course, Shaping a Life was adopted as the Douglass mission course, taken by all entering and transfer students beginning in fall 1995.

During the early 1990s, Dean Hartman also launched a major fund-raising campaign in preparation for Douglass's seventy-fifth anniversary. Douglass development officer Lisa Hetfield worked with the dean and Associate Alumnae of Douglass College executive director Adelaide Zagoren to recruit Gretchen Johnson (DC '63) to serve as volunteer campaign director. Through their energetic efforts, the campaign topped its target goal of $7.5 million, raising $10 million to support key programs, including the Global Village, the Institute for Women's Leadership (IWL), and the construction of the Ruth Dill Johnson Crockett Building, which was to become the new home for the Department of Women's and Gender Studies and the IWL.

With the successful completion of the Douglass seventy-fifth-anniversary campaign, Dean Hartman announced that she would retire from the position of dean at the end of 1994. Looking back on her fifteen years as Douglass dean, she noted that "she never wanted to be a traditional dean"; she wanted "to start things and build new initiatives."[25] She also wanted to give a consistent message to Douglass women: "My concern is that students realize that they're not going to have a happy, fulfilling life unless they love what they do. So, the main choice is, 'What do you care about?' If you can then pick up on what you care about and turn it into a life with a career on the side, that's fine. See what your life passions are and then direct your career accordingly."[26] She continued to launch new initiatives and to inspire students as the founding director of the IWL until her retirement from Rutgers in 2010.

Martha A. Cotter, professor of chemistry and chemical biology at Rutgers and longtime Douglass Fellow, agreed to serve as acting dean in 1995, pledging to preserve and enhance Douglass's strengths as a national search was undertaken for a permanent dean. Preserving equanimity on the Douglass campus was no mean feat during Cotter's eighteen months in the Dean's House. Several key staff members decided to time their

▶ MARTHA A. COTTER, INTERIM DEAN OF DOUGLASS, JANUARY 1995–JUNE 1996

retirement to coincide with Dean Hartman's departure, leaving Dean Cotter to conduct searches for director of the Douglass Campus Center, an associate dean for academic affairs, and a business manager for the college.[27] Dean Cotter also saw Douglass through the tumult around President Francis Lawrence's "misstatement" concerning race and intellectual aptitude (see chapter 10). Dean Cotter quelled campus fears, working with Rutgers and New Brunswick police, fire officials, and the Federal Bureau of Investigation when two bombs were found in the Mabel Smith Douglass Library in April 1995.[28] She raised funds to cover the substantial instructional costs associated with expanding the new mission course to include all incoming and transfer students and recruited faculty to teach the course. In addition, she introduced new recruiting mechanisms to appeal to out-of-state students interested in single-sex education, developing a virtual tour of campus and emphasizing the "Douglass Difference"—the impressive strengths of a major research university combined with the virtues of an elite women's college.

Shoring Up the Foundations: Dean Barbara Shailor

In 1996, Barbara A. Shailor, a classics scholar who specialized in Latin paleography and codicology and the study of Visigoth manuscripts copied and illuminated in northern Spain in the tenth and eleventh centuries, was recruited from Bucknell University to serve as the eighth dean of Douglass. During her years at Bucknell, Shailor had served as associate dean of the College of Arts and Sciences and as associate provost of the university.

In her inaugural convocation address in November 1996, Dean Shailor articulated a vision for Douglass that blended historical college traditions with the demands of the fast-approaching millennium. Reflecting upon the college motto, *Sophia kai sophrosune*, which had long been translated as "Wisdom and Self-Control," Dean Shailor noted: "*Sophia* is, of course, wisdom. . . . *Sophrosune* is the operational aspect of wisdom: the determination, the drive, the self-discipline to set priorities, to overcome obstacles, to use to the best advantage the wisdom we have gained from a Douglass education." Situating the motto in contemporary vernacular, Dean Shailor suggested that it might best be rendered "Smart and Savvy," a fitting reference to what

> Douglass gives its graduates—research skills, technical skills, a taste for discovering, enjoying, and contributing to the wide and wonderful world that lies before her [*sic*]. . . . We cannot actually teach integrity, grace, and dignity; we cannot in any meaningful way mandate involvement, and compassion and open-mindedness. But what we can do and must do and what . . . Douglass is ideally equipped to do is to gather together in one place the people, the ideas, the structures that enable and encourage our women to learn these most important but least tangible things themselves. Those are the lessons of Douglass that last.[29]

▶ BARBARA A. SHAILOR,
DEAN OF DOUGLASS,
1996–2001. PHOTO:
BUCKNELL UNIVERSITY,
1992.

Recognizing the importance of emerging information technology, Dean Shailor wired the residence halls for Internet access and broadcast the first e-mail to all Douglass students. Concerned with certain structural problems with the physical facilities on campus, she raised funds to cover major renovations in the Chemistry Annex (restoring the roof), College Hall (replacing the original slate roof, chimneys, and windows, restoring exterior woodwork, repainting), and rebuilding the terracotta pediments and columns of the chapel. Dean Shailor also reorganized the college administration to place greater emphasis on strengthening relations between the college and its corporate and foundation partners, increasing the visibility of Douglass on the national scene, enhancing mechanisms for student recruitment, and raising funds for scholarships and academic programs.

To evaluate the benefits of the mission course for the largest undergraduate women's college in the United States, Dean Shailor initiated a major study of 3,112 students who had completed Shaping a Life since its inception. Noting that Douglass students were pursuing sixty-nine majors and sixty-five minors, that 70 percent of the students received financial aid, and a large proportion of the students were holding part-time jobs while in college, Dean Shailor sought to discover the measurable benefits of the mission course. The results were telling: Shaping a Life increased retention at the college (attrition rates decreased 30 percent over three years), enhanced academic performance by 10 percent, and improved four-year graduation rates by 5 percent. Students reported that the course fostered a greater sense of community and personal connection to Douglass, heightened their awareness of leadership and academic opportunities, and increased their self-confidence. The students also noted that they had been inspired by the featured women speakers, whose life experiences raised the students' personal aspirations and career expectations.[30] To assist students in their preparation for the labor force, Dean Shailor introduced the Transitional Leadership Program, a seven-week co-curricular program to help students think about life after graduation.

Developing a partnership with Ewha Women's University in South Korea, the largest women's university in world, Dean Shailor began planning two online courses, Psychology of Women, and Leadership in a Global Community, which would enroll students on both campuses, beginning in 2002. In fall 2000, Dean Shailor's recruitment efforts showed palpable results: the entering class of eight hundred students was the largest in a decade, fueled in part by highly positive national publicity. Douglass received glowing reviews in both the *New York Times* and the *Boston Globe*, which characterized the college as "a little-known gem of a school with excellent faculty and access to world-class research facilities; a pioneer in breaking down stereotypes that have deterred many women from pursuing science education." The CBS news show *60 Minutes* produced a segment on the Douglass Project, in conjunction with its report on the newly created Girl Scout Leadership Institute in Science and Technology.

Dean Shailor resigned in 2001 to become director of the Beinecke Rare Book and Manuscript Collection at Yale University. She returned to administration in 2003 as the deputy provost for the arts at Yale, where she served until December 2012, when she retired from administration. She is currently senior research Scholar and senior lecturer in the Department of Classics at Yale.

Douglass Enters the Twenty-First Century with an Alumna at the Helm

In 2001–2002, Linda Stamato (DC '62) became the first Douglass graduate to lead the college as interim dean. As an alumna, faculty member, administrator (co-director of the Center for Negotiation and Conflict Resolution at the Bloustein School for Public Policy), and former chair of the Rutgers Board of Governors, Stamato had an unparalleled record at the university, which she drew upon to shepherd the college through the tumultuous beginning of the twenty-first century. Her term began at a very difficult time for the nation. Fall semester had barely begun when the World Trade Towers and the Pentagon were attacked on September 11. In this moment of terror, when Douglass students were trying to make sense of the enormity of the violence and deal with the loss of friends, family members, and a sense of national security, Dean Stamato sought to restore equanimity. She helped organize "vigils and moments of silence in memory of victims, their families, and friends, as well as blood and clothing drives, classroom and residence hall discussion groups, counseling to help students cope with the trag-edy," and she raised funds to provide a full scholarship for a Douglass student who lost her mother in the attack.[31] She used plenary sessions of Shaping a Life and her Mom's Day talk to connect Douglass women across generations, reinforce bonds, and empha-size the importance of community as a resource in times of adversity. And she helped students see that it is possible to respond to crisis in ways that "affirm the basic good-ness of humanity and our ability to sacrifice for and to be respectful and supportive of each other in times of great distress."[32] Drawing upon her expertise in conflict resolu-tion, Dean Stamato helped students to shift their expectations about peace and peacemaking in a world of growing inequalities.

As a former Douglass student, Dean Stamato drew upon her unique relation to the college to shape her interactions with students, faculty, and staff. She made relation-

◀ LINDA STAMATO (DC '62), INTERIM DEAN OF DOUGLASS, 2001–2002

ship building with the students her top priority, and involved them actively in events at the dean's house. She organized concerts and performances at the dean's house that featured students and invited students to meet women writers (e.g., Joyce Carol Oates), politicians (e.g., Dharani Wiketeleka, Sri Lanka's justice minister), and leaders in various fields at dinners and receptions in her home. To encourage the students to think deeply about contemporary issues, she organized a yearlong series on capital punishment, featuring a talk in the Voorhees Chapel by Sister Helen Prejean, author of *Dead Man Walking,* a panel discussion with Justice Alan Handler of the New Jersey Supreme Court; Raymond Brown, lawyer, scholar, writer and moderator of *Due Process* on PBS; Hiroshi Obayashi, professor of religion at Rutgers; and Mary Hartman. Amherst College professor Austin Sarat, author of *When the State Kills: Capital Punishment and the American Condition,* also gave a lecture in the series and engaged with faculty and students at the dean's home prior to and following his lecture. A film series, launched with *Dead Man Walking,* and an exhibition in the Douglass Library accompanied these debates.

Dean Stamato regularly attended Government Association meetings and "hung out" in the Women's Center, where she engaged with many student groups. To build student confidence in this precarious period, she emphasized the role of Douglass in fostering wisdom and self-determination. Blending a profound respect for Douglass traditions with a nuanced interpretation of the original English translation of the college motto, "Wisdom and Self-Control," Dean Stamato recommended revisiting the most recent iteration of the motto, "Smart and Savvy." She suggested that the Government Association consider substituting "Wisdom and Self-Determination" for "Smart and Savvy" to express more adequately "our expectations of Douglass students . . . gaining knowledge, fine-tuned skills and demonstrated grit and confidence" from their college experience.[33] The Government Association voted enthusiastically to approve the change.[34]

To foster direct faculty involvement with students, Dean Stamato strengthened the Fellows program, building bridges with the Faculty of Arts and Sciences and its new dean, Holly Smith. Through her efforts the number of Douglass Faculty Fellows surpassed four hundred. She increased undergraduate research initiatives and highlighted student research in several venues on campus, in her public talks about Douglass, and in the *Dean's Letter.* She worked with Professor Wise Young in Cell Biology and Neuroscience to create opportunities for students at the W. M. Keck Center for Collaborative Neuroscience who were in the Douglass Project for women in STEM. She broadened the range of majors offered to Douglass students by persuading key administrators in Old Queens that students' academic choices ought not be limited by their chosen college. She strengthened college signature programs, including the Global Village, the honors program, and the Douglass Project. As Douglass's most knowledgeable ambassador, she tried to demonstrate to the central administration that Douglass was "a jewel in Rutgers' crown, not an outlier that 'created problems for the rest of Rutgers.'"[35]

Dean Carmen Twillie Ambar: The Fight to Save Douglass

In 2002, Carmen Twillie Ambar was named the ninth dean of Douglass. At age thirty-three, Ambar was the youngest dean of Douglass and the first lawyer to lead the college. Prior to her appointment, she had served as assistant dean of graduate education at the Woodrow Wilson School of Public and International Affairs at Princeton University and she had worked in the New York City Law Department as assistant corporation counsel.

Dean Ambar's legal expertise was put to good use when both the college and the president's office began receiving phone calls contesting the legitimacy of a women's college at Rutgers. To support their claims that a public university could not allow a women's college to exist, callers routinely cited Title IX of the Education Amendments of 1972, which prohibits sex discrimination in public and private institutions that receive federal financial assistance, the 1974 Equal Educational Opportunity Act, which prohibits the assignment of students to schools on the basis of race, color, religion, national origin, or sex; and *United States v. Virginia,* the 1996 U.S. Supreme Court case

▶ CARMEN TWILLIE
AMBAR, DEAN OF
DOUGLASS, 2002–2008

that declared the all-male admissions policy at Virginia Military Institute unconstitutional. Interpreting these policies to require identical treatment for men and women in public universities, callers claimed that Rutgers had a legal obligation to abolish Douglass. Two lawsuits were filed toward that end. What the callers did not appear to know was that *United States v. Virginia* did not prohibit all single-sex education. The court's ruling drew a distinction between exclusions based on generalizations about the sexes that perpetuate pernicious stereotypes and group-based programs designed to address persisting inequality. Writing for the 7–1 majority, Justice Ruth Bader Ginsburg noted that the justification for a sex-based classification "must not rely on over broad generalizations about the different talents, capacities, or preferences of males and females. . . . Generalizations about 'the way women are,' estimates of what is appropriate for most women, no longer justify denying opportunity to women whose talent and capacity place them outside the average description."[36] Indeed, the decision explicitly endorsed the use of sex-based classifications to "compensate women 'for particular economic disabilities [they have] suffered,' to 'promote equal employment opportunity,' and to advance the full development of the talent and capacities of our Nation's people."[37] In response to the callers' misguided concerns, university counsel crafted a statement for the Visit D.C. website. Rather than drawing attention to unique Douglass programs designed to promote gender equality, university counsel stressed that "Douglass College is only one component of a large coeducational undergraduate population at Rutgers University. All of Rutgers undergraduate students share and have access to the University's educational resources, with Douglass being only one unit of Rutgers' varied undergraduate programs in New Brunswick. Rutgers offers comparable educational opportunities to both male and female undergraduates at its campuses throughout the state."[38] By emphasizing equal access and equal treatment at the university as a whole, Old Queens affirmed the legal ground for Douglass's existence as a women's college.

To ensure that Douglass is "the best and first choice in women's higher education," and to help the college achieve a new level of national and international publicity, Dean Ambar undertook a five-year strategic plan for the college and successfully completed a twenty-nine-million-dollar capital campaign. She launched the teleconferencing course with South Korea's Ewha Women's University and established a partnership with Kiriri Women's University of Science and Technology in Nairobi, Kenya. She strengthened the Global Village, creating a comprehensive living-learning community that incorporated peer leaders to connect academic departments and academic course work with residential living programs, and she worked with the Department of Women's and Gender Studies, the Center for Women's Global Leadership, and the School of Business to shape the academic content and co-curricular components of the living-learning experience, adding the Human Rights House, Leadership House, Mid-East Coexistence House, and Women in Business House. To help students develop a greater global vision, she worked with the Associate Alumnae of Douglass College (AADC) to fund study-abroad scholarships in conjunction with Human Rights House initiatives. Dean Ambar also organized an annual global symposium to discuss issues facing women in a changing world, such as the feminization of poverty both worldwide and in the United States and HIV/AIDS. In 2004, the symposium, "Women in the Era of Globalization," featured Mary Robinson, former president of Ireland and UN high commissioner for human rights (1997–2002), as the keynote speaker.[39]

In 2002, the Douglass Project introduced a comprehensive faculty-mentoring component that paired individual students with eminent Rutgers faculty for intensive funded-research experiences in the first and third years of undergraduate study. Each student also presented her findings at an annual research conference. Both the format and the content of the course, Introduction to Scientific Research, were reshaped in 2003 to feature teaching teams drawn from Rutgers science faculty, who expanded the range of research methods included in the class. Working with the W. M. Keck Center for Neuroscience, the Douglass Project introduced a new seminar series, RUWINS (Rutgers University Women in Neuroscience), which brought prominent women in neuroscience to campus to share their academic research and career experiences with students and faculty.

The Transformation of Undergraduate Education

In 2004, President Richard L. McCormick and the executive vice president for academic affairs, Philip Furmanski, appointed a Task Force on Undergraduate Education, charged to examine all aspects of the undergraduate experience at Rutgers–New Brunswick. Following a year of deliberations involving dozens of faculty and administrators under the direction of Faculty of Arts and Sciences humanities dean, Barry V. Qualls, the task force issued a lengthy report, *Transforming Undergraduate Education* (*TUE*), which recommended the centralization of administrative functions involving student recruitment, admissions, facilities, services, and student life and the standardization of core educational requirements pertaining to academic majors and graduation. In the words of President McCormick, the goal of *TUE* was "to address the insidious competitive hierarchy of former colleges; reorganize on the principle that services for students should be managed centrally but delivered locally, so everyone has nearby access to quality programs; and create a single process of recruitment and admissions, residence halls, recreational facilities, student centers, psychological counseling, and health care."[40] In developing its recommendations, the task force was particularly concerned to ensure equal access of all students to academic and co-curricular programs, eliminate confusing and inequitable requirements set by undergraduate colleges, eliminate the misperception that degrees from some colleges were more valuable or prestigious than degrees from other colleges, ensure equitable resource allocation and consistency in the quality of student services across all campuses, and remove structures that close academic opportunities for some students.[41]

To accomplish these objectives, the task force drew a distinction between schools and campuses: "Schools will denote degree-granting academic units composed of faculty and students; schools set all academic requirements, from admissions to graduation. . . . Campuses will denote student communities (geographical or virtual) cutting across the Schools." In particular, the task force recommended

> the creation of the Rutgers School of Arts and Sciences, which would be responsible for the admission criteria, general education, scholastic standing, honors curricula, and degree certification of all Arts and Sciences students in New Brunswick. Its faculty would comprise the existing Faculty of Arts and Sciences, and its Executive Dean would head that faculty; its students would be students of the Rutgers School of Arts and Sciences.
>
> Our current undergraduate colleges WILL be designated as local campus communities, serving as vital centers for the integration of the academic and co-curricular aspects of undergraduate education. Students in the undergraduate schools would affiliate with one of six such campuses: Busch Campus, Cook Campus, Douglass Campus, Livingston Campus, Queen's Campus (on College Avenue), or UCNB. A Dean, who would report to the Vice President for Undergraduate Education, would serve as the head of each campus. Douglass Campus would be reserved for women; Cook Campus, although distinct from the School of Agriculture and Environmental Sciences, would remain generally focused on programs associated with its land-grant heritage; and UCNB (non-residential) would be reserved primarily for non-traditional students (adult and part-time learners). Campuses would organize smaller learning communities (say of size no larger than 600 students), which would focus on the particular intellectual or artistic interests of groups of faculty and students.[42]

Many at Rutgers saw *TUE* as merely the logical extension of the 1981 reorganization. As Michael Beals, Faculty of Arts and Sciences dean for undergraduate education, noted, "To a great extent since 1981, when the separate college faculties were combined into a single unit, the so-called separate colleges . . . have been residential colleges. And we are not at all proposing that that be changed. The residential campus functions are strong ones that . . . we want to enhance."[43] Across town at Douglass, however, *TUE* recommendations were interpreted as the "abolition" of the undergraduate colleges, a proposal that threatened the very existence of Douglass. To ward off this threat, Dean Ambar, Douglass students, AADC, faculty fellows, staff, and friends of Douglass across New Jersey mobilized to preserve the women's college.

From September 2005 through March 10, 2006, when the Board of Governors approved President McCormick's recommendations, the Save Douglass forces organized debates, demonstrations, petitions, lobbying campaigns in the state capitol and in Washington, and public programs about the importance of women's colleges. Graphically depicted in a photograph of Woodlawn, home of the Eagleton Institute of Politics and the Center for American Women and Politics, with a "Save Douglass" sign prominently displayed on the sloping lawn, *Quair* staff observed, "It is everywhere. On the front page of the *Targum*. Outside the Douglass Student Center. On the wristbands of many students. On Tee shirts. On signs in yards of nearby neighborhoods. 'Save Douglass College.'"[44] Although the students acknowledged that *TUE* recommendations to "streamline applications, eliminate confusion, [and] ensure equal treatment of all Rutgers students" sounded benign, students suggested that they harbored real danger for Douglass: "As the largest public women's college in the nation, Douglass stands to lose a great deal. Current students worry about losing their identity as Douglass students, and alumnae worry about losing their alma mater. All supporters of the college worry about what is to come if the institution is to come to an end. What is to become of everything that Douglass has to offer women?"[45]

As debates about *TUE* continued throughout the academic year, Douglass students turned up at public meetings, sporting T-shirts that proclaimed, "Eliminate my college, eliminate my future." U.S. representative Frank Pallone (D-NJ) wrote an open letter to President McCormick, which was published in the *Targum*, demanding that Rutgers save Douglass: "A degree represents a contract between students and schools. It sets in motion a lifetime bond that provides many benefits to both. For Rutgers, this bond between Douglass and its alumnae has resulted in contributions of $29 million to the University's capital campaign, more than the alumni of any other liberal arts college at Rutgers University."[46] On March 2, AADC organized buses for 150 Douglass students, faculty, alumnae, and friends to carry the Save Douglass campaign to Trenton. Bearing banners saying, "Mabel's treasure should last forever," the demonstrators rallied support for the college among the state legislators. Fifty-two state senators and assembly persons lent their voices to the Save Douglass College campaign in floor debate, culminating in the passage (75–0) of a New Jersey Assembly resolution to retain and strengthen Douglass as a four-year women's college.[47]

During this tumultuous year, Dean Ambar worked with the Save Douglass campaign and behind the scenes to ensure the survival of Douglass. "We want to accomplish both the aims of the task force report and hold on to the benefits of Douglass College."[48] She approached President McCormick with a plan for Douglass Residential College (DRC) that integrated academics, co-curricular programs, internships and externships, and residential living for women students. Dean Ambar was particularly concerned to develop a plan that would help attract students to Douglass. As interest in attending a women's college continued to decline across the United States, fewer students had been applying to Douglass. Some women were "assigned" to Douglass by university admissions staff because there was no space available at Rutgers, Livingston, Cook, or Busch. Through creative programming, Dean Ambar hoped to reverse the trend in declining enrollment. Her proposal envisioned Douglass Residential College as far more than a campus, or physical site, reserved for women. She sought authorization to preserve and create a rich array of academic and co-curricular programs specifically designed for Douglass women.

▲ DOUGLASS STUDENTS CAMPAIGN TO SAVE DOUGLASS AT UNIVERSITY SENATE MEETING

Martha Cotter, president of the university Senate, also drafted a plan for DRC and built support for it within Senate committees that were reviewing *TUE*. Harriet Davidson, associate professor of English and women's and gender studies, played a similar role within the New Brunswick Faculty Council. In his final *TUE* proposal to the Board of Governors, President McCormick included the recommendation that Douglass "provide a single-sex environment for women who choose to live there; offer co-curricular and student life programs consistent with the historic mission of Douglass College, and—with the approval from the new SAS—related curricular opportunities as well."[49]

After securing board approval for *TUE*, President McCormick appointed a special committee to flesh out the possibilities for a residential college, which included longtime Douglass Fellows Cheryl Wall, Lisa Hetfield, Linda Stamato, and Barbara Balliet. Issued in November 2006, their report identified the mission and scope of a residential college at Rutgers:

> Residential Colleges at Rutgers University will promote the intellectual, social and personal growth of undergraduate students by strengthening the relationship between classroom instruction and students' lives outside the classroom.

The purpose is to develop students' intellect, capacity for reason, ability to communicate, and self-knowledge; to broaden their understanding of life; and to bring integration and unification to their college education. The mission of a residential College is to create a supportive and inclusive community of students (both those who live on campus and commuters), staff, and faculty sharing defined academic interests; to build common experiences designed to help students and faculty form a sense of community and mutual support around the residential college's defined interests; to instill in students integrity, independent thought, self-discipline, tolerance, support for diverse cultures and beliefs, a willingness to place others above self for the common good, and a commitment to learning; to connect faculty and students through faculty's commitment to define the residential college and to develop and offer relevant courses; to participate in out-of-classroom activities and to identify relevant academic programs in departments and centers that support the curricular and co-curricular work of the residential college; to sponsor enrichment programs, seminars, lectures and field experiences created to increase opportunities for students to learn together and to enhance their academic, intellectual, professional and personal growth; to further the University's mission of creating an informed and responsible citizenry through civic engagement, community service, and political dialogue.[50]

Although the *Report on Residential Colleges* used generic language, Douglass was the only residential college in New Brunswick until 2015–2016, when the Board of Governors approved the creation of the Honors College on the College Avenue Campus.[51]

In 2008, Dean Ambar announced that she would be leaving Douglass to become president of Cedar Crest College, where she served until 2017, when she was named the fifteenth president of Oberlin College. In her farewell announcement, Dean Ambar emphasized that both pre- and post-*TUE*, Douglass's mission remains constant: "to prepare women for leadership, providing students with a women-centered approach to understanding the world in which they live, helping young women pursue the sciences, and to do so in an ever changing global environment."[52]

Having secured the structural changes that he sought "to reinvigorate the undergraduate experience at Rutgers by creating a more satisfying, more coherent, less frustrating, less confusing, and more rational academic environment for all students," President McCormick faced an additional challenge, the creation of a single association of alumni and alumnae.[53] Prior to 2007, Rutgers had nineteen separate alumni/alumnae associations. Loyal to the undergraduate colleges and professional schools with which they were associated, these units seldom interacted. Although President McCormick acknowledged that Rutgers's "350,000 alums have a perfect right to organize as they see fit," he appointed a task force that recommended the creation of single Rutgers University Alumni/ae Association (RUAA) to which all living Rutgers University graduates belong.[54] The task force recommended increased funding for the RUAA by the university, abolition of dues, and the creation of regional clubs. Acting on these recommendations, President McCormick established the RUAA in 2007. Since its creation, four hundred thousand alumni/alumnae receive *Rutgers Magazine* three times each year; the university regularly communicates with two hundred thousand graduates for whom the RUAA has e-mail addresses; and 150 geographically based alumni/alumnae clubs have been launched, organizing more than one thousand events each year.[55] Douglass alumnae were included in the new RUAA events and clubs, and AADC continued to organize its own programs for Douglass alumnae.

Through 2015, AADC also continued to perform its historic role as the primary fundraiser for Douglass, generating funds for scholarships, fellowships, externships, international programs, and a range of co-curricular programs according to the provisions of a memorandum of understanding negotiated in 2005. Its first campaign of the twenty-first century, Douglass: Always a Leader, raised twenty-nine million dollars for the college. In its second campaign, which concluded in 2014, AADC brought in forty-two million dollars—vital resources in an era of shrinking state budgets.[56] In April 2015, the university terminated the 2005 memorandum of understanding, arguing that AADC should function exclusively as an alumnae association and that the Rutgers University Foundation (RUF) should assume sole responsibility for future fundraising for DRC. When AADC objected to this fundamental change in its historic mission, the university and the AADC entered into a yearlong mediation process.

In July 2016, following a series of thoughtful and productive mediation sessions and subsequent discussions, Rutgers University and the RUF, in partnership with DRC and the AADC, reached a new agreement regarding the fundraising structure and alumnae relations program for DRC and the AADC.

This agreement clarified the relationships among the parties. It specified that DRC will continue in its unique role offering women a single-sex educational opportunity at a major public research university and providing innovative programs to help women students from all backgrounds succeed academically, prepare them to meet the challenges of the global workforce, and pursue career paths with confidence and conviction. The AADC will continue to serve the network of powerful, vibrant Douglass alumnae by providing quality educational, social, and leadership opportunities with lasting impact for Douglass alumnae at every stage of life.

Rutgers University acknowledged AADC's long and successful history of fundraising for and stewardship of gifts to Douglass, enabling the college to grow and fulfill its mission. According to the agreement, after July 2016, Douglass will handle all student educational and fundraising efforts for the college. Fundraising for the college will be managed by DRC, with support from RUF, and they will continue to work to advance the goals and aspirations of Douglass Residential College, the only all-women's college within a major public research university.

The agreement also specified that AADC will fundraise for its alumnae activities, operations, and alumnae fellowships and will continue to steward the Douglass Fund, the endowment that was started by the AADC in 1969 to provide financial support to benefit the college and its students.

The AADC will continue to be a chartered member of the Rutgers University Alumni Association and will remain housed in the Ruth Schilling Hennessy Alumnae Center on the Douglass Campus.

Together, the Associate Alumnae of Douglass College, Douglass Residential College, Rutgers University, and Rutgers University Foundation noted their deep commitment to Douglass's mission of advancing women and the unique experience the college creates for the next generation of female leaders. The parties also encouraged Douglass alumnae to stay connected with the college, the AADC, and each other.

DIVERSIFYING DOUGLASS

AT ONE TIME OR ANOTHER, MANY ASPECTS
OF DOUGLASS LIFE HAVE BECOME CHARGED
WITH RACIAL SIGNIFICANCE.

—*Report of the Commission on
Ethnic and Race Relations*, 1972

In his 2016 commencement address at Rutgers, President Barack Obama characterized the university as a mirror of the demographic riches of this nation:

> Every day, tens of thousands of students come here, to this intellectual melting pot, where ideas and cultures flow together among what might just be America's most diverse student body. Here in New Brunswick, you can debate philosophy with a classmate from South Asia in one class, and then strike up a conversation on the EE Bus with a first-generation Latina student from Jersey City, before sitting down for your psych group project with a veteran who's going to school on the Post-9/11 GI Bill. America converges here. And in so many ways, the history of Rutgers mirrors the evolution of America—the course by which we became bigger, stronger, and richer and more dynamic, and a more inclusive nation.[1]

Featuring a student population that in 2017 is two-thirds students of color, nearly half from families speaking languages other than English at home, and more than one-third first-generation college students, Douglass is not only the most diverse college at Rutgers, but its students also attain the highest academic performance. Thus, Douglass demonstrates that diversity enhances excellence.

Becoming a diverse and inclusive women's college, however, has been the work of a century. From its earliest days, the "Douglass woman" was presumed to be a white Christian—as mandatory chapel attendance made abundantly clear. NJC's acceptance rate for Jewish applicants (31 percent) was about half that of non-Jews (61 percent).[2]

Yet Mabel Smith Douglass complained that too many Jews had been "inadvertently admitted on academic grading solely."[3] To address that concern, during the 1920s, NJC adopted measures similar to those used at Harvard, Yale, Columbia, and the Seven Sisters colleges to restrict Jewish admissions, requiring students to provide place of birth; full names of both parents; a photograph; and a list of extracurricular activities, including "church work," as part of the application process. In making admissions decisions, special weight was given to recommendations, particularly to claims about "personality" and "moral character" to screen out better qualified Jewish candidates as not sufficiently "well-rounded."[4] These measures reduced Jewish enrollment from an average of 17 percent of the entering classes in the late 1920s to 11 percent of the entering class in 1931.[5] In 1936, Dean Margaret Corwin persuaded the trustees to limit the proportion of commuters in the student body to 25 percent, which further reduced Jewish enrollment because the percentage of Jewish students who commuted (68 percent) was more than double that of non-Jews (30 percent).[6] Although NJC rejected Jewish students from Elizabeth, New Brunswick, and Perth Amboy in favor of Christian students with much inferior records, the administration insisted it was not discriminating. On the contrary, it argued that it was preserving "necessary geographic balance within the state" and ensuring that no ethnic group was admitted in proportions significantly higher than its percentage in the state population.[7]

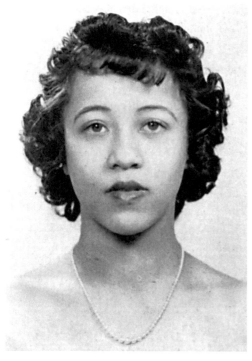

▲ JULIA BAXTER BATES (NJC '38), FIRST AFRICAN AMERICAN ADMITTED TO THE COLLEGE

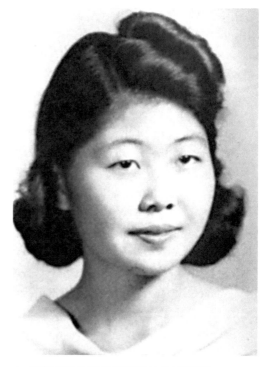

▲ CANADIAN CATHERINE M. KASHIWA (NJC '39), FIRST STUDENT OF JAPANESE DESCENT ADMITTED TO THE COLLEGE

During its first three decades only three African American students were admitted to NJC. One Latina matriculated in 1926 but did not graduate. Several students from China attended NJC, but their presence was sufficiently rare that the arrival of Angela Ahn from Shanghai in 1946 merited a front page news story in the *Caellian*.[8] By the early 1980s, Douglass College had made significant strides in diversifying the student population. The 1982 *Annual Report* indicated that there were 2,748 white students enrolled, 371 black students, 50 Puerto Rican students, 83 "other Hispanic" students, 102 "Oriental" (Asian, Pacific Islander) students, 3 American Indian students, and 125 "other" (no information).[9]

Far more is involved in becoming a diverse and inclusive women's college, however, than discussions of access typically convey. Equitable recruitment and admission programs have been accompanied by transformation of the curriculum, campus climate, and institutional culture to enable diversity to operate as a means to and a mode of academic excellence. This chapter traces the transformation of Douglass from a white-majority institution to a college in which diverse American and international women not only converge but also thrive.

From Access to Equity

Early experiments with coeducation and racial integration across the nation quickly revealed that equal education requires far more than access. As women and students of color "gained equal access to more institutions, it became clear that their presence alone did not ensure the innovations necessary to provide them with truly equal educations. . . . [It] did not seem to alter the attitudes of administrators or instructors . . . nor did it assure equal treatment . . . within the institution."[10] Presumptions concerning white male superiority allowed racism and sexism to permeate the curriculum. In higher education institutions in the United States, the curriculum was "largely about, by and for [white] men. . . . Generalizations about human experience based exclusively on male subjects" circulated as accredited knowledge.[11] Prior to the 1980s, proper English grammar mandated "masculine generics"—the use of male pronouns and terms to refer to all humans.[12] "When small numbers of women and other groups entered the hallowed halls of ivy, they were expected to conform (and often did and do) to the norms already set by the male-dominated institution. . . . Black students were expected to settle in like other students."[13] Yet attempting to assimilate to norms from which one has been intentionally excluded can entail a form of cultural annihilation.[14] "Invisibility and silence are characteristic experiences of subordinated groups, especially in settings created by and controlled by those with structural power . . . those not of the entitled categories may experience a particular kind of silence infused with feelings of not being quite at home, of anxiety, of self-doubt."[15]

In *The Black Student Protest Movement at Rutgers*, Richard P. McCormick notes that Douglass remained an all-white or predominantly white institution throughout the twentieth century: "For two decades after it was founded in 1918, there were no Black graduates; down to 1965 there were fewer than 50."[16] African American students at Douglass during these early decades have spoken about the discrimination and the isolation they experienced. Juanita Wade Wilson (DC '66), the first black student allowed to share a room with a white student, mentioned the

> loneliness of searching for oneself in Blackness in a sea of whites. . . . There was no overt racism because there were so few Blacks on campus—we didn't matter. Isolation was our index of systemic discrimination. . . . There was no mention of Black authors in classes, interested students had to form their own reading groups. . . . Many came from all-black high schools, which had nourished them in the old fashioned way—counseled by adults who cared. By contrast at university, the attitude was more, "you're here, so what?" There were no mentors.[17]

Wilma Harris (DC '66) emphasized that "classwork was hard," but the difficulty was exacerbated because black women "felt an obligation to be successful, to live up to their predecessors and set a standard so other African Americans would be admitted."[18] Arriving at Douglass from a segregated school system in Washington, DC, Barbara Morrison Rodriguez (DC '71), noted that pioneering Black students "paid a price for integration. They lost the 'cocoon'—the warm, loving community of all-Black schools. Before 1969, Black students were expected to be grateful for the educational opportunity Douglass provided . . . to say 'thank you for letting us be here.' Yet they also anticipated being discriminated against, so some self-isolated to avoid rejection."[19]

Black students made their first small enrollment gains in the late 1960s. "By 1968, 115 Black students were among the 2860 women enrolled in the College. . . . Douglass had made more progress in recruiting and meeting the needs of African American students than any of the other undergraduate units at Rutgers."[20] Between 1968 and 1980, African Americans increased from 4 percent to 9.9 percent of the Douglass student population. By 1990, blacks constituted 11.6 percent, growing to 12.4 percent of the student body by 1999—roughly reflecting the composition of the New Jersey population.[21] In the aftermath of the assassination of Dr. Martin Luther King, the attitudes of a growing number of black students on campus changed dramatically. In the words of Juanita Wade Wilson (DC '66). "Students developed militancy. They became determined to change the institution."[22] They organized the Douglass Black Student Congress (DBSC). Drawing lessons from the postcolonial movements across Africa, DBSC insisted that "they must liberate themselves from the inhibitions of subordination to the values of a dominant culture. . . . They must develop their capacity to confront, analyze and articulate another kind of experience, which commands no place in the institutions that are the guardians of the dominant culture."[23] Toward that end, DBSC pointed out that "there was only one Black faculty member of nearly 200 Douglass faculty; one Black counselor, whose duties involved counseling all commuter students.

There were almost no Black secretaries or administrators. There were no Black history courses; only two English courses dealt with Black experience in the United States; there were no Black cultural programs on campus."[24] They met with Dean Margery Somers Foster to demand the hiring of black faculty and the creation of a course on the history of blacks in the United States.[25] Black student activism escalated in late spring 1968 as students staged demonstrations in the dining commons, walked out of classes taught by faculty they deemed insensitive to the needs of black students, refused to speak with white students, and distributed leaflets airing their grievances.[26]

By demanding black studies programs, new student services, hiring of minority faculty and a less Eurocentric curriculum, Black students began educating Douglass administrators, faculty, and students about the complex ways that white privilege is encoded within the practices of a white-dominant institution. Seeking to make visible the forms of marginalization that relegated some to the status of "second class citizens," DBSC offered an important insight:

> To recognize diversity—the condition of being different—with no pejorative connotations attached . . . any educational institution (to be worthy of the name) must create an environment that will nurture, stimulate, and challenge the many members of its community. . . . Respect for diversity demands more than simply infusing a few thoughts or facts about . . . [the marginalized] into what has become known as American History. The concept requires a refocusing of subject matter, a transformation shaped by the full presence of those previously excluded.[27]

In response to the students' demands, Douglass took its first steps to diversify the college.

Dean Foster appointed six committees to address admissions, scholarships, counseling, personnel, curriculum, and lectures. In less than one week, the committees generated twenty-five recommendations, which were approved by the faculty on March 6, 1969, with only minor modifications. Among the commitments: ninety-six spaces in entering class would be reserved for black students, even if this required curtailing out-of-state admissions; fifteen black faculty would be hired over the next two years. Douglass would also hire a black assistant dean, a black counselor-in-residence, and black professionals in admissions and financial aid. An African American studies program was approved and an African American Residence similar to the foreign language houses would be created. A summer orientation program would be extended from two weeks to six weeks. The Black Students Congress's suggestions for cultural programming were also adopted. By October 1969, twenty-three of the faculty commitments had been implemented or were in progress.[28]

Between 1969 and 1971, Douglass "moved more rapidly and with greater success (particularly in terms of low attrition rates) than almost any division of the university and the great majority of other colleges around the state. It . . . approximated its goal of being ethnically representative of the Black population of the state (and show[ed] signs of achieving the same goal for Puerto Rican students in the next few years)."[29] Yet friction between black and white students continued in the early 1970s, as both lodged charges of harassment, belligerent behavior, physical intimidation, gross discourtesy, and exclusionary practices. "White students viewed Blacks as disruptive aggressors; Blacks saw whites as insensitive and domineering."[30] To investigate "racial clashes on campus," Dean Foster appointed a Commission on Ethnic and Race Relations in April 1971.

The commission included students (Evelyn Daniels, chair of the Douglass Black Student Congress; Sara Douglass, president of the Government Association; and Zaida [Josie] Torres, chair, Douglass Puerto Rican Students), faculty (Michael Rockland, American studies, and Harvey Waterman, political science), and an administrator (C. Maxene Summey [DC '70], special assistant to the dean for equal opportunity programs). Holding nine hearings over five weeks in late April and May, the commission invited members of the college community (including students, faculty, administrators, and staff) to testify about their experiences with racism on campus. Over the next seven months, the commission crafted a remarkable document, designed to try to explicate how practices perceived as racially "neutral" by whites are grounded in and reproduce white privilege. Rejecting the view that racism is a matter of individual attitude, the commission sought to make visible both cultural and institutional racism.

Commission members articulated a concern that they found it difficult to fairly represent the diverse views of all who testified at their hearings. They acknowledged that the *Report of the Commission on Ethnic and Race Relations* dealt primarily with black-white relations on campus, "as there seemed to be less tension between Puerto Rican students and Black or White students on campus."[31] They also acknowledged that they were working in a climate of general mistrust. To dispel that mistrust, the commission sought to address "misperceptions [that] stem from crude generalizations on the basis of little evidence, from emotional tension which colors what one sees, and from ideologies which act as blinders to more complex reality.[32] These misperceptions structured views about the commission itself: blacks perceived the commission "as set up in response to white backlash and as incapable of confronting the realities and complexities of institutional racism. Whites tended to see the Commission as having been set up to cover up the role of some Blacks in disruptive behavior."[33] In this challenging environment, the commission's report sought to create the possibility for interracial understanding:

> Many whites seem to be oblivious to the extent to which America is still a racist country and of how apprehensive the average Black is on a minute-to-minute basis that she is about to be exposed to a racial slur. And some Blacks seem to be oblivious to the extent to which rhetoric contemptuous of whites is threatening to those whites. . . . For Blacks, as the minority culture, Black/white

relations are overwhelming, a twenty-four hour a day concern, while for whites, as the majority culture, Black/white relations are a part-time concern. Whites can sometimes turn off the problem; Blacks cannot. This may be one of the reasons for the quite natural turn to separatism by collegiate Blacks precisely at a time when integration was becoming a conventional goal of American society. Integration is probably harder on Blacks than on whites.[34]

In addition to providing a context to help explain racialized misperceptions, the report also traced how behaviors characteristic of many Douglass students had been racialized.

At one time or another, many aspects of Douglass life have become charged with racial significance. For example, rules and values are constantly being tested by students, uncertain of which values the faculty and administration mean to defend and which they are in the process of changing. Part of the testing is a widespread violation of minor, and sometimes major, rules. The simultaneous arrival on campus of large numbers of Black students has engendered the assumption that Black students are the major cause both of discontent and of thefts and other major violations. There seems to exist a myth, primarily subscribed to by older faculty and staff, as well as by alumnae, of "the good old days at Douglass College" when these problems did not exist; implicit is the assumption that, somehow, the problems would not exist today if Black students were not present on campus. These assumptions are faulty because many of the more radical challenges to traditional values in higher education come primarily from whites . . . and there is no persuasive evidence that thefts are primarily attributable to Blacks. Blacks are more visible . . . as are members of any minority group, which is one reason whites perceive Blacks as the troublemakers on campus.[35]

The report denounced "intolerable classroom situations where those who did not conform to the views of the instructor or a vocal and aggressive faction were made to feel unwanted or under attack."[36] Noting that it is the instructor's duty to insure that such situations do not occur, the report suggested that new pedagogical approaches were needed to ensure educational equity. "If instructors are to function effectively in a multi-ethnic college, they must be sensitive to student differences while showing neither prejudice nor favoritism related to ethnicity, politics, or life-styles of their students. The instructors must ensure that no one in the classroom is put down or harassed because of her views."[37]

The commission report recommended the appointment of an ombudsperson to investigate and ameliorate incidents of racial or ethnic significance, open meetings for faculty and students to discuss inclusive pedagogy, antiracism workshops during orientation, efforts by the Government Association to include black students within the organization and address black student concerns, and efforts by the *Caellian* to recruit students of color to the newspaper staff and to increase coverage of events of interest to students of color. In addition to recommending changes in administrative mechanisms, curriculum, pedagogy and student life organizations, the report concluded by insisting that whites and blacks must take responsibility for transforming campus culture:

> Whites need to understand the sources and causes for Black anger; avoid language and behavior that is insensitive or offensive to Blacks; whites must grapple with their own racism and presumption that "crime" is caused by Blacks; civility and cordiality are goals worth striving for, they may enable friendship. Whites should not confuse Black separatism with intimidation or harassment . . . must abandon assimilationist ideals . . . and accept that there is no longer one Douglass lifestyle. This should not need saying in a college community where diversity is supposedly prized.
>
> Blacks face the challenge of seeking education in an environment they perceive as unaware of or unsympathetic to their needs; they should give whites the benefit of the doubt . . . find ways to respond to racism without profanity, harassment or physical aggressiveness . . . communicate grievances to faculty and staff . . . recognize that Black separatism is not viable in a white majority community. They can press for inclusion of Black writers and subject matter in relevant courses, but must accept that not all courses will be amenable to change.[38]

The report included two supplements: appendix A provided a detailed list of racial misperceptions circulating on campus and in the country more generally; appendix B, written by Evelyn Daniels and Maxene Summey, the two African American members of the commission, took up the issue of institutional racism. They pointed out that activities and events sponsored by the college were primarily white oriented, chosen without representation of or input from students of color in decision-making processes. Appendix B also pointed out that subtle presumptions concerning white superiority surfaced in Douglass publicity materials and communications with incoming students.

> The *Douglass Admissions Bulletin* refers to "disadvantaged" minority students, unrealized potential, and latent realization of abilities. Whites are portrayed as qualified and possessing positive traits; Blacks are "deficient and in need of remediation." Letters of admission to Douglass chronicle "conditions," and deficiencies, situating students of color as second-class citizens, admitted on sufferance. Black students are greeted with stares, avoidance, even hostility on the part of many whites. White students are affirmed and welcomed; they see that the administration shares their negative view of Black students.[39]

Daniels and Summey also provided recommendations to remedy these problems: including students of color in event planning, changing the language in recruitment materials to reflect and be supportive of a diverse student body, developing flexible admissions criteria, avoiding all references to disadvantage, making academic support services such as tutoring and lightened academic loads available to all students to remove the stigma from black students who used such services.

Douglass took the *Report of the Commission on Ethnic and Race Relations* seriously, renewing efforts to recruit increasing numbers of students of color and to develop administrative, curricular, and co-curricular programs that would affirm and empower diverse students. Latinas grew from 3.3 percent of the student population in 1981 to 4.9 percent in 1990, 7.7 percent in 1999, and 19 percent in 2016; Asian American students increased from 2.5 percent of the student body in 1981 to 15 percent in 1999 and 23 percent in 2016; and African Americans increased from 9.9 percent to 12.4 percent in 1999 and 20.6 percent in 2016.[40] Progress in changing institutional and academic practices, however, was neither quick nor systemic. Each new class of students encountered challenges in their efforts to grapple with racism, sexism, and homophobia.

In April 1978, Douglass students of color again organized protests against persistent racism on campus. The *Targum* reported:

> Minorities at Douglass feel the pressure of prejudice ensconced in the "Debbie Douglass" stereotype; white students don't talk or interact with students of color or Spanish speakers; white students complain of loud music in dorms but never ask black students to turn it down, allowing the issue to fester; white students think black students inferior and manifest surprise when Blacks perform well in class or in athletics. . . . Professors are more prejudiced than students. . . . A Speech teacher said that 'Blacks can't speak proper English because they have thick tongues and dialect.[41]

Dean Jewel Plummer Cobb initiated an investigation of the students' complaints. In her 1979 *Report on Minority Concerns*, Nancy Richards, Douglass dean of students, validated the students' charges. Her analysis of the expenditure of student activity funds indicated disproportionate support for white student organizations. Although African American and Latina students repeatedly requested funds for cultural events, the Student Activities Board allocated them far less than $9,429 that students of color had paid in student fees. Dean Richards also endorsed the students' proposal to enhance Puerto Rican studies at Douglass, increasing the number of instructors from one to two to facilitate student completion of courses needed for the Certificate in Puerto Rican Studies.[42]

In 1979, to devote greater attention to the needs of students of color, Dean Jewel Plummer Cobb appointed the Douglass Equal Opportunity Board (DEOB). Their first major undertaking was to address student demands for the hiring and retention of faculty of color. In response to student demonstrations across New Brunswick in spring 1979, Provost Wheeler asked each department to respond to a series of issues about minority affairs. The DEOB seized this opportunity to request to meet with faculty in all Douglass academic departments. In 1980, board members visited fifteen departments to discuss minority hiring plans, as well as student perceptions of bias in departmental courses. Their report chronicles the casual dismissal of minority student concerns by many white faculty: "Some departments are unaware of any bias, indifference, or insensitivity of classroom instructors to members of minority groups or their special problems."[43] Where students reported faculty comments in class that made them uncomfortable and failure to include relevant work by scholars of color in course material as reasons for avoiding certain classes, faculty attributed low minority student enrollment to students' "lacking the educational skills to thrive in the field, writing difficulties, and inability to successfully complete course work."[44] Seeing no problem with their own academic practices, these departments also saw no reason to recruit scholars of color. When questions were asked specifically about the absence of minority faculty in the departments, routine responses suggested that there were "no qualified candidates.... Douglass salaries were too low.... [or] minority scholars recruited by Douglass were not accepted by the New Brunswick discipline."[45] Poor records of retention in departments that had hired scholars of color were explained in terms of the scholars' lack of publications, their devotion of too much time to students, or their recruitment to schools that offered higher salaries.[46] Tracing these stock responses across science, social science, and humanities departments, the DEOB drew attention to the sizable task that lay ahead if Douglass was to transform its academic and institutional culture.

Drawing insights from critical race scholarship, the DEOB emphasized that the presumption of inferiority is one of the most persistent barriers to minority achievement. Singular attention to the "deficiencies of minority or women or poor students ... [fails to] consider the inadequacies of the institution. As important as academic support programs are for many of these students, the total learning environment is just as critical: institutional expectations of these students; faculty attitudes; number of female and minority role models in administrative, faculty, and staff ranks; opportunities to learn about the multicultural heritage of this country, and many other elements contribute to intellectual development."[47] Despite the magnitude of the challenge, the DEOB committed itself to the task of institutional transformation: "Under the leadership of Professor Emily Alman, the DEOB was more vigorous than similar committees at the other colleges and could call on a large number of faculty members for volunteer services as recruiters and advisers."[48]

Working with the newly appointed assistant dean for minority affairs and special programs, the DEOB purchased the film *Impact: Racism, the Dividing Line* and organized group discussions with white students, staff, and faculty groups. It organized a four-hour antiracism seminar in late August for house chairwomen, student advisers, and commuter advisers. It organized a special orientation for black and Latino students and held workshops on institutional racism with the Student Government Association and peer counselors. It also monitored student government funding for projects to ensure equitable distribution of student activity fee monies, which led to a 100 percent increase in funding for minority student organizations.[49] Over the decade, students of color created a number of organizations such as the Asian Students Association, the Chinese Students Society, Sociedad de Estudiantes Cubana, and the West Indian Student Organization, which along with the Douglass Black Student Congress and the Puerto Rican Student Association (renamed the Latin American Women's Organization in 1988) sought to build solidarity, celebrate diversity, and "inform and educate the academic community" about the diverse histories and cultures of the United States.[50]

Acknowledging that racism is a systemic problem that requires an active role by whites to resolve, the DEOB pledged to continue work to educate and convert the entire college community. Toward that end, it organized a number of programs designed to familiarize white students with pervasive racist tropes in popular culture, ranging from a film series designed to illuminate themes explored by Donald Bogle in *Toms, Coons, Mulattoes, Mammies and Bucks: An Interpretive History of Blacks in Film* and lectures by Michelle Wallace, author of *Black Macho and Myth of the Superwoman*, and Benjamin Hooks, president of the NAACP, to gospel concerts; and performances by a jazz composer and performer and by Ballet Majeico, a dance troop from Paterson. The DEOB also hosted a reception for minority students and faculty in October and held regular meetings with minority faculty and staff to discuss common concerns and coordinate programming efforts.[51]

▲ DOUGLASS BLACK STUDENT CONGRESS, 1981

Working with the University Affirmative Action Office, the DEOB began monitoring the underrepresentation of faculty of color. In 1980, there were four black tenured faculty at Douglass College, six untenured black faculty, seven contingent black faculty, and four black teaching assistants. There were no tenured or untenured Latino faculty. Despite student mobilizations for minority faculty hiring, no new faculty of color had been hired that academic year. The DEOB noted that deficiency narratives alleging that there were no qualified minority applicants for open positions was closely linked to the assumption of many departments that only graduates of Ivy League schools were qualified to teach at Rutgers. Such a narrow focus replicated pro-white hiring bias as the Ivy Leagues were the institutions least likely to admit students of color.

With university reorganization in 1981, faculty of color and women faculty began to lose ground. The Affirmative Action Office noted that "since 1981–1982, the representation of both minorities and females among full-time faculty *decreased* by one percent. The *decrease* in minority representation occurred in Camden and New Brunswick; of females in New Brunswick and Newark."[52] The 1989 *Report of the Office of Affirmative Action and Employment Research* once again documented losses on the part of African American and Latino faculty, while indicating an increase in the representation of Asian Americans: "Since 1985–86, the increase in minority faculty representation can be attributed to a rise in the number and representation of Asians/Pacific Islanders. During the five year period, their number increased by 32 to 166, resulting in an increase in their representation to 6.7%. The numbers of Black and Hispanic faculty *decreased* slightly, by three and five respectively."[53] While noting that the representation of women faculty had increased by 0.2 percent over the past five years, the report pointed out that "among junior faculty, the number of females decreased by 15, resulting in a 0.2% decrease in their representation."[54] The decrease in women faculty was particularly painful to the DEOB because one decade earlier, women constituted 54 percent of the Douglass faculty, compared with 7 percent at Rutgers College and 13 percent at Livingston.[55]

Despite the DEOB's varied efforts, racial tensions again flared in fall 1987. On December 11, black Douglass students staged a sit-in at Jameson, which was precipitated in part by the closing of Africana House. Dean Mary Hartman appointed the Dean's Advisory Committee on Minority Recruitment and Retention, which recommended the development of a new program for orientation to heighten awareness of cultural diversity. For advice about the proposed program, Dean Hartman turned to the National Coalition Building Institute (NCBI), an international nonprofit leadership development network dedicated to the elimination of racism and other forms of oppression. NCBI conducted a needs assessment at Douglass and returned in March 1988 to conduct a two-day training workshop in prejudice reduction, which was attended by six faculty, nine university police, and thirty-one staff members. NCBI organized two additional workshops that spring to increase awareness of unconscious bias and how it negatively affects students of color. More than two hundred student workers participated in these racial awareness workshops. Following this training, Douglass created multiracial conflict mediation teams to respond to campus issues. The Dean's Advisory Committee noted that Douglass students seldom manifested overt racism, but covert racism remained a problem. Characterizing these programs as a "small start to address manifestations of covert racism," the committee members expressed their "hope at a minimum to establish a climate that enables victims of prejudice to speak openly about their experiences and express their concerns more readily. Such freedom carries its own burdens, since the discussions of racist acts breed anger."[56]

In the early 1990s, Douglass launched special efforts to address racism on campus, presenting a four-week anti-racism training program and a year-long lecture series. The Student Government Association passed a Resolution against Bigotry and Prejudice, and sent copies to all students, encouraging them to participate in campus programs to address bigotry and prejudice related to race, religion, disability and sexual orientation. With training provided by Cheryl Clarke, Director of the Rutgers Office of Diverse Community Affairs, the DEOB organized an Anti-Bias Team in academic year 1992–1993, whose goal was "to anticipate and prevent bias incidents, or when incidents occur to respond and restore positive relations."[57] Acting as the Anti-bias Team for Douglass, the Equal Opportunity Board sponsored an anti-bias poster contest to breathe life into a new Help Stop Hate campaign. They created a new system to report bias complaints, placed a suggestion box for innovative anti-bias interventions in the Student Center, and formed a new Multicultural Student Life Committee. They also organized a town meeting to inform students about the kinds of bias incidents being reported, noting the increase in homophobic episodes, the intersection of racist and heterosexist incidents, and the emergence of anti-Islamic statements in a classroom context.

In 1994–1995, Douglass launched the Multicultural Peer Educators program with the goal of celebrating cultural diversity and reducing the incidence of biased behavior and attitudes. Patterned after Sexual Health Advocates, who had pioneered peer education at Douglass and Rutgers, multicultural peer educators became an effective means of promoting awareness of cultural biases and behavioral change. Seventeen students in the inaugural cohort participated in a six-month training program to prepare them to conduct workshops for house chairs and student advisers in residences. The Multicultural Peer Educators created a video, *Living Together on Campus*, which addressed bias incidents at Rutgers and was used extensively in anti-bias workshops. They also designed Human Relations 101, an orientation session for all incoming students, and they incorporated their findings about bias on campus and anti-bias strategies in a 1.5-credit house course, Intro to American Cultures, taught by Suzan Armstrong West and Margaret Klawunn. After the first year of this highly successful program, the DEOB invited students from other New Brunswick campuses to participate in the trainings.[58]

Given such a strong commitment to antiracism, Douglass students were profoundly disturbed by a statement made by President Francis Lawrence at a meeting with thirty faculty on the Camden campus to discuss post-tenure review. On November 11, 1994, in response to a question about standardized testing, President Lawrence raised the issue of lower SAT scores of African Americans, asking, "Do we refuse to admit anybody below a national standard or do we deal with a disadvantaged population that doesn't have the genetic hereditary background to have a higher average?" When the *Star-Ledger* picked up the story in January 1995, President Lawrence's words gained national attention, creating a furor on campus and across the country. President Lawrence issued a statement saying that he "misspoke and said the opposite of what he believes," but that did not quell the student uproar.[59]

The Douglass College Government Association passed a Resolution Demanding the Resignation of President Lawrence on January 31, 1995. The resolution provides powerful insight into the profound change in student values at Douglass since the 1970s and early 1980s. Denouncing the explicit racism of the president's statement, the resolution noted that "racism and prejudice, especially when promoted by public figures in esteemed positions, serves to separate the working people of New Jersey by ethnicity, sexual orientation, gender, and religion," and it insisted that there should be "no place for this blatant disrespect for people of color and women" within the higher education community in New Jersey.[60] Douglass students were also actively involved in campus demonstrations that called for the removal from office of President Lawrence and for additional efforts to diversify Rutgers. Douglass junior Eubiza Jorge was a key leader of the campus-wide mobilization, which involved more than four hundred students of all races and ethnicities, who demanded that the Board of Governors become more diverse, increasing the number of black and Latino and Latina members. The students also demanded heightened efforts to recruit and retain blacks and Latinos, including removal of the ACT and SAT from admission criteria. And they called for the expansion of Africana, Puerto Rican, and Hispanic Caribbean studies. Insisting, "No racist statement should go unchallenged," the students organized a walk-out from classes on February 8, 1995, which culminated in an occupation of the streets of New Brunswick, including an effort to block the Lynch Bridge across the Raritan River.[61]

Although the students' activism did not secure the removal of President Lawrence, it did generate the President's Multicultural Student Life Recommendations, which sought to improve the classroom climate for minority students by changing curriculum and promoting dialogue as one of its key goals. Noting the concerns of the Douglass Curriculum Committee that it oversees requirements for graduation but lacks authority to ensure that faculty incorporate material on race, gender, and ethnicity in all courses, Monica Devanas began offering workshops through the Teaching Excellence Center on multicultural issues in the classroom and teaching methods to enhance the performance of culturally diverse students.[62]

In the late 1990s, Douglass students continued to campaign to "help stop the hate," naming bias, bigotry, heterosexism, homophobia, racism, misogyny, anti-Semitism, and stereotyping as the target of their efforts. In fall 1997, a National Coming-Out Day poster and several Douglass College Government Association election posters in residence halls were defaced with anti-queer slurs. Again in the residence halls in spring

1998, posters for LABIA (Lesbians and Bisexuals in Action) and a poster for the Douglass Black Students Congress were defaced with homophobic and racist slurs. More than two hundred students signed a petition protesting the college's slow response to these bias incidents.[63] Suzan Armstrong West, dean of minority affairs, and Joan Lemoine, dean of students, held closed forums in the residence halls to discuss the incidents. Rutgers University police offered a five-hundred-dollar reward for information leading to apprehension of the perpetrator. In February 1998, Douglass dean Barbara Shailor created a Task Force on Future Bias Intervention Strategies, which recommended programming, staff development, new residence life protocols, and a comprehensive review of Douglass's multicultural plan. One consequence of this review was the multicultural transformation of the Yule Log ceremony, one of Douglass's oldest traditions. Originally called the Christmas Festival when initiated in 1918, by 2000 it was renamed Share the Light: Celebrate Together. Instead of presenting Christmas carols alone, the ceremony expanded to feature readings from Rig Veda, the Story of Chanukah, the Bible, the Qu'ran, and the Statement of Kwanzaa.

A second important outcome of the comprehensive review was far greater attention to the needs of lesbian, gay, bisexual, and transgender (LGBT) students on campus. Recognizing the stigma associated with lesbianism, particularly in a women's college, Douglass worked with student organizations, professional staff, and the Office of Social Justice Education and Diverse Community Affairs to develop peer support for coming out, and campaigns to break down homophobic stereotypes among the majority student population. Training was provided to ensure that counseling and health services were respectful of students' sexual choices and encouraged self-acceptance. Residence hall staff were trained to know how to deal with the homophobia of heterosexual students. The college pledged to take strong disciplinary action in cases of harassment. Women's Studies developed a series of courses on sexualities and introduced a Critical Sexualities Studies minor.

By taking student complaints seriously, creating commissions, boards, and task forces to devise innovative efforts to resolve intractable problems, and trying to implement fresh approaches, Douglass has diversified its student population and worked to become a site for solidarity and empowerment for all its students. As a women's college, its belief in gender equity committed it to a different way of thinking about difference: "A Western pattern has been to organize human differences of both sex and race hierarchically. White has been different from, and superior to, other colors. Men have been different from, and superior to, women. Any call for equity asks us to accept differences and then, in a far more difficult psychic and cultural task, to organize them as if each element had equal weight and value."[64]

To appreciate the scope of Douglass's shift from access to equity, then, it is helpful to consider the minimalist agenda for coeducation initially articulated by Rutgers College in the early 1970s. Rutgers College dean of arts and sciences Arnold B. Grobman anticipated three kinds of curricular changes resulting from coeducation. Existing courses would be altered to reflect the career interests of women: "in the biological sciences for example, a shift from premedical preparation to secondary school biology teaching preparation." Some courses would reflect the "traditional interests of women: "art history, religion, foreign languages, and anthropology." And the college would need some courses to specifically address women, such as "the role of women in American society."[65] By contrast, to paraphrase Mabel Clarke Peabody (DC '31), Douglass has long recognized how important it is to "avoid creating a 'composite Douglass woman.' The . . . differences of conditions and interests . . . are far too numerous to make such a character trustworthy or interesting."[66] Through arduous efforts over a century, Douglass has crafted an institutional environment and an academic culture that gives equal weight and value to its diverse students, helping each to construct an educational pathway suited to her intellectual interests.

▶ YULE LOG
CEREMONY, 2003

DOUGLASS RESIDENTIAL COLLEGE
Revitalizing Women's Education in the Twenty-First Century

DOUGLASS HAS PROVEN TO BE THE
SUSTAINABLE MODEL FOR WOMEN'S
HIGHER EDUCATION.

—Douglass Residential College
Strategic Plan, 2016–2023

In 2007, Douglass began its new incarnation as the only residential college at Rutgers.[1] Once again college administrators faced the challenge of advancing an empowering model of women's education within a changing research university.

Brainstorming with members of the board of the Institute for Women's Leadership (IWL), Dean Carmen Ambar had sketched a proposal for "democratizing women's education at Rutgers by reinventing Douglass College."[2] The proposal called for the development of "creative programs designed to enable women and minority students to understand the challenges posed by continuing inequality and to equip them to address those challenges."[3] Indeed, it recommended that Douglass expand its educational mission, "offering to all interested students a distinctive feminist curriculum tailored to fulfill the core distribution requirements identified in the Qualls Report, providing residential opportunities for those who seek the benefits of a supportive and intellectually-stimulating women's college experience, and providing an enhanced array of co-curricular opportunities involving students, faculty, and staff."[4] With Dean Ambar's departure, it was left to her successors to transform a blueprint into a vital undergraduate experience. This chapter traces the innovations of interim dean Dr. Harriet Davidson and the tenth dean of Douglass, Dr. Jacquelyn Litt, to cultivate curriculum and co-curricular programs, research opportunities, and sustained faculty-student interactions and thereby ensure that Douglass Residential College (DRC) offered students far more than a physical site and residence halls.

Transitioning to a New Era:
Interim Dean Harriet Davidson, 2008–2010

Longtime Douglass Fellow Harriet Davidson jointly appointed to the Departments of English and Women's and Gender Studies, was tapped by President McCormick in 2008 to serve as interim dean of the college. Like many of her predecessors, Dean Davidson faced "the continuing challenge" articulated by Acting Dean Margaret Judson in the 1960s: "To move ahead with courage and a spirit of adventure—to experiment with new curricula and new approaches to learning—to introduce new areas of knowledge—to work out ways for more students to work independently."[5] DRC faced the particular challenge of how to thrive without the academic functions it once had as a college, such as setting admission and graduation requirements and mounting academic courses, and without direct control over the funds and facilities relating to student life, such as housing and campus centers. Making the best of a reduced staff and budget, Dean Davidson looked back to the initiatives of Deans Cobb and Hartman and focused the work of the college on women's leadership and equality, partnering with the Department of Women's and Gender Studies to provide academic resources for a stimulating education in issues of gender justice. She also developed a campaign to demonstrate the continuing need for and the benefits of a women's college at Rutgers.

As discriminatory laws were struck down in the final decades of the twentieth century and women became the majority of students enrolled in higher education in the

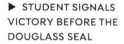

▶ STUDENT SIGNALS
VICTORY BEFORE THE
DOUGLASS SEAL

early twenty-first, many assumed that there was no longer any need for single-sex education for women. Yet women continued to be underrepresented in positions of leadership in public and private sectors, to experience pay inequality and sex-based job segregation, and to be overrepresented among minimum wage workers (76 percent) and the adult poor (80 percent). Despite their advances in enrollment in STEM fields, women continued to be underutilized in the professional ranks of scientists and engineers and to experience significant sexual harassment when employed in these fields.

Dean Davidson hired a new assistant dean for recruitment, Tania Castenada, who began working with Courtney McAnuff, the vice president for enrollment management, to develop recruitment materials and recruitment efforts that positioned DRC as a critical resource in addressing continuing inequities. Capitalizing on Douglass's history and mission, Dean Davidson began publicizing DRC as a college that taught diverse women students about the challenges posed by contemporary forms of inequality, preparing them to address those challenges and excel regardless of their academic specializations.

Under the new centralized admissions process, all Rutgers recruiters began to share information about Douglass with prospective women students, emphasizing that Rutgers is the only major research university that includes a women's residential college. Only after students were admitted to the university did they make a decision about academic programs and housing. Women were provided additional information about Douglass and its mission to offer a distinctive women-centered educational experience; providing residential opportunities for those who seek the benefits of a supportive and intellectually stimulating women's college experience; and providing an enhanced array of co-curricular opportunities involving students, faculty, and staff.

Recruitment studies document that entering students typically choose a college on the basis of the attractiveness of the residence halls and physical facilities. Dean Davidson worked with Barry Qualls, the vice president for undergraduate education, and teams of feminist faculty who had been energized by the Save Douglass campaign to demonstrate that DRC has far more to offer women students than a campus and residence halls. As the home of nationally and internationally renowned research centers and institutes on women; one of the best women's studies programs in the nation; and award-winning programs on women in math, science, and engineering, Douglass had expertise in women's education, an extensive network of faculty committed to its feminist mission, generous alumnae and friends devoted to its distinctive programs, and energy and innovative ideas. Building on these strengths, Davidson enhanced capacity-building programs and living-learning communities that offer students courses, research opportunities, internships, externships, and international study possibilities designed to prepare them for the challenges of contemporary life and for the responsibilities of leadership.

During the transition year of 2007–2008 as Douglass became Douglass Residential College, Dean Ambar had asked Professor Davidson to work with Women's and Gender Studies to develop a new mission course for DRC. Davidson and Dr. Barbara Balliet, then undergraduate program director in that department, and subsequently appointed associate dean of DRC in 2008, developed a new course called Knowledge and Power: Issues in Women's Leadership that was piloted in 2007–2008. Dr. Balliet handled the hiring and training of instructors for the course. The course introduces students to structures of power in the contemporary world that operate through race, gender, ethnicity, class, and nationality, with readings that cover an interdisciplinary range of works, from texts in sociology, political theory, and science studies to personal memoirs. Student assignments are designed to encourage students to see themselves as knowledge producers, not consumers, and to encourage their confidence in public speaking and writing. To facilitate faculty-student interaction, the course combines small group discussion sections limited to 22 students, with plenary sessions featuring lectures by women of extraordinary accomplishment, who talk about their routes to power, obstacles encountered along the way, and strategies they devised to overcome those obstacles.

To connect new students more closely with the activities at Douglass and the university, Dean Davidson, working with Associate Alumnae of Douglass College (AADC), raised funds to establish the Barbara Voorhees Mentor Program, which places an upper-level DRC student as a peer teaching assistant to work with the instructor in each discussion section of the Knowledge and Power course.

Barbara Voorhees mentors gain important leadership and teaching experience, completing a course designed to cultivate their mentoring skills and enhance their peer mentoring with first-year and transfer students at DRC. The Barbara Voorhees mentors serve as role models both through their academic achievement and their high level of engagement with the Douglass community. Inside the class, they help facilitate discussions and assist students with various aspects of course assignments, including the interview project, through which each DRC student crafts a paper on a woman leader that includes material from a personal interview with that leader. Outside of class, mentors accompany students to public lectures and events; meet with them one on one; and encourage them to become involved in student activities, organizations, and special programs. Students responded with enthusiasm to the new mission course for DRC. Knowledge and Power was approved by the Women's and Gender Studies faculty to serve as a gateway course to the department's major and by the Arts and Sciences faculty to fulfill a core general education requirement on twenty-first-century challenges.

This successful collaboration with Women's and Gender Studies was repeated with courses connected with the living-learning houses of Bunting Cobb and the Global Village strengthening the academic element as well as the co-curricular and student-life activities. Working with the Institute for Women and Art and with the Margery Somers Foster Center, the new Women and Creativity house offered students new opportunities to work in visual culture and social media. With scholarship support from AADC, two Global Village houses each year were funded to participate in an international service learning experience designed to foster global awareness and understanding. Dean

▲ HARRIET DAVIDSON, INTERIM DEAN OF DOUGLASS, 2008–2010,
WITH RED PINE AMBASSADORS

Davidson also worked with AADC on a major funding initiative that generated the initial gift from Kathleen W. Ludwig for the construction of the Global Village Learning Center, which opened in 2016.

Dean Davidson and the Douglass Project staff also began a stronger outreach to STEM students through initiatives on the environment, women's health, and engineering. Women students enrolled in the School of Environmental and Biological Sciences, located next to Douglass on the Cook campus, were recruited to Douglass to benefit from the mentoring provided by the Bunting Cobb House and the Douglass Project. Douglass staff devoted a year to environmental themes, organizing lectures and co-curricular activities. A highlight of the year was the campus visit of Majora Carter, the urban revitalization strategist and founder of the nonprofit environmental justice solutions organization Sustainable South Bronx. Douglass also hosted the first major women's health conference at Rutgers and began working with the Women and

Engineering Club to establish connections with women engineers, who were housed at the Busch campus.

To assist students to benefit fully from focused co-curricular activities in conjunction with their academic work, DRC's assistant dean Rebecca Reynolds worked with Associate Dean Barbara Balliet to create an advising system that helped students select "educational pathways" that combined course work, civic engagement, leadership training, and internships appropriate for particular majors. These pathways encouraged students to seek out diverse curricular and co-curricular experiences, and helped to clarify the often overwhelming number of opportunities available at a large university. To connect student work with career planning, the externship program was expanded as students were required to complete one or more short experiences shadowing an alumna in a field of interest. DRC also pioneered at Rutgers the first e-portfolio, an online platform that enables students to track their diverse curricular and co-curricular experiences, create a professional résumé, and save samples of their best work to facilitate job placement.

Like many of her predecessors, Dean Davidson opened the dean's house to many student activities, frequently hosting faculty, staff, and student dinners and receptions. She worked closely with student organizations, meeting with student clubs and governing organizations on issues and activist campaigns (such as changing the exclusively male-focused language of the Rutgers University alma mater), always encouraging students to make a difference. Dean Davidson demonstrated that DRC offered students a personal touch; plenty of time to get to know deans and college staff; multiple opportunities for academic, personal, and career advising; the familiarity and supportiveness of a small college combined with access to the vast resources of a major research university.

DRC's early initiatives were highly successful. Enrollment began to rise, as did diversity and academic excellence. The entering class of DRC in 2010 was more diverse and had a higher first-year GPA than any other unit at Rutgers.

Revitalizing Women's Education in the Twenty-First Century

Following a national search, Jacquelyn Litt, a sociologist specializing in medicalized motherhood, gender and care work, and survival strategies of low-income women, was named the tenth dean of Douglass in 2010. Dean Litt had served as the principal investigator for a National Science Foundation ADVANCE grant at the University Missouri and developed a national reputation as an expert in faculty mentoring. Her expertise was well suited to Douglass's strengths, particularly at a time when more than 50 percent of Douglass students were majoring in STEM fields. Drawing upon her work to promote gender equity in science, technology, engineering and mathematics, Dean Litt began to think creatively about how to extend the benefits of the "Douglass difference" to women students across the university.

Through her early interactions with university administrators, Dean Litt discovered that there was widespread misunderstanding of DRC. Although DRC had a strong

▶ JACQUELYN LITT,
DEAN OF DOUGLASS,
2010–

circle of loyal supporters, beyond that circle some university leaders were uncertain that the college could thrive and others were unclear about how DRC would function in Rutgers's new organizational structure. To secure the long-term success of DRC, Dean Litt sought to create innovative partnerships that would expand Douglass initiatives into new territories. Toward that end, she launched collaborative ventures within and beyond the School of Arts and Sciences to open more of Rutgers's world-class academic programs to Douglass students, while also demonstrating the importance of women's education and integrating DRC inextricably into a fast-changing university. In these ventures, President Richard McCormick; vice president of undergraduate education Barry Qualls; and Qualls's successor, Gregory Jackson, played pivotal roles, helping to clarify and secure DRC's position and providing strategic as well as financial support. Chancellor Richard Edwards and vice president for academic affairs and administration Karen Stubaus also contributed significant resources and helped Dean Litt chart the path forward.

A new partnership between DRC and the School of Engineering (SOE) was Dean Litt's first initiative to expand Douglass's mission. Working with Thomas Farris, dean of the SOE; Elaine Zundl, assistant dean of the Douglass Project for Rutgers Women in Math, Science, and Engineering; Ilene J. Rosen, SOE associate dean for student services; and Candice White, SOE assistant dean of undergraduate education, Litt created a living-learning community (LLC) for Douglass women engineering students. With financial support from Public Service & Gas in New Jersey, the LLC was designed to help redress the underrepresentation of women in engineering fields by incorporating Douglass's expertise in women's education and its hallmark STEM programs into the SOE.

Because marginalization plays such a critical role in women's decisions to quit engineering, SOE and DRC staff suggested that success in increasing retention rates required that the LLC be located on the Busch campus (i.e., the "science campus" at Rutgers). Expanding DRC's mission to benefit women engineering students, then, required a reconceptualization of the college. Dean Litt conceived Douglass not only as a physical location but also as a distinctive mode of women's education that could be exported to other sites across the university. After careful consideration, Dean Litt created a DRC satellite on the Busch campus, the first time that Douglass housing and programs were located beyond the Douglass campus.

Opening in 2012 with twenty students, the DRC LLC on Busch enrolled first-year women engineering students in both the Douglass mission course, Knowledge and Power, and a special section of Introduction to Engineering taught by Helen Buttner, professor of chemical, biochemical, and biomedical engineering. In addition to formal course work, LLC students participated in hands-on engineering projects that afforded intensive interaction with faculty, special research, and internship opportunities; professional development workshops; site visits to industry; tutoring opportunities; peer mentoring; and mentoring by graduate students and SOE faculty and alumnae.

In keeping with long-established Douglass traditions, the LLC students themselves created a vibrant environment for peer learning and support. Students in the first cohort requested expansion of the LLC to a four-year model. With financial and institutional support from the Office of the Vice-President for Undergraduate Education, DRC and SOE adapted key features of the LLC to include enhanced co-curricular activities throughout the participants' undergraduate engineering experience. With the establishment of an endowment for the LLC in 2016, the LLC was named the Reilly Douglass Engineering Living-Learning Community (Reilly DELLC). What had begun as a one-year program with 20 women students in 2012 evolved into a four-year program enrolling 114 women by 2017. Ninety-six percent of the first cohort graduated; of these, some found professional positions with corporations such as Bechtel, Corning, Nestle, and the Norfolk Naval Shipyard; others went on to graduate engineering programs, including at Rutgers, the University of California–Berkeley, and the University of Maryland. As national data indicates, LLCs for women cultivate a strong sense of efficacy, which contributes to high retention rates.[6] A Douglass Project survey in 2013 documented that the LLC experience afforded participants resilience, confidence, and an unwavering identification both as engineers and as "Douglass women." The rich opportunities provided by this LLC also helped to attract additional engineering students to Douglass: by 2017, engineering students constituted 8 percent of the DRC student body.

On the basis of the success of the Reilly DELLC, DRC worked with Rebecca Wright, professor of computer science and director of Rutgers Center for Discrete Mathematics and Theoretical Computer Science (DIMACS) to create a new LLC for women in computer science. In 2014, women comprised only 25% of computing professionals and 17% of computer science majors in the United States.[7] According to the National Science Foundation, computer science lags behind other STEM disciplines where the percentage of women earning bachelor's degrees reached 51% in 2004–5, up from 39% percent in 1984–85.[8] The DRC-Computer Science LLC was designed to cultivate interest in computer and technology careers and to recruit and retain women in these majors at Rutgers.

With support from the National Science Foundation, and in partnership with the School of Arts and Sciences and the Department of Computer Science, the DRC Computer Science Living-Learning Community (CS LLC) launched in 2017 with 17 women students. Under the leadership of Douglass Assistant Dean Geraldine Cochran, the CS LLC combines academic coursework taught by Professor Wright, staff and peer mentoring, career and leadership development, and research opportunities within a residential environment. Adopting intergenerational mentoring—a core feature of the Douglass Project—the CS LLC cultivates the talent of women undergraduates in computing science while affording them opportunities to mentor young girls in New Jersey via the Douglass-DIMACS Computing Corps (DDCC). With support from AT&T and Verizon, members of the CS LLC mentor students at the Woodrow Wilson Elementary School in New Brunswick, Theodore Schor Middle School in Piscataway, the Jonas Salk Middle School and Carl Sandburg Middle School in Old Bridge, devising activities to inspire the girls to explore careers in computer science and technology. Combining mentoring from faculty and DRC peers with mentoring of elementary and middle-school students, CS LLC heightens DRC students' commitment to succeed in this professional field, while helping to recruit the next generation of women to computer science.

To increase the number of women majoring in environmental science, another field in which women remain underrepresented, Dean Litt collaborated with Dean Robert Goodman and Associate Dean Richard Ludescher to create the Douglass-School of Environmental and Biological Sciences (SEBS) Environmental Science Living-Learning Community. Housed in the newly renovated Woodbury Residence Hall on the Douglass campus, this LLC combines course work, internships, community-impact projects, and field trips to environmental work sites and conferences. In keeping with Douglass's women-centered curriculum, participants in this LLC investigate contemporary environmental problems and their effects on women's health, developing interventions to mitigate negative health consequences. Co-curricular programs help students explore careers in environmental protection and remediation, while also preparing them for graduate studies in the field.

To enhance the career development of DRC students across a range of STEM fields, Project Super affords research opportunities in faculty labs in conjunction with a course designed to strengthen research skills. By 2016, DRC was supporting sixty students annually in laboratory and fieldwork sites, supervised by distinguished Rutgers faculty. Since its inception, the retention rate for science majors participating in Project Super has been 100 percent. Supported by Colgate and Douglass alumnae, Project Super has achieved university-wide recognition for successfully involving undergraduates in pathbreaking research.

Dean Litt has also strengthened DRC programs in the Global Village. Under the direction of Gwendolyn Beethem, the Global Village has expanded to include new houses: Leadership Education at Douglass; Women and Creativity; Women and Business; Women and Global Education; Women in Medicine; Women, Media, and Technology; Women and Public Health; and Sexualities. House courses and co-curricular programs are designed to foster global thinking, community engagement, and a social justice approach to education. Global thinking encourages students to understand the interconnectedness of the global and local, situating contemporary problems and their potential solutions within larger geopolitical frames, and thereby countering ethnocentrism and parochialism. Whether analyzing climate change, poverty, homelessness, or gender-based violence, students probe transnational power dynamics that perpetuate local and global inequalities and consider how constructive solutions must encompass families, neighborhoods, communities, cities, regions, nations, and global forces. The houses in the Global Village also forge partnerships with community organizations to cultivate equitable relations between students and community. In contrast to hostile "town and gown" relations that have haunted many colleges and universities in the United States, the forms of community engagement provided within the Global Village encourage students to identify, reflect upon, and move beyond stereotypes that shape interactions between groups. Through this dual focus on the global and the local, the LLCs of the Global Village bring Douglass women together across diverse fields of academic specialization, fostering intercultural appreciation, global awareness, and a sense of community.

The Women and Creativity House also affords students an opportunity to present their artworks in an annual exhibition in conjunction with the Mary H. Dana Women Artists Series. Since 2015, Connie Tell, the administrative director of the Center for Women in the Arts and Humanities has worked with the students in the Women and Creativity House to catalog their artworks and exhibit them in a professional gallery, thereby helping to support new generations of women artists.

Building upon initiatives created by Dean Carmen Twillie Ambar, Dean Litt has increased study-abroad opportunities, enabling more students in the Global Village to participate in international-service learning. Combining service learning with language and cultural studies, these international experiences have been developed in relation to the house mission of specific units within the Global Village such as Africana House, Casa Hispanica, East Asia House, and Human Rights House. Recent house trips have taken Global Village students to Cambodia, the Dominican Republic, Mexico, Peru, Romania, South Africa, and Thailand. With funding provided by Douglass alumnae, DRC provides scholarships for participants in these house trips, thereby removing the financial barriers that preclude students from overseas studies.

Douglass further developed its global reach by creating the first college chapter of the Friends of the United Nations Population Fund (UNFPA). Initiated with the support of alumna Wendy Cai Lee (DC '96), then chair of the UNFPA board, this student organization addresses issues of gender and development, focusing on pressing global issues such as reproductive and maternal health and infant mortality. It has also raised funds to assist women in disaster areas.

In fall 2016, the opening of the Kathleen W. Ludwig Global Village Learning Center in the Jameson Complex on the Douglass campus created a new hub for the Global Village and global education at DRC. Funded by gifts of 265 Douglass alumnae, raised by the AADC, and funds from Rutgers, the nineteen thousand-square-foot facility includes residences for thirty-six students, an apartment for a visiting scholar, several classrooms and lounges, advanced technologies for global communications, and an assembly space that can accommodate over two hundred people. Adorned with artwork from members of the Women and Creativity House and photographic exhibits documenting the service learning endeavors of DRC students, the Ludwig Center provides a Douglass locale to celebrate global programs and foster engagement with global issues. Home to the Douglass's Global Summit (an annual conference devoted to issues of global justice), Global Village plenary speakers, who address topics of major significance, joint programs with Rutgers GAIA Centers, and collaborations with external partners focused on global issues, the Ludwig Center initiates a new chapter in Douglass's global outreach.

During the ribbon-cutting ceremony, Chancellor Richard Edwards captured some of the excitement about the Ludwig Center and the DRC:

> Douglass adds to Rutgers' ethic of innovation and advancement: no other university can boast a center devoted exclusively to educating women on global issues; no other university can claim a 30 year-old project designed to advance women in STEM, and no other university can boast about the College's newest initiative—The BOLD Center at Douglass for women's career and leadership development. . . . The Ludwig building is the next step in Douglass's success. It will serve as a hub for Douglass, Rutgers, and surrounding communities to come together to explore challenges and work on solutions to problems of women's status in our increasingly globalized world.[9]

▲ GROUNDBREAKING CEREMONY FOR THE KATHLEEN W. LUDWIG GLOBAL VILLAGE
LIVING-LEARNING CENTER

Dean Litt established an Alumnae Advisory Board in 2013 to help plan for the future of DRC, provide advice about strategies to improve facilities, and increase alumnae engagement and fund-raising. Led initially by Wendy Cai Lee (DC '96), who was succeeded by Julie Domonokos (DC '83), the board advises the dean and liaises with students and industry partners in support of DRC programs.

In 2015 with these initiatives in place, Dean Litt conducted a strategic-planning process to identify DRC strengths and forge its future. The process included surveys and focus groups with students, alumnae, staff, and faculty and creative suggestions from a university-wide task force. Student responses to questions about "Douglass's greatest successes" indicate the power of DRC programs. At the top of the students' list of the college's successes were Douglass signature programs, including the Global Village, Knowledge and Power, the Douglass Project for Women in STEM, Douglass in D.C., PLEN, summer research stipends in Project Super, and internships and externships, and the emphasis on women's empowerment. Students praised the "incredible networking opportunities," the leadership opportunities, and the ability of the college to "create a niche for every student." Students cited their "pride and ownership" of DRC as a space where "student voice matters." And they celebrated its diversity, "high morale," and "traditions that connect past to present and future." Calling Douglass a "community" and a "sisterhood of confident, intelligent women," contemporary DRC students embraced their identity as Douglass women, just as their predecessors have done for a century.[10]

The strategic review culminated in the publication of *Douglass Residential College Strategic Plan 2016–2023: A Transformative Future; Building on 100 Years of Success*. The plan calls for the continued integration of the college into the university and identifies six critical priorities for the years ahead: (1) advancing intellectual excellence in the core curriculum; (2) enhancing the transformative student experience by creating a new BOLD Center for leadership, career, and personal development; (3) establishing Douglass's prominence as a leader in STEM education for women; (4) furthering the Douglass emphasis on fostering inclusiveness; (5) promoting Douglass as a leader in women's education at Rutgers University, in the United States, and around the world; and (6) developing the resources needed to support growth and innovation at Douglass.

As a result of the strategic planning process, the college instituted new requirements for all DRC students, including involvement in staff and peer-mentoring programs and participation in an "experiential education" project in the form of primary research, externships, internships, service work, or leadership training. Both requirements seek to foster individual resilience, a sense of community, and academic success, while also helping students prepare for careers, advanced study, and leadership. To enable students to fulfill these new requirements, DRC created the BOLD (Building Opportunities for Leadership and Development) Center, which offers individualized staff and peer mentoring, internship and externship placements, and workforce preparation and leadership development programs. In accordance with the maxim "Lead Well, Work Well, Live Well," the center facilitates student exploration of identity and confidence building as a means to achieve aspirations, and development of critical skills such as public speaking, team building, negotiation, organizational management and fund-raising, which are essential to diverse personal and professional settings. Partnering with, yet differentiating itself from, Rutgers Career Services, the BOLD Center emphasizes the unique challenges women face in navigating the workforce, planning careers, undertaking leadership, and managing work-life integration. From matriculation to graduation, the center assists students in clarifying their personal, academic, and professional objectives and forging positive relationships with peer and alumnae mentors, faculty, and professional organizations in diverse fields.[11]

To implement the strategic plan, responsibilities in College Hall were reorganized. Associate Dean Ellen Lieberman assumed oversight of undergraduate programs, including the Global Village and Academic Programs, directed by Dr. Elizabeth Gunn; Recruitment and Student Engagement, led by Amanda Hardie; and the Douglass Project for Rutgers Women in Math, Science, and Engineering. The BOLD Center at Douglass for Career, Leadership, and Personal Development is directed by Dr. Leslie Danehy, who reports directly to Dean Litt. In 2018, the undergraduate programs moved to the Carpender House, on the corner of Nichol Avenue and George Street, which was renovated with financial support from Chancellor Richard Edwards as part of the New Brunswick Strategic Plan.

Dean Litt also created the DRC Office of Institutional Advancement, with responsibility for communications, fund-raising, and student-alumnae engagement. To ensure growing enrollments and thriving student programs, this office seeks to publicize DRC's successful model of women's higher education; cultivate alumnae involvement; and heighten Douglass's reputation locally, nationally, and internationally. Led by assistant dean of development Maureen Mollohan, the Office of Institutional Advancement organizes fund-raising for DRC, including for student scholarships and academic and co-curricular programs. The office also raises major gifts for capital improvements.

While developing these initiatives at DRC, Dean Litt has also been serving as an ambassador for Douglass to the larger university community during a period of intense and rapid change. During the first two years of his administration (2012–2014), President Robert Barchi devoted considerable resources and effort to the incorporation of the University of Medicine and Dentistry of New Jersey into the new Rutgers Biomedical and Health Sciences in compliance with the New Jersey Medical and Health Sciences Restructuring Act.[12] The significant costs of the merger tightened budgets across other Rutgers's units and heightened competition for scarce resources. In this difficult fiscal environment, Dean Litt launched a campaign to demonstrate the importance of Douglass to the university. She partnered with the Schools of Arts and Sciences, Engineering, and Environment and Biological Sciences, and the new Honors College on a host of programs to help deans and faculty see the value added by Douglass's expertise in women's education. She recruited sixty faculty mentors from the sciences and health services to supervise DRC students' summer research placements in labs across the university. She worked with the New Brunswick Chancellor's Office to make visible gendered implications of programs and proposals that appeared to be gender neutral. She assisted the Office of the Vice President for Enrollment Management in national and international recruitment efforts, which resulted in impressive increases in the number of students requesting to enroll in Douglass. Through these strategic engagements during her first five years in office, Dean Litt succeeded in almost doubling the resources that Rutgers provides to DRC.

Annual surveys of students enrolled in the Douglass mission course, Knowledge and Power: Issues in Women's Leadership, indicate that students appreciate the DRC model for women's education: 66 percent of the students report that the course has helped them see themselves as leaders and increased their understanding of issues facing women and women of color; 69 percent indicate that the course has encouraged them to get involved in the community; and 79 percent note that it has motivated them to attend DRC programs and events. In the words of one student, "This is a great time for me to network, to get to know more about myself and my place in the world. I feel empowered as a result of being a Douglass woman and I am forever grateful!" Another noted, "I have an incredible sense of belonging to the DRC and an overwhelming sense of support from everyone. You have made me feel at home in the university. I am happy and proud to be a Douglass woman." A final student comment demonstrates the critical role that Douglass plays at Rutgers: "Douglass Residential College is the best part of my first semester at Rutgers."[13] By providing a supportive, women-centered educational experience, DRC enables students to embrace a dual identity as Douglass women and as Rutgers students. Transcending tensions of earlier eras that pitted Douglass against Rutgers, DRC is fostering a "both/and" identity that empowers Douglass women to excel at Rutgers and in the world following graduation.

Growing enrollments, academic excellence, and diversity at DRC are the best indicators of Douglass's revitalization. The number of students has increased from 1,812 in 2011 to 2,545 in 2016–2017.[14] DRC students have higher secondary school GPAs than entering students in other Rutgers–New Brunswick units; 8.9 percent of DRC students participate in the School of Arts and Sciences Honors Program, compared with 6 percent of students in other undergraduate units. Douglass women were admitted to Rutgers's new Honors College at twice the rate of students from any other undergraduate program.[15] Indeed, Douglass students compose 25 percent of the women students in the Rutgers's Honors College, and through a new Honors College/ Douglass Residential College Community on College Avenue, DRC provides innovative programming to these high-achieving students. The academic excellence of DRC students is incontestable: Douglass students were inducted into Phi Beta Kappa at three times the rate of students in the School of Arts and Sciences—an achievement all the more remarkable in light of the fact that the largest number of Douglass students now major in biology and biomedical sciences. Diversity is also the hallmark of the new DRC: 67 percent of Douglass students are women of color, 51 percent come from families who speak a language other than English at home, and 8 percent are of nontraditional age.[16]

DRC demonstrates what is possible within a women's college that embraces equality and social justice as central to twenty-first-century education. By identifying the obstacles to women's equality and preparing students to address them, Douglass continues to groom women to wrestle with adversity and to overcome it, to analyze inequity and redress it. Building a curriculum on feminist and critical race scholarship, using feminist pedagogy to empower and inspire, inculcating global consciousness and solidarity through engaged service learning, involving students in research and internship experiences, forging community across Douglass generations through mentoring and externship programs, DRC offers a "sustainable and exportable model of women's education."[17] The importance of this model of women's education was affirmed on February 13, 2017, when the New Jersey Senate passed a Resolution on the Occasion of Douglass's 100th Anniversary, which commended "Douglass Residential College at Rutgers–the State University of New Jersey in New Brunswick, an outstanding educational organization that serves as the only all-female residential college at a flagship public research university in the nation."

THE DOUGLASS DIFFERENCE

WOMEN NEED A SENSE OF WHAT A
WOMEN'S PLACE CAN BE—NOT SOME-
WHERE TO RETIRE AND BE PROTECTED,
BUT TO BECOME EMPOWERED, GO
FORTH FROM, SURE OF THEIR OWN
VALUE AND INTEGRITY...NOT JUST
HAVING BEAUTIFUL RESIDENCE HALLS
AND GARDENS, BUT A SOUL.

—Adrienne Rich

"Alumnae observe that Douglass is always changing—and they are right!"[1] Each class of entering students is distinctive, bringing with it new hopes, fears, and interests influenced by a rapidly changing world. Yet Douglass has always been far more than "an organization of students"—the conception of a college offered by President Mason Gross in 1964. Through all its various transformations over the past century, Douglass has been "a community . . . composed of individuals with different talents, faults, and dreams . . . not an amorphous entity," as the preface to the 1972 *Redbook* so aptly characterized the college. The Douglass experience engenders an identity and a sense of belonging. In the words of a 2011 first-year student, "My first-year Douglass experience chokes me up every time I think about it. I feel a part of something so much bigger than I am."[2] Introducing students to a wider world, Douglass is the kind of "women's place" envisioned by Adrienne Rich—a physical space, a mode of life, an opening of the mind, a development of expertise, a sense of community, an ethos, an attitude, a forging of friendships, an accumulation of memories. For students, alumnae, deans, faculty fellows, and professional staff, Douglass is a women's college that "encourages women to think in terms of possibilities rather than limitations and provides the kind of education that turns possibilities into realities."[3] This chapter explores differences and continuities at Douglass, comparing Douglass with other women's colleges and examining changes in Douglass women across decades to explicate the illusive "Douglass difference."

Distinguishing Douglass from Other Women's Colleges

The growth of coeducation in the twentieth century has made survival a pressing issue for all women's colleges. Recent surveys indicate that only 3–4 percent of young women say that they would consider attending a women's college.[4] Facing this constraint, women's college administrators have accentuated the historical strengths of their institutions, while connecting them to new circumstances.[5] They have devised innovative strategies to enable their colleges to flourish. Some have encouraged more research on women, some have become an institute for advanced study (Radcliffe) or an institute for women's leadership (Newcomb), some have emphasized women's continuing education (Sarah Lawrence), some have developed ties with other educational agencies and institutions (the Boston Consortium), some have cultivated an integrated curriculum that recognizes the importance of gender in all forms of endeavor (Barnard), and some have admitted male students (Vassar).[6]

In charting its survival strategies, Douglass has differed from other women's colleges from the outset, combining public and private initiatives to establish the college. Indeed, its founding and survival benefited from state and federal funding and from a

▶ GEORGE STREET BRIDGE, DOUGLASS CAMPUS

grassroots subscription campaign orchestrated by the New Jersey State Federation of Women's Clubs, as well as donations from private philanthropists. Douglass has combined a strong liberal arts curriculum with career preparation attuned to realities of women's lives, while also initiating pathbreaking programs for women in nontraditional careers in STEM fields and in public and global leadership. Far more than any other women's college, Douglass has cultivated a diverse student population. In 2016, 67 percent of Douglass students were women of color, compared with an average of 48 percent at other women's colleges. Through arduous efforts, it has developed mechanisms to support women's diverse identities and cultivate inclusiveness in a single-sex environment.[7] Unlike any other women's college, Douglass has flourished within a major public research university, helping to launch and providing a home for an unparalleled set of research centers and institutes that focus on women's lives, livelihoods, and leadership. And with the exception of two brief periods when it was administered by acting deans (Albert E. Meder, 1932–1934, and John L. Swink, May 1–June 30, 1960), Douglass has been led by women.

As it has preserved and enhanced its mission as a women's college, Douglass has also taken on a crucial role, pressing to transform the larger university of which it is a part, so that women students across all units benefit from changes in curriculum that reflect new scholarship on women, race, gender, and sexuality. It has also pressed the university to diversify its faculty and administrative ranks and to develop policies that promote gender and racial equity.[8] Douglass has not only shaped equity policies across the university; it has also developed academic excellence that has laid the groundwork for the creation of new schools at Rutgers. In the 1950s, its library school became the Graduate School of Library Science and its education department significantly augmented the faculty and the budget of the University School of Education.[9] In the 1970s, its arts faculty became the nucleus for the Mason Gross School of the Arts. No other women's college can claim such transformational effects.

Differences and Continuities across Generations

The transformations Douglass has experienced over the past century have been shaped by changes in the world that have profoundly altered the roles of women, opening new possibilities in their public and private lives. Women are now better educated than men. In 2014, women ages twenty-five to thirty-four were 21 percent more likely than men to be college graduates and 48 percent more likely to have completed graduate school.[10] The contours of women's work have expanded dramatically. Composing 46.8 percent of the total U.S. labor force, 73 percent of contemporary working women are employed full time, 27 percent part time. Although the most prevalent occupations for women continue to be secretaries and administrative assistants, nurses, and elementary and middle school teachers, 41 percent of employed women now work in management, professional, and related occupations. Women now constitute 52.7 percent of the students graduating from law schools, 20 percent of law school deans, 33.3 percent of lawyers practicing in the United States, and almost half of law firm associates. Women are 48 percent of medical students, 40 percent of hospital residents, and 33 percent of the medical doctors in the nation, concentrated in general practice, internal medicine, dermatology, and obstetrics/gynecology. Women account for 38 percent of faculty members in colleges and universities, making up 46 percent of assistant professors, 38 percent of associate professors, and 23 percent of full professors.[11]

Private lives have also undergone notable change. According to the General Social Survey in 2014, 40 percent of women over the age of eighteen were married, compared with 43 percent in 2000, and 64 percent in 1975.[12] Family forms are far more diverse: single parenting is now the modal family form; 34 percent of U.S. families involve single parents raising their children, and 84 percent of single parents are women. More than 40 percent of mothers are now the sole or primary source of income for the household and about two-thirds of children live in a family with a co-breadwinner or breadwinner mother, up from less than 30 percent in 1967.[13]

Surveys of alumnae indicate that Douglass graduates have differed from national trends—sometimes in surprising ways. Reflecting on NJC graduates from 1922 to 1943, Rosamond Sawyer Moxon (NJC '29) noted that "the personality of the College lives uninterruptedly in the alumnae: her product, her best friend, and her severest critic." Culling the memories of two decades of Douglass women, she made some fascinating observations.[14]

Dangerous as it is to yield, the temptation to do some generalizing is irresistible. The student body of any year is fundamentally similar to that of any other year, but the surface is colored by the few, the vivid ones most affected by outside influences. Thus it can be said that the girls of the '20s were interested in independence, in proving their ability to match the achievements of men, in careers, experiment, and the defiance of convention. Those of the '30s were disillusioned, eager to find and adopt new ideas, understandably bitter, a little better aware that the world was not one bright place. By the end of the '30s both of these eras had spent themselves. NJC undergrads were calmer, anxious to know and to understand, to learn how to pull their own weight. They were uninhibited, but not self-consciously so. They hoped to find jobs worth doing and they considered marriage in that category.[15]

Thirty-seven percent of the women who graduated from Douglass between 1922 and 1943 responded to the survey conducted by the Alumnae Association in conjunction with the twenty-fifth anniversary of NJC. The profile of alumnae created by Mabel Clarke Peabody (NJC '31) indicates that 63.9 percent of Douglass graduates married, "very much higher than the national average for college women" (56.9 percent) at that time.[16] Yet they had far fewer children. "If all married alumnae had families of the same size, there would be 1.008 children in every home. If the children were distributed

▲ COMMENCEMENT, 1924

evenly, though fractionally, among the married alumnae who have children, there would be 1.7 children for each."[17] Douglass graduates' participation in the waged labor force was higher than national averages, growing from 36 percent (1922–1927) to 49 percent (1934–1939) to 70 percent (1940–1942).[18]

The value of a Douglass degree was apparent in the kinds of occupations that alumnae took up: 51 percent held professional positions. Although teaching remained the "principal occupation" of Douglass graduates, by 1943, the percentage of alumnae in the teaching profession was 29 percent, compared to 40 percent in 1935, and 53 percent in 1931. World War II opened new occupational possibilities: 11 percent of alumnae were working in commerce or trades, 11 percent in manufacturing, 10 percent in libraries; 7 percent in social welfare agencies and hospitals, 7 percent as executives or minor officials, 7 percent in government, 2 percent in transportation, 2 percent in the armed services, 1 percent in agriculture, and 8 percent in "fields that do not lend themselves to easy classification."[19] The love of music nurtured by the Douglass music department had lifelong influence: three of four alumnae reported an abiding interest in music and 30 percent reported that playing the piano was their favorite hobby.[20] Early Douglass graduates committed significant energy to civic engagement: 84 percent were involved in volunteer activities, ranging from the Red Cross, civilian defense, United Services Organizations, and other war work (rationing, registration, war bonds) to the PTA, cultural associations, and community organizations.[21]

Two surveys of the class of 1945, collected in conjunction with their forty-fifth and fiftieth reunions, indicate that marriage rates soared for Douglass women after World War II—as they did for American women in general—with 71 percent married. The

members of the Class of '45 had 2.7 children on average (3.04 if the average is calcu-
lated on the basis of those who bore children).[22] Proving that "our 1945 Commencement
was truly a beginning," 32.5 percent of the class completed graduate degrees, an additional 8 percent earned professional certifications and licenses, and another 33 percent
completed graduate courses but did not earn a graduate degree.[23] Teaching continued
to be the prevalent occupation, although only 19.5 percent of the Class of '45 entered
the teaching profession; 9 percent pursued careers in social work and 8 percent in scientific research; 8 percent were librarians; 3.4 percent worked in business, accounting,
or administration; and 12.6 percent chose homemaking as a profession.[24] Regardless of
profession, Douglass women in the Class of '45 devoted considerable time to community affairs: "90 percent participated in a multitude of causes. A list consisting of each
specific activity would total over 200."[25]

Questions concerning political party identification revealed that 39 percent of the
Douglass Class of '45 identified as Democrats, 29 percent as Republicans, and 30 percent as Independents.[26] Beyond party affiliation, however, these Douglass alumnae held
markedly similar views on women's issues: 73 percent supported the women's liberation movement, 72 percent favored the Equal Rights Amendment, and 78 percent were
pro-choice.[27] Two subsequent studies of multiple generations of Douglass women,
comparing students from the mid-1950s and the mid-1970s with Douglass students in
2000, document continuing support for women's liberation. Roberta Sigel and John
Reynolds surveyed all Douglass alumnae whose daughters were attending Douglass in
1975–1976; forty-six "mother-daughter dyads" answered questions about seventeen
feminist issues.[28] In keeping with the demographics of that era, the respondents were
predominantly white, middle-class, well-educated women. Over 90 percent of both
mothers and daughters understood the women's movement primarily as a movement
that seeks the legal and economic equality of women: 58 percent of the mothers and 67
percent of the daughters supported it unequivocally, an additional 30 percent of the
mothers and 20 percent of the daughters articulated support mixed with some ambiva-
lence, and only 12 percent of the mothers and 13 percent of the daughters opposed the
women's movement.[29] The daughters were over twice as likely to indicate the strongest
possible support for the movement; the mothers were more reticent, but the difference
was in intensity, not in direction of support. There was little generational difference on
employment issues: mothers and daughters agreed that employment discrimination
must end and pay equity be secured. Mothers and daughters also agreed that abortion
should be legal and that birth control should be available to college women. The
younger generation of Douglass women were, however, more feminist on questions
pertaining to "sexuality, reproduction, and physical contact with men. . . . The areas in
which the generations differ most are areas where the traditional social mores governing the conduct of women have been strictest."[30] The issues of widest disagreement
between Douglass women of the 1950s and those of the 1970s "center around new
views of what it means to be a woman and what women want out of life. The daughters

▲ COMMENCEMENT, 1960S

do not value marriage and motherhood as highly as do their mothers, or perhaps it would be more accurate to say they do not see these institutions as the main avenue for self-fulfillment. Nor do the daughters see women as so very different from men, at least as far as sex drive and emotional differences are concerned."[31]

Of the forty-seven Douglass students interviewed by Sigel and Reynolds in 1975, twenty-three subsequently had daughters who also attended Douglass, matriculating in 2000. Krista Jenkins conducted a study of these mother-daughter dyads to explore changing perceptions of the women's movement and how views of feminism influenced women's work life and private life. Jenkins's study provides fascinating insights about two intimately connected generations of Douglass women. As with earlier Douglass women, "two-thirds (65%) of mothers and nine-tenths (92%) of daughters had favorable views of the women's movement, believing that change for women had been great in magnitude and good for women overall. . . . 80% reported that the women's movement remains a necessary part of the social and political landscape."[32] When interviewed in 2000, members of the 1975 cohort were even more supportive of the women's move-ment than they had been when first interviewed. They associated the women's movement with equal opportunities, especially in the workforce and with equal pay; some "emphasized women's empowerment, the coming of age for women, the blos-soming of an awareness, a sense of unity."[33] Members of the Class of 1975 had struggled with sex discrimination and sexual harassment in the workplace and with the double shift that comes with working outside the home and returning at the end of a workday to a full set of gendered household responsibilities. They had a clear sense that "women were not yet equal—they were asked to do more than their fair share, more than men are asked to do."[34] Their exposure to political movements devoted to peace, civil rights, black liberation, student power, and gender equality gave the Class of '75 an under-standing of the importance of collective action. "They were far more cognizant of the many different issues involved in women's liberation . . . over and above equal opportu-nity—abortion rights, improved health, safer environments, equality in the home . . . and had a clear sense of women working together to make positive change in women's lives."[35] Within the 1975 cohort of Douglass women, 65 percent reported that they had been involved in some form of protest.

Among the Douglass students in 2000, feminism was "a positive attribute, encom-passing those who were working for the rights of women, or had realized their power and were doing something about issues they believed in. . . . Feminism meant strength in yourself, confidence and respect for yourself and for other women."[36] Yet Jenkins sug-gests that the younger cohort had a more restricted view of the women's movement than had their mothers: "Daughters saw the movement primarily as seeking equal opportunity to hold any position that a man may hold . . . equal rights as equal oppor-tunity in the labor force. . . . Collective action was absent from their understanding of the women's movement. . . . It was less a movement than individual women acting to bring about change . . . individual women going out and grasping their dreams, becom-ing a doctor or an engineer."[37] Their reduction of feminism to individual opportunity in nontraditional fields had a corollary where public policies were concerned: 60 percent of the Douglass women interviewed in 1975 supported affirmative action; only 48 per-cent of those interviewed in 2000 did so.[38]

Members of the 1975 cohort found that challenging gender roles at home was more difficult than challenging them in public life. Expressing "healthy doses of both pessimism and realism . . . their observations about what they had planned and how their lives had turned out reflected an awareness of the difficulty of moving beyond traditional gender roles. Many had planned careers, but had made compromises to assist their husband's career or meet family needs."[39] The majority of women who were educated in the 1970s entered traditionally female professions such as teaching, nurs-ing, and librarianship—fields that were supposed to facilitate the demands of both workplace and family, yet they discovered that "having it all was more fantasy than real-ity. At best, it was attainable through 'sheer smartness and grit'; at its worst, designing a

▲ COMMENCEMENT, TWENTY-FIRST CENTURY

life with this goal in mind could result in the woman herself suffering 'heart attacks, strokes, serious physical problems, and stress-related problems.'"[40]

In contrast to their mothers and grandmothers, Douglass students in 2000 aspired to nontraditional careers in the corporate sector, management, science, and engineering: 61 percent said employment was as important to women as to men (compared with 48 percent in 1975).[41]

Yet they described career plans that implicitly endorsed the traditional division of labor in the home, anticipating taking time off to raise children during their formative years. Like their mothers, the students in 2000 had "internalized a belief that children do best when reared at home with one parent [devoting full-time to childrearing] . . . and that the best way to pursue their goals was to scale back on career expectations in order to meet needs of their future children."[42]

Like most U.S. women, Douglass women were more likely to identify with the Democratic Party: 37 percent of the 1975 cohort and 48 percent of the 2000 cohort declared themselves to be Democrats; 22 percent of the mothers and 13 percent of the daughters identified as Republican. The numbers of Independents decreased from 41 percent in 1975 to 35 percent in 2000, although 4 percent of the younger cohort identified with a third party.[43] Like earlier generations of Douglass women, members of the 1975 and 2000 cohorts reported high levels of volunteer work: 78 percent volunteered their time to various public and private organizations; 89 percent of this activism among the younger cohort involved social justice issues such as hunger (soup kitchens, food drives), rape prevention, and social welfare; 65 percent of Douglass women in the 2000 cohort indicated that they devoted five hours or fewer each week to volunteer activities; 24 percent reported spending more than eleven hours weekly on social justice activism.[44]

At least since 1939, when Dean Margaret Corwin began providing "grants-in-aid" for students on the basis of "good citizenship," the college has linked women's education to civic involvement as a powerful means to cultivate leadership and a sense of competence while also contributing to social justice.[45] Recent graduates have framed the Douglass difference in relation to that linkage. In the words of Gabrielle Rossi (DRC '14), "The Douglass difference . . . means that Douglass gives her students the resources, opportunities, advising, and advantages to take the world by storm. Douglass women graduate with confidence, poise, and leadership skills they need to go on to do truly exceptional things."[46] Margaret Frimpong (DRC '14) concurred, noting that Douglass "inspired me to go after my dreams. The Douglass Difference meant leadership, academic support, and financial support from our associate alumnae, and endless friendship for life!"[47] Khoobi Gangdev (DRC '14) credits Douglass with making her "bolder and more willing to take risks," affording her "the ability to look at things from a very different perspective than four years ago."[48] As Dawn Angelicca Barcelona (DRC '14) put it:

> The Douglass Difference . . . meant having a chance to try new things in a supportive environment. . . . The deans, fellow students, and the all-women's living environment created an amazing environment for me to step out of my comfort zone with things like public speaking. Douglass gave me a chance to become a better leader and learn how to work with other leaders. Douglass was also the first place I felt I had a "voice" that mattered and found people who were willing to listen to my input and fuse their ideas with mine to make an even greater vision and plan happen.[49]

Separated from Mabel Smith Douglass by nearly a century, these recent Douglass graduates manifest the possibilities for empowerment envisioned by the founding dean: "The age has created almost unlimited opportunities for women. It is our duty to bring about an intellectual quickening, a cultural broadening in connection with specific training so that women may go out into the world fitted not only for positions on the lower rung of the ladder of opportunity but for leadership as well in the economic, political, and intellectual life of this nation."[50]

Overcoming manifold challenges in each of its ten decades, Douglass has persevered, providing transformative experiences that educate women "to lead the world with conviction, creativity, and critical insight."[51] Planning for the college's second century, Dean Jacquelyn Litt sees the Douglass mission to be as important as ever: "Women in the 21st century are poised to have unprecedented influence on the course of world affairs. Their education is essential to securing a future of peace, well-being, and justice in our nation and around the globe. The unique combination of a Douglass education—a mission-focused education for women's advancement—within a pre-eminent national research university sets the stage for women's contribution to this future."[52]

AFTERWORD

One hundred years ago, fifty-four women students stepped into the halls of the New Jersey College for Women (NJC). They were seeking something uncommon in that day—but something long overdue—the opportunity for public higher education. They were pioneers, and their legacy is a long and unbroken line of women leaders. Since that day, Douglass has given us one hundred years of excellence, one hundred years of opportunity, and one hundred years of access. The founders of NJC, the members of the New Jersey State Federation of Women's Clubs, were committed to creating a great public institution of learning for women. And thanks to countless faculty, staff, alumnae, donors, students, and administrators over the years, that's exactly what they achieved.

The Douglass Century takes us through an uncommon journey. Douglass has undergone many changes in its long history, some driven internally and others externally. Ours is a history of opportunities and challenges and, most of all, adaptation, resilience, and innovation. All through its history, Douglass has provided education that fits with its originating mission—to create the best education for women in the nation.

The New Jersey State Federation of Women's Clubs saw a clear need for public education and broader access in New Jersey, revealing a vision well ahead of its time. Yet even at NJC, exclusions occurred, as Jewish and Catholic women were tracked for religion and African Americans by racial status, leading to exclusions from admittance and marginalization at NJC itself.

The landscape of higher education has changed dramatically over the course of the past one hundred years, creating new challenges and opportunities to advance women's education both at Rutgers and nationwide. Since the middle of the twentieth century, higher education has come to be understood as a lever for equal opportunity across a broad spectrum of the population. The past sixty years alone have seen the civil rights movement, the women's movement, Title IX, Black Lives Matter, and Deferred Action for Childhood Arrivals (DACA), all resulting in new access to higher education. The coeducation system exploded in the late 1960s and early 1970s, admitting women to the most elite institutions in the country and later to virtually all colleges and universities. The numbers of students enrolling in post-secondary education has grown from four million in 1960 to more than eighteen million in 2012. Nearly 80 percent of all high school graduates will enter college, although far fewer will graduate.[1]

The system of universal education and the coeducational movement have affected the status of women's colleges and women's education. Today, women constitute the majority of students on campuses across the county, both in under-graduate and in some graduate and professional schools. Over the past one hundred years, the nation's undergraduate population has become more diverse in gender, age, faith, race/ethnicity, geographic and economic background, and abil-ity. In the future, we expect that people of color will become the majority of students in our higher education system. Douglass now is among the most diverse entities at Rutgers, which is one of the most diverse universities in the country.

Given the value—if not the full achievement—of universal education and the radical increase in the numbers of women attending institutions of higher educa-tion, do we still need women's colleges? "Is it time," as Agnes Scott College president Elizabeth Kiss asked in 2015, "for us to declare victory in the fight for women's equal educational opportunity and let women's colleges go the way of buggies and white gloves?"

Kiss responds, as I do, with a resounding *no*. Women's colleges, born in the nine-teenth century, have seen a decline—from 260 in 1960 to fewer than 40 today. The coeducation movement has opened up opportunities to women that were unheard of when NJC opened. Yet women's colleges continue to have a central place in the higher education landscape.

Women's colleges today lead four-year institutions in the percentage gain of African American, first-generation, and lower-income students and boast higher graduation rates for women of color. In comparison with coeducational institutions, women's colleges provide students with greater opportunities for participation in leadership, build higher self-esteem in their students, and provide better prepara-tion for women's first jobs. Graduates of women's colleges display more confidence and leadership skills, higher levels of social and historical awareness, and a greater tendency to engage in nonprofit work and are twice as likely to earn a graduate degree compared with graduates of flagship public universities. Women's colleges today represent less than 1 percent of all women undergraduates, but our graduates are highly represented in the leadership ranks across the country.

Yet questions remain: Can we bring this advantage into coeducational institu-tions in which 99 percent of women receive their education? Can we foster the exceptional outcomes of women's colleges in institutions that have a broader reach and mission? From social psychologist Virginia Valian's groundbreaking work on unconscious bias, which documented the unintentional if powerful persistence of gender schemas in evaluations of women, to the thorough social science research of today, we have learned that women, particularly women of color, do not have equal access to educational opportunity in coeducational colleges and universities. In these environments, women remain underrepresented in the leadership of student clubs and governments. Women are less likely than men to major in the physical and math sciences and engineering. And women are more likely to have lower confidence in their academic abilities than are men.

University "access programs" across the country and at Rutgers itself are sterling examples that can address the individual needs of first-generation and low-income students to help them succeed in college. Yet in most institutions, the distinct needs of women students, the impact of the intersections of gender with race/ethnicity, socioeconomic status, and sexuality on women's opportunities, are not identified as central to the diversity mission. If our diversity programs do not identify women as a category, where can we develop the supports and programs that are essential to women's success?

At Rutgers, Douglass serves that purpose, providing an education for women that is unique in the nation and, I would argue, possible at other coeducational institutions. Douglass has institutional status as the organization at Rutgers that is devoted exclusively to undergraduate women's advancement and success within the context of its larger coeducational setting. Douglass brings together a comprehensive, four-year curricular and co-curricular education; career and leadership development; science, technology, engineering, and math (STEM) education; and equity programs. While partnering with the excellent access programs and the academic departments and schools at Rutgers, Douglass stands as the site that forges excellence in women's education.

Much of our success is rooted in the institutional status of the college itself. The institutional position as a distinct but central part of the undergraduate program at Rutgers serves as a focus point for university partners that are also committed to women's education and success. Douglass's position as a fixed and permanent organization allows for resource mobilization both within and outside the university. Douglass's separate governance and resource structure offer our students the organizational experiences to create new understandings of efficacy, confidence, and innovation.

Has Douglass led to change in the wider university? Douglass Residential College today enrolls twenty-five hundred women, or 15 percent of all women undergraduates at the New Brunswick campus. The dramatic increase in our enroll-ment since our students have been able to co-enroll at Rutgers and at Douglass signals that young women today—in this age of coeducation—understand the dis-tinct appeal of single-gender institutions. Our students are perhaps the best evidence of what women's education can accomplish; Rutgers's faculty see first-hand the confidence and ambition of Douglass students, opening the faculty up to new ideas about what women's education can achieve.

Women's education challenges many of the taken-for-granted assumptions that govern the university gestalt nationwide: assumptions about women's equal inclusion and opportunity. A separate institution for women's education in a coedu-cational setting signals and addresses the distinct needs of women in higher education. In an era when questions about women's education appear to be answered simply through a look at the demographics, Douglass's impact reminds us that women's education remains an unfinished revolution. Douglass itself keeps women's education on the radar—and I believe this has changed Rutgers, just as Douglass has been changed by Rutgers.

Through its wide array of academic opportunities, Rutgers University is perhaps one of the best places to spearhead this new model for higher education—a world-class research university that includes an institution focused entirely on the success and advancement of undergraduate women. Yet Rutgers is not the only place in which this model of women's education can develop. Indeed, the structure of Dou-glass Residential College may well be the prototype for women's education in the century to come, bringing students the best of both worlds: an education devoted to their success within a college or university with a broad array of academic options and the resources to support them.

Women in the twenty-first century are poised to have unprecedented influence on the course of world affairs. Their education is essential to securing a future of peace, prosperity, and well-being. The unique combination of a mission-focused women's education within our system of higher education institutions can set the stage for women's contributions to this future.

JACQUELYN LITT

Dean, Douglass Residential College and Douglass Campus

Professor of Sociology and Women's and Gender Studies

ACKNOWLEDGMENTS

In the twenty-first century, discussions of women's education have often focused on the Global South, receiving far less attention in the North, where women constitute the majority of undergraduate students. Indeed, in some advanced economies, the sheer number of women in colleges and universities has been taken as proof that gender equality is no longer an issue. Yet an examination of debates about women's higher education over the past two centuries suggests that women's education per se, as well as an appropriate model for women's education, have been and continue to be matters of significant controversy in all regions of the globe. *The Douglass Century* explores the history of the women's college at Rutgers University in relation to these ongoing debates and as an example of what a single-sex "coordinate college" for women can enable both in higher education and in knowledge production.

As we have undertaken research for this volume, we have benefited greatly from the ideas and assistance of many within the Douglass and Rutgers communities. Colleagues on the Board of the Institute for Women's Leadership under the inspiring leadership of Alison Bernstein and Lisa Hetfield, and the Douglass College 100th Anniversary Committee offered creative suggestions and encouragement for a "new" history of the college. Dean Jacquelyn Litt and Marlie Wasserman, then director of Rutgers University Press, concretized the possibilities for the book and helped chart its contours. Krisellen Maloney, vice president for information services and university librarian, warmly supported the project. University archivist Thomas J. Frusciano, archivist Erika B. Gorder, archive research manager Flora Boros, and archival intern Alex Plante provided invaluable assistance throughout the research process. Mary S. Hartman, former dean of Douglass (1981–1994) and founding director of the Institute for Women's Leadership, generously shared materials from her private papers, records, and speeches, as well as her recollections of life at Douglass over the past five decades. We are also grateful to the Barnard College Archives and the Jersey City Free Public Library for access to their collections.

We owe a special debt of thanks to Rutgers students Kelly Hannavi (history and women's/gender studies), Allison Manolis (journalism and media studies and women's/gender Studies), Meaghan Moody (library and information science, School of Communication and Information), Maegan Kae Sunaz (political science and women's/gender studies), Meryem Uzumcu (public policy, Middle Eastern studies, and women's/gender studies), who enrolled in our team-taught directed-research course, From Exclusion to Inclusion: 250 Years of Women at Rutgers, in fall 2015 and unearthed a wealth of archival material, which helped shape our thinking about this historical narrative in relation to women at Rutgers. Price Family Fellow Autumn Oberkehr (psychology and women's/gender studies) has provided superb research assistance for the volume in academic years 2015–2016 and 2016–2017, searching for illusive content, images, and bibliographic materials.

The draft manuscript benefited greatly from meticulous readings and insightful comments by Dr. Barry V. Qualls (Department of English and former vice president for undergraduate education), Dr. Paul G. E. Clemens (Department of History and author of *Rutgers since 1945*), and Dr. Richard L. McCormick (Rutgers president emeritus and author of *Raised at Rutgers: A President's Story*). We are also grateful to former acting deans of Douglass Dr. Martha Cotter (Department of Chemistry), Linda Stamato (DC '62, co-director of Rutgers Center for Negotiation and Conflict Resolution), and Dr. Harriet Davidson (Departments of English and Women's/Gender Studies), who shared personal reminiscences of their administrations as well as feedback on individual chapters of the book. Marjorie Munson, former assistant dean for research, evaluation, and scholarships at Douglass, and Assistant Dean Rebecca Reynolds provided critical guidance in finding copies of Associate Dean Louise Duus's unpublished manuscript on the history of Douglass from 1968 through 1985, which Associate Alumnae of Douglass College executive director Valerie Anderson (DC '81) kindly shared with us. Dr. Gwendolyn Beetham, DRC dean for the Global Village and academic programs, directed our attention to the Casa Boriqua scrapbooks, which provided a wealth of information about Latinas experiences at the college. Dr. Ferris Olin (DC '70), founding head of the Margery Somers Foster Center and the Institute for Women and Art), drew upon her unparalleled knowledge of the history of Douglass to flesh out periods and projects scarcely documented in the archives. Dr. Carolyn Williams, Douglass Fellow and professor of English, provided vital information about the origin of Shaping a Life, the first Douglass mission course.

Douglass alumnae have also contributed significantly to the volume. We are grateful to Mary Cook Craig (NJC '49), Flora Buchbinder Cowen (DC '59), Inez Phillips Durham (DC '57), Sandra Harding (DC '56), Wilma Harris (DC '66), Lola Fuchs Kamp (DC '56), Anne Spiegel Lipner (DC '62), Susan Gordan Marchand (DC '61), Ivette Mendez (DC '75), Reiko Fukuyama Ohye (DC '56), Irene Figarotta Pearse (DC '59), Marissa Rodriguez (DRC '11), Barbara Morrison-Rodriguez (DC '71), Aya Sakar (DRC '15), Susan Cower Schwirck (DC '71), and Juanita Wade Wilson (DC '66) for sharing their reminiscences about daily life at the college. Ann Heuer, who served as a graduate research assistant in Dean Mary Ingraham Bunting's laboratory, provided helpful information about the involvement of Douglass undergraduate students in the dean's research projects. Terrese Williams Martin (DC '69) not only shared her memories but provided crucial research assistance on the history of Douglass women who won regional and national recognition as members of the Scarlet Knights Women's Basketball team in

1978–1979 and 1979–1980. AADC executive director Valerie Anderson (DC '81), AADC president Jeanne Fox (DC '75), and AADC past president Tina B. Gordon (DC '72) graciously granted permission to use the AADC Oral History Archives as a resource for our investigation of the student and alumnae experiences at NJC and Douglass. Rutgers Art Librarian Megan Lotts added to this treasure by conducting an interview with alumna Anne (formerly Camilla Joseph) Hill (NJC '36) on the eve of her hundredth birthday. Rutgers alumni Lynn Whately (RC '70) and alumnae Sondra Korman (RC '77) and Kaylan Michas (RU '16) also shared recollections and research with us.

We would also like to thank Maria E. De Pina, senior department administrator, and Merrie Snead, senior public relations specialist, at Douglass, and Nick Romanenko and Jane Hart of University Relations Creative Services for their assistance in finding images for the book and Richard Sandler, senior technical coordinator at Rutgers University Libraries Media Center, for contributing his talents as a photographer. Andrew Ruggiero, unit computing specialist at Douglass Library, provided guidance on image file sizes and access to the interviews of the Associate Alumnae of Douglass College Oral History Project.

We are deeply indebted to artist Margaret Bailey Doogan and the Tucson Art Museum for permission to include *Five-Fingered Smile,* 2010 (charcoal on printed paper, 72" x 52", purchased with funds provided by Robert J. Greenberg), in chapter 8.

We have benefited greatly from the expertise of Elisabeth Maselli, Victoria Verhowsky, Anne Hegeman, and Jennifer Blanc-Tal at Rutgers University Press, who have contributed their impressive talent to facilitate the production process, and from Romaine Perin for her meticulous copyediting of the manuscript.

Rich intellectual collaboration across disciplines and academic units is a hallmark of Douglass. Over the past century, the college has enabled rewarding friendships and creative knowledge production by and about women—the conditions that made this book possible. In undertaking a "new" history of Douglass on the occasion of its one hundredth anniversary, we hope to illuminate the remarkable character of a college dedicated to the education of women, and provide glimpses of the lives, leadership, and transformative scholarship it has enabled.

KAYO DENDA
Head, Margery Somers Foster Center and Women's Studies Librarian,
Rutgers University Libraries

MARY HAWKESWORTH
Distinguished Professor, Political Science and Women's/Gender Studies

FERNANDA PERRONE
Archivist and Head, Exhibitions Program, Curator of the William Elliot Griffis
Collection, Special Collections/University Archives, Rutgers University Libraries
February 2017

Chapter 1   Inventing Douglass:
The Challenge of Women's Higher Education

1   Message from Dean Mabel Smith Douglass, *Quair: The Yearbook of the New Jersey College for Women*, 1932, 255. Hereafter, *Quair*. This chapter's epigraph is from John M. Thomas, *The Expansion of Public Education in New Jersey* (address at his inauguration as president of Rutgers University, October 14, 1925) (New Brunswick, NJ: Rutgers University, 1925), 13.

2   This figure captures the enrollment in 2016–2017. Demographic data is drawn from Rutgers Research and Enrollment Information Services (REIS), December 6, 2016.

3   Mabel Smith Douglass, "Personal Recollections," *Quair*, 1929, 64.

4   J. M. Thomas, 13.

5   Women's College Coalition, The Truth about Women's Colleges: Comparative Enrollment Trends of Women's Colleges and Private, Coeducational Colleges, June 2014, http://www.womenscolleges.org/sites/default/files/report/files/main/wcc01_trendsreport_final_interactive.pdf.

6   Mabel Newcomer, *A Century of Higher Education for Women* (New York: Harper and Brothers, 1959), 171. For an overview of women's employment in the United States, see Alice Kessler Harris, *Out to Work: A History of Wage-Earning Women in the United States* (New York: Oxford University Press, 1982).

7   Joseph A. Hill, *Women in Gainful Occupations, 1870 to 1920* (Washington, DC: Bureau of the Census, 1929).

8   The quote is taken from Mary Wollstonecraft, *A Vindication of the Rights of Woman*, 1792 (New York: W. W. Norton, 1975), 189. For a full exploration, see Linda Kerber, *Women of the Republic: Intellect and Ideology in Revolutionary America* (Chapel Hill: University of North Carolina, 1980).

9   Lucia McMahan notes that no figures exist concerning the numbers of these schools or the numbers of girls who attended them. "Common estimates citing 'thousands' of women seem at once vague and conservative because individual academies maintained enrollments ranging from hundreds to thousands." *Mere Equals: The Paradox of Educated Women in the Early Republic* (Ithaca, NY: Cornell University Press, 2012), 22.

10   William H. Demarest, in *A History of Rutgers College, 1766–1924* (New Brunswick, NJ: Rutgers University), refers to the female academy twice (194, 224), in both instances referring to the school as a project of Reverend Ira Condict, trustee, then (1811) serving as vice president of Queens College. It appears, however, that Demarest conflated two different schools, Miss Hoyt's Female Seminary and the New Brunswick Female Academy, then operating under the direction of Mr. Preston and later run by Hannah Hoyt. For efforts to differentiate these schools, see McMahan; and Women's Project of New Jersey, Inc., *Past and Promise: Lives of New Jersey Women*, Joan Burstyn,

ed. (Metuchen, NJ: Scarecrow Press, 1990).

11   Cited in Susan L. Poulson, "A Quiet Revolution: The Transition to Coeducation at Georgetown and Rutgers Colleges, 1960–1995" (PhD diss., Georgetown University, Washington, DC, 1989), 3.

12   Robert Fletcher, *A History of Oberlin College: From Its Foundation through the Civil War* (Chicago: R. R. Donnelley & Sons, 1943), 291. Oberlin was one of the first institutions of higher education to admit African American students, who were also treated somewhat differently from the white male students, although all were being trained for "ministry and missionary work."

13   Rutgers Female Institute (New York, N.Y.), Catalogue of the Rutgers Female College, 1867–1868 (New York: Agathynian Press, 1867), 13.

14   Ibid., 23–24.

15   Henry Miller Pierce, *President's Address to the First Graduating Class of Rutgers Female College,* June 2, 1867 (New York: Agathynian Press, 1867), 5.

16   Ibid.

17   Ibid., 18.

18   New Jersey designated Rutgers Department of Agriculture the land grant college for the state in 1864. Rutgers trustees accepted federal and state funds, but considered Rutgers a private men's college and chose not to admit women.

19   Poulson, 11.

20   Marie Marmo Mullaney, "The New Jersey College for Women: Middle-Class Respectability and Proto-Feminism, 1911–1918," *Journal of Rutgers University Libraries* 42, no. 1 (1980): 26–39, 28.

21   Poulson, 16–17.

22   Newcomer, 13.

23   Edward Hammond Clarke, *Sex in Education; or, A Fair Chance for the Girls* (Boston: James R. Osgood, 1873), 17–18.

24   Eliza Lo Chin, *This Side of Doctoring: Reflections from Women in Medicine* (Thousand Oaks, CA: Sage, 2002), 3.

25   Ibid., 103–104.

26   Mary Putnam Jacobi, "Women in Medicine," in A. N. Meyer, ed., *Woman's Work in America* (New York: Henry Holt, 1891), 143.

27   Newcomer, 31.

28   Thomas Woody, *A History of Women's Education in the United States,* 2 vols. (New York: Octagon Books, 1929), vol. 2, 290; see also Barbara Miller Solomon, *In the Company of Educated Women: A History of Women and Higher Education in America* (New Haven, CT: Yale University Press, 1985), 63, table 3.

29   Poulson, 17.

30   M. Carey Thomas, "Present Tendencies in Women's College and University Education," AAUW, *Association of Collegiate Alumnae Magazine,* series III, no. 17 (January 1908): 43–62, 53.

31   Cited in Patricia Palmieri, "From Republican Motherhood to Race Suicide: Arguments on the Higher Education of Women in the United States, 1820–1920," in Carol Lasser, ed., *Educating Men and Women Together: Coeducation in a Changing World* (Champaign-Urbana: University of Illinois Press, 1987), 59; anglicized spelling in the original.

32   Ibid., 59.

33   Poulson, 17.

34   William Rainey Harper Papers, University of Chicago Library, July 21–23, 1902, cited in Poulson, 24–26.

35   Poulson notes that Chicago had difficulty enforcing sex segregation and gradually, over the course of several years, the colleges abandoned the effort, 29.

36 According to Hall, "The first danger to a woman is over-brainwork. It affects that part of her organism which is sacred to heredity. This danger is seen in the diminishing number of marriages. The postponement of marriage is very unfortunate in its influence upon civilization." G. Stanley Hall, *National Education Association Proceedings* 1903:460, cited in Woody, vol. 2, 274. Hall's arguments were also influential in Britain, where they were used to justify women's exclusion of women from Cambridge, Oxford, and other universities.

37 G. Stanley Hall, *Adolescence: Its Psychology and Its Relations to Physiology, Anthropology, Sociology, Sex, Crime, Religion, and Education*, 2 vols. (New York: D. Appleton, 1904).

38 Julius Sachs, "Coeducation in the United States," *Educational Review* 33 (March 1907): 303.

39 Poulson,15.

40 Ibid., 31–32.

41 Ibid., 32–34.

42 Andrea Walton, "Rekindling a Legacy: Barnard College Remains a Women's College," in Leslie Miller-Bernard and Susan L. Poulson, eds., *Challenged by Coeducation: Women's Colleges since the 1960s* (Nashville, TN: Vanderbilt University Press, 2006), 289.

43 Rima Dombrow Apple, *The Challenge of Constantly Changing Times: From Home Economics to Human Ecology at the University of Wisconsin, 1903–2003* (Madison: University of Wisconsin Library Parallel Press, 2003), 2.

44 Ibid.

45 Ibid., 107–108.

46 Woody, vol. 2, 282.

47 Mullaney, 38. It is worth noting that the act specified that "not more than twenty per centum of the money appropriated under this Act for payment of teachers of trade, home economics and industrial subjects in any given year, shall be expended for the salaries of teachers of home economics subjects." See Smith-Hughes Act (Vocational Education Act) of 1917, Public Law 347, 64th Cong., 2d sess., February 23, 1917, reprinted in The Statutes at Large of the United States of America from December, 1915, to March, 1917, vol. 39, part 1 (Washington, DC: GPO, 1917), 929–936.

48 Poulson, 27.

49 Woody, vol. 2, 288.

50 Elizabeth Deering Hanscom, "The Ethical Purpose of a Woman's College," *Educational Review* 22 (October 1901): 312.

51 M. C. Thomas, 55.

52 J. M. Thomas, 13. Thomas points out that that in 1860, there were only four public high schools in New Jersey; sixteen years later, there were eleven high schools enrolling 1,607 students.

53 Poulson, 132.

54 Richard P. McCormick, *Rutgers: A Bicentennial History* (New Brunswick, NJ: Rutgers University Press, 1966), 98.

55 Ibid.

56 Demarest, 485.

57 Mullaney, 29.

58 Ibid., 28.

59 Ibid.

60 Ibid., 31.

61 Ibid., 32.

62 Ibid.

63 Ibid., 34.

64   Ibid., 35.

65   Ibid., 32–33.

66   Ibid., 36.

67   Ibid., 37. The conception of the "Teutonic" or "Saxon" race was narrowly construed during this time period. African Americans, Asian Americans, Irish Americans, Italian Americans, Mexican Americans, and American Jews were all racialized as threats to the purity of the white race nation.

68   Palmieri, 57.

69   Woody, vol. 2, 301.

70   Ibid. For details about Alice Freeman Palmer's extraordinary life, see George H. Palmer, *The Life of Alice Freeman Palmer* (Boston: Houghton Mifflin, 1908); and Ruth Borden, *Alice Freeman Palmer: The Evolution of a New Woman* (Ann Arbor: University of Michigan Press, 1993).

71   Palmieri, 57. In his 1897 essay, "National Life and Character," Roosevelt asserted that "nineteenth century democracy needs no more complete vindication for its existence than the fact that it has kept for the white race the best portions of the new world's surface, temperate America and Australia." But the victory achieved by the "white race" was not secure. On the contrary, Roosevelt argued that it was under dire threat from the proliferating population and migration of "inferior" races. The census had documented that population growth was not evenly distributed: the "lower races of men" were increasing faster than the "higher." Anticipating a clash that pitted "East" against "West" and "South" against "North," Roosevelt noted with alarm that "the dark races are gaining on us, as they have already done in Haiti and are doing throughout the West Indies and our Southern States." Characterizing this emerging global racial competition as "the warfare of the cradle," Roosevelt insisted that "no race has any chance to win a great place unless it consists of good breeders and good fighters." Thus Roosevelt demanded that "the woman must be the housewife, the helpmeet, the homemaker, the wise and fearless mother of many healthy children. . . . When men fear righteous war, when women fear motherhood, they tremble at the brink of doom." It should be noted that the boundaries of whiteness were narrowly construed in this era. Irish, Italians, Jews, and Slavs were often subsumed under the "darker races."

72   Mary Hartman, "Baccalaureate Address," Douglass College, New Brunswick, NJ, 1977, 4.

73   George P. Schmidt, *Douglass College: A History* (New Brunswick, NJ: Rutgers University Press, 1968), 61. Membership in the National Society of the Daughters of the Revolution of 1776 (DRs) was restricted to women over the age of eighteen who were direct descendants of Revolutionary War soldiers and statesmen of the Revolution; the membership of the Daughters of the American Revolution (DARs) was a bit less restrictive, including women who were directly descended from a person involved in the struggle for independence. As this list suggests, supporters of NJC spanned the political spectrum of the period.

74   Ibid., 12.

75   Ibid., 10, 12.

76   Demarest, 535–537.

77   After inheriting the fortunes of her father, John Rodman, and her uncle, Robert Woodruff Rodman, Elizabeth Rodman Voorhees (1841–1924) devoted her life to philanthropy. Although she never received a formal education, she strongly believed in the benefits of higher education and donated significant sums to colleges, including NJC; Hope College; the Voorhees Normal and Industrial School, created for African American students in South Carolina; and the Voorhees School for the Blind in Bombay, India.

78   Schmidt, 26–27.

79 Ibid., 20.
80 "Diversity" file, Rutgers University Records Management, Box #5, 10542195, Special Collections and University Archives (SC/UA).
81 Schmidt, 75.
82 Ibid., 73.
83 Ibid., 54. See also McCormick, *Rutgers*, 207.
84 Jill Kerr Conway, "Coeducation and Women's Studies: Two Approaches to the Question of Woman's Place in the Contemporary University," *Daedalus* 103, no. 4 (1974): 239–249, 239.

Chapter 2   New Jersey College for Women: Establishing a Tradition, 1918–1929

1   Delight Wing Dodyk, "Historical Overview: 1866–1920," in Women's Project of New Jersey, Inc., *Past and Promise: Lives of New Jersey Women,* 2nd ed., edited by Joan N. Burstyn (Syracuse, NY: Syracuse University Press, 1997), 101.
2   On the youth culture of the 1920s, see Paula S. Fass, *The Beautiful and the Damned: American Youth in the 1920s* (New York: Oxford University Press, 1979).
3   Nancy K. Bristow, *American Pandemic: The Lost Worlds of the 1918 Influenza Epidemic* (New York: Oxford University Press, 2012), 3–4. Total deaths in the United States are estimated at 675,000.
4   Richard P. McCormick, *Rutgers: A Bicentennial History* (New Brunswick, NJ: Rutgers University Press, 1966), 166.
5   Mabel Smith Douglass, *The Early History of New Jersey College for Women* (New Brunswick: New Jersey College for Women, 1929), 21.
6   Birth certificate, Mabel Smith Douglass Papers, Box 1, Folder 1a, Special Collections and University Archives (hereafter SC/UA); and Louise Duus, "Mabel Smith Douglass," in Women's Project of New Jersey, Inc., 126.
7   Lynn Gordon, "Annie Nathan Meyer and Barnard College: Mission and Identity in Women's Higher Education, 1889–1950," *History of Education Quarterly* 26, no. 4 (1986): 504.
8   *Mortarboard* (Barnard College yearbook), 1899, Barnard College Archives, New York, NY.
9   Unlike NJC, Barnard was granted the right to appoint its own trustees in the agreement of affiliation with Columbia signed in 1900. See Andrea Walton, "Rekindling a Legacy: Barnard College Remains a Women's College," in *Challenged by Coeducation: Women's Colleges since the 1960s,* edited by Leslie Miller-Bernal and Susan L. Poulson (Nashville, TN: Vanderbilt University Press, 2006), 291.
10 Undated newspaper clipping, 1904, Mabel Smith Douglass Papers, Box 1, Folder 1b, SC/UA.
11 *Report to the Trustees of the Board of Managers* (June 11, 1920), RG 04/11/01, Office of the Rutgers University President, William H. Demarest, Box 27, folder 1, SC/UA.
12 Douglass, 22–23.
13 McCormick, 171.
14 Alumni Biographical File, Leonard F. Loree, Box 53, SC/UA.
15 McCormick, 175.
16 Board of Managers Minutes, January 28, 1921, RG 19/A0/01, Douglass College, Dean's Records. Mabel Smith Douglass, Box 12, Folder 15, SC/UA; and Douglass, 27.
17 Douglass, 28.
18 Helen Lefkowitz Horowitz, *Alma Mater: Design and Experience in the Women's Colleges from Their Nineteenth-Century Beginnings to the 1930s,* 2nd ed. (Amherst: University of Massachusetts Press, 1993), 5, 88–89, and 346.

19   George P. Schmidt, *Douglass College: A History* (New Brunswick, NJ: Rutgers University Press, 1968), 47–48.
20   Schmidt, 41–43.
21   Schmidt, 51–52.
22   McCormick, 189–190.
23   Kayo Denda, "Jessie Gladys Fiske: A Pioneer in STEM Fields at Douglass College," *Diversity Almanac 2015* (New Brunswick, NJ: Rutgers University Office of Institutional Diversity and Inclusion, 2015).
24   McCormick, 173.
25   Schmidt, 56.
26   Marie L. Casteen to William Demarest, August 12, 1919, RG 04/A11, Office of the Rutgers University President, William Demarest, Box 26, Folder 36, SC/UA.
27   Mabel Smith Douglass to William Demarest, January 16, 1922, RG 19/A0/01, Douglass College, Dean's Records. Mabel Smith Douglass, Box 60, Folder 2, SC/UA.
28   Leonor Loree to Mabel Smith Douglass, June 1, 1925, RG 19/A0/01, Douglass College, Dean's Records. Mabel Smith Douglass, Box 60, Folder 2, SC/UA.
29   Schmidt, 53; and New Jersey College for Women, *Announcement*, 1927–1928, SC/UA.
30   *Daily Home News* (New Brunswick, NJ), July 19, 1917, and October 17, 1921; and Francis Bazely Lee, *Genealogical and Memorial History of the State of New Jersey*, vol. 2 (New York: Lewis Historical Publishing, 1910), 467.
31   Frieda Finklestein Feller (NJC '41), oral history interview, March 27, 1998, by G. Kurt Piehler and Elizabeth Wyatt, Rutgers Oral History Archives, http://oralhistory.rutgers.edu/social-and-cultural-history/31-interviewees/910-feller-frieda-finklestein (last accessed February 7, 2017).
32   Patricia Palmieri has written of the unique intellectual, social, and emotional community that developed at Wellesley in the early twentieth century. See Patricia A. Palmieri, "Here Was Fellowship: A Social Portrait of Academic Women at Wellesley College, 1895–1920," *History of Education Quarterly*, Summer 1983, 195–214.
33   New Jersey College for Women, *Announcement*, 1928–1929, SC/UA.
34   Schmidt, 32.
35   Margaret A. Judson, *Breaking the Barrier* (New Brunswick, NJ: Rutgers University, 1984), 40–41.
36   John W. Chambers II and Larayne J. Dallas, "Emily Gregory Hickman," in Women's Project of New Jersey, Inc., 319–320.
37   Schmidt, 53–54.
38   Minutes, Faculty-Executive Council, December 1, 1930, and October 16, 1931, RG 19/A0/01, Douglass College, Dean's Records. Mabel Smith Douglass, Box 110, Folder 13, SC/UA.
39   Minutes, Faculty-Executive Council, November 30, 1931, RG 19/A0/01, Douglass College, Dean's Records. Mabel Smith Douglass, Box 110, Folder 13, SC/UA.
40   Notes on Careers for Women, Mabel Smith Douglass Papers, Box 3, Folder 1, SC/UA.
41   Paul R. Marthers, "Did the Women's Colleges Founded in the Progressive Era Represent a New Model?" *American Educational History Journal* 40, no. 2 (2013): 223–239.
42   New Jersey College for Women, *Announcement*, 1918–1919, SC/UA.
43   New Jersey College for Women, *Announcement*, 1919–1920, SC/UA.
44   Rutgers College, *Catalog*, 1919–1920, 48.
45   McCormick, 186. On Bryn Mawr, see Horowitz, *Alma Mater*, 115–119.
46   Schmidt, 95–96.
47   These slides have now been digitized as part of the Rutgers Department of Classics Initiative. Carla Cantor, "Classics Department Pieces Together a Mystery," *Rutgers Focus*, February 20, 2006.

48   Schmidt, 94–97.

49   Extracts from the *Reports of the Divisional Executives*, Division of Languages and
     Literature, ca. 1930, RG A01/01, Douglass College, Dean's Records. Mabel Smith
     Douglass, Box 79, Folder 11, SC/UA.

50   Louise Franck ('30), "Inauguration of French House," RG 19/10/01, Douglass
     College, Dean's Records. Mabel Smith Douglass, Box 65, Folder 6, SC/UA.

51   Marjorie East, *Home Economics: Past, Present and Future* (Boston: Allyn and Bacon,
     1980), 5.

52   Shana Groeschler and Fernanda Perrone, "The Study of Home Economics at Douglass
     College," in Thomas J. Frusciano and Fernanda Perrone, eds. *A New Generation Looks
     Back: Historical Essays on Douglass College* (New Brunswick, NJ: Douglass College,
     2000), 24.

53   New Jersey College for Women, *Announcement*, 1919–1920, SC/UA. In September
     1924, of 540 registrants, there were 107 home economics majors. Addendum, Memo-
     randum of Opening, September 15–16, 1924, RG 19/A0/01, Douglass College, Dean's
     Records. Mabel Smith Douglass, Box 12, Folder 15, SC/UA.

54   Marthers, 232. On home economics, known as "euthenics" at Vassar, see Horowitz,
     Alma Mater, 295–302.

55   Megan J. Elias, *Stir It Up: Home Economics in American Culture* (Philadelphia: Univer-
     sity of Pennsylvania Press, 2008), 20–51.

56   New Jersey State Agricultural College, "Courses in Home Economics, 1921–1922,"
     State College Publication 2, no. 1 (1921), 19. RG 19/A0/01, Douglass College, Dean's
     Records. Mabel Smith Douglass, Home Economics Department, Box 60, Folder 2.

57   Helen W. Hazen, Director, Department of Home Economics, Report to the Dean, June
     30, 1931, 1-5. RG 19/A0/01, Douglass College, Dean's Records. Mabel Smith
     Douglass, Box 2, Folder 7.

58   New Jersey State Agricultural College, 11.

59   Ibid., 5.

60   Lynn D. Gordon, *Gender and Higher Education in the Progressive Era* (New Haven, CT:
     Yale University Press, 1990), 35 and 99–101.

61   Roberta Park, "Sport, Gender, and Society in a Transatlantic Victorian Perspective,"
     British Journal of Sports History 2, no. 1 (1985): 11–20.

62   Schmidt, 39.

63   Indian Clubs were (and are) heavy club-shaped weights used in strength-building
     exercises. Originally known as *jori*, Indian Clubs were adopted by the British military
     in colonial India during in the nineteenth century. See Jan Todd, "The Strength
     Builders: A History of Barbells, Dumbbells, and Indian Clubs," *International Journal of
     the History of Sport* 20, no. 1 (2003): 65–90.

64   Rosamond Sawyer Moxon (NJC '29), "Trends of the First Quarter Century: A History
     of Intangibles," in Rosamond Sawyer Moxon and Mabel Clarke Peabody, *Twenty-Five
     Years: Two Anniversary Sketches of New Jersey College for Women* (New Brunswick: New
     Jersey College for Women, Rutgers University, 1943), 14.

65   Ibid., 16–17.

66   L. Loree to M. S. Douglass, October 14, 1926, RG 19/A0/10, Douglass College,
     Dean's Records. Mabel Smith Douglass, Box 67, Folder 4, SC/UA.

67   Schmidt, 71–72.

68   Park, 19.

69   New Jersey College for Women, *Announcement*, 1928–1929, SC/UA.

70   Brochure, *Physical Education and Recreational Leadership as Profession for the College
     Woman* (New Brunswick: New Jersey College, ca. 1927), 3, Mabel Smith Douglass
     Papers, Box 3, Folder 8, SC/UA.

71 *New Jersey College for Women Medical Report,* October 31, 1925, RG 19/A0/10, Douglass College, Dean's Records. Mabel Smith Douglass, Box 61, SC/UA.

72 Moxon, 17.

73 David Yosifon and Peter N. Stearns, "The Rise and Fall of American Posture," *American Historical Review* 103, no. 4 (1998): 1074–1078.

74 Douglass, 33.

75 McCormick, 186.

76 Douglass, 33.

77 Florence Ayres Mulford, ed., *The Fourth Wall: Reminiscences of the New Jersey College for Women Class of 1925* (New Brunswick, NJ: Douglass College, 1955), 11–13.

78 New Jersey College for Women, *Announcement,* 1928–1929, 59–61, SC/UA.

79 *Fall Report of Work Done in Office of Assistant to the Committee on Admissions,* December 1, 1931, RG 19/A0/01, Douglass College, Dean's Records. Mabel Smith Douglass, Box 105, Folder 7, SC/UA.

80 L. F. Loree to M. S. Douglass, September 29, 1920, RG 19/A0/01, Douglass College, Dean's Records. Mabel Smith Douglass, Box 67, Folder 3, SC/UA.

81 Mulford, 1. For the first time, NJC had four class years on campus.

82 Board of Managers Minutes, NJC, October 6, 1922, RG 19/A0/10, Douglass College, Dean's Records. Mabel Smith Douglass, Box 12, Folder 15, SC/UA.

83 McCormick, 207.

84 Beulah B. Clark, *Annual Report: Admissions,* July 31, 1928, RG 19/A0/01, Douglass College, Dean's Records. Mabel Smith Douglass, Box 5, Folder 1, SC/UA.

85 Emily Gregory Hickman, *An Experiment in Supervised Study for Deficient Sophomores at New Jersey College for Women* (New Brunswick: New Jersey College for Women, 1929).

86 Ibid., Part III, Individual Case Histories. Although there is no information on these students' religious affiliation, none appear to be Jewish.

87 Mabel Smith Douglass to James Neilson (carbon copy), January 24, 1922, RG 19/A0/01, Douglass College, Dean's Records. Mabel Smith Douglass, Box 72, Folder 1, SC/UA.

88 Barbara Miller Solomon, *In the Company of Educated Women: A History of Women and Higher Education in America* (New Haven: Yale University Press, 1985),142.

89 Michael Greenberg and Seymour Zenchelsky, "Private Bias and Public Responsibility: Anti-Semitism at Rutgers in the 1920s and 1930s," *History of Education Quarterly* 33, no. 3 (1993): 305–308.

90 Jeannette Finn Blackman, *Report of Work Done in Office of Assistant to the Committee on Admission,* April 19, 1932, RG 19/A0/01, Douglass College, Dean's Records. Mabel Smith Douglass, Box 105, Folder 7, SC/UA.

91 Greenberg and Zenchelsky, 312–313.

92 Rosalind Rosenberg, "The Legacy of Dean Gildersleeve," *Barnard Alumnae Bulletin,* Summer 1996, 21.

93 Jerome Karabel, *The Chosen: The Hidden History of Admission and Exclusion at Harvard, Yale, and Princeton* (Boston: Houghton Mifflin, 2005), 1.

94 David O. Levine, *The American College and the Culture of Aspiration, 1915–1940* (Ithaca, NY: Cornell University Press, 1986), 146–147.

95 Greenberg and Zenchelsky, 304.

96 Julia Feller Feist (NJC '35), interview with Jocelyn Briddell (DC '81), May 30, 2003. Associate Alumnae of Douglass College Oral History Project, Douglass Library. Used by permission of the Associate Alumnae of Douglass College.

97 Jeannette Finn, *Report of the Work Done in September 1930 by the Assistant to the Committee on Admissions at the New Jersey College for Women,* RG 19/A0/01, Douglass

College, Dean's Records. Mabel Smith Douglass, Box 105, Folder 7, SC/UA.

98   Class of 1922, *In the Beginning . . . Reminiscences of the Class of 1922* (New Brunswick: New Jersey College for Women, 1952), 2.

99   Ibid., 43–44.

100 Ibid., 42.

101 Douglass, 43.

102 New Jersey College for Women, *Red Book: Handbook of Information for* Students (New Brunswick: New Jersey College for Women, 1922), 8–9.

103 Class of 1922, 36.

104 Horowitz, *Alma Mater*, 122–123.

105 Only a few months later, Reverend Hall and parishioner Eleanor Reinhardt Mills were found murdered in a famous unsolved murder case. See Mary S. Hartman, "The Hall Mills Murder Case: The Most Fascinating Unsolved Murder in America," *Journal of the Rutgers University Libraries* 47, no. 1 (1984), 4–15.

106 Schmidt, 68–69.

107 Diary, Florence Marshall ('29), May 10 and 11, 1927, Douglass Library.

108 Elizabeth David, "Traditions of Douglass College: The Transition from Class-Centered to College-Centered Focus," in Frusciano and Perrone, 3–12.

109 New Jersey College for Women, *Red Book*, 1921.

110 Horowitz, *Alma Mater*, 167.

111 New Jersey College for Women, *Red Book*, 1922, 9; and *Cooperative Association of the New Jersey College for Women* (New Brunswick, NJ, 1924), 10.

112 Class of 1922, 45–50.

113 Ibid., 19.

114 New Jersey College for Women, *Red Book*, 1926.

115 Lynn E. Couturier, "Considering *The Sportswoman*, 1924 to 1936: A Content Analysis," *Sports History Review* 41 (2010): 111–112.

116 See Lynn Couturier, "Play With Us, Not Against Us," *International Journal of the History of Sport* 25, no. 4 (2008): 421–442.

117 "Objections to Intercollegiate Sports Explained," *Campus News*, October 14, 1927, 1.

118 Class of 1922, 53.

119 Horowitz, *Alma Mater*, 149.

120 The first student government at a women's college was established at Bryn Mawr in 1892 and followed this model. See Horowitz, Alma Mater, 119–120.

121 Douglass, 40.

122 Leah Boddie, "The Organization of a Department of Student Life in a Coordinate College for Women," in Sarah M. Sturtevant and Harriet Hayes, eds., *Deans at Work* (New York: Harper and Brothers, 1930), 78–80.

123 New Jersey College for Women, *Red Book*, 1930 and 1937.

124 Horowitz, *Alma Mater*, 149–150.

125 Diary, Marshall ('29), February 6, 1927.

126 New Jersey College for Women, *Red Book*, 1922, 20.

127 New Jersey College for Women, *Red Book*, 1924, 43.

128 Mulford, 23.

129 Helen Lefkowitz Horowitz, *Campus Life: Undergraduates Cultures from the End of the Eighteenth Century to the Present* (Chicago: University of Chicago Press, 1988), 127.

130 Class of 1922, 5.

131 Ibid., 46.

132 "Bobbed Heads Are Defended by Pro and Con," *Campus News*, May 25, 1923, 1, as quoted in Suzanne Boyle, "Bob or Behave? How NJC Dealt with the Pressures of Fads and Traditions in the 1920s," in Fernanda Perrone and Thomas J. Frusciano, eds.,

Towards a New History of Douglass College: Essays by Students from the Douglass Scholars Program (New Brunswick, NJ: Douglass College, 2003), http://www.libraries.rutgers. edu/rul/libs/scua/douglass_scholars/introduction.shtml (accessed February 4, 2017).

133   Diary, Marshall, February 9, 1927.

134   New Jersey College for Women, *Red Book*, 1928.

135   New Jersey College for Women, *Red Book*, 1927 and 1928.

136   Mulford, 24.

Chapter 3   Challenges of the 1930s

1   Susan Ware, *Holding Their Own: American Women in the 1930s* (Boston: Twayne, 1982), 56.

2   Calvin B. T. Lee, *The Campus Scene, 1900–1970* (New York: David McKay, 1970), 62–64. The first Red Scare was associated with socialist and anarchist mobilizations in the United States in the aftermath of the Bolshevik Revolution. The Justice Department, under Attorney General A. Mitchell Palmer, created the General Intelligence Division of the Bureau of Investigation on August 1, 1919, under the direction of J. Edgar Hoover to uncover Bolshevik conspiracies and find, incarcerate, or deport "conspirators." The subsequent arrests of thousands of individuals involved in radical organizations were carried out through what were known as the Palmer Raids.

3   Margaret A. Nash and Lisa S. Romero, "'Citizenship for the College Girl': Challenges and Opportunities in Higher Education for Women in the United States in the 1930s," *Teachers College Record* 114 (February 2012): 14.

4   *Daily Home News* (New Brunswick, NJ), September 7, 1923.

5   William H. Leupp to Mabel Smith Douglass, September 11, 1923, RG 19/A0/01, Douglass College, Dean's Records. Mabel Smith Douglass, Box 70, Folder 1, Special Collections and University Archives (hereafter SC/UA).

6   George P. Schmidt, *Douglass College: A History* (New Brunswick, NJ: Rutgers University Press, 1968), 13.

7   L. A. Opdyke, MD, to Mabel Smith Douglass, October 27 and 31, 1925, Mabel Smith Douglass Papers, Box 3, Folder 4, SC/UA.

8   Dr. Imre Weitzner, MD, to Mabel Smith Douglass, March 8, 1930, Box 3, Folder 8, Mabel Smith Douglass Papers, SC/UA.

9   Jane Inge to Mabel Smith Douglass, December 18, 1929, Mabel Smith Douglass Papers, Box 3, Folder 8, SC/UA.

10   Richard P. McCormick, *Rutgers: A Bicentennial History* (New Brunswick, NJ: Rutgers University Press, 1966), 197–198.

11   Mabel Smith Douglass to John Martin Thomas, November 10, 1925, RG 19/A0/01, Douglass College, Dean's Records. Mabel Smith Douglass, Box 75, Folder 7, SC/UA.

12   Mabel Smith Douglass to Leonor F. Loree, December 24, 1926, RG 19/A0/01, Douglass College, Dean's Records. Mabel Smith Douglass, Box 67, Folder 4, SC/UA.

13   McCormick, 211.

14   Ibid., 200–201.

15   Mabel Smith Douglass to Leonor F. Loree, October 14, 1927, RG 19/A0/01, Douglass College, Dean's Records. Mabel Smith Douglass, Box 67, Folder 4, SC/UA.

16   Quoted in McCormick, 211.

17   McCormick, 211–212.

18   McCormick, 212; and Rosemary Sawyer Moxon (NJC '29), "Trends of the First Quarter Century: A History of Intangibles," in Rosemary Sawyer Moxon and Mabel Clarke Peabody, *Twenty-Five Years: Two Anniversary Sketches of the New Jersey College for Women* (New Brunswick, NJ: New Jersey College for Women, Rutgers University, 1943), 4.

19 McCormick, 230; and Schmidt, 72. McCormick gives the 1929 figure for NJC as 1,159.

20 Board of Managers Minutes, May 1, 1931, and June 6, 1931, RG 19/A0/01, Douglass College, Dean's Records. Mabel Smith Douglass, Box 9, SC/UA.

21 McCormick, 229.

22 Telegram, Robert Clothier and Mabel Smith Douglass to members of the State Legislature, June 4, 1932, RG 19/A0/01, Douglass College, Dean's Records. Mabel Smith Douglass, Box 75, Folder 7, SC/UA.

23 New Jersey College for Women, *Announcement*, 1931–1932, 12; and 1933–1934, 9, SC/UA.

24 McCormick, 229.

25 Catherine Landreth, Director, School for Child Study, Report to the Dean, April 14, 1932, RG 19/A0/01, Douglass College, Dean's Records. Mabel Smith Douglass, Box 86, Folder 2, 1–10 SC/UA; and New Jersey College for Women, *Annual Report*, Bulletin no. 11, October 1932, RG 19/A0/01, Douglass College, Dean's Records. Mabel Smith Douglass, Box 10, 14, SC/UA.

26 Helen W. Hazen, Chair, Department of Home Economics, Report to the Dean, June 30, 1931, 1–5, RG 19/A0/01, Douglass College, Dean's Records. Mabel Smith Douglass, Box 2, Folder 7, SC/UA.

27 New Jersey College for Women, *Annual Report*, 1929–1930, 1930–1931, and 1931–1932.

28 "Students Are Urged to Remain in School," *Campus News*, October 6, 1931, 1.

29 Schmidt, 80.

30 *Report to the Committee on the New Jersey College for Women of the Board of Trustees of Rutgers College*, December 2, 1932, RG 19/A0/01, Douglass College, Dean's Records. Mabel Smith Douglass, Box 12, SC/UA.

31 Barbara Sicherman, "Colleges and Careers: Historical Perspectives on the Lives and Work Patterns of Women College Graduates," in John Mack Faragher and Florence Howe, eds. *Women and Higher Education in American History* (New York: W.W. Norton, 1988), 160–162.

32 Lucille Bourath Pogue (NJC '33), interview with Jocelyn Briddell (DC '81), May 30, 2003. Associate Alumnae of Douglass College Oral History Project, Douglass Library. Used by permission of the Associate Alumnae of Douglass College.

33 Moxon, 21–22.

34 Mabel S. Douglass to Leonor F. Loree, June 15, 1931, RG 19/A0/01, Douglass College, Dean's Records. Mabel Smith Douglass, Box 67, Folder 5, SC/UA.

35 Moxon, 23.

36 Trustees Committee, June 29, 1932, RG 19/A0/01, Douglass College, Dean's Records. Mabel Smith Douglass, Box 12; and Minutes, Faculty-Executive Council, December 1, 1930, Box 110, Folder 13, SC/UA.

37 Schmidt, 83.

38 George Christian Ortloff, *A Lady in the Lake: The True Account of Death and Discovery in Lake Placid* (Lake Placid, NY: With Pipe and Book, 1985), 37–38.

39 Memorandum, Robert C. Clothier to Faculty of NJC, May 22, 1933, RG 19/A0/01, Douglass College, Dean's Records. Mabel Smith Douglass, Box 75, Folder 8, SC/UA.

40 Rutgers Faculty Biographical File, Albert E. Meder, Jr., SC/UA and Obituary, Janet Davis Meder, *Bennington Banner*, June 13, 2006.

41 Trustees Committee Minutes, June 3, 1933, RG 19/A0/01, Douglass College, Dean's Records. Mabel Smith Douglass, Box 12, SC/UA.

42 Virginia Lee Block to Mabel Smith Douglass, June 11, 1933, Mabel Smith Douglass Papers, Box 3, Folder 3, SC/UA.

43   Louise Duus, "Mabel Smith Douglass," in Women's Project of New Jersey, Inc., *Past and Promise: Lives of New Jersey Women,* edited by Joan N. Burstyn, 2nd ed. (Syracuse, NY: Syracuse University Press, 1997), 128.

44   Ortloff, 41–47.

45   Minutes, Trustees Committee, March 6, 1936, RG 19/A0/01, Douglass College, Dean's Records. Margaret T. Corwin, Box 13, Folder 1, SC/UA.

46   H. T. Muller, New York State Police to Ruth Adams, September 27, 1963, Mabel Smith Douglass Papers, Box 4, Folder 6, SC/UA.

47   "Miss Edith Douglass to Wed Max A. Roth," *New York Times,* March 8, 1943; and "Woman Kills Herself as Clergyman Waits," *New York Herald Tribune,* May 1, 1948, copy in New Jersey College for Women Collection, Box 2, SC/UA.

48   Ortloff, 51.

49   Frances E. Riche, "Margaret Trumbull Corwin," *Alumnae Bulletin,* Spring 1983, 1–2; and Margaret Trumbull Corwin Faculty Biographical File, SC/UA.

50   Joint Meeting of the Committee on the New Jersey College for Women and the Finance Committee, November 6, 1936, RG 19/A0/01, Douglass College, Dean's Records. Margaret T. Corwin, Box 13, Folder 1, SC/UA.

51   McCormick, 245.

52   Margaret T. Corwin, *Report to the President,* July 10, 1934, RG 19/A0/01, Douglass College, Dean's Records. Margaret T. Corwin, Box 10, Folder 5, 4, SC/UA.

53   Moxon, 9–10.

54   Frieda Finklestein Feller (NJC '41), oral history interview, March 27, 1998, by G. Kurt Piehler and Elizabeth Wyatt, Rutgers Oral History Archives, http://oralhistory.rutgers.edu/social-and-cultural-history/31-interviewees/910-feller-frieda-finklestein (last accessed January 16, 2017).

55   Moxon, 6–7.

56   Ibid., 8.

57   Schmidt, 100.

58   New Jersey College for Women, *Annual Report to President Clothier,* July 23, 1935, RG 19/A0/01, Douglass College, Dean's Records. Margaret T. Corwin, Box 10, Folder 5, SC/UA.

59   *Dean's Report to President Clothier,* 1935–1936, RG 19/A0/01, Douglass College, Dean's Records. Margaret T. Corwin, Box 10, Folder 6, 4, SC/UA.

60   Margaret Corwin to Helena Kees, September 28, 1936, RG 19/A0/01, Douglass College, Dean's Records. Margaret T. Corwin, Box 114, Folder 8, SC/UA. The Jane Addams House was discontinued in the early 1940s when it became too difficult to administer. It also duplicated the resources of Neighborhood House, a nearby New Brunswick settlement. See William La Barre, *Report of the Jane Addams House,* December 1939, RG 19/A0/01, Douglass College, Dean's Records. Margaret T. Corwin, Box 114, Folder 8, SC/UA.

61   Sicherman, 156.

62   Moxon, 7; and Addendum, Memorandum of Opening, September 15–16, 1924, RG 19/A0/01, Douglass College, Dean's Records. Mabel Smith Douglass, Box 12, Folder 15, SC/UA.

63   Minutes, Faculty Executive Council, June 2, 1930, RG 19/A0/01, Douglass College, Dean's Records. Mabel Smith Douglass, Box 110, Folder 13, SC/UA.

64   Sicherman, 153–157.

65   Minutes, Trustees Committee, May 3, 1935, February 7, 1936, and June 1, 1940, RG 19/A0/01, Douglass College, Dean's Records. Margaret T. Corwin, Box 13, Folders 1 and 2, SC/UA. For discussion of NJC students' overall career trajectories and how they changed over time, see chapter 12.

66 Trustees Committee, December 6, 1932, RG 19/A0/01, Douglass College, Dean's Records. Mabel Smith Douglass, Box 12, Folder 15, SC/UA.

67 Minutes, Trustees Committee, May 6, 1938, RG 19/A0/01, Douglass College, Dean's Records. Margaret T. Corwin, Box 13, Folder 1, SC/UA.

68 Margaret Judson, *Breaking the Barrier* (New Brunswick, NJ: Rutgers University, 1984), 100–115.

69 Schmidt, 84.

70 McCormick, 231–232.

71 Minutes, Trustees Committee, April 2, 1937, RG 19/A0/01, Douglass College, Dean's Records. Margaret T. Corwin, Box 13, Folder 1, SC/UA.

72 Alma Geist Cap (NJC '38), interview with Nancy Punchatz Hines ('61), May 30, 2003, Associate Alumnae of Douglass College Oral History Project, Douglass Library. Used by permission of the Associate Alumnae of Douglass College.

73 Michael Greenberg and Seymour Zenchelsky, "Private Bias and Public Responsibility: Anti-Semitism at Rutgers in the 1920s and 1930s," *History of Education Quarterly* 33, no. 3 (1993): 314–318.

74 Minutes, Trustees Committee, June 3, 1939, RG 19/A0/01, Douglass College, Dean's Records. Margaret T. Corwin, Box 13, Folder 1, SC/UA. In earlier years, this policy was applied unofficially.

75 Minutes, Trustees Committee, October 2, 1936, RG 19/A0/01, Douglass College, Dean's Records. Margaret T. Corwin, Box 13, Folder 1, SC/UA.

76 Ida Perlmutter Kamich (NJC '38), interview with Susan Gordan Marchand (DC '61) and Nancy Punchatz Hines (DC '61), February 9, 2005, Associate Alumnae of Douglass College Oral History Project, Douglass Library. Used by permission of the Associate Alumnae of Douglass College.

77 Jerome Karabel, *The Chosen: The Hidden History of Admission and Exclusion at Harvard, Yale, and Princeton* (Boston: Houghton Mifflin, 2005), 111–115.

78 Frieda Finklestein Feller (NJC '41), oral history interview, March 27, 1998, by G. Kurt Piehler and Elizabeth Wyatt, Rutgers Oral History Archives, http://oralhistory.rutgers.edu/social-and-cultural-history/31-interviewees/910-feller-frieda-finklestein (last accessed January 16, 2017).

79 Annette Greenblatt (NJC '45) oral history interview, October 6, 1999, by Shaun Illingworth and Stephanie Katz, Rutgers Oral History Archives, http://oralhistory.rutgers.edu/interviewees/957-greenblatt-annette (last accessed February 6, 2017).

80 Bernice Adler Luxemburg (NJC '41), interview with Rose Ann Bourchewski Howarth (DC '59), May 30, 2008, Associate Alumnae of Douglass College Oral History Project, Douglass Library. Used by permission of the Association Alumnae of Douglass College; Pearl Paterson Thompson, oral history interview, December 18, 2001, by Rutgers Oral History Archives, http://oralhistory.rutgers.edu/alphabetical-index/31-interviewees/1288-thompson-pearl-paterson (last accessed February 6, 2017).

81 David O. Levine, *The American College and the Culture of Aspiration, 1915–1940* (Ithaca, NY: Cornell University Press, 1986), 158–160.

82 Nash and Romero, 6.

83 Margaret T. Corwin to President Clothier, August 8, 1934, RG 04/A14, Rutgers University Office of the President, Robert C. Clothier, Box 85, Folder 8, SC/UA.

84 Patti Verbanas, "Julia Baxter Bates: Proving the Scientific Case for Public School Desegregation," *Rutgers Today,* May 9, 2016, http://news.rutgers.edu/feature/julia-baxter-bates-proving-scientific-case-public-school-desegregation/20160508 (last accessed October 2, 2016)

85 Aya Sakar (DRC '15), "Perspectives on Diversity and Multiculturalism on Douglass Campus, from the 1920s to the 1950s" (Aresty Research Project, Rutgers University, 2015).

86   See Linda M. Perkins, "The African American Female Elite: The Early History of African American Women in the Seven Sisters Colleges, 1880–1960," *Harvard Educational Review* 67, no. 4 (1997): 718–756.

87   February 22, 1935, "Teddy" Kunst/Theresa Kerr Diaries, Accn. 2015.003, SC/UA.

88   *Dean's Report to President Clothier*, June 24, 1936, RG 19/A0/01, Douglass College, Dean's Records. Margaret T. Corwin, Box 10, Folder 6, SC/UA.

89   McCormick, 232.

90   Schmidt, 140–145.

91   McCormick, 232–233.

92   Schmidt, 150.

93   Robert Cohen, *When the Old Left Was Young: Student Radicals and America's First Mass Student Movement, 1929–1941* (New York: Oxford University Press, 1993), xiii.

94   Ibid., 91–93.

95   April 12, 1935, "Teddy" Kunst/Theresa Kerr Diaries, Accn. 2015.003, SC/UA.

96   Cohen, 152–153; and *Dean's Report to President Clothier*, June 24, 1936, RG 19/A0/01, Douglass College, Dean's Records. Margaret T. Corwin, Box 10, Folder 6, SCUA.

97   The story of the Bergel-Hauptmann affair has been told in David M. Oshinsky, Richard P. McCormick, and Daniel Horn in *The Case of the Nazi Professor* (New Brunswick, NJ: Rutgers University Press, 1989). See also Michael Greenberg and Seymour Zenchelsky, "Confrontation with Nazism at Rutgers: Academic Bureaucracy and Moral Failure," *History of Education Quarterly* 30, no. 3 (1990): 325–349. The account below is taken primarily from these two sources.

98   Lee, 68.

99   May 3, 1935, "Teddy" Kunst/Theresa Kerr Diaries, Accn. 2015.003, SC/UA.

100   May 21, 1935, "Teddy" Kunst/Theresa Kerr Diaries, Accn. 2015.003, SC/UA.

101   Oshinsky, McCormick, and Horn, 99. In 1985, the fiftieth anniversary of the hearings, Rutgers College alumnus Alan Silver, who had been one of Bergel's student supporters in the 1930s, launched a press campaign to convince Rutgers to apologize to Lienhard Bergel. President Edward Bloustein appointed a panel of historians to reexamine the case. Although the group uncovered many interesting facts, including Hauptmann's flight to Germany and its cover-up by Rutgers officials, the historians ultimately supported the Ashmead Committee's conclusion that Bergel was not dismissed because of political prejudice. Oshinsky, McCormick, and Horn's *The Case of the Nazi Professor* is a published version of the historians' findings. Other scholars have challenged that conclusion; see Greenberg and Zenchelsky, "Confrontation with Nazism."

102   Cohen, xiv–xv.

103   Schmidt, 151–53.

104   *Dean's Report to President Clothier*, June 24, 1936, RG 19/A0/01, Douglass College, Dean's Records. Margaret T. Corwin, Box 10, Folder 6, SC/UA.

105   Ida Perlmutter Kamich (NJC '38), interview with Susan Gordan Marchand (DC '61) and Nancy Punchatz Hines (DC '61), February 9, 2005, Associate Alumnae of Douglass College Oral History Project, Douglass Library. Used by permission of the Associate Alumnae of Douglass College.

106   Schmidt, 154 and Adelaide Marcus Zagoren (NJC '40), interview with Linda Cohen (DC '66), March 20, 2012, Associate Alumnae of Douglass College Oral History Project, Douglass Library. Used by permission of the Associate Alumnae of Douglass College.

107   Schmidt, 154.

108   January 14, 1935, "Teddy" Kunst/Theresa Kerr Diaries, Accn. 2015.003, SC/UA.

109   See "Plan Campus Yule Fete: Jersey Girls' College Students Name Leaders as Log Bearers," *New York Times*, December 3, 1933.

110 "Democracy?" *Campus News*, October 28, 1938, 2.

111 Schmidt, 155–156.

112 Ilanit Sluzak, "The Abolition of *Campus News*" (honors thesis, Rutgers University, 1994), 8–13.

113 Sluzak, 16–34. Ilanit Sluzak (DC '95) interviewed Campus News editors Marion Short Sauer (NJC '36), Enda Sweeney Slack (NJC '40) and Dorothy Taylor Durand (NJC '40) in the research for her thesis.

114 Quoted in Sluzak, 1.

115 Cohen, 28–30 and 57–65.

116 McCormick, 234.

117 Audrey Brown Walton (NJC '38), interview with Susan Gordan Marchand (DC '61), May 30, 2003, Associate Alumnae of Douglass College Oral History Project, Douglass Library. Used by permission of the Associate Alumnae of Douglass College.

118 McCormick, 234.

119 Helen Erickson (NJC '31), interview with Rose Ann Borichewski Howarth (DC '59), May 30, 2003, Associate Alumnae of Douglass College Oral History Project, Douglass Library. Used by permission of the Associate Alumnae of Douglass College.

120 Isolde Musterman Byrne (NJC '34), interview with Linda Cohen (DC '66), February 19, 2003, Associate Alumnae of Douglass College Oral History Project, Douglass Library. Used by permission of the Associate Alumnae of Douglass College.

121 *Dean's Report to President Clothier*, June 24, 1936, RG 19/A0/01, Douglass College, Dean's Records. Margaret T. Corwin, Box 10, Folder 6, SC/UA.

122 Sluzak, 44; and Schmidt, 160.

Chapter 4   World War II and Its Aftermath: New Jersey College for Women, 1940–1950

1   "WWII by the Numbers," National World War II Museum, New Orleans, http://www.nationalww2museum.org/learn/education/for-students/ww2-history/ww2-by-the-numbers/.

2   D'Ann Campbell, *Women at War with America: Private Lives in a Patriotic Era* (Cambridge, MA: Harvard University, 1984), 20.

3   Ibid., 103.

4   Susan M. Hartmann, *The Home Front and Beyond: American Women in the 1940s* (Boston: Twayne, 1982), 80–82 and 40–41.

5   V. R. Cardozier, *Colleges and Universities in World War II* (Westport, CT: Praeger, 1993), 4–5.

6   Ibid., 215–228.

7   Shirley Friedlander and Margaret Lauer, eds., *Quair: The Yearbook of the New Jersey College for Women*, 1942, 93 (hereafter, *Quair*).

8   Laura Micheletti, "'Carrying On': Students at New Jersey College for Women and World War II" (history honors thesis, Rutgers University, 1999), 15–16.

9   George P. Schmidt, *Douglass College: A History* (New Brunswick, NJ: Rutgers University Press, 1968), 161.

10 Margaret T. Corwin, New Jersey College for Women, *Annual Report*, July 1940, RG 19, Douglass College, Annual Reports, Box 2, 3–6, SC/UA.

11 Margaret T. Corwin, New Jersey College for Women, *Annual Report*, 1941, RG 19, Douglass College, Annual Reports, Box 2, 1, SC/UA.

12 Micheletti, 16–17.

13 Laura Micheletti Puaca, *Searching for Scientific Womanpower: Technocratic Feminism and the Politics of National Security, 1940–1980* (Chapel Hill: University of North Carolina Press, 2014), 17.

14   Margaret T. Corwin, New Jersey College for Women, *Annual Report*, 1941, RG 19, Douglass College, Annual Reports, Box 2, 2–3, SC/UA.

15   Margaret Corwin to M. Phillip Stotts, Field Secretary, Regional Plan Association, March 5, 1941, RG 19/A0/01, Douglass College, Dean's Records. Margaret T. Corwin, Box 109, Folder 5, SC/UA.

16   Pearl Paterson Thompson, oral history interview, December 18, 2001, by Greg Kupsky, Rutgers Oral History Archives, http://oralhistory.rutgers.edu/social-and-cultural-history/31-interviewees/1288-thompson-pearl-paterson (last accessed January 16, 2017).

17   Margaret Judson to Margaret T. Corwin, January 27, 1941, RG 19/A0/01, Douglass College, Dean's Records. Margaret T. Corwin, Box 109, Folder 5, SC/UA.

18   Richard P. McCormick, "Rutgers in World War II," *Journal of the Rutgers University Libraries* 58 (1997): 4.

19   Margaret T. Corwin, New Jersey College for Women, *Annual Report*, 1941, RG 19, Douglass College. Annual Reports, Box 2, 2–3, SC/UA. Margaret Corwin to M. Phillip Stotts, Field Secretary, Regional Plan Association, March 5, 1941, RG 19/A0/01, Douglass College, Dean's Records. Margaret T. Corwin, Box 109, Folder 5, SC/UA.

20   Puaca, 29–30.

21   McCormick, "Rutgers in World War II," 4.

22   Bernice Adler Luxemburg (NJC '41), interview with Rose Ann Bourchewski Howarth (DC '59), May 30, 2008, Associate Alumnae of Douglass College Oral History Project, Douglass Library. Used by permission of the Associate Alumnae of Douglass College.

23   Ruth Sheeler Moncrief, oral history interview, October 5, 2007, by Sandra Stewart Holyoak, Sabeenah Arshad, and Hanne Ala-Rami, Rutgers Oral History Archives, http://oralhistory.rutgers.edu/social-and-cultural-history/31-interviewees/1123-moncrief-ruth-sheeler (last accessed January 1, 2017).

24   Barbara Waters Kramer, oral history interview, March 23, 1998, by G. Kurt Piehler and Donovan Bezer, Rutgers Oral History Archives, http://oralhistory.rutgers.edu/social-and-cultural-history/31-interviewees/1045-kramer-barbara-waters (last accessed January 1, 2017).

25   Margaret T. Corwin, New Jersey College for Women, *Annual Report*, 1942, RG 19, Douglass College, Annual Reports, Box 2, 3, SC/UA.

26   Puaca, 21.

27   McCormick, "Rutgers in World War II," 4–7.

28   Hartmann, 101–104.

29   Margaret T. Corwin, New Jersey College for Women, *Annual Report*, 1945, RG 19, Douglass College, Annual Reports, Box 2, SC/UA.

30   Micheletti, 27. Indeed during the war, women were admitted to twenty-nine previously all-male engineering programs, including those at Columbia, Purdue, and Cornell. See Margaret W. Rossiter, *Women Scientists in America: Before Affirmative Action, 1940–1972* (Baltimore: Johns Hopkins University Press, 1995), 14; and Amy Sue Bix, *Girls Coming to Tech! A History of American Engineering Education for Women* (Cambridge, MA: MIT Press, 2013), 103–111.

31   Thomas J. Frusciano, "'A Truly Cooperative Effort': New Jersey College for Women and the War Effort as Documented in the Rutgers Oral History Archives of World War II," paper presented at the annual meeting of the Society of American Archivists, Los Angeles, CA, August 21, 2003, 14. Used by permission.

32   Schmidt, 164–165.

33   Margaret T. Corwin, New Jersey College for Women, *Annual Report*, 1942, RG 19, Douglass College, Annual Reports, Box 2, 3, SC/UA.

34 Nancy Petersen Godfrey, oral history interview, February 14, 1997, by G. Kurt Piehler and Barbara Tomblin, Rutgers Oral History Archives, http://oralhistory.rutgers.edu/social-and-cultural-history/31-interviewees/941-godfrey-nancy-petersen (last accessed January 1, 2017).

35 Rosamond Sawyer Moxon (NJC '29), "Trends of the First Quarter Century: A History of Intangibles," in Rosamond Sawyer Moxon and Mabel Clarke Peabody, *Twenty-Five Years: Two Anniversary Sketches of New Jersey College for Women* (New Brunswick: New Jersey College for Women, Rutgers University, 1943), 23 and 42.

36 Ibid., 15.

37 Jean C. Comeforo, oral history interview, April 10, 1996, by G. Kurt Piehler, Maria Mazzone, and Melanie Cooper, Rutgers Oral History Archives, http://oralhistory.rutgers.edu/social-and-cultural-history/31-interviewees/868-comeforo-jean-c (last accessed January 1, 2017).

38 Ibid, 162.

39 Margaret T. Corwin, New Jersey College for Women, *Annual Report*, 1944, RG 19, Douglass College, Annual Reports, Box 2, 4–5, SC/UA.

40 Margaret T. Corwin to Robert C. Clothier, June 21, 1943, and July 14, 1943, RG 04/A14, Office of the Rutgers University President, Robert C. Clothier, Box 85, Folder 9, SC/UA.

41 Micheletti, 27.

42 Fredericka Belknap to Margaret T. Corwin, January 12, 1943, RG 19/A0/01, Douglass College, Dean's Records. Margaret T. Corwin, Box 74, Folder 1, SC/UA.

43 Rossiter, 2–3.

44 "Home Ec Alumnae Inspect Food for U.S. Government," *Caellian*, May 6, 1943, 3.

45 Frusciano, 13–14.

46 Nancy Squire Christensen, oral history interview, November 7, 2008, by Shaun Illingworth and Ellie MacPherson, Oral History Archives, http://oralhistory.rutgers.edu/social-and-cultural-history/31-interviewees/859-christensen-nancy-squire (last accessed January 10, 2017).

47 Margaret T. Corwin, New Jersey College for Women, *Annual Report*, 1945, RG 19, Douglass College, Annual Reports, Box 2, SC/UA. Barbara Sicherman notes the long-term trend in which college-educated women gradually entered fields other than teaching as an additional contributing factor. See Barbara Sicherman, "College and Careers: Historical Perspectives on the Lives and Work Patterns of Women College Graduates," in John Mack Faragher and Florence Howe, eds. *Women and Higher Education in American History* (New York: W.W. Norton, 1988), 153.

48 Quoted in Micheletti, 30.

49 Adelaide Marcus Zagoren (NJC '40), interview with Linda Cohen (DC '66), March 20, 2012, Associate Alumnae of Douglass College Oral History Project, Douglass Library. Used by permission of the Associate Alumnae of Douglass College.

50 Rossiter, 13–14.

51 Richard P. McCormick, *Rutgers: A Bicentennial History* (New Brunswick, NJ: Rutgers University Press, 1966), 260.

52 Jean O'Grady Sheehan, oral history interview, September 21, 2006, by Sandra Stewart Holyoak, Rutgers Oral History Archives, http://oralhistory.rutgers.edu/social-and-cultural-history/31-interviewees/1240-sheehan-jean-ogrady (last accessed January 14, 2017).

53 Nancy Petersen Godfrey, oral history interview, February 14, 1997, by G. Kurt Piehler and Barbara Tomblin, Rutgers Oral History Archives, http://oralhistory.rutgers.edu/social-and-cultural-history/31-interviewees/941-godfrey-nancy-petersen (last accessed January 17, 2017).

54   Margaret Harriet Waugh, oral history interview, January 28, 1999, by Laura Micheletti and Barbara Tomblin, Rutgers Oral History Archives, http://oralhistory.rutgers.edu/social-and-cultural-history/31-interviewees/1312-waugh-margaret-harriet (last accessed January 17, 2017).

55   Michael Ojeda and James Bongi, "Some Gave All: World War II," http://oralhistory.rutgers.edu/related-documents/19-some-gave-all/1409-some-gave-all-world-war-ii, Related Documents, Rutgers Oral History Archives (last accessed January 15, 2017).

56   Schmidt, 168–169.

57   Cardozier, 125.

58   ". . . My Last Word," *Caellian*, April 27, 1944, 2.

59   Micheletti, 40.

60   Margaret T. Corwin, New Jersey College for Women, *Annual Report*, 1945, RG 19, Douglass College, Annual Reports, Box 2, SC/UA.

61   "Mrs. Roosevelt to Give Two Talks Monday on Youth in World at War," *Caellian*, January 13, 1944, 1.

62   Hartmann, 6.

63   "HEPS Committee Works to Better Race Relations," *Caellian*, May 18, 1944, 1, 3.

64   Ibid.

65   Aya Sakar (DRC '15), "Perspectives on Diversity and Multiculturalism on Douglass Campus, from the 1920s to the 1950s" (Aresty Research Project, Rutgers University, 2015).

66   Eleanor Oliven, "Minorities' Chairman Discusses Tolerance," *Caellian*, March 21, 1945, 2.

67   Nancy Petersen Godfrey, oral history interview, February 14, 1997, by G. Kurt Piehler and Barbara Tomblin, http://oralhistory.rutgers.edu/social-and-cultural-history/31-interviewees/941-godfrey-nancy-petersen, Rutgers Oral History Archives (last accessed January 2, 2017).

68   Irene Prager (NJC '44), "Where N.J.C. Can Win," *Caellian*, December 9, 1943, 2.

69   Evelyn Field (NJC '49), interview with Susan Schwirck (DC '71), December 28, 2007, Associate Alumnae of Douglass College Oral History Project, Douglass Library. Used by permission of the Associate Alumnae of Douglass College.

70   Mary Lou Norton Busch, oral history interview, August 17, 2007, by Shaun Illingworth, Matthew Lawrence and Jessica Thomson Illingworth, Rutgers Oral History Archives, http://oralhistory.rutgers.edu/social-and-cultural-history/31-interviewees/837-busch-mary-lou-norton (last accessed January 2, 2017).

71   Nancy Squire Christensen, oral history interview, November 7, 2008, by Shaun Illingworth and Ellie MacPherson, Oral History Archives, http://oralhistory.rutgers.edu/social-and-cultural-history/31-interviewees/859-christensen-nancy-squire (last accessed January 2, 2017).

72   Micheletti, 44.

73   Mary Lou Norton Busch, oral history interview, August 17, 2007, by Shaun Illingworth, Matthew Lawrence and Jessica Thomson Illingworth, Rutgers Oral History Archives, http://oralhistory.rutgers.edu/social-and-cultural-history/31-interviewees/837-busch-mary-lou-norton (last accessed January 2, 2017).

74   Schmidt, 163.

75   Mabel Clarke Peabody (NJC '31), "Portrait of the Alumnae: Some Facts and Figures," in Moxon and Peabody, 51.

76   Sicherman, 143.

77   Jean C. Comeforo, oral history interview, April 10, 1996, by G. Kurt Piehler, Maria Mazzone, and Melanie Cooper, Rutgers Oral History Archives, http://oralhistory.rutgers.edu/social-and-cultural-history/31-interviewees/868-comeforo-jean-c (last

accessed January 15, 2017).

78   Nancy Petersen Godfrey, oral history interview, February 14, 1997, by G. Kurt Piehler and Barbara Tomblin, http://oralhistory.rutgers.edu/social-and-cultural-history/31-interviewees/941-godfrey-nancy-petersen, Rutgers Oral History Archives (last accessed January 15, 2017).

79   Cardozier, 130.

80   Margaret T. Corwin to Robert Clothier, August 4, 1942, RG 04/A14, Office of the Rutgers University President, Robert C. Clothier, Box 85, Folder 8, SC/UA.

81   Jean C. Comeforo, oral history interview, April 10, 1996, by G. Kurt Piehler, Maria Mazzone, and Melanie Cooper, Rutgers Oral History Archives, http://oralhistory.rutgers.edu/social-and-cultural-history/31-interviewees/868-comeforo-jean-c (last accessed January 15, 2017).

82   McCormick, *Rutgers*, 260.

83   Miriam Null, oral history interview, August 23, 2006, by Shaun Illingworth and Jonathan Wolitz, Rutgers Oral History Archives, http://oralhistory.rutgers.edu/social-and-cultural-history/31-interviewees/1146-null-miriam (last accessed January 15, 2017).

84   McCormick, *Rutgers*, 260.

85   Paul G. E. Clemens, *Rutgers since 1945: A History of the State University of New Jersey* (New Brunswick, NJ: Rutgers University Press, 2015), 5.

86   McCormick, *Rutgers*, 268–269 and Schmidt, 171–172.

87   Interfaith Committee, 1944–1945, RG 19/A0/01, Douglass College, Dean's Records. Margaret T. Corwin, Box 114, Folder 2, SC/UA.

88   McCormick, *Rutgers*, 276.

89   Ibid., 271.

90   Margaret T. Corwin, New Jersey College for Women, *Annual Report*, 1947, RG 19, Douglass College, Annual Reports, Box 2, SC/UA.

91   Margaret T. Corwin, New Jersey College for Women, *Annual Report*, 1944, RG 19, Douglass College, Annual Reports, Box 2, 16, SC/UA.

92   Clemens, 6.

93   Schmidt, 172–73.

94   Linda Eisenmann, *Higher Education for Women in Postwar America, 1945–1965* (Baltimore: Johns Hopkins University Press, 2006), 28.

95   Barbara Miller Solomon, *In the Company of Educated Women: A History of Women and Higher Education in America* (New Haven, CT: Yale University Press, 1985), 194–195.

96   Mary Lou Norton Busch, oral history interview, August 17, 2007, by Shaun Illingworth, Matthew Lawrence, and Jessica Thomson Illingworth, Rutgers Oral History Archives, http://oralhistory.rutgers.edu/social-and-cultural-history/31-interviewees/837-busch-mary-lou-norton (last accessed January 16, 2017).

97   New Jersey College for Women, *Announcement*, 1945–1946.

98   Mary Hance Owen, oral history interview, July 24, 1997, by Sandra Stewart Holyoak and Melanie Cooper, Rutgers Oral History Archives, http://oralhistory.rutgers.edu/social-and-cultural-history/31-interviewees/1149-owen-mary-hance (last accessed January 16, 2017).

99   "Duke Sociologist Calls Marriage 'a Creative Career': Gives Hints," *Caellian*, April 7, 1949, 1, 3.

100   Puaca, 37.

101   New Jersey College for Women, *Annual Report*, "Personnel Bureau," 1947–1948, RG 19/A0/01, Douglass College, Dean's Records. Margaret T. Corwin, Box 8 Folder 2, SC/UA.

102   Ibid.

103   Nancy Squire Christensen, oral history interview, November 7, 2008, by Shaun
      Illingworth and Ellie MacPherson, Oral History Archives, http://oralhistory.rutgers.
      edu/social-and-cultural-history/31-interviewees/859-christensen-nancy-squire (last
      accessed January 16, 2017).

104   Micheletti, 51.

105   Frieda Finklestein Feller, oral history interview, March 27, 1998, by G. Kurt Piehler
      and Elizabeth Wyatt, Rutgers Oral History Archives, http://oralhistory.rutgers.edu/
      social-and-cultural-history/31-interviewees/910-feller-frieda-finklestein (last
      accessed, January 16, 2017).

106   Evelyn Field (NJC '49), interview with Susan Schwirck (DC '71), December 28, 2007,
      Associate Alumnae of Douglass College Oral History Project, Douglass Library. Used
      by permission of the Associate Alumnae of Douglass College.

107   Mike Deak, "Somerset County Mourns Pioneer Evelyn Field," myCentralJersey.com,
      http://www.mycentraljersey.com/story/news/local/somerset-county/2015/12/07/
      somerset-county-mourns-pioneer-evelyn-field/76926094/.

108   Margaret T. Corwin, New Jersey College for Women, *Annual Report*, 1955, RG 19,
      Douglass College, Annual Reports, Box 2, 3, SC/UA.

109   Adelaide Marcus Zagoren (NJC '40), interview with Linda Cohen (DC '66), March
      20, 2012, Associate Alumnae of Douglass College Oral History Project, Douglass
      Library. Used by permission of the Associate Alumnae of Douglass College.

Chapter 5   From NJC to Douglass College

1   J. Edgar Hoover, "Mothers . . . Our Only Hope," *Women's Home Companion*, January
      1944, 20–21. Cited in Elaine Tyler May, *Homeward Bound: American Families in the
      Cold War Era* (New York: Basic Books, 1988), 69.

2   Alice E. Courtney and Sarah Wernick Lockeretz, "A Woman's Place: An Analysis of
      Roles Portrayed by Women in Magazine Advertisements," *Journal of Marketing
      Research* 8, no. 1 (1971): 92–95.

3   Susan Hartmann, "Women's Employment and the Domestic Ideal in the Early Cold
      War Years," in Joanne Meyerowitz, ed., *Not June Cleaver: Women and Gender in Postwar
      America* (Philadelphia: Temple University Press, 1994).

4   Lynn White Jr., *Educating Our Daughters* (New York: Harper and Brothers, 1950).

5   Susan Lynn, "Gender and Progressive Politics: A Bridge to Social Activism of the
      1960s," in Meyerowitz, 104.

6   Elaine Yaffe, *Mary Ingraham Bunting: Her Two Lives* (Savannah, GA: Frederic C. Beil,
      2005), 123. Bunting's tenure home was in the Institute of Microbiology on Busch
      Campus, where her lab was also located. Kayo Denda's personal communication with
      Ann Heuer (July 28, 2016).

7   George P. Schmidt, *Douglass College: A History* (New Brunswick, NJ: Rutgers Univer-
      sity Press, 1968), 200.

8   *Douglass Alumnae Bulletin* 35, no. 1 (1955), 1.

9   *Douglass Alumnae Bulletin* 30, no. 3 (1955): 16.

10   Reiko Fukuyama Ohye, Sandra Harding, and Lola Fuchs Kamp, Douglass College
      Class of 1956, personal communication with Kayo Denda (November 10–11, 2016).

11   Schmidt, 179.

12   Ibid., 188. Schmidt notes that NJC students were fined for missing classes immediately
      before or after holidays and they were denied credit for courses if they had missed a
      certain number of classes. These rules were abolished only in 1964.

13   Linda Stamato (DC '62), personal communication with Mary Hawkesworth, June 18,
      2016.

14 Douglass College, *Annual Report*, 1958–1959, 3. Mabel Smith Douglass Library.

15 Richard P. McCormick, *Rutgers: A Bicentennial History* (New Brunswick, NJ: Rutgers University Press, 1966), 272.

16 Margaret Judson, *Breaking the Barrier: A Professional Autobiography by a Woman Educator and Historian before the Women's Movement* (New Brunswick, NJ: Rutgers University Press, 1984), 43–44.

17 Ibid., 74.

18 Schmidt, 173.

19 Ibid.

20 Ibid.

21 Ibid., 176.

22 Ibid., 175.

23 Ibid., 221.

24 McCormick, *Rutgers*, 295.

25 Ibid., 296. See also Paul Clemens, *Rutgers since 1945* (New Brunswick, NJ: Rutgers University Press, 2015), 12–13; and Ellen W. Schrecker, *No Ivory Tower: McCarthyism and the Universities* (New York: Oxford University Press, 1986), 171–179, 195–197.

26 Richard P. McCormick, *Academic Reorganization in New Brunswick, 1962–1978: The Federated College Plan* (New Brunswick, NJ: Rutgers University, 1978), 2.

27 Letter from Mary Bunting to the Alumnae of Douglass (November 15, 1957). Printed in *Douglass Alumnae Bulletin* 33, no. 1 (1957): 2.

28 Schmidt, 217.

29 Douglass College, *Annual Report*, 1958–1959, 7. Mabel Smith Douglass Library.

30 Judson, 60.

31 *Quair: The Yearbook of Douglass College*, 1927 (hereafter, *Quair*).

32 Interview with Linda Stamato by Mary Hawkesworth, June 29, 2016. See also Yaffe, 124.

33 *Douglass Alumnae Bulletin* 36, no. 2 (1961): 1–3.

34 Irene Figarotta Pearse (DC '59), personal communication with Kayo Denda.

35 Anne Spiegel Lipner, personal communication with Mary Hawkesworth, July 2, 2016. Special thanks to Linda Stamato for reaching out to her classmates for memories of Dean Adams.

36 Schmidt, 217–218.

37 Douglass College, *Annual Report*, 1959–1960, 1. Mabel Smith Douglass Library.

38 Ibid.

39 Schmidt, 208.

40 *Douglass Alumnae Bulletin* 36, no. 5 (1961): 14–17. A substantial gift came from the Class of 1927 and the bequest of one of their members, Edith Shipman Roth, the daughter of Mabel Smith Douglass.

41 "College Libraries: Bridges to Learning," *Progressive Architecture* 44 (March 1963): 134–137. Clemens, 268–269.

42 Schmidt, 203

43 John W. Chambers, "Emily Gregory Hickman, 1880–1947," in Women's Project of New Jersey, Inc., *Past and Promise: Lives of New Jersey Women* edited by Joan N. Burstyn (Metuchen, NJ: Scarecrow, 1990), 319–320.

44 Schmidt, 229.

45 Douglass College, *Annual Report*, 1964–1965, 4. Mabel Smith Douglass Library.

46 Douglass College, *Annual Report*, 1965–1966, 1–2. Mabel Smith Douglass Library.

47 Schmidt, 230.

48 *Douglass Alumnae Bulletin* 36, no. 3 (1961): 10–11, 14.

49 Joan Marter, *Off Limits: Rutgers University and the Avant-Garde* (Newark and New

Brunswick: Newark Museum and Rutgers University Press, 1999), 3.

50   Ferris Olin and Joan Marter, *Artists on the Edge* (New Brunswick, NJ: Rutgers University, Dana Women's Art Series, 2005), 3–4.

51   Erika B. Gorder, *Archival Assemblages: Rutgers and the Avant-Garde, 1953–1964* (exhibition catalog) (New Brunswick, NJ: Special Collections and University Archives, Rutgers University, 2001), http://dx.doi.org/doi:10.7282/T3S180K7.

52   Olin and Marter, 2. For a detailed discussion of the innovative art scene at Douglass, see Joan Marter, *Women Artists of the Leading Edge,* forthcoming from Rutgers University Press.

53   *Douglass Alumnae Bulletin* 38, no. 1 (1962): 25.

54   Douglass College, *Annual Report,* 1965–1966, 2. Mabel Smith Douglass Library.

55   Pamphlet, Admissions to Rutgers, the State University, Douglass College New Jersey, 20–21, 36. Mabel Smith Douglass Library.

56   Shana Groeschler, "The Study of Home Economics at Douglass College," in Thomas Frusciano and Fernanda Perrone, eds., *A New Generation Looks Back: Historical Essays on Douglass College* (New Brunswick, NJ: Douglass College, 2000), 29.

57   This material is based on research conducted by Autumn Oberkehr (DRC '18). "Home Economics: An Unsung Hero of Women's Education," paper presented at the symposium "From Exclusion to Inclusion: 250 Years of Women at Rutgers," Mabel Smith Douglass Library, March 8, 2016.

58   Clemens, 304–305.

59   Interview with Rita Kay Thomas by Marissa Rodriguez (DRC '11), Leadership Scholar at the Institute for Women's Leadership, Rutgers University, 2008.

60   Douglass College, *Annual Report,* 1967–1968, 6. Mabel Smith Douglass Library.

61   After working at the Agricultural Experimental Station as a seed analyst, Fiske was hired by NJC in 1918 as a laboratory assistant in botany. She rose through the faculty ranks, becoming a full professor. In 1942, the botany and zoology fields merged, with Professor Fiske as the chair of the joined department, and in 1959 under her stewardship it became the Department of Biological Sciences. She retired in 1960 after forty-two years of service.

62   Douglass College, *Annual Report,* 1965–1966, 3. Mabel Smith Douglass Library.

63   Department of Chemistry and Bacteriology, Annual Report, 1952-1953. Records of the Dean of Douglass College (Group I), 1887–1973 (RG19/A0/01), Box 1, Folder 7, SC/UA.

64   "Three Major Departments Today," in *Douglass Alumnae Bulletin* 37, no. 3 (1962): 13–14.

65   Elaine Showalter, "Only the Conception: Becoming a Feminist Critic," *Douglass Alumnae Bulletin* 66, no. 4 (1993), 1–5.

66   Douglass College, *Annual Report,* 1967–1968, 6. Mabel Smith Douglass Library.

67   *Douglass Alumnae Bulletin* 38, no. 2 (1963): 4–5, 13.

68   Ibid., 6–7.

Chapter 6   Preserving Douglass's Special Mission

1   Richard P. McCormick, *Academic Reorganization in New Brunswick, 1962–1978: The Federated College Plan* (New Brunswick, NJ: Rutgers University, 1978), 1.

2   Ibid., 4.

3   President Edward Bloustein referred to the intensive exchanges surrounding reorganization in the 1970s as "the Great Debate." As pressures for coeducation increased in New Brunswick, Douglass deans adopted the rhetoric of Douglass's "special mission" in their various attempts to preserve the college as a single-sex institution.

4   *Douglass Alumnae Bulletin* 36, no. 1 (1960): 1.

5   Douglass College, *Annual Report,* 1964–1965, 6. Mabel Smith Douglass Library.

6   McCormick, 7.

7   Ibid., 8.

8   Ibid., 7.

9   Ibid., 31, 35.

10   Ibid., 4–5.

11   Petition from Douglass faculty to Provost Schlatter, January 27, 1964, quoted in McCormick, 7.

12   Ibid., 8.

13   Ibid., 9. For further discussion of the long-term consequences of this memorandum of understanding, see chapter 9.

14   Ernest Lynton served as dean of Livingston until 1973.

15   McCormick, 15.

16   Ibid., 47-48.

17   As the ninth president of Wellesley College, in 1969 Ruth Adams introduced Hillary Rodham, later Clinton, at the ninety-first commencement exercise. Rodham was the first student commencement speaker in the history of the college.

18   McCormick, 35.

19   Douglass College, *Annual Report*, 1966–1967, 5. Mabel Smith Douglass Library.

20   Jean Burton, Douglass professor of psychology, cited in Gloria Negri, "Margery Foster, 93, Dynamic Dean of Women's College," Boston Globe, October 10, 2007.

21   Margery Somers Foster, *"Out of Smalle Beginnings . . .": An Economic History of Harvard College in the Puritan Period, 1636–1712* (Cambridge, MA: Belknap Press of Harvard University Press, 1962).

22   Philip Conkling, president of the Island Institute, a community development group in Rockland, Maine, cited in Negri.

23   Douglass College, *Annual Report* 1966–1967, 2. Mabel Smith Douglass Library.

24   McCormick, 44.

25   The College of Agriculture and Environmental Science was one of four "men's colleges" at Rutgers, New Brunswick.

26   McCormick, 44.

27   Ibid., 47.

28   Ibid.

29   Dean Foster sent a confidential memorandum to Henry Torrey, dean of the Graduate School, indicating that she did not object to this transfer. Changing perceptions of the field of home economics during the 1950s and 1960s convinced the dean that this major was far from ideal in a progressive women's college. Records of the Dean of Douglass College (Group II), 1965–1981, Box 8, Folder 5, Special Collections, SC/UA; and Oberkehr, "Home Economics: An Unsung Hero of Women's Education." Paper presented at the symposium "From Exclusion to Inclusion: 250 Years of Women at Rutgers," March 8, 2016. Mabel Smith Douglass Library.

30   McCormick, 60.

31   Ibid., 65.

32   Ibid., 63.

33   Ibid., 65.

34   Margery Somers Foster, "Tentative Responses to Wheeler—Questions," February 5, 1974, Records of the Dean of Douglass College (Group II), 1965–1981, Box 10, Folder 11, SC/UA.

35   Records of the Dean of Douglass College (Group II), 1965–1981, Box 10, Folder 11, SC/UA.

36   Douglass College, *Annual Report*, 1968–1969, 2. Mabel Smith Douglass Library.

37   Douglass College, *Annual Report*, 1970–1971, 6. Mabel Smith Douglass Library.

38   Letter from Margery Somers Foster to Lois Banner and Mary Hartman, March 27, 1973. Records of the Dean of Douglass College (Group II), 1965–1981, Box 8, Folder 4, SC/UA.

39   Interview with Susan Cower Schwirck (DC '71), Associate Alumnae of Douglass College Oral History Project, October 14, 2014. Used by permission of the Associate Alumnae of Douglass College. After serving as chair of the theater arts department, Jack Bettenbender became the first dean of the Mason Gross School of the Arts, 1976–1988.

40   Following her resignation as dean, Margery Somers Foster returned to the faculty as a member of the Douglass Department of Economics, where she taught until her retirement in 1980. She died on September 22, 2007, at the age of ninety-three.

41   Paul Clemens, *Rutgers since 1945* (New Brunswick, NJ: Rutgers University Press, 2015), 4.

42   Ibid., 73n19.

43   Paula Brownlee subsequently went on to serve as dean of faculty and then president of Union College before becoming president of the American Association of Colleges and Universities. In 1986, she was named one of the hundred most effective presidents by the Council for the Advancement and Support of Education.

44   Jewel Plummer Cobb, Connecticut Women's Hall of Fame, http://cwhf.org/induct-ees/science-health/jewel-plummer-cobb#.V3l7u6Ko3Bk.

45   Louise Hartman, *Finding Aid of the Inventory of the Records of the Dean of Douglass College (Group II) 1965–1981*, SC/UA. May 1995, http://www2.scc.rutgers.edu/ead/uarchives/douglass_deans_2f.html

46   "Biological Sciences," Records of the Dean of Douglass College (Group II), 1965–1981, Box 3, Folder 2, SC/UA.

47   "Basic Skills," Records of the Dean of Douglass College (Group II), 1965–1981, Box 2, Folder 8, SC/UA.

48   Records of the Dean of Douglass College (Group II), 1965–1981, Box 6, Folder 6 and Box 11, Folder 8, SC/UA.

49   Her priorities are articulated in the Douglass College Master Plan, 1977–1982, May 19, 1977.

50   Records of the Dean of Douglass College (Group II), 1965–1981, Box 10, Folder 12, SC/UA.

51   Correspondence between Jewell P. Cobb and George A. Carrol, university librarian, April 24, 1978. Records of the Dean of Douglass College (Group II), 1965–1981, Box 9, Folder 3, SC/UA.

52   Douglass College Master Plan, 1977–1982, May 19, 1977, ii. Mabel Smith Douglass Library.

53   Information about the Black Alumnae Network was provided by Flora Buchbinder Cowen (DC '59) in personal communication with Kayo Denda.

54   "Wheeler Proposal: Why Go in Circles?" *Caellian*, February 15, 1980, 2.

55   Michele M. Guarino (DC '80), letter to the editor, *Caellian*, February 22, 1980, 2, 3.

56   "Recommendation of Douglass College Government Association concerning University Reorganization," undated. Group Number 23/D1/3, Box 16, File: "McCormick: Academic Reorganizations 1979–1980," SC/UA.

57   University Senate candidate Annie Greenberg (DC '81), "Government Association Elections: Candidates Speak," *Caellian*, February 28, 1980, 3.

58   The students' premonitions concerning travel time and the negative impact of reorganization on Women's Studies proved to be thoroughly correct. Faculty who had been hired on women's studies lines were forced into discipline-based departments, as part of the consolidation of the college faculties into one Faculty of Arts and Sciences. The

newly combined discipline-based departments were often dominated by the more conservative faculty from Rutgers College, simply because there were more of them. Hence, they could determine the outcome of departmental votes when they chose to vote as a bloc. Of the faculty involved in women's studies who were transferred into discipline-based departments, several failed to be awarded tenure—contributing to a significant brain drain for women's studies. The feminist scholars denied tenure at Rutgers went on to have eminent careers in the United States and Europe.

59   President Edward J. Bloustein, An Open Letter to the Academic Community in New Brunswick, April 3, 1980, 1–2, Group number 23/D1/3, Box 16, File: "McCormick: Academic Reorganizations 1979–1980," SC/UA.

60   Ibid., 2, 3.

61   The Associate Alumnae of Douglass College, "Set of Principles on University Reorganization," November 20, 1979, Group Number 23/D1/3, Box 16, File: "McCormick: Academic Reorganizations 1979–1980," SC/UA.

62   Pamella R. Lach, "The Survival of a Women's College: Douglass College and Reorganization" (Mabel Smith Douglass Honors Thesis, Douglass College, 1998), 58–59.

63   Ibid.

64   Louise Duus, "Schmidt Chapter," unpublished manuscript, 28. Records of the Associate Alumnae of Douglass College, n.d., provided through the courtesy of Marjorie Munson, Rebecca Reynolds, and Valerie Anderson. Paul Clemens also provided helpful background information about the formation of the Douglass College Fellows (e-mail communication to Kayo Denda, Fernanda Perrone, and Mary Hawkesworth, November 2, 2016).

65   Lach, 66.

66   Ibid.

67   Reubena L. Spence, "Campus Views: On Reorganization," Caellian, September 18, 1980, 7. Caellian editors posed the question "The Board of Governors has passed a reorganization bill for the university. How do you feel about it as Douglass students?" and published responses of nine students.

68   Douglass College, Red Book, 1953. Mabel Smith Douglass Library.

69   Admissions to Douglass College, 1961. Mabel Smith Douglass Library. Language houses, later called cultural houses, were units unique to the Corwin campus that included living-learning experiences. They had house chairs who reported to a counselor in residence. In addition to the French, German, Russian, and Spanish Houses, the African and Afro-American House was established in 1970 in response to the demands by the Douglass Black Student Congress. A few years later, addressing the demands of the Douglass Puerto Rican Students, the Casa Boriqua was also inaugurated on the Corwin campus, adding diversity and more living options for Douglass students. The residents of both houses negotiated the boundaries of belonging in an overwhelmingly white college, while the houses also served a diverse coalition of minority students across the Rutgers campuses.

70   Quair, 1964, 67.

71   Ibid.

72   Caellian, April 26, 1963.

73   Ibid., April 12, 1963.

74   Ibid., December 8, 1967.

75   Ibid.

76   Ibid., February 23, 1968.

77   Douglass College, Annual Report, 1967–1968, 3. Mabel Smith Douglass Library.

78   Ibid., 1.

79   Caellian, February 5, 1968.

80   Douglass College, *Annual Report*, 1967–1968. Mabel Smith Douglass Library. The commission members included one alumna; five students, including the president of the Government Association; four faculty; one member of the Douglass College Committee of the Rutgers University Board of Trustees; the college physician; Margery Trayes, dean of students; and Dean Margery S. Foster, dean of the college. *Report of the Commission on Douglass as a Resident College*, 45. Mabel Smith Douglass Library.

81   Marjorie M. Trayes, "Report of the Dean of Students," in Douglass College, *Annual Report*, 1969–1970. Mabel Smith Douglass Library.

82   *Report of the Committee on Douglass as a Resident College*, appendix G (1969), 70–79.

83   Douglass College, *Red Book*, 1970–1971, 75.

84   *Douglass Alumnae Bulletin* 36, no. 2 (1961): 6.

85   Susan Jacobs, "The Changing American University," Douglass College, *Red Book*, 1970–1971, 6.

86   Gloria Bonilla-Santiago, *Organizing Puerto Rican Migrant Farmworkers: The Experience of Puerto Ricans in New Jersey* (New York: Peter Lang, 1988), 32.

87   *Douglass Alumnae Bulletin* 38, no. 1 (1962): 10–11, 17.

88   Ibid.

89   *Douglass Alumnae Bulletin* 39, no. 6 (1964): 40. Interview with Juanita Wade Wilson, Associate Alumnae of Douglass College Oral History Project. Used by permission of the Associate Alumnae of Douglass College.

90   Some scholarships and program funds were also supported by donors through contributions to the university.

91   *Quair*, 1967, 85; *Caellian*, October 14, 1966, 3.

Chapter 7   Douglass in Two Turbulent Decades: Student Activism and Institutional Transformation

1   Paul Clemens, *Rutgers since 1945: A History of the State University of New Jersey* (New Brunswick, NJ: Rutgers University Press, 2015), 35.

2   Douglass College, *Red Book*, 1960, 65.

3   Richard P. McCormick, *The Black Student Protest Movement at Rutgers* (New Brunswick, NJ: Rutgers University Press, 1990), 6.

4   Aya Sakar (DRC '15), *Perspectives on Diversity and Multiculturalism on Douglass Campus, from the 1920s to the 1950s*. Poster presented at the Aresty Undergraduate Research Symposium, April 24, 2015.

5   Interview with Inez Phillips Durham by Paul Clemens and Rudy Bell, May 2015.

6   Agnoli's parents were notified in advance of this "unorthodox" assignment; Wade's parents were not.

7   Interview with Juanita Wade Wilson, Associate Alumnae of Douglass College Oral History Project, June 12, 2012. Used by permission of the Associate Alumnae of Douglass College.

8   *Targum*, November 4, 1963. November 4, 1963; Susan Kass, "Why Has Everyone Forgotten So Soon?" *Douglass Alumnae Bulletin* 39, no. 3 (1963): 4–5, 20.

9   Kass, 4–5.

10   Ibid.

11   Letter from Donald Harris to the students of Rutgers and Douglass (October 19, 1963) in Records of the Rutgers Chaplain Bradford S. Abernathy, 1928–1974, Rutgers University Special Collections and University Archives (hereafter SC/UA). Abernathy was one of the leaders in the efforts to release Harris from prison.

12   Kass, 4.

13   *Caellian*, November 8, 1968, 7.

14   McCormick, 18–19.

15   Ibid., 24.

16   *Caellian,* February 21, 1969, 4. See also February 28, 1969, 1–2.

17   McCormick, 56.

18   Ibid.

19   *Caellian,* April 24, 1970, 8.

20   McCormick, 75–77.

21   *Report of the Commission of Ethnic and Race Relations* (New Brunswick, NJ: Douglass College, 1972), 25.

22   Ibid., 31.

23   McCormick, 93.

24   B. Robert Kreiser, "Championing Academic Freedom at Rutgers: The Governance Affair and the Teach-In on April 1965," *AAUP Journal of Academic Freedom* 7 (2016): 1.

25   The Douglass chapter of Young Americans for Freedom was founded in 1953. Douglass College, *Red Book* 1953, 39.

26   Clemons, 24.

27   Ibid., 25.

28   *Douglass Alumnae Bulletin* 45, no. 4 (Summer 1970), 2–3.

29   Douglass College, *Annual Report,* 1969–1970, 4. Mabel Smith Douglass Library.

30   Some Douglass students were actively engaged in the protests organized by Rutgers College. For a fuller account, see Clemens, Chapter 6, "Student Protest."

31   Douglass College, *Annual Report,* 1969–1970, 5. Mabel Smith Douglass Library.

32   *Brown v. Board of Education* 347 U.S. 483 (1954).

33   Susan Poulson, "'A Quiet Revolution': The Transition to Coeducation at Georgetown and Rutgers Colleges, 1960–1995" (PhD diss., Georgetown University, Washington, DC, 1989), 50.

34   Leslie Miller-Bernal, *Separate by Degree: Women Students' Experiences in Single-Sex and Coeducational Colleges* (New York: Peter Lang. 2000), 6.

35   Ibid., 53.

36   Richard P. McCormick, chair of the Rutgers College Committee for Coeducation, worked behind the scenes to ensure that Rutgers was named in the WEAL complaint. His committee sought to persuade the Board of Governors that single-sex education at Rutgers violated the Equal Protection Clause of the U.S. Constitution and they enlisted the aid of Ruth Bader Ginsburg, then a member of the Law School Faculty in Newark to help craft ten legal arguments to present to the board. See Rabeya Rahman, "The Price of Higher Admission: Coeducation and Some Change" (honors thesis, Rutgers College, 2010).

37   Poulson, "'A Quiet Revolution,'" ix.

38   "Fact Sheet on Coeducation," SC/UA, http://njdigitalhighway.org/enj/lessons/social_protest_60s_70s/?part=pro_coeducation. The other male-only school was the Virginia Military Institute. At the time there were twelve hundred state-supported colleges and universities in the United States.

39   Student Council Motion, February 2, 1969, SC/UA, http://njdigitalhighway.org/enj/lessons/social_protest_60s_70s/?part=anti_coeducation.

40   Letter from Albert W. Twitchell, Director of Athletics, to Arnold B. Grobman, Dean of Rutgers College, September 23, 1969, SC/UA, http://rci.rutgers.edu/~kdenda/hist_coll_life/HTML/anti-coeducation/content/index.html

41   Twitchel was right that women admitted to Rutgers College would have higher academic qualifications than their male counterpart. The 544 women (411 first-year students and 133 transfer students) who entered Rutgers in 1972 were all in the top 15

percent of their high school graduating class; Rutgers men represented far wider class rankings. Rahman, 51.

42 Poulson, "'A Quiet Revolution,'" 186.

43 Ibid., 187.

44 Ibid., 188.

45 Diane Kiesel, "The View from across Town," *Caellian*, December 10, 1971, 9.

46 Letter from Dean Margery Somers Foster to President Mason Gross and the Board of Governors, May 7, 1971. Records of the Office of the Dean of Douglass College, SC/UA, http://njdigitalhighway.org/enj/lessons/social_protest_60s_70s/?part=anti_coeducation.

47 Poulson, "'A Quiet Revolution,'" 151–152.

48 Douglass College, *Annual Report*, 1969–70, 5. Mabel Smith Douglass Library.

49 Letter to the editor from Cheri Connell, Kathryn Conner, Janet Cottrell, and Barbara Oettle, *Targum*, December 10, 1969, 6.

50 *Douglass Alumnae Bulletin* 46, no. 2 (1970): 23.

51 Louise Duus, "Schmidt Chapter," unpublished manuscript, 16. Records of the Associate Alumnae of Douglass College, n.d.; provided through the courtesy of Marjorie Munson, Rebecca Reynolds, and Valerie Anderson.

52 *Douglass Alumnae Bulletin* 46, no. 2 (1970–71): 22.

53 Douglass College Ad Hoc Committee on the Education of Women, *A College Education for Women* (New Brunswick, NJ: Douglass College, 1970). Mabel Smith Douglass Library. Mary Howard and Elaine Showalter chaired the committee. In addition to the two students, committee members included Emily Alman, David Burrows, Jean Burton, Alice Crozier, and Helen Davis.

54 Elaine Showalter, "Only the Conception: Becoming a Feminist Critic," in *Douglass Alumnae Bulletin* 66, no. 4 (1993): 1–4.

55 Douglass College, *Red Book*, 1971–1973, 9. Mabel Smith Douglass Library.

56 Clemens, 45.

57 Barbara Balliet, Mary Hawkesworth, Lisa Hetfield, Jennifer Morgan, and Lillian Robbins, "Feminist Interventions: Creating New Institutional Spaces for Women at Rutgers," in *Re-affirming Action: Designs for Diversity in Higher Education; Report to the Ford Foundation* (New Brunswick, NJ, Institute for Women's Leadership, 2005), 91–92. In the College of Arts and Sciences at Rutgers-Newark, a small group of tenured women faculty filed a class-action sex-discrimination complaint with the U.S. Department of Health, Education, and Welfare in May 1971. Constituting themselves as the Committee on the Status of Women, they collected meticulous data to demonstrate multiple dimensions of sex discrimination on campus, devoting particular attention to serious pay inequities. Salary data indicated that women faculty were paid less than their male counterparts in every discipline at every level. Women instructors were paid on average four hundred dollars less per course than their male counterparts; women full professors earned on average four thousand dollars less than their male colleagues at a time when average male salaries were twenty thousand dollars. One African American woman faculty hired by the psychology department was given a full-time teaching load, but paid only part-time wages. Women were significantly underrepresented across all departments and, where present, were concentrated at lower faculty ranks, especially at the nontenurable ranks of instructor, assistant instructor, and lecturer. Only eight of the fifty-four women then teaching at Rutgers-Newark were tenured despite long years of service. Investigation of promotion practices revealed that the average time from PhD to professor for male faculty in one department was eight years, while it took eighteen years for the lone tenured woman to reach that rank. Men were awarded tenure with full support from their departments

and college committees, while women with better credentials were routinely denied tenure and had to fight through long and difficult grievance mechanisms to have those decisions reversed. Analysis of workload practices demonstrated that women faculty carried far heavier teaching and service loads. Men were promoted to full professor with fewer publications than those of women whose promotion efforts were turned down. Males awarded graduate fellowships were given research assignments; women fellows were assigned secretarial duties, such as typing faculty papers and answering correspondence. Moreover, women faculty were subjected to marginalization, "condescension, and slurs that men are unlikely to experience" (Memorandum on the Status of Faculty Women at Rutgers-Newark, November 1971, 3). In 1972, there were only five tenured women on the faculty at Rutgers College. When one newly recruited associate professor developed an affirmative action plan, at the dean's request, to assist with the implementation of coeducation at Rutgers College, the department chairs, an all-male enclave, reacted with anger and refused to support the plan. Moreover, the woman faculty member who authored the plan was fired by her department chair, who retroactively claimed that her appointment as associate professor did not include tenure. She too filed sex discrimination complaints with the Equal Opportunities Commission and the Civil Rights Division of DHEW.

58   The Training Institute for Sex Desegregation of the Public Schools was a project led by Rebecca L. Lubetkin and established with a Title IV grant from the Office of Education, U.S. Department of Health, Education, and Welfare. It was sponsored jointly by the University Extension Division and the Women's Studies Institute. The purpose of the training institute was "to improve the ability of school personnel to deal effectively with the educational change occasioned by federal and state sex desegregation mandates."

59   *Douglass Alumnae Bulletin* 50, no. 3 (1975): 2, 5.

60   Douglass College, *Annual Report*, 1975–1976, "Advisory Services for Women (formerly Women's Center)." Mabel Smith Douglass Library.

61   Douglass College, Announcement, 1973-1974, 8. Mabel Smith Douglass Library.

62   *Douglass College Women's Studies Program* (pamphlet), [1975–1976]. Mabel Smith Douglass Library.

63   Douglass College, *Red Book*, 1976–1977, 7.

64   E-mail from Sondra Korman (RC '77), founding member of *Labrys*, to Kayo Denda.

65   Responding to the evolving nature of Latina/o and Caribbean migration and the fields of Latina/o and Caribbean studies, the Program in Puerto Rican Studies was created in fall 1970. It became a department at Livingston College in 1973. It was renamed Puerto Rican and Hispanic Caribbean Studies in the mid-1980s, Latino and Hispanic Caribbean Studies in 2005–2006, and Latino and Caribbean Studies in January 2016.

66   Diane Miranda (DC '71) Douglass College, *Casa Boriqua Scrapbook*, 1973–1974, Office of the Dean for Academic Programs and the Global Village, Douglass Residential College.

67   *Caellian*, March 5, 1971, 9.

68   Lourdes Santiago, "Who I Am? What I Am? Where Do I Belong? *Casa Boriqua Scrapbook*, 1973–1974, Office of the Dean for Academic Programs and the Global Village, Douglass Residential College.

69   "Racial Identity Dilemma," *Caellian*, December 13, 1973, 1, 3, 6.

70   Ivette Mendez (DC '75), paper presented at the "Remembering the Rutgers Puerto Rican Student Movement of the 1970s" conference and celebration, Rutgers University, Piscataway, NJ, October 14, 2016.

71   Janet Yocum, *Casa Boriqua Scrapbook*, 1975–1976. Office of the Dean for Academic Programs and the Global Village, Douglass Residential College.

72   Nancy Richards, Douglass College, *Casa Boriqua Scrapbook*, 1975–1976. Office of the

Dean for Academic Programs and the Global Village, Douglass Residential College.

73   Elizabeth Fraenkel (NJC '44), "Peer Counseling the Lesbian," *Douglass Alumnae Bulletin* 49, no. 4 (1974): 5–7.

74   Kaylan Michas, "Seeds of Revolution: Progressive Student Activism at Rutgers, 1968–1972" (honors thesis, Rutgers University, 2016).

75   David Nichols and Kafka-Hozschla, "The Rutgers University Lesbian/Gay Alliance, 1969–1989: The First Twenty Years," *Journal of the Rutgers University Libraries* 51, no. 2 (1989): 63.

76   Ibid., 66.

77   Meryem Uzumcu (DRC '17), "Intersectionality within LGBTQ Activism at Rutgers through the Years," paper presented at the symposium "From Exclusion to Inclusion: 250 Years of Women at Rutgers," Mabel Smith Douglass Library, March 8, 2016.

78   Nichols and Kafka-Hozschlag, 80–81.

79   Clemens, 198–199.

80   In the early 1990s, the organization changed its name once again to the Rutgers University Gay, Lesbian, and Bisexual Alliance (RUGLBA), reflecting a broader identity within the community.

81   Nichols and Kafka-Hozschlag, 85.

82   For more on this topic, see the Susan Cavin Papers (R-MC007), SC/UA.

83   Unpublished inventory to the records of the Bisexual, Gay and Lesbian Alliance at Rutgers University, 1965–1995, 48/H7/01, SC/UA.

84   "RU LGBTQA History," Center for Social Justice Education and LBGT Communities, Rutgers University Office of Student Affairs, http://socialjustice.rutgers.edu/about-us/history/ (accessed July 29, 2016).

85   Mabel Smith Douglass, "Tenth Anniversary Address" (1929), microform. Mabel Smith Douglass Papers, Mabel Smith Douglass Library.

Chapter 8   Creating Knowledge about, by and for Women

1   This chapter's epigraph is from Mary Howard and Elaine Showalter, Letter of Transmittal to Dean Margery Somers Foster, accompanying the *Report of the Ad Hoc Committee on the Education of Women*, February 1, 1971.

2   Report of the Ad Hoc Committee on the Education of Women: A College Education for Women (New Brunswick, NJ: Douglass College, Fall 1970), 1. Mabel Smith Douglass Library. Other members of the committee included Emily Alman, David Burrows, Jean Burton, Alice Crozier, Helen Davis, Barbara Dildine (DC '71), Geoffrey Hendricks, and Lynn Tannenbaum (DC '71). At the time of her appointment to this committee, Elaine Showalter was a specialist in Victorian literature. She went on to create a distinctive methodology for feminist literary criticism, "gynocritics," which sought to "construct a female framework for the analysis of women's literature, to develop new models based on the study of female experience, rather than to adapt male models and theories. Gynocritics begins at the point when we free ourselves from the linear absolutes of male literary history, stop trying to fit women between the lines of the male tradition, and focus instead on the newly visible world of female culture." Showalter, "Toward a Feminist Poetics," in *Women's Writing and Writing about Women*, edited by Mary Jacobus (London: Croom Helm, 1979), 1379.

3   *Report of the Ad Hoc Committee on the Education of Women*, 2.

4   Ibid., 11.

5   Ibid., 12.

6   As a result of the federated college system, three women's studies programs began to emerge at Rutgers in the late 1960s—at Douglass, at Livingston, and later at Rutgers College.

7   According to George P. Schmidt, the first women's studies course at NJC was taught in 1948 by Dr. Ida Bobula, Hungarian scholar and war refugee, whose class, History of the Social and Economic Position of Women in Western Culture beginning with Ancient Greece, was attended by faculty and students. *Douglass College: A History* (New Brunswick, NJ: Rutgers University Press, 1968), 104.

8   The disciplines included English, French, history, religion, and sociology.

9   *Report of the Ad Hoc Committee on the Education of Women*, 6.

10   Nancy Bazin, letter to John Salapatas, September 9, 1974. Janet Todd, a Rutgers literary critic specializing in women writers, created the Mary Wollstonecraft Newsletter, which in 1976 metamorphosed into the journal *Women & Literature*, the first journal of its kind. Todd went on to become the Herbert JC Grierson professor of English and director of the Centre for the Novel at the University of Aberdeen.

11   Nancy Bazin, letter to John Salapatas, Kenneth Wheeler, and Paul Pearson, April 19, 1975.

12   Judith Walkowitz, letter to Kenneth Wheeler, March 19, 1975. Walkowitz's first book, *Prostitution and Victorian Society* (1980), examined the system of medical and police regulation of prostitution, a system first established in 1864 and abolished in 1886, to control the spread of venereal disease among enlisted men. After leaving Rutgers, Professor Walkowitz had a distinguished career at Johns Hopkins University, where she taught for thirty years.

13   Barbara Balliet, Mary Hawkesworth, Lisa Hetfield, Jennifer Morgan, and Lillian Robbins, *Feminist Interventions: Creating New Institutional Spaces for Women at Rutgers* (New Brunswick, NJ: Institute for Women's Leadership, 2006), 37.

14   Richard P. McCormick values the Eagleton bequest at $2 million in *Rutgers: A Bicentennial History* (New Brunswick, NJ: Rutgers University Press, 1966), 302.

15   Proposal for the Center for the American Woman and Politics at the Eagleton Institute of Politics, Appendix A, quoted in the *Report of the Ad Hoc Committee on the Education of Women*, Douglass College, Fall 1970, 27.

16   Interview with Ida Schmertz by Ruth Mandel, September 14, 2014, https://www.youtube.com/watch?v=op4ub0AIhVM.

17   *Women in Public Office: A Biographical Directory and Statistical Profile* (New York: R. R. Bowker, 1976; reprinted by Metuchen, NJ: Scarecrow Press, 1978). Later, between 1989 and 1997, CAWP collaborated with the National Women's Political Caucus to issue directories of women elected officials. With the advent of the Internet, CAWP began publishing lists (with web links) of women candidates and officeholders, along with current and historical statistics, on its award-winning web-site. Reflecting debates within feminist scholarship and heightened awareness of the diversity of American women, the name was changed to Center for American Women and Politics in 1999.

18   Jeane J. Kirkpatrick, *Political Woman* (New York: Basic Books, 1974), 217, 244.

19   *Report of the Ad Hoc Committee on the Education of Women*, Douglass College, Fall 1970, 17.

20   In her article "The Mary H. Dana Women Artists Series: From Idea to Institution," Beryl Smith, Rutgers University art librarian, notes that Joan Snyder was encouraged by her former Douglass sociology professor, Emily Alman, to "do something," given Joan's criticisms of the lack of female faculty in the visual arts program and the fact that the college gallery showed works by only male artists, when the students were all female. *Rutgers University Libraries Journal* 54, no. 1 (1992): 4–17. I am grateful to Ferris Olin for calling this to my attention.

21   Nell Smithers, a professor in the English department, provided funds to endow the series in honor of her friend Dana.

22   For a discussion of the manifold accomplishments of the women in the Douglass art

department, see Joan Marter, *Women Artists of the Leading Edge*, forthcoming from Rutgers University Press.

23   *IRW Network,* Spring 1997, 3. Digitized copies of this newsletter are available at http://irw.rutgers.edu/images/Newsletters/newsletterspring97.pdf.

24   After directing the institute, Kate Stimpson went on to serve as dean of the Graduate School and vice provost for graduate education at Rutgers, director of the Fellows Program at the MacArthur Foundation, and university professor and dean of the Graduate School of Arts and Science at New York University.

25   Letter of the Nominating Committee to Provost Kenneth Wheeler, February 24, 1981, Douglass College Dean's Records. Jewel Plummer Cobb, Box 6, Rutgers Special Collections and University Archives (hereafter SC/UA).

26   Balliet et al., 39.

27   Ibid.

28   Ibid.

29   Lourdes Beneria also served as acting director of the IRW the year after Kate Stimpson's term ended. I am grateful to Ferris Olin for this information.

30   *IRW Network,* Spring 1997, 4.

31   Carol H. Smith and Ferris Olin, eds., *The New Jersey Project: Integrating the Scholarship on Gender, 1986–1989* (New Brunswick, NJ: Institute for Research on Women, 1990).

32   Fund for the Improvement of Secondary Education Grant, Junior Year at Douglass, CO-PIs Mary Hartman and Ellen Mappen, Douglass College Dean's Records, Mary Hartman, Box 6, SC/UA.

33   The original mission statement appeared on the IWA website in 2006. Although the statement changed when IWA was reconfigured as the Center for Women in the Arts and Humanities, the original version is still available at http://womens-studies.rutgers.edu/resources/the-institute-for-women-s-leadership-consortium.

34   In recent years, the IWL expanded, adding two units, the Office for the Promotion of Women in Science, Engineering and Mathematics and the Center on Violence against Women and Children. Although the work of these units is vital to the IWL's mission, they are not based at Douglass College. For this reason, they have not been included in this chapter.

35   CAWP NEW Leadership Alumnae Survey Findings, http://www.cawp.rutgers.edu/education_training/NEW_Leadership/new-leadership-alumnae-survey-key-findings.

36   CAWP's NEW Leadership Network partners can be found in Arizona, Idaho, Illinois, Iowa, Maine, Mississippi, Missouri, Nevada, New York, New England, Ohio, Oklahoma, Oregon, Pennsylvania, South Carolina, Texas, and Washington.

37   CAWP Fact Sheet, Women in State Legislatures, http://www.cawp.rutgers.edu/women-state-legislature-2016.

38   Diane Erbe-Maltabes, *Center for Women's Global Leadership History: 1989–1995* (New Brunswick, NJ: Center for Women's Global Leadership, 2003), 17.

39   Ibid.

40   Mary Trigg and Alison Bernstein, *Junctures in Women's Leadership: Social Movements* (New Brunswick, NJ: Rutgers University Press, 2016).

41   Lisa Hetfield and Dana Britton, *Junctures in Women's Leadership: Business* (New Brunswick, NJ: Rutgers University Press, 2016).

42   *Report of the Ad Hoc Committee on the Education of Women*, 1.

Chapter 9   Reinventing Douglass: From University Reorganization to the Transformation of Undergraduate Education

1   Richard P. McCormick, *Rutgers: A Bicentennial History* (New Brunswick, NJ: Rutgers University Press, 1966), 179. This chapter's epigraph is from Carmen Twillie Ambar,

Douglass College and Douglass Campus: A Model for a 21st Century Women's College at Rutgers University (New Brunswick, NJ, Douglass College, April 2005), 1.

2   Ibid., 211.

3   John Martin Thomas, 1925–1930, RG 04/A12, Records of the Office of the President, Special Collections and University Archives, Rutgers University Libraries; hereafter SC/UA.

4   R. P. McCormick, 211; George Schmidt, *Douglass College: A History* (New Brunswick, NJ: Rutgers University Press, 1968, 73.

5   Ambar, 1. A footnote identifies the following "weaknesses": "Traditionally, women's colleges have only offered single-sex experiences, a limited number of majors, a narrow resource base, and are not connected with the quality of faculty present at a research university."

6   Dean's Newsletter, August 1980, Douglass College Dean's Records. Jewel Plummer Cobb, Box 4, SC/UA. In her celebration of Douglass's star athletes, Dean Cobb overlooked one Livingston student and one Rutgers student who participated on the winning women's teams. The participants in two consecutive winning seasons included the following:

> 1978–1979 (28–4)
> EAIAW Mid-Atlantic Region Tournament Champion
> AIAW Eastern Satellite Tournament Participant
> Mary Coyle—Douglass College
> Denise Kenney—Livingston College
> Sandy Tupurins—Rutgers College
> June Olkowski—Douglass College
> Kathy Glutz—Douglass College
> Top Subs: Patty Delehanty—Douglass College
> Patti Sikorski—Douglass College
>
> 1979–1980 (28–5)
> EAIAW Mid-Atlantic Region Tournament Runner-Up
> AIAW National Tournament Final Eight
> Mary Coyle—Douglass College
> Patty Coyle—Douglass College
> Sandy Tupurins—Rutgers College
> Kathy Glutz—Douglass College
> June Olkowski—Douglass College
> Top Subs: Joanne Burke—Douglass College
> Patty Delehanty—Douglass College
>
> Special thanks to Terrese Williams Martin (DC '69) for her research to correct this record.

7   1980 Douglass College Brochure, Women's College Brochures, Douglass College Dean's Records. Jewel Plummer Cobb, Box 4, SC/UA.

8   Joe Anne Adler, 1991–1993, ARCO Guide to Women's Colleges, Women's College Brochures, Douglass College Dean's Records. Mary S. Hartman, Box 4, SC/UA.

9   Suzanne Boyle (DC '03), "Academic Reorganization at Douglass College: New Perspectives for a New Era," in Fernanda Perrone and Thomas J. Frusciano, *Toward a New History of Douglass: Essays by Students from the Douglass Scholars Program*, http://www.libraries.rutgers.edu/rul/libs/scua/douglass_scholars/introduction.shtml.

10   Ibid.

11   1979–1980 Brochure, "Career-Related Experiences at Douglass," Women's College

Brochures, Douglass College Dean's Records. Jewel Plummer Cobb. Box 4, SC/UA; and interview with Mary Hartman by Mary Hawkesworth, May 9, 2016.

12   Douglass Student Affairs, Douglass College Dean's Records. Jewel Plummer Cobb, Box 6, SC/UA.

13   *WON Newsletter* at Rutgers 1, no. 1 (1980): 1. Douglass College, Dean's Records. Jewel Plummer Cobb, Box 6, SC/UA.

14   WON Newsletter at Rutgers 3, no. 2 (1983), 3. Douglass College, Dean's Records. Jewel Plummer Cobb, Box 6, SC/UA.

15   Jewel Plummer Cobb served as president of California State University, Fullerton, from October 1981 to August 1990. She then served as Trustee Professor at California State University, Los Angeles, where she directed the ACCESS Center, established to increase the number of economically disadvantaged students pursuing careers in math, science, and engineering. Over the course of her career she was the recipient of more than twenty honorary degrees. In 1993 she received a Lifetime Achievement Award from the National Academy of Science. The Center for Excellence selected her to receive the Achievement in Excellence Award in 1999, and in 2001, she was the first recipient of the Reginald Wilson Award for significant and noteworthy accomplishments in the area of diversity in higher education. She died on January 1, 2017, at age ninety-two.

16   "From Dean Jewel Plummer Cobb to Class of 1981," *Quair: Yearbook of Douglass College,* 1981, 240. Hereafter, *Quair.*

17   "Reorganization—Part I: The Administration View," *Douglass Bulletin,* Fall 1983, 2.

18   Interview with Mary Hartman by Mary Hawkesworth, May 9, 2016.

19   Douglass College, *Annual Report,* 1988–1989. Mabel Smith Douglass Library.

20   Dean's Newsletters, August 1987, Douglass College Dean's Records. Mary S. Hartman, Box 4, SC/UA.

21   Ibid.

22   *The Report of the Provost's Committee on Undergraduate Education* (New Brunswick, NJ: Rutgers University, August 30, 1990). Quoted in the Douglass College, *Annual Report,* 1990–1991, n.p.. Mabel Smith Douglass Library.

23   Douglass College, *Annual Report,* 1993–1994. Mabel Smith Douglass Library.

24   Professor Carolyn Williams, personal communication with Mary Hawkesworth, May 10, 2016.

25   Interview with Mary Hartman by Mary Hawkesworth, May 9, 2016.

26   "An Interview with Mary S. Hartman," by IWL scholar Nancy Santucci, Class of 2010, http://iwl.rutgers.edu/translives_interviews/transcript/transcript_maryhartman.pdf.

27   Interview with Martha Cotter by Mary Hawkesworth, June 10, 2016.

28   Neil MacFarquhar, "Bomb Is Found in Rutgers Library Three Days after a Small Blast," *New York Times,* April 8, 1995.

29   Deans on Leadership, November 1996, Douglass College, Dean's Records. Barbara A. Shailor, Box 3, SC/UA.

30   *A Newsletter for Friends of Douglass College,* Fall 1999, Douglass College, Dean's Records. Barbara A. Shailor, Box 3, SC/UA.

31   Linda Stamato, "A Letter to New and Old Friends of Douglass," Spring 2002, 4. Papers of Linda Stamato, shared with Mary Hawkesworth.

32   Ibid.

33   Linda Stamato, personal communication with Mary Hawkesworth, June 11, 2016.

34   College Symbols, Notes of Associate Dean Marjorie Munson, November, 10, 2003, Douglass College, Dean's Records, Linda Stamato, Box 5, SC/UA.

35   Linda Stamato, personal communication with Mary Hawkesworth, June 18, 2016.

36   *United States v. Virginia,* 518 U.S. 515, pp. 533, 550.

37   Ibid., 533.

38   Memo from Joan Apple Lemoine to Carmen Twillie Ambar and Kim Owens, October 30, 2002, Douglass College, Dean's Records, Carmen Twillie Ambar, Box 4, SC/UA.

39   Douglass by the Decade, Douglass College, Dean's Record's, Carmen Twillie Ambar, Box 5, SC/UA.

40   Richard L. McCormick, *Raised at Rutgers: A President's Story* (New Brunswick, NJ: Rutgers University Press, 2014), 110.

41   *Transforming Undergraduate Education: A Report of the Task Force on Undergraduate Education* (New Brunswick, NJ: Rutgers University, 2005).

42   Ibid., 139.

43   Michael Beals, "The Case for Scrapping Rutgers' Separate Colleges," *NJBIZ Interview*, October 10, 2005, 13.

44   *Quair*, 2006, 14.

45   Ibid.

46   *Targum*, February 24, 2006.

47   Ibid., March 3, 2006.

48   Ibid., February 7, 2006

49   R. L. McCormick, *Raised at Rutgers*, 112.

50   *Report of the Task Force on Residential Colleges*, November 27, 2006, Douglass College, Dean's Records, Carmen Twillie Ambar, Box 6, SC/UA.

51   The Honors College provides a four-year living-learning experience for students from the liberal arts and professional schools at Rutgers–New Brunswick: the School of Arts and Sciences, School of Environmental and Biological Sciences, School of Engineering, Rutgers Business School, Ernest Mario School of Pharmacy, and Mason Gross School of the Arts. It enrolls five hundred students a year.

52   Farewell Announcement, 2008, Douglass College, Dean's Records, Carmen Twillie Ambar, Box 5, SC/UA.

53   "Transforming Undergraduate Education: History," Rutgers, New Jersey, http://urwebsrv.rutgers.edu/transform_ru/history.shtml#focus.

54   R. L. McCormick, *Raised at Rutgers*, 114.

55   Ibid.

56   I am grateful to Valerie Anderson, AADC executive director, for providing these figures (e-mail to Mary Hawkesworth, December 19, 2016).

Chapter 10 Diversifying Douglass

1   President Barack Obama, Commencement Address, Rutgers University, New Brunswick, NJ, May 15, 2016. This chapter's epigraph is from Commission on Ethnic and Race Relations, *Report of the Commission on Ethnic and Race Relations* (New Brunswick, NJ: Douglass College, January 1972), 8.

2   Stephen H. Norwood, *The Third Reich in the Ivory Tower: Complicity and Conflict on American Campuses* (Cambridge, UK: Cambridge University Press, 2011), 169.

3   Ibid.

4   Ibid.

5   Michael Greenberg and Seymour Zenchelsky, "Private Bias and Public Responsibility: Anti-Semitism at Rutgers in the 1920s and 1930s," *History of Education Quarterly* 33, no. 3 (1990): 304.

6   Norwood, 169.

7   Ibid., 170. Norwood points out that the Nazis used this same argument to limit Jewish admission to German universities to 1 percent, the proportion of Jews in the German population. Both Rutgers and NJC claimed that Jews composed 6 percent of the New Jersey population but 12 percent of student body. When Jewish organizations

complained of discrimination, they were told that their "misunderstanding" arose from their "erroneous assumption that scholastic standing is the sole test" in the college admissions process (170–171). Four Jews served on the faculty of NJC in the mid-1930s.

8   Mary Coakley (NJC '48), "Angela Ahn Finds U.S. Strange but Wonderful," *Caellian*, October 3, 1946, 1.

9   Douglass College, *Annual Report*, 1982–1983, 2. Mabel Smith Douglass Library.

10   Carol Lasser, *Educating Men and Women Together: Coeducation in a Changing World* (Champagne-Urbana: University of Illinois Press, 1987), 3–4.

11   Marilyn Boxer, "Women's Studies, Feminist Goals, and the Science of Women," in Carol R. Pearson, Donna L. Shavlik, and Judith G. Touchton, eds., Educating the Majority: How Women Are Changing Higher Education (New York: ACE/Macmillan, 1989), 192.

12   Barrie Thorne, "Rethinking the Ways We Teach," in Pearson et al., 312.

13   Margaret Wilkerson, "Majority, Minority, and the Numbers Game," in Pearson et al., 26, 28.

14   Lynn Whately (RC '70), comments presented at "Black on the Banks: African American Students at Rutgers in the 1960s," a conference organized by historian Douglas Greenberg in conjunction with Rutgers 250th Anniversary Celebration, November 6, 2015, Neilson Dining Commons, Douglass Campus.

15   Thorne, 313.

16   Richard P. McCormick, *The Black Student Protest Movement at Rutgers* (New Brunswick, NJ: Rutgers University Press, 1990), 56. In 1938, Julia Baxter Bates was the first black woman to graduate from Douglass (see chapter 3). By comparison, James Dickson Carr was the first black graduate of Rutgers College in 1892. Over the next fifty years, he was followed by no more than twenty others. From 1945 to 1965, blacks were less than 1 percent of the student population (7).

17   Juanita Wade Wilson (DC '66), *Black on the Banks: African American Students at Rutgers in the 1960s*, November 6, 2015.

18   Wilma Harris (DC '66), *Black on the Banks: African American Students at Rutgers in the 1960s*, November 6, 2015.

19   Barbara Morrison Rodriguez (DC '71), *Black on the Banks: African-American Students at Rutgers in the 1960s*, November 6, 2015.

20   McCormick, *The Black Student Protest Movement at Rutgers*, 56.

21   Diversity, Douglass College, Dean's Records. Mary Hartman, Box 4, Rutgers Special Collections and University Archives, hereafter SC/UA.

22   Wilson.

23   Jill Kerr Conway, "Coeducation and Women's Studies: Two Approaches to the Question of Woman's Place in the Contemporary University," *Daedalus* 103, no. 4 (1974): 239–249, 240–241.

24   McCormick, *The Black Student Protest Movement at Rutgers*, 56.

25   Ibid., 25.

26   Ibid., 57.

27   Wilkerson, "Majority, Minority, and the Numbers Game," 29–30.

28   McCormick, *The Black Student Protest Movement at Rutgers*, 58.

29   Commission on Ethnic and Race Relations, 20.

30   McCormick, *The Black Student Protest Movement at Rutgers*, 59.

31   Commission on Ethnic and Race Relations, 6. Lesser animosity toward Latina students might well have been related to their small numbers on campus. Less than a decade later as the number of Puerto Rican students increased, racial tensions escalated, as noted in chapter 7.

32   Commission on Ethnic and Race Relations, 7.

33   Ibid., 6.

34   Ibid., 11.

35   Ibid., 8.

36   Ibid., 13.

37   Ibid.

38   Ibid, 29–30.

39   Ibid., 34–35.

40   Douglass College, *Annual Reports*, 1981, 1990. Mabel Smith Douglass Library; *A Newsletter for Friends of Douglass College,* Fall 1999. Douglass College, Dean's Records, Barbara A. Shailor, Box 3, SC/UA. Figures for 2016–2017 are taken from Rutgers Research and Enrollment Information Services (REIS), provided December 6, 2016, courtesy of Dean Litt. It should also be noted that 4.4 percent of Douglass students reported in 2016 that their racial identity involved more than one race.

41   *Targum*, April 12, 1978, 3

42   Nancy Richards, *Report on Minority Concerns*, November 20, 1979. Douglass College, Dean's Records. Jewel Plummer Cobb, Box 4, SC/UA.

43   Douglass Equal Opportunity Board Report, 1980, Douglass College, Dean's Records. Jewel Plummer Cobb, Box 4, SC/UA.

44   Ibid.

45   Ibid.

46   Ibid.

47   Wilkerson, "How Equal Is Equal Education: Race, Class, and Gender," in Lasser, 137, 139.

48   McCormick, *The Black Student Protest Movement at Rutgers,* 56.

49   Douglass Equal Opportunity Board Report, 1980, Douglass College, Dean's Records. Jewel Plummer Cobb, Box 4, SC/UA.

50   Douglass College Government Association, *Redbook*, 1984, 21. By 1984, a disability rights group, Friends of 504, was also active at Douglass.

51   Ibid.

52   *Report of the Office of Affirmative Action and Employment Research* (1983), quoted in Barbara Balliet, Mary Hawkesworth, Lisa Hetfield, Jennifer Morgan, and Lillian Robbins, *Feminist Interventions: Creating New Institutional Spaces for Women at Rutgers* (New Brunswick: Institute for Women's Leadership, 2006); emphasis added.

53   Ibid.; emphasis added.

54   Ibid.

55   *Report of the Ad Hoc Committee on the Education of Women: A College Education for Women* (New Brunswick, NJ: Douglass College, 1970). Mabel Smith Douglass Library.

56   *Fellows Folio* 2, no. 1 (1988): 1. See also Douglass College, *Annual Report*, 1988–89. Mabel Smith Douglass Library.

57   Douglass College, *Annual Report*, 1992–1993. Mabel Smith Douglass Library.

58   Douglass College, *Annual Report*, 1994–1995. Mabel Smith Douglass Library.

59   The front page story in the *Star-Ledger*, January 31, 1995, was subsequently picked up by Dale Russkoff, "Racial Remark Has Rutgers Roiling," Washington Post, February 9, 1995, https://www.washingtonpost.com/archive/politics/1995/02/09/racial-remark-has-rutgers-roiling/2868700f-4341-4c2d-abc8-4eedd9bd805f/?utm_term=.871da1aef594; and Doreen Carvajal, "Taking Back His Words: Rutgers President Faces Wall of Skeptics," New York Times, February 10, 1995, http://www.nytimes.com/1995/02/10/nyregion/taking-back-his-words-rutgers-president-faces-wall-of-skeptics.html). 1.

60   Douglass College Government Association, "Resolution Demanding the Resignation of President Lawrence," January 31, 1995. Douglass College, Dean's Records. Martha Cotter, Box 6, SC/UA.

61   Ibid. Martha Cotter, acting dean of Douglass, recollects that Piscataway police came to Douglass following the bridge incident, demanding the Douglass administrators identify the Douglass students who had been photographed on the bridge. Douglass College staff and Douglass Fellows claimed not to recognize any of the students captured on film. Interview with Martha Cotter by Mary Hawkesworth, June 10, 2016.

62   Douglass College, *Annual Report*, 1996. Mabel Smith Douglass Library.

63   *Targum*, February 26, 1998, 3.

64   Catharine Stimpson, "New Consciousness, Old Institutions, and the Need for Reconciliation," in Lasser, 163.

65   Susan Poulson, "'A Quiet Revolution': The Transition to Coeducation at Georgetown and Rutgers Colleges, 1960–1975" (PhD diss., Georgetown University, Washington, DC, 1989), 167.

66   Mabel Clarke Peabody, "Portrait of the Alumnae: Some Facts and Figures," in Rosamond Sawyer Moxon and Mabel Clarke Peabody, *Twenty-Five Years: Two Anniversary Sketches of New Jersey College for Women* (New Brunswick: New Jersey College for Women, Rutgers University, 1943), 47.

Chapter 11   Douglass Residential College: Revitalizing Women's Education in the Twenty-First Century

1   In 2015–2016, the Honors College opened as the second residential college at Rutgers. This chapter's epigraph is from Douglass Residential College, Douglass Residential College Strategic Plan, 2016–2023: *A Transformative Future; Building on 100 Years of Success*, http://douglass.rutgers.edu/sites/douglass.rutgers.edu/files/Combined%20 High%20Res%20Strategic%20Plan.pdf.

2   Barbara Balliet, Mary Hawkesworth, Lisa Hetfield, and Jennifer Morgan, "Democratizing Women's Education at Rutgers by Re-inventing Douglass College," Institute for Women's Leadership, September 19, 2005, 1.

3   Ibid.

4   Ibid, 1–2.

5   Margaret Judson, *Breaking the Barrier: A Professional Autobiography by a Woman Educator and Historian before the Women's Movement* (New Brunswick, NJ: Rutgers University Press, 1984), 139–140.

6   Karen Kurotsuchi Inkelas and Jennifer Weisman, "Different by Design: An Examination of Student Outcomes among Participants in Three Types of Living-Learning Programs," *Journal of College Student Development* 44, no. 3 (2003): 335–368; and Ajda Kahveci, Sherry Southerland, and Penny Gilmer, "From Marginality to Legitimate Peripherality: Understanding the Essential Functions of a Women's Program," *Science Education* 92, no. 1 (2008): 33-64.

7   National Science Foundation, "Women and Minorities in the S&E Workforce," Science and Engineering Indicators 2016, https://nsf.gov/statistics/2016/nsb20161/#/ report/chapter-3/women-and-minorities-in-the-s-e-workforce; Catherine Ashcroft, Brad McLain, and Elizabeth Eger, Women in Tech: The Facts, National Center for Women in Information Technology, 2016, https://www.ncwit.org/sites/default/files/ resources/womenintech_facts_fullreport_05132016.pdf.

8   Randall Stross, "What Has Driven Women Out of Computer Science?" *New York Times*, November 16, 2008, Business section, 4.

9   Richard Edwards, remarks at the dedication of the Kathleen W. Ludwig Global Village Learning Center, Douglass Residential College, September 18, 2016.

10   Douglass Residential College Strategic Planning Committee, "Summary of Student Responses: Envisioning Questions," February 19, 2015.

11   To ensure that all DRC students fulfill these requirements, the BOLD Center has consolidated and expanded several signature Douglass programs, most notably the Douglass Externship Experience, which provides ten hours of professional development training to prepare students for a two-week "job shadowing" experience with Douglass and Rutgers alumnae and with women professionals across the nation. DRC students have been placed in diverse work sites ranging from Google and JibJab, to Merck, AT&T, Tiffany & Co., and the New Jersey Conservation Foundation. The BOLD Center now hosts an annual career conference, featuring alumnae and women professionals in diverse fields. Participating organizations have included Johnson & Johnson, Bayer Health Care, Forbes, Colgate, Facebook, Wells Fargo, and the Center on Islamic Study. The BOLD Center also organizes leadership retreats and summits. Attended by 250 student leaders, the retreats teach team building, inclusion in the workplace, leading for social justice, and other skills essential to women's leadership. The BOLD EMPOWER program, launched in 2017 with funding from the Chancellor's Office Strategic Initiative Fund, creates opportunities for first-generation university students to assist them in navigating the college experience. Created as part of the RU 1st Initiative in the Office of Undergraduate Academic Affairs, EMPOWER builds on the college's strategic initiative to advance diversity and inclusion at DRC.

12   A neuroscientist and neurologist, Dr. Robert Barchi was appointed the twentieth president of Rutgers University in July 2012. Prior to this appointment, he had served as president of Jefferson University in Philadelphia (2004–2012) and as provost and chief academic officer of the University of Pennsylvania (1999–2004), where he had served on the faculty since 1974.

13   Quotations in this paragraph are taken from the 2011 Survey of the Douglass mission course, Knowledge and Power. Box #31—10541886, Rutgers University Records Management.

14   DRC enrollment figures for 2016–2017 were provided by Rutgers Research and Enrollment Information Services (REIS). Special thanks to Dean Litt for sharing this information.

15   These figures are drawn from the Douglass Residential College Academic Report, 2011–2015. Special thanks to Dean Litt for sharing this information.

16   The Bunting students receive significant scholarship support from the Charlotte W. Newcombe Foundation.

17   Interview with Jacquelyn Litt by Mary Hawkesworth, May 18, 2016.

Chapter 12   The Douglass Difference

1   Interview with Mary Hartman, May 9, 2016. This chapter's epigraph is from Adrienne Rich, *Blood, Bread, Poetry* (New York: W. W. Norton, 1986), 196.

2   Survey of first-year students enrolled in the Douglass mission course, Knowledge and Power, 2011. Douglass College, Dean's Records, Jacquelyn Litt, Box 31, Rutgers Special Collections and University Archives; hereafter SC/UA.

3   May Metz, president of Mills College, cited in Leslie Miller-Bernal and Susan L. Poulson, eds., *Challenged by Coeducation: Women's Colleges since the 1960s* (Nashville, TN: Vanderbilt University Press, 2006), 183.

4   Ibid., 11.

5   Ibid., 319.

6   Ibid., 307–308.

7   Douglass demographic data taken from Rutgers Research Enrollment Information Services (REIS) Enrollment Management, December 6, 2016. Data for other women's

colleges is provided by Linda Sax, *Who Attends a Women's College?* Identifying Unique Characteristics and Patterns of Change, 1971–2011 (Los Angeles: University of California, September 2014, updated April 2015), 10, http://www.womenscolleges. org/sites/default/files/report/files/main/students_at_womens_colleges_final_ report.pdf.

8   Douglass Fellows and Dean Barbara Shailor constituted a majority of the FAS Gender Equity Committee that investigated persisting gender inequalities on campus and issued a report in 2001. Mary Hartman chaired the FAS Task Force on Race and Ethnicity in 2003–2004. Mary Hartman and Cheryl Wall served as Principal Investigators for a multi-year Ford Foundation grant to promote diversity efforts at Rutgers and 12 other colleges and universities across the United States. Cheryl Wall served for years as the Chair of the President's Committee on Diversity and Inclusion.

9   George P. Schmidt, *Douglass College: A History* (New Brunswick, NJ: Rutgers University Press, 1968), 175.

10   Executive Office of the President of the United States, Eleven Facts about American Families and Work, 2014, https://s3.amazonaws.com/s3.documentcloud.org/docume nts/1350164/11familyworkfacts.pdf.

11   U.S. Department of Labor, Women's Bureau, "25 Most Common Occupations for Women, 2014," https://www.dol.gov/wb/stats/most_common_occupations_for_ women.htm.

12   NORC at the University of Chicago, "General Social Survey (GSS)," 2014 Reports, http://www.norc.org/Research/Projects/Pages/general-social-survey.aspx.

13   Executive Office of the President, 4.

14   Rosamond Sawyer Moxon (NJC '29), "Trends of the First Quarter Century: A History of Intangibles," in *Two Anniversary Sketches of the New Jersey College for Women* (New Brunswick: New Jersey College, 1943), 41.

15   Ibid., 33–34.

16   Mabel Clarke Peabody (NJC '31), "Portrait of the Alumnae: Some Facts and Figures," in Rosamond Sawyer Moxon and Mabel Clarke Peabody, *Twenty-Five Years: Two Anniversary Sketches of NJC* (New Brunswick: New Jersey College for Women, Rutgers University, 1943), 49.

17   Ibid., 53.

18   Ibid., 57.

19   Ibid., 57–59.

20   Ibid., 65–66.

21   Ibid., 67.

22   Jean Comeforo and Jay Comeforo, Douglass Class of 1945: 50th Reunion (New Brunswick, NJ: Douglass College, 1995), 1.

23   Jean Raff Comeforo and Jay E. Comeforo, Douglass College Class of 1945: 45th Reunion (New Brunswick, NJ: Douglass College, 1990), 8.

24   Ibid.; employment figures computed from biographical sketches.

25   Comeforo and Comeforo, Douglass College Class of 1945: 45th Reunion, 3.

26   Comeforo and Comeforo, Douglass College Class of 1945: 50th Reunion, 7.

27   Comeforo and Comeforo, Douglass College Class of 1945: 45th Reunion, 8.

28   Roberta S. Sigel and John V. Reynolds, "Generational Differences in the Women's Movement," *Political Science Quarterly* 94, no. 4 (1979–1980): 635–648.

29   Ibid., 639.

30   Ibid., 640.

31   Ibid., 641.

32   Krista Jenkins, *Mothers, Daughters, and Political Socialization: Two Generations at an American Women's College* (Philadelphia: Temple University Press, 2013) 31.

33   Ibid., 34.

34   Ibid.

35   Ibid., 42–44.

36   Ibid., 39.

37   Ibid., 42–43.

38   Ibid., 46.

39   Ibid., 54–55.

40   Ibid., 60–61.

41   Ibid., 64.

42   Ibid., 67–69.

43   Ibid., 96.

44   Ibid., 96, 143n3.

45   Moxon, 23. For a discussion of the effects of civic engagement on the cultivation of leadership at women's colleges, see D. G. Smith, L. E. Wolf, and D. Morrison, "Paths to Success: Factors Related to the Impact of Women's Colleges" *Journal of Higher Education* 66, no. 3 (1995): 245–266.

46   Quoted in Diane Propsner, "Graduating College Women Talk about 'The Douglass Difference,'" Huff Post: The Blog, http://www.huffingtonpost.com/diane-propsner/douglass-difference-womens-colleges_b_5413423.html

47   Quoted in ibid.

48   Quoted in ibid.

49   Quoted in ibid.

50   Mabel Smith Douglass, "New Jersey College for Women Tenth-Anniversary Address" (1929). Mabel Smith Douglass Papers (microform), Mabel Smith Douglass Library.

51   "Douglass Mission Statement," Rutgers: Douglass Residential College, https://douglass.rutgers.edu/mission-statement.

52   Jacquelyn Litt, quoted in Rutgers, Douglass Residential College, Douglass Residential College Strategic Plan, 2016–2023: *A Transformative Future; Building on 100 Years of Success*, ii, http://douglass.rutgers.edu/sites/douglass.rutgers.edu/files/Combined%20High%20Res%20Strategic%20Plan.pdf.

Afterword

1   Derek Bok, *Higher Education in America* (Princeton, NJ: Princeton University Press, 2013).

BIBLIOGRAPHY

PRIMARY SOURCES

ARCHIVAL SOURCES

Unless otherwise stated, all collections are located in New Brunswick, New Jersey.

Alumni Biographical Files. Special Collections and University Archives, Archibald S. Alexander Library, Rutgers University Libraries.

Associate Alumnae of Douglass College, Douglass Alumnae Oral History Project, Mabel Smith Douglass Library.

Douglass College, Annual Reports.
> 1950–1967, Mabel Smith Douglass Library.
> 1918–2001, Special Collections and University Archives, Rutgers University Libraries.

Douglass College, Casa Boriqua Scrapbooks, 1973–1976, Office of the Dean for Academic Programs and the Global Village, Douglass Residential College.

Douglass College, Florence Marshall Diary, Mabel Smith Douglass Library.

Douglass College, Office of the Dean, Jewel Plummer Cobb, 1976–1981, Special Collections and University Archives, Rutgers Universities Libraries.

Douglass College, Office of the Dean, Mary Hartman, 1981–1994, Special Collections and University Archives, Rutgers University Libraries.

Douglass College, Office of the Dean, Barbara Shailor, 1996–2000, Special Collections and University Archives, Rutgers University Libraries.

Douglass College, Office of the Dean, Carmen Twillie Ambar, 2002–2008, Special Collections and University Archives, Rutgers University Libraries.

Douglass College, "Teddy" Kunst/Theresa Kerr Diaries, Special Collections and University Archives, Rutgers University Libraries.

Faculty Biographical Files, Special Collections and University Archives, Rutgers University Libraries.

RG 04/A11, Rutgers University Office of the President (William H. S. Demarest), 1890–1928, Special Collections and University Archives, Rutgers University Libraries.

RG 04/A12, Rutgers University Office of the President (John Martin Thomas), 1902–1932 (1925–1930, bulk), New Jersey College for Women, Box 23, Special Collections and University Archives, Rutgers University Libraries.

Mabel Smith Douglass Papers
> Mabel Smith Douglass Library (microform).

Special Collections and University Archives, Rutgers University Libraries (originals).

New Jersey College for Women Collection, Special Collections and University Archives, Rutgers University Libraries.

RG 04/A14, Rutgers University Office of the President, Inventory to the Records of the Robert C. Clothier Administration, 1925–1952, Boxes 84–87, Box 137, Special Collections and University Archives, Rutgers University Libraries.

RG 19/G1/01, Inventory to the Records of the Douglass College Council, 1928–1970 (academic regulations). http://www2.scc.rutgers.edu/ead/uarchives/DouglassCouncilf.html

RG 19/A0/01, Inventory to the Records of the Dean of Douglass College (Group I), 1918–1973. http://www2.scc.rutgers.edu/ead/uarchives/douglass_deans_1f.html

RG 19/A0/02, Inventory to the Records of the Dean of Douglass College (Group II), 1965–1981. http://www2.scc.rutgers.edu/ead/uarchives/douglass_deans_2f.html

RG 19/A0, Douglass College, Office of the Dean, Mary Hartman, Special Collections and University Archives, Rutgers University Libraries.

RG 23/D1/3, Rutgers College, Office of the Dean, Recommendation of Douglass College Government Association Concerning University Reorganization, Undated, Box 16, File "McCormick: Academic Reorganizations, 1979–1980," Special Collections and University Archives, Rutgers University Libraries.

RG 23/HC, Rutgers College, Office of the Dean, Rutgers University Chaplain (Bradford S. Abernethy), 1928–1974. http://www2.scc.rutgers.edu/ead/uarchives/abernethyf.html and Box 6, "Harris Case, 1963–1965," Special Collections and University Archives, Rutgers University Libraries.

R-MC 079, Elizabeth W. Durham Papers, Member of Class of 1922, Journals, Box 2, Special Collections and University Archives, Rutgers University Libraries.

R-MC 50, Richard P. McCormick Papers, Special Collections and University Archives, Rutgers University Libraries.

R-MC 041, Mary Clara Kangler Papers, 1917–1955, Special Collections and University Archives, Rutgers University Libraries.

Class of 1938, Box 3, class notebooks and scrapbook, Special Collections and University Archives, Rutgers University Libraries.

Access Databases (searchable at Special Collections and University Archives).
> Rutgers University Archives Photograph Collection (R-Photo).
> Rutgers Faculty Files (R-Bio-Faculty).
> Rutgers Vertical File (R-Vert).

Douglass Women's File, vertical (subject-based) paper files on women, Mabel Smith Douglass Library.

Rutgers Graduate School of Applied and Professional Psychology, Douglass Developmental Disabilities Center, 2013. http://dddc.rutgers.edu/mission.html

Rutgers Oral History Archives.
> Interviews with women: http://oralhistory.rutgers.edu/.
> Women's history index: http://oralhistory.rutgers.edu/social-and-cultural-history/787-womens-history-index.

PUBLICATIONS

Admissions to Douglass College (pamphlet), 1960–1970. Mabel Smith Douglass Library, Rutgers University Libraries.

Alumnae Magazine, 1926– . Publication of the Douglass Alumnae Association. Bound Periodicals section, Mabel Smith Douglass Library.

Announcement (includes requirements for admission, description of courses, tuition, etc.), 1956–1981. Mabel Smith Douglass Library and Special Collections and University Archives, Rutgers University Libraries.

Caellian (Douglass College student newspaper). Index available for 1921–1955. Special Collections and University Archives, Rutgers University Libraries.

Campus News, Special Collections and University Archives, Rutgers University Libraries.

Cantor, Carla. "Classics Department Pieces Together a Mystery." *Rutgers Focus,* February 20, 2006.

Class of 1922. *In the Beginning . . . Reminiscences of the Class of 1922.* New Jersey College for Women, 1952. Mabel Smith Douglass Library.

Commission on Ethnic and Race Relations. *Report of the Commission on Ethnic and Race Relations.* New Brunswick, NJ: Douglass College, January 1972. Mabel Smith Douglass Library.

Courier News. Obituary, Evelyn S. Field, December 7, 2015.

Daily Home News (New Brunswick, NJ), July 19, 1917, and October 17, 1921.

Douglass, Mabel Smith. *The Early History of New Jersey College for Women: Personal Recollections.* Reprinted from *Quair,* 1929. New Brunswick: New Jersey College for Women, 1929. Special Collections and University Archives, Rutgers University Libraries.

Douglass College Ad Hoc Committee on the Education of Women. *A College Education for Women.* New Brunswick, NJ: Douglass College, 1970. Mabel Smith Douglass Library.

Gorder, Erika B. *Archival Assemblages: Rutgers and the Avant-Garde, 1953–1964* (exhibition catalog). Special Collections and University Archives Gallery, Rutgers University, New Brunswick, NJ, 2001. http://dx.doi.org/doi:10.7282/T3S180K7.

Hickman, Emily Gregory. *An Experiment in Supervised Study for Deficient Sophomores at New Jersey College for Women.* New Brunswick: New Jersey College for Women, 1929. Mabel Smith Douglass Library.

Horn Book, Literary Quarterly (student publication). Special Collections and University Archives, Rutgers University Libraries.

Labrys. Douglass Library Women's File, Mabel Smith Douglass Library.

McCormick, Richard L., Philip Furmanski, and Douglass College. *Douglass College and Douglass Campus: A Model for a 21st Century Women's College at Rutgers University.* New Brunswick, NJ: Rutgers University, 2005. Special Collections and University Archives, Rutgers University Libraries.

Mortarboard (Barnard College yearbook), 1899. Barnard College Archives, New York, NY.

Mulford, Florence Ayres, ed. *The Fourth Wall: Reminiscences of the New Jersey College for Women Class of 1925.* New Brunswick, NJ: Douglass College, 1955.

New Jersey College for Women. *Annual Report,* 1929–1930, 1930–1931, 1931–1932. Special Collections and University Archives, Rutgers University Libraries.

New Jersey State Agricultural College. "Courses in Home Economics, 1921–1922." *State College Publication* 2, no. 1 (1921). Special Collections and University Archives, Rutgers University Libraries.

Pierce, Henry Miller. *President's Address to the First Graduating Class of Rutgers Female College.* June 2. New York: Agathynian Press, 1867.

Quair: The Yearbook of New Jersey College for Women, 1922–1955 / *The Yearbook of Douglass College,* 1956–2006 (with gaps). Mabel Smith Douglass Library and Special Collections and University Archives, Rutgers University Libraries.

Red Book (handbook of information for students). Mabel Smith Douglass Library, 1928–1943, and Special Collections and University Archives, Rutgers University Libraries.

Rutgers College. *Catalog,* 1919–1920. Special Collections and University Archives, Rutgers University Libraries.

Rutgers College and the State University of New Jersey. *The College for Women Announcement,* 1918–1919. Special Collections and University Archives, Rutgers University Libraries.

Rutgers Female Institute (New York, NY). Catalogue of the Rutgers Female College, 1867–1868. New York: Agathynian Press, 1867.

Rutgers University. *Rutgers University Bulletin.* New Brunswick, NJ: Rutgers University, 1928–. Special Collections and University Archives, Rutgers University Libraries.

Thomas, John M. *The Expansion of Public Education in New Jersey.* Address at his inauguration as president of Rutgers University, October 14, 1925. New Brunswick, NJ: Rutgers University, 1925. Special Collections and University Archives, Rutgers University Libraries.

SECONDARY SOURCES

Apple, Rima Dombrow. *The Challenge of Constantly Changing Times: From Home Economics to Human Ecology at the University of Wisconsin, 1903–2003.* Madison: University of Wisconsin Library Parallel Press, 2003.

Bix, Amy Sue. *Girls Coming to Tech! A History of American Engineering Education for Women.* Cambridge, MA: MIT Press, 2013.

Bok, Derek. *Higher Education in America.* Princeton, NJ: Princeton University Press, 2013.

Boddie, Leah. "The Organization of a Department of Student Life in a Coordinate College for Women." In Sarah M. Sturtevant and Harriet Hayes, eds., *Deans at Work,* 78–80. New York: Harper and Brothers, 1930.

Bonilla-Santiago, Gloria. *Organizing Puerto Rican Migrant Farmworkers: The Experience of Puerto Ricans in New Jersey.* New York: Peter Lang, 1988.

Bristow, Nancy. *American Pandemic: The Lost World of the 1918 Influenza Epidemic.* New York: Oxford University Press, 2012.

Campbell, D'Ann. *Women at War with America: Private Lives in a Patriotic Era.* Cambridge, MA: Harvard University Press, 1984.

Cardozier, V. R. *Colleges and Universities in World War II.* Westport, CT: Praeger, 1993.

Chin, Eliza Lo. *This Side of Doctoring: Reflections from Women in Medicine.* Thousand Oaks, CA: Sage, 2002.

Clarke, Edward Hammond. *Sex in Education; or, A Fair Chance for the Girls.* Boston: James R. Osgood, 1873.

Clemens, Paul G. E. *Rutgers since 1945: A History of the State University of New Jersey.* Rivergate Regionals Collection. New Brunswick, NJ: Rutgers University Press, 2015.

Cohen, Robert. *When the Old Left Was Young: Student Radicals and America's First Mass Student Movement, 1929–1941.* New York: Oxford University Press, 1993.

"College Libraries: Bridges to Learning." *Progressive Architecture* 44 (March 1963): 134–137.

Couturier, Lynn E. "Considering *The Sportswoman*, 1924 to 1936: A Content Analysis." *Sports History Review* 41 (2010): 111–112.

———. "Play with Us, Not against Us." *International Journal of the History of Sport* 25, no. 4 (2008): 421–442.

David, Elizabeth. "Traditions of Douglass College: The Transition from Class-Centered to College-Centered Focus." In Thomas J. Frusciano and Fernanda H. Perrone, eds., *A New Generation Looks Back: Historical Essays on Douglass College*, 1–21. New Brunswick, NJ: Douglass College, 2000.

Demarest, William H. *A History of Rutgers College, 1766–1924*. New Brunswick, NJ: Rutgers College, 1924.

Duus, Louise. "Schmidt Chapter." Unpublished manuscript, Associate Alumnae of Douglass College, n.d. Courtesy of Marjorie Munson, Rebecca Reynolds, and Valerie Anderson.

East, Marjorie. *Home Economics: Past, Present and Future*. Boston: Allyn and Bacon, 1980.

Eisenmann, Linda. *Higher Education for Women in Postwar America, 1945–1965*. Baltimore: Johns Hopkins University Press, 2006.

———. "A Time of Quiet Activism: Research, Practice, and Policy in American Women's Higher Education, 1945–1965. *History of Education Quarterly* 45, no. 1 (2005): 1–17.

Elias, Megan J. *Stir It Up: Home Economics in American Culture*. Philadelphia: University of Pennsylvania Press, 2008.

Faehmel, Babette. *College Women in the Nuclear Age: Cultural Literacy and Female Identity, 1940–1960*. New Brunswick, NJ: Rutgers University Press, 2012.

Faragher, John Mack, and Florence Howe. *Women and Higher Education in American History*. New York: W. W. Norton, 1988.

Fletcher, Robert. *A History of Oberlin College: From Its Foundation through the Civil War*. Chicago: R. R. Donnelley & Sons, 1943.

Foster, Margery Somers. *"Out of Smalle Beginnings . . ." An Economic History of Harvard College in the Puritan Period (1636 to 1712)*. Cambridge, MA: Belknap Press of Harvard University Press, 1962.

Freedman, Estelle. "Separatism as Strategy: Female Institution Building." *Feminist Studies* 5 (1979): 512–529.

Frusciano, Thomas J. "'A Truly Cooperative Effort': New Jersey College for Women and the War Effort as Documented in the Rutgers Oral History Archives of World War II." Paper presented at the Annual Meeting of the Society of American Archivists, Los Angeles, CA, August 21, 2003.

Frusciano, Thomas J., and Fernanda H. Perrone. *Towards a New History of Douglass College Essays by Students from the Douglass Scholars Program*, 2003. http://www.libraries. rutgers.edu/rul/libs/scua/douglass_scholars/introduction.shtml.

Frusciano, Thomas J., Fernanda H. Perrone, and Douglass Scholars Program. *A New Generation Looks Back: Historical Essays on Douglass College*. New Brunswick, NJ: Douglass College, 2000.

Gatta, Mary. *Not Just Getting By: The New Era of Flexible Workforce Development*. Lanham, MD: Lexington Books, 2005.

Goldstein, Carolyn M. *Creating Consumers: Home Economists in Twentieth-Century America*. Chapel Hill: University of North Carolina Press, 2012.

Gordon, Lynn D. "Annie Nathan Meyer and Barnard College: Mission and Identity in Woman's Higher Education, 1889–1950." *History of Education Quarterly* 26, no. 4 (1986): 503–522.

———. *Gender and Higher Education in the Progressive Era.* New Haven, CT: Yale University Press, 1990.

Greenberg, M., and S. Zenchelsky. "The Confrontation with Nazism at Rutgers: Academic Bureaucracy and Moral Failure." *History of Education Quarterly* 30, no. 3 (1990): 325–349.

———. "Private Bias and Public Responsibility: Anti-Semitism at Rutgers in the 1920s and 1930s." *History of Education Quarterly* 33, no. 3 (1993): 295–319.

Groeschler, Shana. "The Study of Home Economics at Douglass College." In Thomas J. Frusciano and Fernanda H. Perrone, eds., *A New Generation Looks Back: Historical Essays on Douglass College,* 23–35. New Brunswick, NJ: Douglass College, 2000.

Hanscom, Elizabeth Deering. "The Ethical Purpose of a Woman's College." *Educational Review* 22 (October 1901): 312.

Hartman, Mary S. "From Professor to Dean." *Alumnae Bulletin* 58, no. 2 (1983): 2.

———. "The Hall Mills Murder Case: The Most Fascinating Unsolved Murder in America." *Journal of the Rutgers University Libraries* 47, no. 1 (1984): 4–15.

Hartmann, Susan M. *The Home Front and Beyond: American Women in the 1940s.* Boston: Twayne, 1982.

Holsten, George H., Jr. *Bicentennial Year: The Story of a Rutgers Celebration.* New Brunswick, NJ: Rutgers University Press, 1968.

Horowitz, Helen Lefkowitz. *Alma Mater: Design and Experience in the Women's Colleges from Their Nineteenth-Century Beginnings to the 1930s.* 2nd ed. Amherst: University of Massachusetts Press, 1993.

Hyer, Lauren. "The Impact of the Women's Liberation Movement on Douglass College." In Thomas J. Frusciano and Fernanda H. Perrone, eds., *A New Generation Looks Back: Historical Essays on Douglass College,* 61–71. New Brunswick, NJ: Douglass College, 2000.

Jenkins, Krista. *Mothers, Daughters, and Political Socialization: Two Generations at an American Women's College.* Philadelphia: Temple University Press, 2013.

Judson, Margaret. *Breaking the Barrier: A Professional Autobiography by a Women Educator and Historian before the Women's Movement.* New Brunswick, NJ: Rutgers University Press, 1984.

Karabel, Jerome. *The Chosen: The Hidden History of Admission and Exclusion at Harvard, Yale, and Princeton.* Boston: Houghton Mifflin, 2005.

Kerber, Linda. "Separate Spheres, Female Worlds, Woman's Place," *Journal of American History* 75, no. 1 (1988): 9–39.

Kerr Conway, Jill. "Coeducation and Women's Studies: Two Approaches to the Question of Woman's Place in the Contemporary University." *Daedalus* 103, no. 4 (1974): 239–249.

Kirkpatrick, Jeane J. *Political Woman.* New York: Basic Books, 1974.

Kreiser, Robert B. "Championing Academic Freedom at Rutgers: The Governance Affair and the Teach-In on April 1965." *AAUP Journal of Academic Freedom* 7 (2016): 1.

Lach, Pamela R. "The Survival of a Women's College: Douglass College and Reorganization." Mabel Smith Douglass Honors Thesis, Douglass College, 1998.

Lasser, Carol, *Educating Men and Women Together: Coeducation in a Changing World.* Champaign-Urbana: University of Illinois Press, 1987.

Lee, Calvin B. T. *The Campus Scene, 1900–1970.* New York: David McKay, 1970.

Levine, David O. *The American College and the Culture of Aspiration, 1915–1940.* Ithaca, NY: Cornell University Press, 1986.

Ling, Huping. "A History of Chinese Female Students in the United States, 1880s–1990s." *Journal of American Ethnic History* 16, no. 3 (1997): 81–109.

Lucas, Mark Langley. "The Origins of Student Life: A History of the Colonial College Extra-curriculum at Rutgers and Princeton, 1800–1870." PhD dissertation, Rutgers, The State University of New Jersey, 1996.

Lukac, George J. *Aloud to Alma Mater*. New Brunswick, NJ: Rutgers University Press, 1966.

Manekin, Sarah. "Gender, Markets, and the Expansion of Women's Education at the University of Pennsylvania, 1913–1940." *History of Education Quarterly* 50, no. 3 (2010): 298–323.

Marbury, Elizabeth. "Education of Women." *Education* 8 (December 1887): 236–237.

Marter, Joan. *Off Limits: Rutgers University and the Avant-Garde*. Newark and New Brunswick, NJ: Newark Museum and Rutgers University Press, 1993.

Marthers, Paul P. "Did the Women's Colleges Founded in the Progressive Era Represent a New Model?" *American Educational History Journal* 40, no. 1/2 (2013): 221–239.

Maudsley, William. *Sex in Mind and Education*. Syracuse, NY: C. W. Bardeen, 1884.

May, Elaine Tyler. *Homeward Bound: American Families in the Cold War Era*. New York: Basic Books, 1988.

McCormick, Richard L. *Raised at Rutgers: A President's Story*. New Brunswick, NJ: Rutgers University Press, 2014.

McCormick, Richard P. *Academic Reorganization in New Brunswick, 1962–1978: The Federated College Plan*. New Brunswick, NJ: Alexander Library, 1978.

———. *The Black Student Protest Movement at Rutgers*. New Brunswick, NJ: Rutgers University Press, 1990.

———. *Rutgers: A Bicentennial History*. New Brunswick, NJ: Rutgers University Press, 1966.

———. "Rutgers in World War II." *Journal of the Rutgers University Libraries* 58 (1997): 1–10.

McMahon, Lucia. *Mere Equals: The Paradox of Educated Women in the Early Republic*. Ithaca, NY: Cornell University Press, 2012.

Meyerowitz, Joanne. *Not June Cleaver: Women and Gender in Postwar America*. Philadelphia: Temple University Press, 1994.

Micheletti, Laura A. "Carrying On: Students at New Jersey College for Women and World War II." Honors thesis, Rutgers University, 1999.

Miller-Bernal, Leslie. *Separate by Degree: Women Students' Experiences in Single-Sex and Coeducational Colleges*. New York: Peter Lang, 2000.

Miller-Bernal, Leslie, and Susan Poulson. *Challenged by Coeducation: Women's Colleges since the 1960s*. Nashville, TN: Vanderbilt University Press, 2006.

Milstein, Sarah. "Foundations: A History of the First Ten Years of Women's Studies at Rutgers University." Honors thesis, Rutgers University, 1993.

Minnich, Elizabeth. *Reconstructing the Academy: Women's Education and Women's Studies*. Chicago: University of Chicago Press, 1988.

Moxon, Rosamond, and Mabel Clarke Peabody. *Twenty-Five Years: Two Anniversary Sketches of New Jersey College for Women*. New Brunswick: New Jersey College for Women, Rutgers University, 1943.

Mullaney, Marie Marmo. "The New Jersey College for Women: Middle Class Respectability and Proto-Feminism, 1911–1918." *Journal of the Rutgers University Libraries* 42, no. 1 (1980): 26–39.

Nash, Margaret A., and Lisa Romero. "'Citizenship for the College Girl': Challenges and Opportunities in Higher Education for Women in the United States in the 1930s." *Teachers College Record* 114, no. 2 (2012): 1–35.

Newcomer, Mabel. *A Century of Higher Education for Women.* New York: Harper and Brothers, 1959.

Nichols, David, and M. J. Kafka-Hozschlag. "The Rutgers University Lesbian/Gay Alliance, 1969–1989: The First Twenty Years." *Journal of the Rutgers University Libraries* 51, no. 2 (1989): 55–95.

Norwood, Stephen H. *The Third Reich in the Ivory Tower: Complicity and Conflict on American Campuses.* Cambridge, UK: Cambridge University Press, 2011.

Olin, Ferris, and Joan Marter, *Artists on the Edge: Douglass College and the Rutgers MFA.* Dana Women's Art Series. New Brunswick, NJ: Rutgers University, 2005.

Olin, Helen Maria Remington. *The Women of a State University: An Illustration of the Working of Coeducation in the Middle West.* New York and London: G. Putnam's Sons, 1909.

Olsen, Deborah M. "Remaking the Image: Promotional Literature of Mount Holyoke, Smith, and Wellesley Colleges in the Mid to Late 1940s." *History of Education Quarterly* 40, no. 4 (2000): 418–459.

Ortloff, George Christian. *The Lady in the Lake: The True Account of Death and Discovery in Lake Placid.* Lake Placid, NY: With Pipe and Book, 1985.

Oshinsky, David M., Richard P. McCormick, and Daniel Horn. *The Case of the Nazi Professor.* New Brunswick, NJ: Rutgers University Press, 1989.

Palmieri, Patricia A. "From Republican Motherhood to Race Suicide: Arguments on the Higher Education of Women in the United States, 1820–1920." In Carol Lasser, ed., *Educating Men and Women Together: Coeducation in a Changing World,* 49–64. Urbana-Champaign: University of Illinois Press, 1987.

———. "Here Was Fellowship: A Social Portrait of Academic Women at Wellesley College, 1895–1920." *History of Education Quarterly* 23, no. 2 (1983): 195–214.

———. *In Adamless Eden: The Community of Women Faculty at Wellesley.* New Haven, CT: Yale University Press, 1995.

Parelius, Ann P. "Emerging Sex-Role Attitudes, Expectations, and Strains among College Women." *Journal of Marriage and the Family,* February 1975, 146–153.

Park, Roberta. "Sport, Gender and Society in a Transatlantic Victorian Perspective." *British Journal of Sports History* 2, no. 1 (1985): 11–20.

Perkins, Linda M. "The African American Female Elite: The Early History of African American Women in the Seven Sisters Colleges, 1880–1960." *Harvard Educational Review* 67, no. 4 (1997): 718–756.

Poulson, Susan L. "'A Quiet Revolution': The Transition to Coeducation at Georgetown and Rutgers Colleges, 1960–1975." Ph.D. diss., Georgetown University, Washington, DC, 1989.

———. "The Uses of Women for the Education of Men: The Coeducation Debate at Rutgers, 1960–1972" *New Jersey History* 116, no. 1/2 (1998): 59–79.

Powers, Jane Bernard. *The Girl Question in Education: Vocational Education for Young Women in the Progressive Era.* New York: Falmer Press, 1992.

Puaca, Laura Micheletti. *Searching for Scientific Womanpower: Technocratic Feminism and the Politics of National Security, 1940–1980.* Chapel Hill: University of North Carolina Press, 2014.

Radke-Moss, Andrea G. *Bright Epoch: Women and Coeducation in the American West*. Lincoln: University of Nebraska Press, 2008.

Rahman, Rabeya. "The Price of Higher Admission: Coeducation and Some Change." Honors thesis, Rutgers College, 2010.

Reuben, Jeff. "NYC's Forgotten Rutgers Female College on 5th Avenue, Harlem, and Lower East Side." Untapped Cities, 2015. http://untappedcities.com/2015/08/27/nycs-forgotten-rutgers-female-college-on-5th-avenue-harlem-and-lower-east-side/.

Rhea, John Mark. "Creating a Place for Herself in History: Anna Lewis' Journey from Tuskahoma to the University of Oklahoma, 1903–1930." *Great Plains Journal* 45, no. 1 (2009): 26–51.

Rice, Suzanne. "Toward an Understanding of the Educational Significance of 'Niceness' for Girls and Women," *Initiatives: The Journal of the National Association of Women in Education* (e-journal) 59, no. 3 (2000). http://www.nawe.org/initiatives.

Ritter, Kelly. *To Know Her Own History: Writing at the Woman's College, 1943–1963*. Pittsburgh: University of Pittsburgh Press, 2012.

Roosevelt, Theodore. "National Life and Character." In *American Ideals and Other Essays Social and Political*, 293–294. New York: Putnam & Sons, 1897.

———. *Strenuous Life: Essays and Addresses*. London: Grant Richards, 1902.

Rosenberg, Rosalind. "The Legacy of Dean Gildersleeve." *Barnard Alumnae Bulletin*, Summer 1996.

Rossiter, Margaret. *Women Scientists in America*. Baltimore: Johns Hopkins University Press, 1982.

Sakar, Aya. "Perspectives on Diversity and Multiculturalism on Douglass Campus from the 1920s to the 1950s." Aresty Research Project, Rutgers University, 2015.

Schmidt, George P. *Douglass College: A History*. New Brunswick, NJ: Rutgers University Press, 1968.

Schrecker, Ellen W. *No Ivory Tower: McCarthyism and the Universities*. New York: Oxford University Press, 1986.

Scott, Joan Wallach. *Only Paradoxes to Offer: French Feminists and the Rights of Man*. Cambridge, MA: Harvard University Press, 1996.

Shay, Patricia Dougher. "The Founding of the New Jersey College for Women: The Struggle for Women's Access during the Progressive Era, 1870–1930." EdD dissertation, Harvard University, 2010.

Sicherman, Barbara. *Women and Higher Education in American History: Essays from the Mount Holyoke College Sesquicentennial Symposia*. New York: Norton, 1988.

Sluzak, Ilanit. "The Abolition of Campus News." Honors thesis, Rutgers University, 1994.

Smith, D. G., L. E. Wolf, and D. Morrison. "Paths to Success: Factors Related to the Impact of Women's Colleges." *Journal of Higher Education* 66, no. 3 (1995): 245–266.

Solomon, Barbara Miller. *In the Company of Educated Women: A History of Women and Higher Education in America*. New Haven, CT: Yale University Press, 1985.

Stage, Sarah, and Virginia Bramble Vincenti. *Rethinking Home Economics: Women and the History of a Profession*. Ithaca, NY: Cornell University Press, 1997.

Stimpson, Catharine. "New Consciousness, Old Institutions, and the Need for Reconciliation." In Carol Lasser, ed., *Educating Men and Women Together: Coeducation in a Changing World*, 155–168. Champaign-Urbana: University of Illinois Press, 1987.

Susman, Warren I. *The Reconstruction of an American College: Some Proposals for Rutgers College*. New Brunswick, NJ: Rutgers University, 1968.

Thomas, M. Carey. "Present Tendencies in Women's College and University Education," *Association of Collegiate Alumnae Magazine* 17 (January 1908): 43–62.

Tischler, Hace, and Harold W. Demone, Jr. *Social Work Past: A Twenty-Five Year History of the Graduate School of Social Work.* New Brunswick, NJ: University Publications, Rutgers, the State University of New Jersey, 1983.

Todd, Jan. "The Strength Builders: A History of Barbells, Dumbbells and Indian Clubs." *International Journal of the History of Sport* 20, no. 1 (2003): 65–90.

Van der Beck, Shanna Lynn. "Douglass College and the Fight to Prevent Coeducation at Rutgers College." Honors thesis, Rutgers University, 2001.

Verbanas, Patti. "Julia Baxter Bates: Proving the Scientific Case for Public School Desegregation." Rutgers Today, May 9, 2016. http://news.rutgers.edu/feature/julia-baxter-bates-proving-scientific-case-public-school-desegregation/20160508.

Vicinus, Martha. *Independent Women: Work and Community for Single Women, 1850–1920.* Chicago: University of Chicago Press, 1988.

Ware, Susan. *Holding Their Own: American Women in the 1930s.* Boston: Twayne, 1982.

Weigley, Emma Seifrit. "It Might Have Been Euthenics." *American Quarterly* 26, no. 1 (1974): 79–96.

Wein, Roberta. "Women's Colleges and Domesticity, 1875–1918." *History of Education Quarterly*, Spring 1974, 31–47.

Wheaton, Kimberley Dolphin. "Challenging the 'Climate of Unexpectation': Mary Ingraham Bunting and American Women's Higher Education in the 1950s and 1960s." EdD dissertation, Harvard University, 2001.

Wilkerson, Margaret B. "How Equal Is Equal Education: Race, Class, and Gender." In Carol Lasser, ed., *Educating Men and Women Together: Coeducation in a Changing World*, 132–141. Urbana-Champaign: University of Illinois Press, 1987.

Women's Project of New Jersey, Inc. *Past and Promise: Lives of New Jersey Women*, ed. Joan N. Burstyn. Metuchen, NJ: Scarecrow Press, 1990.

Woody, Thomas. *A History of Women's Education in the United States.* Vol. 2. 1929. New York: Octagon Books, 1980.

Yaffe, Elaine. *Mary Ingraham Bunting: Her Two Lives.* Savannah, GA: Frederic C. Beil, 2005.

Ye, Weili. "'Nü Liuxuesheng': The Story of American-Educated Chinese Women, 1880s–1920s." *Modern China* 20, no. 3 (1994): 315–347.

Yosifon, David, and Peter N. Stearns. "The Rise and Fall of American Posture." *American Historical Review* 103, no. 4 (1998), 1074–1078.

ABOUT THE AUTHORS

KAYO DENDA is the head of the Margery Somers Foster Center and women's studies librarian at Rutgers University Libraries. She is the liaison librarian to the Department of Women's and Gender Studies, the Institute for Women's Leadership, the Institute for Research on Women, the Center for Women's Global Leadership, and Douglass Residential College.

MARY HAWKESWORTH is Distinguished Professor of Political Science and Women's and Gender Studies at Rutgers University. Her most recent books include *Embodied Power: Demystifying Disembodied Politics* (Routledge, 2016), the *Oxford Handbook of Feminist Theory* (Oxford University Press, 2016), and *Gender and Power: Towards Equality and Democratic Governance* (Palgrave Macmillan, 2016).

FERNANDA PERRONE, archivist and head, Exhibitions Program, and curator of the William Elliot Griffis Collection, Special Collections/University Archives, Rutgers University Libraries, specializes in women's manuscript collections, especially the documentation of women's higher education and women's organizations. Her research focuses on the history and archives of women's colleges and religious communities.